# Men, Women, and God(s)

# Men, Women, and God(s)

Nawal El Saadawi and
Arab Feminist Poetics

Fedwa Malti-Douglas

UNIVERSITY OF CALIFORNIA PRESS

*Berkeley / Los Angeles / London*

University of California Press
Berkeley and Los Angeles, California

University of California Press, Ltd.
London, England

Library of Congress Cataloging-in-Publication Data

Malti-Douglas, Fedwa.
    Men, women, and God(s) : Nawal El Saadawi and Arab feminist
poetics / Fedwa Malti-Douglas.
        p.   cm.
    "A Centennial book."
    Includes bibliographical references and index.
    ISBN 0-520-20071-3 (alk. paper).—ISBN 0-520-20072-1 (pbk.
: alk. paper)
    1. Sa'dawī, Nawāl—Political and social views.   2. Feminist litera-
ture—Arab countries.   3. Feminism and literature—Arab
countries.   4. Women authors, Arab—Political and social views.   5.
Feminism in literature.   I. Title.
    PJ7862.A3Z78   1995
    892.73´6—dc20                                                      94-44255
                                                                            CIP

Printed in the United States of America

9 8 7 6 5 4 3 2 1

*To All My Tats*

# Contents

# Acknowledgments

My relationship with Nawal El Saadawi, both intellectual and personal, goes back decades. It was in 1975, while meandering through bookstores in Damascus, that I first encountered Nawal El Saadawi the novelist. I bought two of her novels at the famous Syrian bookstore, the Maktabat al-Nûrî: *Mudhakkirât Tabîba* (Memoirs of a woman doctor) and *Imra'a 'ind Nuqtat al-Sifr* (Woman at point zero). The female heroes of those two novels installed themselves in my library and in my mind. It was a few years later, in Cairo, that I would encounter Nawal El Saadawi the person. Twenty-five Murad Street in Giza became a normal stop for me whenever I arrived in the Egyptian capital.

The seed that eventually became this book on Nawal El Saadawi planted itself in my mind, seemingly on its own, and would not go away. Every time I taught one of her novels in a course, whether in Arabic or in English, I would ask myself why I had not yet written the book. The Saadawian prose would pull on one side, the disparaging comments of friends and colleagues would pull on the other. After all, I was constantly hearing from these well-meaning good wishers, El Saadawi did not write Literature (with a capital *L*) but Polemics (with a capital *P*). The power of her prose spoke another message. It was the latter I finally chose to listen to. I would hope that the resulting study will rehabilitate Nawal El Saadawi in the minds of my discouraging friends and colleagues.

But slipping into what I knew would be unfriendly waters was a slow process: an article here, an interview there. In an article I wrote in 1983 for an Arabic monthly, I evoked the name of Nawal El Saadawi. She herself advised me in Cairo to eliminate her name for fear that my article would not appear. When I was invited in 1988 to write something for the cultural page of an Arabic daily, I proposed a review of one of her novels. The editor hemmed and hawed and kindly suggested I might wish to consider another topic. I did.

As an Arab woman, writing about an Arab feminist has meant participating in one of the most highly charged dialogues in our Arab culture. Writing a study of a living author proved to be an intense experience all its own. This exercise could not have been accomplished without Nawal El Saadawi and Sherif Hetata. Their friendship and generosity were more than I could have imagined. They opened up their home and their library to me. I will never forget that wonderful weekend spent in their home in the Egyptian countryside. Nor will I forget those intellectually stimulating evenings spent in the seminars of the Jamʿiyyat Tadâmun al-Marʾa al-ʿArabiyya (Arab Women's Solidarity Association) in Cairo—alas, now a victim of the political process. Simply, I could not have written this book without Nawal's and Sherif's help. This does not mean, however, that either would agree with all that I have written here.

Many are the friends whose names are better left out but they should know that my writing this book does not mean that I did not consider long and hard their sincerely meant attempts to dissuade me from it. But many are also the friends who were encouraging. To name them all might compromise them. Nevertheless, I would like to isolate Evelyne Accad, Etel Adnan, Amel Ben Aba, Simone Fattal, Jane Marcus and Susan Napier for special thanks. I could always count on their unswerving encouragement. Not to forget Jaroslav Stetkevych and Suzanne Pinckney Stetkevych, whose general support and friendship have been a constant. Those friends and colleagues who over the years kindly provided me with forums in which I could present my ideas on Nawal El Saadawi also deserve mention: Leila Ahmed, Roger Allen, Teirab AshShareef, Halim Barakat, Sandra Bem, Ross Brann, William Brinner, Priscilla Parkhurst Ferguson, Adel Gamal, Helen Hardacre, William Hanaway, Peter Heath, Dore Levy, Jane Marcus, Piotr Michalowski, Jan Monk, Magda al-Nowaihi, Susan Slyomovics, Jeanette Wakin, Jay Wright, Farhat Ziadeh. In Bloomington, Hasan El-Shamy has been an invaluable source with his unparalleled in-depth knowledge of Arab folklore.

As with any book whose gestation is years long, this one traveled the world with me. The physical trajectory of its writing crosses continents. It would not be what it is without long and numerous residences in Cairo and other parts of the Middle East and North Africa. Nor would it be what it is without those few weeks spent in Wales thanks to the generosity of my dear friend, James Piscatori. Unbeknownst to him, he encouraged me greatly simply by his passion for El Saadawi's fiction. The Rockefeller Foundation Bellagio Study and Conference Center on Lake Como gave the writing its impetus, with five weeks of an absolutely idyllic existence that can barely be imagined in an academic's dream. Alberta Arthurs, Susan Garfield, Pasquale Pesce, Tomás Ybarra-Frausto, and Lynn Szwaja know how grateful I am to them. But, most of all, it was the presence at the Villa Serbelloni of other fellows who never tired of listening to descriptions of one's research that made the once-in-a-lifetime experience just that. Andrew Billingsley, Margaret Coady, Tony Coady, Alfred Corn, Chris Corwin, Robert Ferguson, Priscilla Parkhurst Ferguson, Anne Fausto-Sterling, Eric Gamalinda, Henry Louis Gates Jr., David Iyornongo Ker, Tanya León, John Malmstead, David Rosand, Ellen Rosand, Paula Vogel, Eileen Wolpert, Julian Wolpert: the annual reunions with these, and sometimes other, Bellagini remind me how sweet can be the life of the mind.

Other friends have also inadvertently made this book happen. As a previous chair of a department, Ross Brann understood my unspoken need to temporarily escape administrative madness. He was instrumental in my being invited to be Senior Fellow at the Society for the Humanities at Cornell University. But without the help of Jonathan Culler, Dominick LaCapra, Mary Ahl, Linda Allen, Aggie Sirrine, and the wonderful staff of the Society, the all-too-short visit to the A. D. White House would never have materialized. Having Natalie Kampen in residence as a Senior Fellow at the same time was a special pleasure.

As always, I am indebted to all those longtime friends who never complain when I impose yet one more book manuscript on them. Judith Allen, Roger Allen, Michael Beard, Helen Hardacre, Susan Jeffords, Jan Johnson, Renate Wise: whether they read the entire text or part of it, I hope they know how much I count on their expertise and deep knowledge.

The enthusiasm of my friend Lynne Withey, Associate Director of the University of California Press, went beyond the call of duty. From the moment we first discussed the idea for the book until its completion, her support never waned. I consider myself lucky to have had her behind the project. Her intimate knowledge not only of the world of publishing but also of the world of Middle Eastern academic politics eliminated many of the anxieties inherent in publishing a book of this sort. The final preparation of the manuscript could not have been accomplished without the patience, good cheer, and watchful eye of Douglas Abrams Arava. At the last minute, it was my ever-helpful student assistant at Indiana University, Susan French, who came to the rescue. She never tired of running to the library on those hot and humid Bloomington summer days to check yet one more bibliographical reference.

Allen Douglas has been a guiding light that kept me on the right path. He dispelled many of the fears and hesitations—intellectual and other—that seem to set in with the writing of any book. His deep and unswerving commitment to feminism coupled with his discerning mind meant that I could count on him to be my harshest, and yet most supportive, critic.

How do I express what I felt for S. P.-T. who kept me company while I read and reread El Saadawi's books? Her presence on or near the computer was always a great comfort. D. P.-T. picked up the tradition started by her sister. How often she sat next to the printer, staring at me, inspiring me as I wrote and rewrote the chapters! 'A. P.-T. was always there too, especially during those pre-dawn hours, warming the computer, and at once reassuring me and making me aware that there is more to life than simply long hours of screen work. The deciphering of many of the Saadawian works could not have been done without all three of them. Their beauty, calm, and affection continue to be an inspiration.

# Note on Translation
# and Transcription

All translations in the text are my own, unless otherwise indicated, and all references are to the Arabic originals. When English translations of El Saadawi's works are available, these are noted in the first mention, both in the text and in the notes. For the convenience of the general reader, references to El Saadawi's works in the body of the text use the titles of the published English translations.

I have used a simplified transcription system in which the lengtheners on lowercase vowels are indicated with the French circumflex accent. The *'ayn* and the *hamza* are represented by the conventional symbols. Specialists should be able to easily identify the Arabic words. Since Nawal El Saadawi has anglicized her name, I use that anglicized form in the text. I have, however, transcribed her name in the notes and bibliography when referring to the Arabic originals of her works.

# Introduction

*Paradigms of Violation*

---

No Arab woman inspires as much emotion as Nawal El Saadawi. No woman in the Middle East has been the subject of more polemic. Certainly, no Arab woman's pen has violated as many sacred enclosures as that of Nawal El Saadawi. Is it any wonder that many an Arab male intellectual has dismissed her in my presence as at best an opportunist and at worst a whore? Or that many Western critics of the Middle East, including gender-conscious ones, persist in ignoring, when not occulting, her literary corpus? Her fiction has been castigated as mere propaganda, as a tireless repetition of her radical message. Yet in the Middle East her books have gone into multiple editions in their Arabic originals, and in the West she has become a household word in feminist circles. In a Cairo religious bookstore in 1988, her just-released novel *The Fall of the Imam* (Suqût al-Imâm) sat alongside books by the popular blind preacher Shaykh Kishk. At the time, this juxtaposition surprised me. Yet I was even more shocked in May 1993 to discover a religious Shî'î bookstore on Rue Jean-Pierre Timbaud in Paris, a street famous for its Islamist bookstores,[1] where one could purchase books by Nawal El Saadawi under the watchful and, apparently, pleased eye of the Imam Khomeini.

Indeed, irony seems to be part and parcel of Nawal El Saadawi's life. The Egyptian government that shut down her organization, the Arab Women's Solidarity Association, is the same government that found itself protecting her (and other secular intellectuals) from the Islamist radical groups that issued threats to her life after the assassination of Faraj Fûda in 1992.[2] A leftist male writer from another part of the Arab world (whose name I omit out of affection and deference) once declared to me in an impassioned tone when I raised the topic of El Saadawi the writer: "She has ruined our daughters!"

How could the Egyptian feminist and physician Nawal El Saadawi (b. 1931) have ruined not just the daughters of the Nile but those of the entire Middle East? What is so dangerous in her writing? Oddly enough, the only available book-length study on El Saadawi in English is a Freudian attack on her work.[3] Her enormous literary corpus, ranging from novels, short stories, and plays to prison memoirs, autobiographical texts, and travel memoirs, has remained, when viewed in its totality, largely uncharted territory.

This critical reaction—or lack thereof—is fascinating. Of all living Arabic writers, none more than Nawal El Saadawi has his or her finger so firmly on the pulse of Arab culture and the contemporary Middle East. (It is perhaps no accident that she is a practicing physician.) Little escapes her gender-conscious pen. Male-female relations, sexuality and the body, politics and government, theology and religion: these combine with a deceptively simple style to shape some of the most powerful narratives in contemporary Arabic—and world—letters.

How does one approach the widely diverse writings of a radical feminist like Nawal El Saadawi? We will begin our exploration of the Saadawian corpus by delving into the biographical and critical domain that today defines Nawal El Saadawi (Chapter 1). Because she is an important player on the contemporary Arab intellectual scene, El Saadawi's name is evoked by writers authoring works on subjects as diverse as intellectual history and the contemporary religious revival. She has the dubious honor of being discussed—and attacked—by Arab polemicists of widely divergent ideological positions. Issues of East and West, of authenticity and canonicity: these are but some of the theoretical questions that El Saadawi's mere textual presence generates.

Nawal El Saadawi was trained as a physician and practiced medicine. The science of the body has always been an important force in her writings (Chapter 2). Although there are other physician-writers in the Arab world—of whom probably the most famous is El Saadawi's compatriot and fellow medical student Yûsuf Idrîs (1927–1991), whose works have been widely translated[4]—these writers are of the male gender. El Saadawi stands in a category of her own. In her work, medicine allows the female physician to question games of power and social hierarchy.

El Saadawi's medical eye is never far from her literary pen. Michel Foucault has made us all conscious of the power of medical discourse.[5]

In El Saadawi, this discourse assumes a distinctive form, one that is tied to gender and social roles, subverting and redefining them. The female physician is more than a physical healer in the feminist's literary corpus. She becomes a modern-day Shahrazâd, giving voice in short stories and novellas to characters whose narratives would otherwise remain hidden.

How interesting it then becomes to have the role of narrator usurped from this powerful female physician by a prostitute. In *Woman at Point Zero* (Imra'a 'ind Nuqtat al-Sifr), the female psychiatrist frames the engrossing narrative of Firdaws, a prostitute condemned for the murder of her pimp. The primary forces driving her are both corporal and social, as woman's body becomes the elusive object whose control is in question. Yet *Woman at Point Zero* is more than a novel about a woman's recuperation of the body social and corporal; it also lays out a relationship between two women from opposite social classes, a Saadaw-ian duo that eloquently articulates the dilemma of women in a class-based society. Rather than being antagonists, the physician and the prostitute of *Woman at Point Zero* find themselves intimately drawn to each other. Chapter 3 of *Men, Women, and God(s)* investigates the dynamics of this female-female relationship, a relationship that ends in the corporal destruction of the lower-class character. By her existence and her death, Firdaws reminds us that her reality is indissolubly tied to her body. In this sense she is not too far from the narrator-heroine of *Memoirs of a Woman Doctor* (Mudhakkirât Tabîba), whose saga opens with a declaration of radical incompatibility between that narrator and her female body.

These two heroines signal an important—and pervasive—element in El Saadawi's creative writings: the corporal. But the body in the Saadawian literary corpus is more than a source of conflict. It is inti-mately tied to a discourse of gender and sexual definition (Chapter 4). What, in fact, constitutes the male body? What constitutes the female body? Nowhere are these questions more central than in Nawal El Saadawi's hauntingly poetic novel *The Circling Song* (Ughniyyat al-Atfâl al-Dâ'iriyya). The identical twins in this work, Hamîdû and Hamîda, are but two sides of a single coin, separated only by gender; their paral-lel trajectories in both village and urban environments highlight the cor-poral as this combines with the social. When Hamîda is impregnated through rape, she is banished from the village. Her brother, Hamîdû, is then sent to kill her and wipe out the shame. Brother and sister, a potentially explosive heterosexual duo in Arabo-Islamic civilization, play out a different story on the Saadawian stage.

Through rape Hamîda joins other of El Saadawi's literary heroines who undergo the same physical violation. She is also, by virtue of her low social class, Firdaws's counterpart. The very meaning of Firdaws's name—Paradise—calls attention to her hellish life. But the irony of the religious signifier is even sharper in the case of another Saadawian heroine: Bint Allâh, Daughter of God.

Bint Allâh and her literary neighbors in *The Fall of the Imam* herald a new type of Saadawian narrative. A highly complex literary work—perhaps El Saadawi's most complex—*The Fall of the Imam* has first-person and third-person narrators of both genders sitting side by side, sometimes in the same chapter. Bint Allâh stars in the novel with the Imam, both being woven into the fabric of a postmodern novel. He is the patriarchal ruler who governs with the usual paraphernalia of male power. His recurrent murder in the text is paralleled by the recurrent killing of Bint Allâh. Male body and female body are both subject to destruction.

*The Fall of the Imam* is an ambitious rewriting of patriarchy. Among its literary and religio-cultural games, the novel exploits the famous frame of *The Thousand and One Nights*, redefining the problematic relationship between Shâhriyâr and Shahrazâd. Chapter 5 of *Men, Women, and God(s)* will demonstrate the significance of this literary violation. El Saadawi's recasting is neither that of Eastern writers (e.g., Tawfîq al-Hakîm) nor that of Western writers (e.g., John Barth, Ethel Johnston Phelps). Hers is a radical vision that ties together both Eastern and Western patriarchal structures under the sign of the powerful literary serial murderer Shâhriyâr.

In the Saadawian system, patriarchy is an all-inclusive system that informs social, political, and religious structures. The Imam by his name, of course, reminds us of the religious side of his character. Thus Bint Allâh, we shall discover, is not only playing a literary game with *The Thousand and One Nights*. She is involved as well in an infinitely more complex and important game, that of redefining male theology and constructing an alternate, feminist religious mythology. Of course, the religious intertext was not alien to El Saadawi, who had already exploited it in some of her short stories. In *The Fall of the Imam*, however, this intertext becomes a dominant part of the narrative, even altering the quality of the Arabic language itself.

With her penultimate novel, *Jannât wa-Iblîs* (Jannât and Iblîs; the title of the English translation is *The Innocence of the Devil*), Nawal El Saadawi boldly continued the project begun with *The Fall of the Imam*. Whereas in *The Fall* the political dominated, redefining the social and religious structures with which it came in contact, in *The Innocence of the Devil* the religious intertext leads, redefining the political and social orders (Chapter 6). The setting of the book is an insane asylum, where Satan (Iblîs) and God are confined together as patients. As in *The Fall of the Imam*, events repeat and characters intertwine one with the other. Who is the Deity? Who is the Devil? More is at stake when we realize that Jannât's very name means Paradises (in the plural). In effect, this ambitious Saadawian narrative redefines not only the relationship between God and Devil, but also that between Adam and Eve, between man and woman. Christianity and Islam are both guilty here, and the Devil, like woman, becomes but another victim of the patriarchal order. Once again, the body is a central player, with the physical rape of the female merely one of its articulations.

If the dominance of patriarchy renders the vision in *The Innocence of the Devil* somewhat bleak, such is not the case in El Saadawi's play *Izîs* (Isis) (Chapter 7). A deliberate rewriting of Tawfîq al-Hakîm's play by the same title, the Saadawian *Izîs* constructs an alternate feminist view of the Isis legend. Here society is newly governed by a patriarchy that has self-consciously eliminated matriarchy. Two of El Saadawi's favored subjects are treated here: the frame of the *Nights*, clitoridectomy— though, in a violent twist, the play adds to this female corporal mutilation male castration. The bodies of slaves, like those of women, are not immune to the patriarchal deities. Violations here are multiple: corporal violations mirror the literary violation that consists in casting aside al-Hakîm's male vision of the ancient Egyptian goddess.

*Izîs* and *The Fall of the Imam* share a great deal, not the least of which is the dominance of a patriarchal ruler. Is it an accident that both works directly followed Nawal El Saadawi's prison memoirs? That incarceration was such a powerful experience for El Saadawi that it engendered not just *Memoirs from the Women's Prison* (Mudhakkirâtî fî Sijn al-Nisâ') but a play as well, *al-Insân* (The human being). *Memoirs* is not a mere chronicling of an imprisonment and subsequent liberation. Rather, the first-person narrator of this text weaves an intricate tale in which prostitutes and political prisoners sit side by side, in which fictional elements blend with nonfictional ones, and in which past and present merge as childhood memories redefine the incarceration. A female homosocial environment results. More important, the entire project that is the prison memoirs is one of metaphorical and literary violation. Investigation of these multiple violations will make it clear that the death of Sadat was a necessary act whose consequences go beyond the mere liberation of the narrator. The initial violation that set the book in motion is rectified gradually throughout the narrative, culminating logically with the death of the male ruler (Chapter 8).

The violations in El Saadawi's textual corpus are more than literary and metaphorical. They are also social. When a divorced Nawal El Saadawi ventures out of Egypt alone, she is subjected to harassment by airport officials. While it is not unusual for a Western woman to travel on her own, in the Middle East it is a different matter altogether. For Nawal El Saadawi, though, the issue is not merely travel; it is also travel writing, the creation of a discourse of discovery that crosses not only geographical boundaries, but historical and social ones as well (Chapter 9). When Nawal El Saadawi, the world traveler, traverses these borders, intricate games of identity are played out as the narrator uses various locales to make savage social commentary, for example on racism in the American South. For an Arabic reader, however, the crossing of these boundaries is not nearly as dramatic or provocative as the crossing of the gender boundary, as when the female traveler dresses as a man.

The insolence of the travel text is likewise a violation. *My Travels Around the World* (Rihlâtî fî al-'Alam) does not just tell of a woman venturing out most of the time alone. It tells us, for example, of an Arab woman sitting in a European café sipping a beer. A violation? It is more than that. The challenge this act represents is difficult to convey to Western readers unfamiliar with Arabo-Islamic culture on its many levels.

Such a depiction reminds us, lest we be prone to forget, that Nawal El Saadawi's writing must be seen as part of the literary, religious, and social discourses in the contemporary Middle East (Chapter 10). The textual battlegrounds on which she is fighting are quite Middle Eastern; if we ignore this fact, we denude her texts of much of their power and specificity. For example, one can hardly comprehend the literary danger (a devout Muslim called it blasphemy in my presence) of *The Fall of the Imam* without understanding Islam. (Some might draw a parallel between El Saawadi's novel and Salman Rushdie's *Satanic Verses*. Although the two books appeared at roughly the same time, El Saadawi's literary project is clearly different from Rushdie's.) *The Innocence of the Devil*, too, is based on close readings of the Islamic tradition.

Even the medical dilemmas that El Saadawi's patients face, whether in the fiction or in the programmatic works, are clearly—and intimately—tied to the society that gave the Egyptian feminist birth. This is part of what makes Nawal El Saadawi an Egyptian writer.

El Saadawi's concern with an overarching patriarchy whose roots are social, religious, and political combines with her treatment of gender and the body in a formula that is nothing short of feminist. Her political activism, however, is but one aspect of the war she has devoted her life to fighting. Her plots, her linguistic games, her literary allusions, her religio-legal intertextual references: these, too, are part and parcel of what makes Dr. Nawal El Saadawi a powerful Arab—and Arabic—writer.

# CHAPTER ONE

# Theorizing an Iconoclast

From a modest family background in an Egyptian village, Nawal El Saadawi went on to become a leading figure on the international feminist stage.[1] Her saga, both biographical and intellectual, is dramatic, traversing continents and propelled by some of the central theoretical issues of our age. Few other Arab intellectuals, and in particular women intellectuals, have had the dubious honor of being negatively singularized at once in the West and in the Middle East by writers of varying political allegiances. On the one hand is the distinguished scholar and Palestinian leftist activist Edward W. Said, who, writing in English in the *Nation*, calls El Saadawi "overexposed (and overcited)."[2] On the other hand is Dr. 'Abd al-Wadûd Shalabî, the Islamist thinker and activist, who, in his book on the contemporary Muslim world, blasts Nawal El Saadawi in Arabic.[3] Neither Shalabî nor Said stands alone. Many voices have been raised against the Egyptian feminist. Hisham Sharabi puts it most honestly: "It is difficult to explain to the non-Arab reader the effect . . . [El Saadawi's writings] can have on the Arab Muslim male."[4]

Despite such negative publicity, Dr. El Saadawi boasts an enormous readership both inside and outside the Arab world. As an important player on the contemporary Arab and Middle Eastern intellectual scene, her work always appears first in her native Arabic. Thereafter, Western advocates of cultural studies and women's studies devour El Saadawi's books in translation with seeming insatiability. Rare is the publication dealing with modern Arab letters, women's writing, or general intellectual trends in the region that omits the name of the Egyptian feminist.[5] She has even been the subject of doctoral study.[6]

Nevertheless, the first book written about El Saadawi in her native Arabic is not a book *about* her. It is a book *against* her: a Freudian-based argument that her writings contradict true womanhood. Its Arabic title, *Unthâ Didd al-Unûtha* (A female against femininity), accurately reflects its politics. In its English translation as *Woman Against Her Sex*, the book is the only extended work on El Saadawi in a European language.[7] Such a situation is most extraordinary for a Middle Eastern intellectual.

The wide familiarity of El Saadawi's name has its disadvantages, however. There is perhaps no other writer about whom so much misinformation has been propagated by critics, some of whom no doubt consider themselves favorably disposed to the Egyptian feminist.

To err is human, of course, but that is not the point. The point is that this controversial figure seems to have attracted more than her fair share of misrepresentation, and often of a sort that tends to have a marginalizing effect. It is almost as if critics felt the need to create an alternate biography of El Saadawi. Her year of birth has been changed.[8] Her medical specialization has been transformed into the one most closely attached to women's bodies and the one that befits the physician's own gender: gynecology. This speciality—which, oddly enough, El Saadawi never practiced—is then used to explain some of her work on sexuality and gender.[9] The translation of the feminist's works has been misattributed.[10] Finally, her own relationship to the Egyptian publishing industry—a not insignificant fact for an Arab intellectual—has been misrepresented. The publication of her prison memoirs, undertaken by the well-known Nasserite Muhammad Fâ'iq and his Cairo publishing house, Dâr al-Mustaqbal al-'Arabî, was transposed from Cairo to Beirut, an error that casts an undue shadow of censorship (and foreignness) over the work.[11]

Nawal El Saadawi was born in 1931 in the village of Kafr Tahla in the Egyptian Delta, and "grew up in a large family of nine brothers and sisters."[12] Her father believed strongly in education, which helped him to become a high official in the Egyptian Ministry of Education. El Saadawi, for her part, attended public schools before going on to study in the faculty of medicine at the University of Cairo. In other words, El Saadawi's formal education took place in native Egyptian Arabic-language schools.[13] This is hardly a given for Arab intellectuals, many of whom received substantial amounts of their education either outside the region or in foreign (and generally foreign-language) schools in the Middle East. Nor was Nawal the only child in her family to attend college: all her siblings did as well. But El Saadawi did not choose to pursue medicine for its own sake. Rather, as she puts it, "the Faculty of Medicine takes the best students, those with the highest grades." One of approximately fifty women among hundreds of men,[14] she graduated in 1955.[15] As a physician, El Saadawi practiced in the areas of thoracic medicine and psychiatry. She was appointed to the Ministry of Health in 1958, but in August 1972 she was dismissed from the ministry and from her post as Egypt's national public health director owing to her frank writings on sexuality, specifically in *Woman and Sex*.[16]

But the dangers that El Saadawi would face because of her uncompromising views became even more dramatic. In 1981, she was imprisoned by Egyptian president Anwar Sadat as part of his massive round-up and incarceration of Egyptian intellectuals. This period, though quite brief, had a powerful artistic impact on El Saadawi. Inspired by her carceral experience, she wrote *The Fall of the Imam*, a novel that helped place her name on the death lists circulated by conservative Islamist groups.[17]

It was also after her imprisonment that Nawal El Saadawi founded, in 1982, the Arab Women's Solidarity Association (AWSA), an international organization dedicated to "lifting the veil from the mind" of the Arab woman. In 1985, the association was granted "consultative status with the Economic and Social Council of the United Nations as an Arab non-governmental organization."[18] The AWSA organized conferences and weekly seminars and functioned as a locus for frank discussions of various topics related to gender analysis and women's status. In June 1991, however, the Egyptian government closed down the Arab Women's Solidarity Association and diverted its funds to a religious women's organization. El Saadawi, with her customary energy and convictions, took the Egyptian government to court, but to no avail. The association's magazine, *Nûn*, has also disappeared from public life.[19] El Saadawi chronicled this final phase of the AWSA's saga in *Ma'raka Jadida fi Qadiyyat al-Mar'a* (A new battle in woman's cause), using the occasion as well to demonstrate the world support that her organization received from international groups.[20]

These activities make Nawal El Saadawi perhaps the most visible woman intellectual in the Arab world. In addition, she is supposedly the only Arab woman whose name has been placed on the Islamist death lists. After the assassination of the Egyptian secularist intellectual Faraj Fûda in 1992, El Saadawi began to take these death threats more seriously. Although many Arab leftist intellectuals, whose names likewise appear on the death lists, have confidently declared to me that no Islamist group would ever kill a woman, this is not a chance that Dr. Nawal El Saadawi seems willing to take. She presently divides her time between Europe and the United States, with frequent but brief visits to her native Egypt.

If there is a single activity that has sustained the Egyptian feminist throughout her years in medical school, government employ, even prison, it is writing. Nawal El Saadawi tells with great pride of how she left her second husband, a lawyer. When his colleagues complimented him on a short story his wife had published, he presented her with an ultimatum: choose between him or her writing. "Well," she said, "I choose my writing."[21] This is a dramatic step for an Arab woman, for whom marriage still fulfills a socially sacred and legitimizing function. But such a step should not surprise anyone who knows Nawal El Saadawi. The demons of writing inhabited her even as a child. In 1944, at age thirteen, she had already penned a novel, *Mudhakkirât Tifla Ismuhâ Su'âd* (Memoirs of a female child named Su'âd).[22]

In the half-century since she penned that childhood story, El Saadawi has imposed herself on the world literary scene. Her latest novel, *al-Hubb fî Zaman al-Naft* (Love in the time of oil), appeared in 1993, almost fifty years after *Mudhakkirât Tifla*.[23] The corpus of fictional and nonfictional texts that the feminist physician-writer boasts is enormous: medical texts, short stories, novels, plays, prison memoirs, travel texts, critical essays. No other Arab woman (and few Arab men) approaches El Saadawi in the breadth of her writing. Nor has the Egyptian feminist ever shied away from controversial subjects. Her literary obsessions, ranging as they do from male-female relations to physical gender boundaries, make of her a literary iconoclast—in part, perhaps, because in El Saadawi's discourse the scalpel is never far from the pen.

If medicine is less prominent than art in El Saadawi's life, both are played out against the backdrop of politics. The Egyptian feminist tells, for example, of how as a secondary-school student she led demonstrations against the British and Egypt's King Farouk. Her political activities continued when she became a university student. Yet despite her strong and unswerving allegiances to political causes, including that of the Palestinians, Nawal El Saadawi has never joined a political party.[24]

For a Middle Eastern intellectual, this absence of overt political allegiance might seem inconsistent. In fact, however, El Saadawi's position simply foregrounds the complicated relationship that exists between politics and women's liberation in a non-Western and a nondominant cultural context.[25] In a seminal work now almost twenty years old, Fatima Mernissi argued that since women's liberation in the contemporary Middle East is associated with westernization, the entire issue becomes entangled in political and cultural debates.[26] For most Arab intellectuals (both of the Middle East and of North Africa), to be a leftist or a Marxist means to be politically (though not necessarily culturally) anti-Western, specifically anti-American. And while leftist politics in a third world context normally implies support for the general idea of women's equality, in fact such politics is frequently compatible with hostility to active movements advocating equality for women. Cultural critics are by now only too familiar with the story of women's active role in the Algerian War against French occupation. It is also clear by now that the expulsion of the foreigner freed Algerian women to move from the battlefield to the kitchen, and this under a leftist, modernizing, anti-imperialist, FLN government. Similar gender dynamics have appeared in the Palestinian struggle, which was until recently a consensus issue among Arabs worldwide. Liana Badr, a prominent Palestinian woman writer, eloquently lays out what she perceives to have been the weaknesses of the Palestine Liberation Organization vis-à-vis women's issues. Her conclusion? "Like all Arab regimes, the PLO has a cautious, perhaps reactionary attitude towards women."[27]

Hence, in the Middle East, to be a supporter of liberation causes does not necessarily indicate effective support for women's liberation. Nawal El Saadawi has often been questioned about political priorities. Should not the political struggle of oppressed and occupied peoples, like the Palestinians, take precedence over women's issues? After the expulsion of the foreigner, or after the revolution (or, for some, after the creation of the Islamic society), we will be able to sit down and work out these vestigial problems among ourselves. El Saadawi's replies have been consistent and categorical: women's oppression must be fought in the context, and as an integral part, of all other struggles for human liberation in the region, and indeed worldwide.[28] Her opposition to imperialism and the Western powers has been unvarying throughout her career, as seen most recently in her condemnation of the Gulf War as oil-inspired Western imperialism.[29]

It is not just that to El Saadawi, the refusal to adjourn women's issues to some future time is pragmatically essential in a region with so many other national, social, and political claims. The Egyptian writer's understanding of the relations of gender with class and other forms of oppression (a relationship clearly reflected in her writing) reverses the usual masculine political priorities. Without an attack on gender oppression, she argues, no lasting blows can be delivered against the other citadels of injustice. In a way, nationalist-based arguments against the urgency of women's concerns are local variants of a more general challenge, elegantly refuted by Mary Daly in her *Beyond God the Father*. As she puts it, the tactic of asking, "But isn't the real problem *human* liberation?" is simply a way to "make the problem [of women's liberation] disappear by *universalization*."[30]

Westerners like Mary Daly or Joanna Russ in her book *How to Suppress Women's Writing*, however, have not imagined all the ways in which an Arab feminist, such as Nawal El Saadawi, can be dismissed.[31] Nawal El Saadawi's detractors are made uncomfortable by her writings largely because they threaten many of the existing discourses on women in the Middle East. Discourses on Arab women in both the Middle East and the West are "privileged" (not necessarily a positive factor!) by being entangled with many other discourses, ranging from Orientalism, imperialism, and postcolonialism to world feminism and postfeminism.[32] To discuss the situation of Arab women today is to be dragged willy-nilly into these debates. The fiery nature of many of these discussions is rendered even more explosive by other political and religious developments in the region, such as the rise of the Islamist movement. Nawal El Saadawi, by inserting religion into many of her recent textual creations, has placed herself in the heart of the fray.[33]

All these debates have one thing in common: a concern with the problem of the West—as oppressor of the region, as purveyor of negative stereotypes (seen as linked to the first), and, most pointedly, as the source of a foreign movement called feminism, which, because of its foreignness, is either inapplicable or detrimental to Arab-Islamic culture and society. El Saadawi becomes in this view, despite her consistent opposition to Western imperialism (an opposition that her critics usually manage to avoid recalling), objectively a tool of Western imperialism. At the very least she can be labeled an outsider. How convenient it is symbolically to expel from the tribe the person one does not wish to hear. And how ironic, because what is most devastating about the arrows shot by this daughter of the Egyptian countryside is that their points are sharpened by an insider's knowledge.

Thus, many object that through her writings Nawal El Saadawi is giving the Arabs a bad name (read: in the West). In this view, even critics who discuss the Saadawian corpus are guilty, since they give exposure—and maybe even credence—to her positions.[34] After all, we all know that the Arabs have a far from favorable press in the West; discussing the likes of Nawal El Saadawi simply feeds that negative fire.[35]

These arguments seek to force the discussion of Arab women (whether by Arabs or by non-Arabs) into a rigid and politically loaded binarism: on the one hand, positive appreciations that easily turn into apologetics, and on the other, critical assessments that are characterized as attacks. A pernicious label has even begun to be attached to such critical assessments: Orientalist feminism.[36] Yet a defensive apologetic slides too easily into a defense of those in power—when it does not become a particular form of cultural arrogance which holds that Arabs cannot survive a frank discussion of their own social problems. Dr. El Saadawi has more confidence in the cultural and intellectual vitality of her people than that.

The message behind these arguments is a simple one: feminists like El Saadawi should be silenced lest they reveal dark secrets about the Arab world to non-Arab readers. I have talked about the implications of this silencing, an act that is nothing short of censorship, elsewhere.[37] Suffice it to say here that this silencing occurs when questions of gender are at stake, but it is rarely deemed necessary when class or other forms of oppression are called into question. No one accuses the leftist writer who denounces the upper classes or political despotism of giving the Arabs a bad name. Of course, none of this is meant to suggest that El Saadawi skirts issues of class. Far from it. As we shall see, class perspectives dynamically inform her gender analyses. Rather, the point is that El Saadawi treats gender problematics with a directness that is rare, not only in Arabic letters but in mainstream media throughout the world. It is this directness that makes her so threatening. The image-of-the-Arabs-in-the-West argument is but a smokescreen. What really matters is the attack she is waging on values long cherished—and not only in the Middle East.

The accusation of stoking anti-Arab fires, however, almost always carries other charges in its wake. Is not Nawal El Saadawi writing for a Western audience? Does this not make her a "Western" feminist? It would then follow that El Saadawi's writings do not provide their reader with an "authentic" vision of Arab women and the Arab world.

Any reasonable discussion of the applicability of an intellectual or political ideology in a non-Western context must consider not only feminism but other ideologies and movements as well. The most obvious of these is Marxism. While many Middle Easterners, notably neotraditionalists, reject Marxism as foreign and irrelevant, most of those, both inside and outside the region, who question the applicability of feminism have no objections to applying concepts like class, imperialism, capitalism, and exploitation to Middle Eastern societies.[38] Advocates of the "shouldn't be used there because not invented there" school of thought most often direct their objections not to ideologies that they themselves embrace but to ideologies that they find distasteful. Gender analyses seem to generate much more intellectual squeamishness than arguments derived from other social problematics.[39]

Yet gender consciousness is hardly new to Middle Eastern society. Social, cultural, historical, and legal questions relating to male-female roles, equality of women, and so forth have been part and parcel of Arabo-Islamic discourse for centuries.[40] This is one area where the culture had no need of a Western import.

Nawal El Saadawi has locked her powerful pen on many of the gender obsessions in her own culture and has woven memorable narratives around them. Her work demonstrates that it is possible to denounce women's oppression without taking a pro-Western stance and without forgetting the reality that class differences make in the varying patterns of that oppression.

But to seek to exclude feminist perspectives (that is, the reality that as groups males dominate females across the planet) from particular geopolitical zones—in this case the Arab world, the Middle East, or the world of Islam—is automatically to privilege patriarchal discourses within these zones. Anti-imperialism can easily become a trap through which nationalism, while seeking to defend the native against the outsider, really defends those in power in the native society. A feminism that is not internationalist will find itself powerless because it will allow nationalisms to be used against the empowerment of women in each separate society.

Can we dismiss as "Western feminism" the entire intellectual and artistic venture that examines these gender constructs? El Saadawi's very concrete discussions, her often sociological novels based on her personal observations of the lives of women in the city and the country, in the upper classes and the lower classes, stand as an eloquent refutation of this position.

The problem, however, lies deeper than the sociological specificity of Dr. El Saadawi's work. Rather, it goes to the very heart of the problematic notions of East-versus-West and authenticity. In 1991, the University of Texas Press advertised a translated novel by a Moroccan woman, maintaining that this work was "uniquely Moroccan," as opposed to "most novels by women of the Middle East that have been translated[, which] reflect Western views, values, and education."[41] At the time, the largest number of "novels by women of the Middle East" available in English translation were, indeed, by El Saadawi. But it is not important whether she was intended in this depiction. For this advertising copy simply articulates in writing what many voices utter in corridors or in closed gatherings: novels that present problematic images of the Middle Eastern woman "reflect Western views." The phrase "uniquely Moroccan" in the University of Texas Press advertising copy also implies that the reader will receive a more intimate and authentic look at the lives of Middle Eastern women.

But in fact both our Moroccan author and Nawal El Saadawi are circulating in an international world, one in which the East-West dichotomy is often misleading. To be sure, both writers begin in a regional context that is linguistically defined. They do this by deciding to write in Arabic. At the same time, they are swiftly drawn, more willingly than not, into a transnational circulation of cultural products.[42] Most successful Arab writers and scholars become part of an international market. I know of no Arabic author who does not wish to see his or her work translated and integrated into the world literary scene. Anyone who thinks this phenomenon is limited to the secularists—or the leftists, or the Westernized intellectuals—needs but walk into the Islamist bookstores of Paris and London, where one can find loving translations (into the languages of the colonizers) of the works of the most anti-Western Islamic neotraditionalists. And this is to say nothing of the Middle Eastern intellectuals whose lives are spent in exile in Western countries, hence partaking of at least two cultures. It is difficult to walk through the corridors of the Institut du Monde Arabe in Paris without bumping into some of the Arab world's most beloved thinkers and artists. And what of the many literary genres, such as the novel and the short story, in which non-Western writers (like our Moroccan friend) indulge—and which likewise are originally Western?[43] Universities around the globe are also sites of such cultural hybridization . . . but there is no need to belabor the obvious.

To speak of authenticity in this context is as vain as the tourist search for the authentic, unspoiled site, which ceases to be authentic as soon as the tourist sets foot in it. For there is no authentic modern Arab world (or discourse) if that means one untainted by Western culture.[44] Modern Arab culture, from its most secular to its most religious manifestations, from its most elite to its most popular products, bears the inescapable imprint of Western cultural exports. More important, there is no contemporary intellectual figure, be he or she the most neotraditionalist of Islamic revivalists, whose thought has not been powerfully affected by modern European ideas.

Furthermore, the discourse of authenticity plays two related political roles in the region. The first is the attempt to discredit as foreign one's ideological opponent. The second is a plea for recognition on the part of the budding artist or intellectual who has yet to gain access to the more lucrative international markets.

When El Saadawi writes, she does not speak for all Arab women. Hers is one voice. That does not mean that on a certain level of generality some of her fictional situations do not speak *about* all Arab women, indeed potentially about all women. Yet El Saadawi's texts, whatever their potential implications, are always firmly grounded and have as their first referents the realities of the condition of Arab women (and men, of course, in the process) in her own society. Though not all of her work is realistic in the literary sense, her texts are overwhelmingly based on her own direct knowledge and experience.

By the same token, to call attention to the transnational role played by many of El Saadawi's writings is not to deny their linguistic specificity. Nawal El Saadawi's narratives are intricately woven tapestries in which the choice of a word, like the color of a thread, becomes a vital marker. The rich linguistic specificity of these narratives can suffer when they are transposed into another language, such as English. A translation is a new cultural product, one that speaks to new audiences and new cultural concerns. Hence, translations can never be a truly adequate guide to the subtleties of El Saadawi's art.

But what about the Middle Eastern specialists, those able to read El Saadawi in her original Arabic? Too often, rather than analyzing this feminist literature, they have acted as if they wished to isolate it from the mainstream of Arabic letters. Consider, for example, this recent assessment by a Middle East specialist:

> The Egyptian physician, polemicist and authoress [sic] Nawal al-Saadawi has several works in English translation: some of these are extended in length and partly imaginative and are therefore considered to be novels. These include *Woman at Point Zero* . . . ; *God Dies by the Nile* . . . ; *Two Women in One* . . . ; *Memoirs of a Woman Doctor* . . . ; *The Fall of the Imam* . . . ; and *The Circling Song.* In each case these works combine autobiographical references and personal opinions with fictional representations of persons either real or imagined in a radical

feminist context with heavily emotional, anti-establishmentarian and anti-Islamic overtones. They are highly controversial in the Arab world.[45]

The implication here that snippets of autobiography and polemical journalism have been spread out with some imaginative material to the length of virtual novels is both methodologically questionable and factually inaccurate. Yet this assessment is not isolated. Sabry Hafez, speaking of *Memoirs of a Woman Doctor* and *The Fall of the Imam*, writes: "I hesitate to call them novels."[46] One could ask: if they are not novels, what are they? What the critic is really trying to do, of course, is to call into question their literary worth. Are we seeing in the begrudging attribution of the designation "novel" to a corpus that in fact is dominated by that genre a form of condescension not unknown to other women writers?[47]

But still more is at issue. Does the frankly polemical force of so much of the Saadawian corpus mean that the feminist's work is somehow not fully literary? The debate over art and political engagement is an old one. Nawal El Saadawi is clearly an *engagé* writer. But her writing is not limited to her political engagement. Indeed, its artfulness supports its politics. It is as complex as the Arabo-Islamic heritage that gave it birth.

# CHAPTER TWO

# Social Power, Body Power

*The struggle between me and my femininity began very early . . .
before my femininity sprouted and before I knew anything about
myself, my sex, or my origin . . . indeed, before I knew what
hollow had enclosed me before I was tossed out into this wide
world.*[1]

Thus does Nawal El Saadawi enter the domain of modern
Arabic novelists.[2] This statement, rich in corporal and social allusions, is
the opening line of her first published novel, *Memoirs of a Woman Doc-
tor* (Mudhakkirât Tabîba).[3] This struggle, whose evocation launches the
novel with the force and directness of cannon fire, dominates the work,
to be resolved only at its conclusion.

What about the physician of the title? Medicine and the physician
play key roles in the saga of the female protagonist. Medicine stands in
this first novel, as in many other of El Saadawi's works, at the intersec-
tion of social power and corporal consciousness. That social power per-
mits the female to overcome the power of the male. As such, the
woman doctor becomes the prototype of one of El Saadawi's most
common character types: the upper-class woman able to struggle
through to a position of relative autonomy and liberation. The corporal
consciousness is linked to a body knowledge that subverts claims of
patriarchal superiority by showing the artificiality of socially created gen-
der distinctions. The social power and body knowledge thematics give
revolutionary force to a novel that might otherwise seem conservative in
its general plot structure. After all, this is the story of a protagonist who

20

finds a successful resolution in the context of existing society. But as we shall see in this and subsequent chapters, the social power associated with such happy endings is not available to all women.

Several of the most sophisticated and most influential writers of the contemporary Arab world are or have been practicing physicians. There is a societal reason for this: in the Egyptian educational system, for example, the best secondary school graduates frequently entered the faculty of medicine, the career path that was at once the most demanding and the most prestigious. Further, different branches of the Arab intellectual elite are far closer to one another than is the case in the West (more like the situation in nineteenth-century Europe, for example). Hence, the designation "physician-writer" does not have the sense of duality or even possible contradiction that it has in the United States today. Among male physician-writers in Arabic, the best known is certainly the Egyptian fiction writer Yûsuf Idrîs, who died in 1991. Others include the Syrian 'Abd al-Salâm al-'Ujaylî and the Egyptians Mustafâ Mahmûd and Sherif Hetata. In the oeuvre of each of these men, medicine and/or the physician plays an important role.[4]

Much the same phenomenon exists in the fiction of medical practitioners in the West, like Richard Selzer and William Carlos Williams. But relative to her Western colleagues, the Egyptian feminist doctor makes less of disease and cures, focusing more often on the social role of medicine and the physician.[5] Striking, indeed, is her de-emphasis of the therapeutic process. Often, fictional situations that could lead to the medical treatment of physical maladies are resolved without professional intervention.[6] This Saadawian de-emphasis denudes medicine and science of part of their magical, technological power.

If the medical interaction between physician and patient is not the primary concern in these narratives, what is? In fact, the most pervasive function of medicine (and the physician) in the Saadawian fictional corpus is that of a repository of social power.[7]

In *Memoirs of a Woman Doctor* El Saadawi sets forth the major issues related to medicine and the physician that would dominate the rest of her fictional corpus. Despite its title and first-person narration, which suggest an autobiographical account (especially for those who know that its author is a female medical practitioner), the text nowhere formally presents itself as autobiography. Those crucial generic features identified by Philippe Lejeune as constituting the "autobiographical pact" are absent.[8] Despite some similarities, the life described is not that of the author.[9]

*Memoirs of a Woman Doctor* is a female *Bildungsroman* that adopts the fiction of autobiography.[10] Its opening expresses the long-standing and continuing conflict between the protagonist and her femininity. These sentiments extend to her female body as well, giving rise to resentment and hatred of its physical peculiarities.

The hero of the novel, who is first in her secondary school class, rejects her family's designs for her marriage and decides to enter the faculty of medicine. Science appeals to her greatly, but eventually this fascination is transferred to nature, when she moves to a peaceful country village. The accompanying partial resolution permits the hero to make peace with other figures in her life.[11]

Yet still something is missing, as we see in the novel's chronicling of the young woman's relationships with men. The first, with an engineer, ends in disaster when he tries to block her career. The second, with a physician, also fails. Only the third, with a musician/artist, finally permits her to come to terms with her career, her sexuality, and her feelings toward men.

*Memoirs of a Woman Doctor* tells a story of conflict and conquest. The language of its first-person narration is deceptively simple, consisting of short, choppy sentences generously interspersed with ellipses. The ellipses are not without meaning; they signal a hesitation on the part of the narrator, an uncertainty in the process of discovery of self.[12] Surmounting society's obstacles, the protagonist goes on to a successful, personally fulfilling career. To do so, social barriers are broken, ones associated with the body. Biology, we discover, is not destiny for this precocious narrator. Medicine provides the escape from the social and professional roles that the narrator's physical reality dictates.

As a child, the hero of *Memoirs* hated

> . . . the ugly, limited world of women, from which emanated the odor of garlic and onion.
>
> No sooner would I escape to my small world than my mother would drag me to the kitchen, saying, "Your future lies in marriage . . . You have to learn to cook . . . Your future lies in marriage . . . Marriage! Marriage!"
>
> That loathsome word that my mother repeated every day until I hated it . . . And I never heard it without imagining in front of me a man with a big belly inside of which was a table of food . . . [13]

When, in the opening chapter of El Saadawi's text, the narrator defines the limiting or negative nature of her femininity, she does so in a comparison with her brother:

And there was only one meaning for the word "girl" in my mind . . . that I was not a boy . . . I was not like my brother . . .

My brother cuts his hair and leaves it free, he does not comb it, but as for me, my hair grows longer and longer. My mother combs it twice a day, chains it in braids, and imprisons its ends in ribbons . . .

My brother wakes up and leaves his bed as it is, but I, I have to make my bed and his as well.

My brother goes out in the street to play, without permission from my mother or my father, and returns at any time . . . but I, I do not go out without permission.

My brother takes a bigger piece of meat than mine, eats quickly, and drinks the soup with an audible sound, yet my mother does not say anything to him . . .

As for me . . . ! I am a girl! I must watch my every movement . . . I must hide my desire for food and so I eat slowly and drink soup without a sound . . .

My brother plays . . . jumps . . . turns somersaults . . . but I, whenever I sit and the dress rides up a centimeter on my thighs, my mother throws a sharp, wounding glance at me.[14]

Not only is the hero defined by what she cannot do, by her unfreedom, but, perhaps even more important, her femininity is conceived not as an essence but as a difference—a difference grounded in and articulated through the body.

The first object the narrator focuses on is hair: hers (chained, imprisoned) versus her brother's (free). Braids and ribbons are normally external signs of femininity. El Saadawi's narrator thus effects a change of registers: external signs of femininity are turned into acts of confinement for the young girl. Perhaps it is not accidental, then, that her first overt act of rebellion should consist in her going to a beauty shop to have her hair cut. "Woman's crown" falls at her feet.

*Memoirs* chronicles three adolescent sexual encounters between the hero and members of the opposite sex. The first involves a doorkeeper who approaches her when she is sitting on a bench and attempts to explore her sexual parts with his hand. She stands up in terror and runs away.[15] The second episode involves a friend of her father's. She is asked to meet him, as a matrimonial prospect. When her father announces that she is first in her class, she expects the guest to show some admiration. But all she sees is the man scrutinizing her body, his eyes settling finally on her chest. She runs from the room, again in terror.[16] The third encounter is with her cousin, with whom she played as a child. They take a walk together and decide to run a race. When she is about to win, however, he pulls her down and tries to kiss her. For a moment, she wishes that he would embrace her fiercely, but when she comes back to her senses she becomes angry and slaps him.[17]

These three early encounters display the same dynamics: physical violation, be it overt or covert, of woman's body. The first example, with the doorkeeper, is a clear trespass. The second, that with the father's friend, is apparently more complex. Normally, in middle-class Egyptian society such an encounter would be viewed as socially licit, or at least free of violation. The narrator does not experience it that way, though, and so she runs away with the same terror. Hence this encounter must also be understood as an illicit one, representing a physical violation, though one more subtle than that committed by the doorkeeper. In the incident with her cousin, likewise, she interprets his advances as physical transgression, despite her own initial desire.

Notwithstanding their varying degrees of social acceptability, these three incidents are all treated in the text as more or less open forms of physical violation, as the exercise of unwanted male sexual power over woman. In the hero's adult experiences, however, it is she who determines the fate of her encounters with men, initiating and terminating relationships. The balance of power has shifted.

The rite of passage that separates the child from the adult is the hero's medical training. Medicine equals power; in fact, it is this power that motivates the narrator to attend the faculty of medicine in the first place.

The submissive domestic existence in the kitchen that must be rejected, the long braided hair that must be cut, the illicit sexual advances that must be countered: all these are dictated by the narrator's being a girl—in a word, by her female body. Nor is it mere coincidence that all these repudiations occur before the narrator decides to pursue medicine, a career centered on the body.

Responding to the societal limits and frustrations to be overcome, the narrator of *Memoirs* ends the first chapter by insisting that she will show her mother "that I am smarter than my brother, than man, than all men . . . and that I am capable of doing all that my father does, and still more . . . "[18] The physical difference will not only be defeated; it will be redefined in such a way as to provide the path to superiority rather than inferiority. The body will be the conquered, not the conqueror.

These declarations of superiority are social and intellectual: the narrator will prove that she is smarter than malekind. And the individual to whom this demonstration will be made is the mother, the upholder of woman's perceived inferiority and domestic role in the first chapter of *Memoirs*.[19] To turn the page on this initial chapter, both literally and figuratively, is to enter the universe that will alter the narrator's existence: the universe of medicine.

> The Faculty of Medicine?! Yes medicine . . .
> The word has a fearful impression on me . . . it reminds me of white shining glasses under which are two penetrating eyes moving with amazing speed . . . and strong tapered fingers holding a sharp frightening long needle . . .
> The first physician I saw in my life . . .
> My mother was trembling in fear and looking at him with supplication and humility . . . And my brother was shaking from fear . . . And my father was lying in bed looking at him with imploration and a plea for mercy . . .
> Medicine is a fearful thing . . . Very fearful . . . My mother, my brother, and my father look at it with a look of reverence and veneration.
> I will be a physician then . . . I will learn medicine . . . I will put on my face white shining glasses . . . I will make my eyes under them penetrating, moving with amazing speed. And I will make my fingers strong, tapered. I will hold with them a sharp frightening long needle.
> I will make my mother tremble in fear and look at me with supplication and humility . . . And I will make my brother shake in front of me from fear . . . And I will make my father look at me with imploration and a plea for mercy . . . [20]

This first exposure to medicine is interesting indeed, for here the science is subsumed in the identity of its practitioner, a male physician. That the physician should be a male may seem logical at first glance. But this gender label has deeper implications. The narrator's choice of medicine as an escape from the confining (and confined) domestic existence of the female sets up a dichotomy between the world of science and the world of the family, exemplified by the mother who ceaselessly advocates marriage and a life spent in the kitchen. Medicine on the one hand, the traditional world of the mother on the other: these are not foreign pairs on the contemporary Arabic literary scene. The blind Egyptian modernizer Tâhâ Husayn, for example, exploited them in his classic autobiography, *The Days* (al-Ayyâm), when he opposed the mother (and subsequently all women as a category) to the scientific knowledge embodied in modern medicine.[21]

What appeals initially to the female narrator of *Memoirs* is the effect that this man has on her family members: mother, brother, father—all three tremble before the mighty physician. The narrator would have us believe that their trepidation is the direct result of the raw power of the scientist. A closer look reveals, however, that the father is lying in bed. Why? Is he ill? If so, might not his reaction and that of the mother and brother be related to his infirmity? The narrator is oddly silent here.

This cloaking of the father's physical state is not a literary chance. In asserting her decision to become a physician, the young woman speaks of the effect she will have on her three family members: mother, father, and brother. Their response to the to-be female physician will be identical to those they already displayed to the male physician, but with one major difference. This time, the father is not lying in bed. There is no question about his physical state. The reason for his reaction and that of the other family members is clear: it is the female physician.

But what does it mean to be this idolized specialist? The male doctor, when we first meet him, is nothing more than isolated body parts: a set of "white shining glasses" with two darting eyes, strong fingers holding a long sharp needle. These body parts, eyes and fingers, are each linked to instruments external to the body, glasses and a needle. When the female supplants him, she is transformed into those identical corporal and noncorporal parts.

The eyes and the fingers are highly suggestive. The fingers are holding a long needle, an instrument of penetration. When the narrator refers to the eyes moving with speed under the white glasses, she describes them as "penetrating." Medical activity, whether that of the male physician or the female narrator, is redefined: no curative or healing attributes are evident. Power is reduced to its social and (male) sexual components.

And the primary vector of this power is the gaze. The scopic penetrating activity of the physicians operates in a dialectical relationship with the scopic activity of the other family members. Their glance is generated alternately by fear or a desire for mercy. The narrator's scopic game in which everyone's glance becomes significant (she sees the physician; the physician is first defined as someone who looks; the family members look on the physician with fear and a desire for mercy) is eloquent indeed. It becomes even more significant when seen in a Middle Eastern context. With this delicate scopic game, Nawal El Saadawi has entered a gender debate, one quite vigorous in the contemporary Islamic world, over the glance. Men looking at women, women looking at men: these issues plague Muslim religious authorities today. The power of the glance and its potentially destructive nature in creating *fitna*, or chaos provoked by woman's sexuality, is still hotly debated in pamphlets that pepper the streets of Middle Eastern cities (and some Western ones as well).[22]

The debate is a long-standing one in the Arabo-Islamic tradition; its roots go back centuries.[23] What El Saadawi has done, however, is to crystallize the issue in a contemporary literary text and redefine it. When her narrator ties the penetrating activity of the physician's eyes with the physician's needle, she extends the debate. The contemporary Moroccan sociologist Fatima Mernissi notes that the eye is "an erogenous zone in the Muslim structure of reality, as able to give pleasure as the penis."[24] The scopic power of the physician (from which the erotic is never fully absent) becomes a form of penetration that is virtually a violation.

This power, initially the attribute of the male, will become the property of the female through the science of medicine. Effectively, El Saadawi's position here concords with that in a story by Yûsuf Idrîs. In his "On Cellophane Paper," a woman, disgusted with her marital situation, experiences a change of attitude when she watches her husband perform a delicate surgical procedure.[25] If for Yûsuf Idrîs medicine can establish the power of the male gender over womankind, for Nawal El Saadawi it empowers a woman to escape the roles traditionally assigned to her sex. In another of El Saadawi's novels, *The Absent One* (al-Ghâ'ib), the female protagonist is prevented from entering medical school by her poor examination scores. In this case her mother had wished this career for her, since men were "useless."[26]

Medicine will do more for the narrator of *Memoirs*. The science of the body will help the female protagonist to conquer her own body: "Despite what is inside it and outside it of deficiencies [*'awrât*], I will triumph over it. . . . "[27] *'Awrât* is the plural of *'awra*, one of the most central, provocative, and emotionally laden words in *Memoirs*. In literary Arabic, this word signifies something shameful, defective, and imperfect, the genitals, and something that must be covered. As the signifier for the genitalia, it refers to men as well.[28] If the girl's dress rode up while she was sitting, her mother "would give her a sharp look," and she would hide her "*'awra*" "*'Awra*! Everything in me is *'awra*, though I am a child of nine years!"[29]

In El Saadawi's text, the *'awra* of the private parts is made to expand and apply to the female hero's body in its entirety. In large part the concept of *'awra* contributes to the sense of difference that the young woman feels and that sets her apart, that marginalizes her. *'Awra* is thus a sign whose signifieds expand outward in concentric circles from a physically circumscribed reality to the hero's dilemma.

The primary referents of 'awra are corporal: they are the private parts of the hero of *Memoirs*. But this loaded word also stands for the femininity of the female physician. 'Awra can make this semiotic leap because it is, in fact, part of a physico-moral discourse in Arabic culture—a discourse of the body. In this discourse, a physical reality that in itself possesses no necessary moral or social meaning is invested with a moral value. This investment, in turn, dictates social conclusions.

'Awra is central to the predicament of the narrator, the key cultural reality against which she rebels, embodying the sense of physical shame and inadequacy and the restrictions that society places upon her as a female. Her entire body takes on the notions of shame and imperfection. Such a generalization is perfectly consistent with traditional Arabo-Islamic values.[30]

This narrator is treading on provocative ground. What is and is not 'awra in woman—that is, the question of woman's modesty—has been and remains a hotly contested issue in Islamic writings of all periods, drawing men and women, more and less conservative scholars to the question of precisely what 'awra encompasses.[31] The preoccupation in *Memoirs* with the notion of 'awra thus proves to the discerning reader that El Saadawi is well attuned to the course of these debates in the contemporary Middle East.

That medicine helps this narrator overcome her 'awra should probably not surprise us. After all, we are still in the domain of the corporal. But nature is equally important for her ultimate liberation, helping to heal her wounds and lead her to a rebirth. After she completes her medical studies, our hero replaces the god of science with that of nature. In the countryside, she lifts her gaze from the "wide, peaceful, green fields to the pure, blue sky" and "surrendered to the rays of the sun and let them fall on my body." When a light breeze blows the covering from her legs, she is not hit by "that old terror which I used to feel when my legs were bared." This environment, in effect, permits the hero to escape not only from the constraints of the city but also from those associated with her femininity and her body. She disregards, for example, all of her mother's advice on how a girl should eat—compliance with which, as we saw, distinguished her from her brother—but rather fills her mouth with food and drinks noisily. These actions, now performed with unrestrained physicality, show once again the limitations that a female body traditionally places on its subject.

Most important, nature brings about a rebirth: "I felt at that moment that I was born anew."[32] After this awakening, the young physician wonders how her mother had been able to instill in her "that loathsome sensation that my body was 'awra."[33] The presence of nature in the female *Bildungsroman* is certainly nothing new. Annis Pratt and Barbara White have amply shown its predominance in *Archetypal Patterns in Women's Fiction*, stating that "Nature . . . becomes an ally of the woman hero, keeping her in touch with her selfhood, a kind of talisman that enables her to make her way through the alienations of male society."[34] It is also a positive force that, in combination with the narrator's medical education, can help erase social corporal restrictions.

But what an education the narrator receives in medical school! The most powerful manifestation of that education is in the form of cadavers. If for Yûsuf Idrîs the operating table was the locus of male power, a power strong enough to bring the physician's wife back to his fold, for the narrator of *Memoirs* it is the dissection table that holds power, and a power that demonstrates not the superiority of the male over the female, but his vulnerability. Dissection, first of a male corpse and then of a female one, plays an important role in the development of the hero's gender consciousness. Medicine (through dissection) will permit the physical destruction of the two bodies and with them a recasting of many of the issues that earlier plagued the narrator.

There she is in the dissection room in the presence of the two naked bodies. The male corpse lying alongside that of the female raises questions in the narrator's mind. It is as if she were reliving her childhood and reexamining the values that her mother and society tried to instill in her. Even her previous violations will be redefined.

> Why did my mother place these enormous differences between me and my brother and make of man a deity for whom I had to spend all my life cooking food?
>
> Why is society always trying to persuade me that masculinity is a distinction and an honor and femininity a disgrace and weakness?
>
> Is it possible for my mother to believe that I am standing with a naked man in front of me and with a scalpel in my hand with which I will open his stomach and his head?
>
> Is it possible for society to believe that I am contemplating a man's body and dissecting it and cutting it up without feeling that it is a man?
>
> And who is society? Is it not men like my brother whose mother raised him since his childhood as a god? Is it not women like my mother who are weak and useless?

> How is it possible for these people to believe that there is a woman who knows nothing about man except that he is muscles, arteries, nerves, and bones?[35]

Like a series of flashbacks, these questions bring the reader back in time to the childhood experience of the narrator. Moreover, they stand out from much of the prose of *Memoirs* by their lack of ellipses. There is no hesitation here on the narrator's part. We see again the essential differences between her and her brother. We relive the scenes in which the mother attempted to inculcate the values of cooking and marriage in the narrator's young mind. But the questions extend these childhood events into a general social commentary. The mother's actions become those of all women, and her sin, more universal.

One question, inserted among the others, overshadows the rest: "Is it possible for my mother to believe that I am standing with a naked man in front of me and with a scalpel in my hand with which I will open his stomach and his head?" Certainly a woman contemplating a male stranger's naked body is provocative in a Middle Eastern context: one can well imagine the mother's response. But that is only half of it. The scalpel and the opening of the stomach and the head will reappear in the book like an obsession.

> Man's body! That dreadful thing with which mothers frighten their young daughters, so they are consumed by the fire of the kitchen for the sake of his satiation and they dream of his spectral figure night and day! There he is, man, thrown in front of me, naked, ugly, torn to pieces . . .
> I did not imagine that life would disprove my mother to me so quickly . . . Or would avenge me of man in this way . . . That dejected man who looked at my breasts one day and saw nothing of my body but them . . .
> There I am returning his arrow back to his chest . . .
> There I am looking at his naked body and feeling nauseated . . .
> There I am bending over with my scalpel and tearing him to pieces . . .
> Is this man's body?![36]

Once again, mothers are to blame, for they instill the values of domesticity in their daughters. The result? The young women "are consumed by the fire of the kitchen." But this is not any fire. The word used is *nâr*, a word also used for hellfire. More than polysemy is involved here, however. Daughters would not normally be "consumed by the fire of the kitchen" (at least not literally), but they certainly can be by the fire of hell, which is what the kitchen has become. From the world of enforced domesticity, woman moves into the domain of religious punishment, from the world of onion and garlic into that of eternal damnation.

What a stunning reversal of the earlier discourse of marriage inculcated by the mother! Nonetheless, the narrator has still not had her full revenge. This will come about when the male corpse is violated by her scalpel, much as she herself had felt violated by a man's unwanted glance at her chest. The dead male corpse is made to pay for the illicit acts of the male gender in its entirety. Man's body is penetrated and torn to pieces.

The female corpse, whose inanimate existence is framed by her hair, also has a role to play. Both in introducing us to this anonymous young woman and in closing the account of the dissection, the narrator focuses on a single body part: the hair. It begins the description long and soft and ends it in the pail of the dissection room, together with the other discarded body parts, in a striking narrative trajectory. In between, the narrator moves along the body down from the hair to the white teeth and long, painted fingernails, ending at the chest.

Much like her dead male colleague on the dissection table, the female corpse fulfills more than a medical function.

> Her breasts are over her chest but they are thin, hanging down . . .
> The two pieces of flesh that tortured me during my childhood . . . the two that determine the future of girls and occupy the minds and eyes of men . . .
> There they are resting under my scalpel, dried up, wrinkled like two pieces of shoe leather![37]

The narrator describes the breasts of the dead female and, in a stunning shift, begins to speak of her own breasts. These are turned into pieces of meat, independent of the body. They become the active subject of the act of torture, of the delimitation of women's future, and of the preoccupation of men. It is as if woman's body becomes victim of these "two pieces of flesh."

Woman's breasts, like woman's hair, have their own trajectory. They move from the dead body to become attached first to the narrator and then to the entirety of women. When they return to the corpse, it is as two desiccated objects resembling shoe leather. From body parts that elicit such admiration on the part of men (and society), the breasts join the lower body in a less than flattering image.

The hair is equally eloquent. When the female cadaver is first intro-
duced, it is through her "long soft hair." When the "long soft hair"
reappears, it is directly linked to the narrator. "And the long soft hair
over which my mother tortured me the years of my childhood . . .
Woman's crown and the throne of her beauty . . . " The hair effects a
direct identification first between corpse and narrator and then with all
women. The hair as crown is an image that El Saadawi's Egyptian read-
ers recognize. On the opposite side of the religio-cultural spectrum, the
Muslim revivalist Karîmân Hamza in her spiritual autobiography has a
narrative battle over covering her hair. She notes how the women's
magazine *Hawwâ'* (Eve) always exhorted her: "Your Hair . . . Your
Crown."[38]

The power of the hair should come as no surprise. After all, was it
not a basis of difference between the narrator and her brother? And was
not cutting it the narrator's first act of defiance? In this, the narrator of
*Memoirs* is not unlike her literary cousin, the heroine of Laylâ
Ba'labakkî's novel *Anâ Ahyâ*, who also cuts her hair as an act of rebel-
lion.[39] As Nancy Huston has shown, a link between hair and sexuality
has existed from time immemorial.[40] Under the Egyptian feminist's pen
(might we also add scalpel?), the combination takes on special mean-
ing, helping to circumscribe what is and is not the female body (see also
Chapter 4).

Part of the power of these dissection room scenes lies in their
imagery. But more than language and image are at issue here. In ques-
tion is the redefinition of societal gender boundaries. The cadavers are
unwilling pawns in this morbid game. The narrator moves with uncom-
mon swiftness from dead bodies to childhood experiences; from the
kitchen fire to hellfire; from the violation of the male glance to the
female violation of the male body; from a young girl's breasts to the
shriveled breasts of a dead woman. These all seem essential to the rede-
finition of incidents in the narrator's childhood. The identity of sorts
between the narrator and the female corpse means that the narrator has
died as well. In fact, she declares just this ("Ah . . . I have died") before
jumping up to run out of the dissection room.[41] Yet she fights this iden-
tification with death: "No! I will never die and become a corpse like
these corpses stretched out in front of me on the tables."[42]

It is as if only death could fully exorcise the traumatic experiences of
her youth. But this is not just any death. It is death seen through the
prism of medicine. The medical universe has once again united the
social and the corporal.

The process of dissection, along with the rest of the medical school experience, leads the narrator to the conclusion, proven by science, that woman is like man, and man like animals. "Woman has a heart, a brain, and nerves, exactly like man . . . And an animal has a heart, a brain, and nerves, exactly like a human . . . "[43] The body as physical entity is the great equalizer.

Yet there is more to medicine in *Memoirs* than the power of knowledge. Although at first the hero conceives of medicine as science and as an all-powerful deity, she begins to change her mind when she sees one of the physician instructors slap a patient; she now decides that this medicine, at least, lacks compassion.[44]

In fact, medicine is not only the catalyst that redefines childhood experiences (in the dissection of the two corpses, for example), but it is also the element that will delimit the adult experiences of the female protagonist. This will be accomplished not by the bodies of the dead, however, but by the bodies of the living, in the form of patients.

The first patient the female physician encounters is a young woman afflicted with rheumatism. To add to the complexity of the situation, this patient is pregnant, and we meet her as she is giving birth. Her fate is doomed, though: she dies during childbirth, leaving behind a healthy baby. The physician finds medicine to be particularly ineffective in helping her to understand this mystery that permits life to emanate from death. "How was a living child born from the body of a woman who is dying?" This event permits the conflict in the hero's life to move from the domain of masculinity and femininity to that of humanity in general.[45]

The second patient is an older male peasant carried to the physician's country home in the middle of the night. Like the pregnant woman, this man has a greater role to play than that of simple patient, the object merely of professional duty. His diseased existence permits the hero to feel pain for the first time in her life. Her outbreak of tears elicits an emotional response from the patient, who tries to reassure her. She comments, "It is as though the disease of the body diminishes next to the disease of the soul, so I feel that he is the physician and I am the patient."[46]

This role reversal has its function. The sick old man bears a gift for the hero: he helps her regain her faith in humanity. And as if this were not enough, his smile causes her to become aware of her love for life. She realizes that she is but a twenty five year old child, "a child who wants to run and play and be free and love."[47]After the incident with this patient, moreover, the physician finds herself able to cast aside her earlier medical knowledge of man's body, a necessary prerequisite for her love quest: "It is as though I had not dissected the body of a man . . . as though I had not laid him bare . . . as though I had not seen his repulsiveness and his ugliness."[48]

Is it a surprise, then, that medicine and patients become coterminous with the amorous relationships of this woman doctor? It is two o'clock in the morning, and the young physician is awakened by a voice: "Save my mother from death, Doctor." The hero responds to the call and discovers an older woman, her heart weak from age. The son has to ask twice whether his mother's state is serious. "No," the hero responds, "it is not serious . . . She is only dying." The son is, of course, shocked by her response, but she entreats him to let his mother die in peace.

This man, an engineer, reappears in the physician's life, not as the son of a patient, but as her future husband. Their relationship begins as one of mutual misunderstanding. He has an idea of a woman doctor that, interestingly enough, has some similarity to the first scopic image of a physician the narrator exposed us to: "I used to imagine that a female physician had to be ugly or old . . . Wearing on her eyes thick white glasses . . . " It is difficult for this man to conceive of a woman who is at once beautiful and intelligent.[49] By the same token, the narrator responds to the engineer's marriage proposal with her received notions tying marriage to food. When he asks her a second time if she will marry him, she has a flashback and thinks about the meaning of the word marriage: "A man with a big stomach inside of which is a table of food." She responds by asking the engineer if he likes food. His surprised reaction elicits this explanation: "Man gets married so he can eat."[50]

The union is doomed. It was created by her professional status as a physician called upon to save the engineer's mother. When he asks the narrator if she wishes to live with him forever, she notes that he looks at her "with the look of an orphan child." It is her sense of motherliness that is initially stimulated. Once locked into the relationship, however, the physician finds her husband urging her to abandon her clinic and her medical career. Her response? She leaves him.

This amorous failure described in *Memoirs* fits only too well into Pratt's archetypal patterns, but with one major difference. In the prenuptial stages of the relationship, the man offers more than he is in fact willing to deliver. The woman is lured into what she believes is a relationship of mutual equality; the marriage, however, proves to be the opposite. This is the first part of the archetypal structure. But unlike the protagonists discussed by Pratt, El Saadawi's female hero will not allow her health (read, her body) to atrophy. Instead, she leaves her husband and continues her quest.

Before the narrator finally meets the right partner, she must have a second negative relationship, this time with another physician and instigated by a man afflicted with cancer. The two doctors are in attendance in the operating room where the body of this diseased individual has been "opened." Like other men, the male physician sees the woman only as a physical object. The narrator breaks off this relationship, concluding that she must fight and resist society's pressures on her.[51]

The successful relationship that represents the resolution of the narrator's conflicts is with an artist, and medicine and a patient likewise play a significant role. The couple meet at an official dinner party, where both express an aversion to the traditional trappings of these sorts of gatherings. Fortuitously, the artist is later present at the physician's home when the phone rings. Again an anxious voice pleads: "Save him from death, Doctor. He is dying." This time, however, the physician does not go alone; her companion accompanies her to the bedside of a young man with pulmonary tuberculosis. The young man is in desperate need of a blood transfusion, and the artist goes out to get the blood. He also helps the physician to set up the transfusion. When she urges him to move away from the patient lest he become infected, he replies:

> —And you?
> —This is my duty . . . I have to do it under the worst of circumstances . . .
>
> He looked at me in silence . . . And he did not move from his place until I finished setting up the transfusion equipment . . .[52]

The two then sit next to each other and watch the blood drip into the patient's artery. The physician tells her companion: "If you had not been with me, I could not have done it alone . . . ." He replies that she could indeed have done it. No matter; the patient is saved, and he thanks the duo. He then draws out one Egyptian pound to pay the physician. She, however, faints. We later understand that this response may have been due to the intense shame she feels for having taken money from patients for so many years. The moral of this particular story? Medicine does not consist merely of diagnosing disease, prescribing the appropriate drugs, and collecting money. Rather, medicine means providing succor to those in need, with no strings attached.[53]

This episode leads to the personal fulfillment of the narrator of *Mem-*

*oirs*, a fulfillment that is arrived at neither quickly nor easily. What gives this incident its curative power? This most recent relationship was initiated on nonmedical, neutral ground, at an official dinner party. The medical emergency surfaces only after the couple have declared their love for each other. But this fact does not necessarily seal the relationship. The patient still has an important role to play.

Unlike the earlier phone call in which the doctor is entreated to save a patient from death (the engineer's mother), here the physician actually does cure the patient—but only, as she herself declares, with the help of her male companion. Unlike the first visit, where the narrator in her own car is the lone person on a medical errand, this last visit is accomplished in her male companion's car. He, in fact, does the driving. At the patient's bedside, the medical need for the blood is fulfilled by the male. And he helps to set up the transfusion, remaining with the doctor until the operation proves successful.

When she examines the patient's chest, the narrator realizes that his life depends on a vial of blood. Her companion asks her:

> —Do you need something?
> —A bottle of blood now from the emergency center.
> He ran to the door saying:
> —I will go in the car and get it immediately.
> I sat on a wooden chest next to the patient and injected him with medicine . . . I prepared the blood transfusion equipment . . . and determined the blood type . . . [54]

Did the artist wait long enough before leaving to learn the blood type from the physician? We must assume so, for otherwise how could he get the correct blood? But that is almost beside the point.

This medical ellipsis (if we may call it that) signals that the episode is not so much about medicine as about something else, and that something else is the narrator's relationship with her companion. He goes out and brings blood, the life-giving force. The blood type is irrelevant. The two will participate equally in this activity of giving life. They will cure the patient and allow him to be reborn. As a couple, they are participating in the activity of birth, albeit metaphorically.

We have in a sense come full circle. We are oddly near yet oddly far from the physician's first patient, the young woman afflicted with rheumatism who died as she gave birth. Here, the couple gives birth, in what is for them a life-giving process. Medicine is at last successful. And if we remember that the momentous phone call occurs in the text directly after their mutual declarations of love, after the couple has formed itself, then childbirth seems the logical next step.

It is only because the doctor is able to overcome her obsession with medicine as power that she is also able to transcend her focus on the male-female power struggle and come to terms with both her femininity and medicine. This last is now science *and* art, reason *and* compassion.[55]

One of the interesting elements in the system outlined by the narrative is that while the female physician-heroes integrate these two aspects of medicine, the male physicians do not. The incident with the patient afflicted with cancer is a case in point. Indeed, in *Memoirs*, and in the work of Nawal El Saadawi generally, one really finds two types of physicians: those who are capable of compassion (almost invariably women) and the cold-hearted embodiments of science (always men). In only two short stories by Nawal El Saadawi do male physicians play a central role without being opposed to women doctors in the same narrative. And both these tales appear in her first published collection of short stories, *I Learned Love* (Ta'allamt al-Hubb). In one, "Something Else" (Shay' Akhar), the reader is treated to a day in the life of Dr. Rajab, economically less well off than his neighbor, whose Cadillac he envies. Dr. Rajab insults his staff, has too many patients and not enough beds, and feels that he has wasted his seven years in medicine.[56] In the second text, "This Time" (Hâdhihi al-Marra), the male physicians function as objects of desire for the nurses, who see them as offering an escape from the poverty and squalor of their lives.[57]

The arbitrariness of making the woman doctor caring and her male counterpart uncaring is evident when one looks at the strategy of Sherif Hetata, also a physician-writer (and the husband of Nawal El Saadawi). In *The Eye with the Iron Lid* (al-'Ayn Dhât al-Jafn al-Ma'danî), for example, he pairs off two male doctors, one cold-hearted and cowardly, the other courageous and compassionate.[58]

Nawal El Saadawi develops the sexual politics of medicine in two ways: first, by using it as a vehicle for women to regain their lost power; and second, by making it the focus of her own call for the integration of traditionally male and female qualities.

This complex of elements is not restricted to *Memoirs of a Woman Doctor*. In *Two Women in One*, for example, similar themes emerge. The female hero is a medical student who is torn between her medical training and her career as an artist. The same dichotomy is set up in the young woman's relationships with men: on the one hand there is the medical doctor, a professor in the faculty of medicine, and on the other, the young man who encourages the hero in her artistic endeavors.[59]

The thematic nexus of science and art, entities that pull in opposite directions, pervades the fictional narratives of Nawal El Saadawi, tearing her female heroes apart.[60] In one short story, "A Special Letter to an Artist Friend" (Risâla Khâssa ilâ Sadîq Fannân), the first-person narrator (not surprisingly, a physician) speaks of the conflict that has plagued her since birth: she wanted to become an artist, and wonders what drove her to pursue medicine.[61] That medicine precludes art is also apparent in the novella *al-Khayt* (The Thread). As the patient in this text puts it baldly to the female physician, "You are a physician and not an artist."[62]

This conflict is perhaps most articulately expressed by the woman doctor in the short story "All of Us Are Confused" (Kullunâ Hayârâ). Here, the narrator reveals that she erred in choosing medicine: "I should have been an artist, or a poet, or a writer." The faculty of medicine, she charges, is really the "Faculty of Illness, and Moaning, and Death."[63] Much the same assessment is made by the female hero in the story "When I Am Worthless" (Hînamâ Akûn Tâfiha). Here, the physician narrator expresses her disgust at both her financial and her social status when she wonders how she could possibly have lost her way and entered the field of medicine.[64] The idea of medicine as death is extended even to the accoutrements of the physician. In *Two Women in One*, for example, the metal stethoscope hanging around a physician's neck is likened to a hangman's rope, an image that is repeated in *Memoirs*.[65]

Thus medicine becomes a focus for conflicts and choices in the lives of young women, and these conflicts and choices revolve around medicine as a total system, especially as a career. Nawal El Saadawi's writings explore the relations of power, medicine, and the female condition in other ways than simply by centering on medicine as a career. This she does by focusing on the physician-patient relationship, using a significant, and eminently characteristic, literary technique.

In some highly innovative texts, El Saadawi exploits a narrative technique that, though it brings her close to her medieval literary sister Shahrazâd, is relatively unusual in modern Arabic letters. This technique is one of embedding or enframing, familiar to Eastern and Western readers alike from *The Thousand and One Nights*.[66] A female physician, acting in her professional capacity, becomes the first narrator who enframes a story told, eventually, by the patient.

*Woman at Point Zero* is certainly one of El Saadawi's most powerful novels. Its external narrator is a psychiatrist working in a women's prison. She begins the story by explaining her interest in the case of one of the prisoners, Firdaws, a prostitute convicted of murder and awaiting execution. The bulk of the novel then consists of the convicted killer's narration of her own life. The physician is drawn to this woman—realizing, at the end of the novel, that she herself is no better than the prostitute. We shall examine this duo in detail in Chapter 3.[67]

Firdaws's discourse is oral: it is her physical voice that transmits her story. The voice of many other Saadawian female heroes is epistolary. The physician narrator of the novella *The Thread* tells the reader, in the frame, that she once had occasion to examine a woman with strange symptoms. The physician later receives a letter from this patient, outlining events from her perspective. Thus we see the doctor and medicine through the eyes of this patient, who has had a neurotic relationship with her father. The patient, addressing the physician–external narrator, explains at length that the physician's very occupation precludes her being a woman, that she is incapable of feeling, and then poses the question, Can medicine turn a human being into a stone? The patient's neurosis clearly connects this cold, "scientific" aspect of medicine with patriarchy.

*The Thread* and *Woman at Point Zero* are similar in several respects. In each case a female physician is reflected through the eyes of a female patient, with the patient receiving more narrative space than the doctor. In addition, both works deliberately set the patient up as the social opposite of the physician. Yet the patient's voice, whether oral or epistolary, finally calls this separation into question. In this way, both *The Thread* and *Woman at Point Zero* cast doubt on the role of the physician as an epitome of science and wisdom, superior to, and detached from, the patient.

It is no coincidence that external and internal narrators, doctor and patient, are both women. The literary linkage reflects their common embodiment of the female condition. Physician and patient alike are caught in the coils of sexual politics.

The frames in *The Thread* and *Woman at Point Zero* show us, in a sense, only half the picture. Another Saadawian text, the short story "The Man with Buttons" (al-Rajul Dhû al-Azrâr) uses the framing technique as well, but here there is nothing medical about the internal narrative; it could, in fact, stand on its own, without the external narration of the physician.[68] In this story, the physician narrator explains that she had published a story entitled "My Husband, I Do Not Love You,"[69] to which a reader replied, expressing her dislike of the narrator's story and presenting her own. The owner of this internal epistolary voice is named Firdaws, like the internal narrator of *Woman at Point Zero*. We will compare the sagas of these two women in Chapter 3, when we analyze the story of Firdaws the prostitute.

In both narratives, the doctor is able to liberate the stories and give them forms that will assure their life. Here, then, the physician narrator differs from her literary cousin Shahrazâd, who had to rely on the male to assure that her oral stories were turned into written, permanent narratives.[70]

If these internal narratives could have stood on their own, without help from an external narrator, what is the purpose of the embedding? First, the external first-person narrator adds a second subjectivity to that of the internal narrator. More important, the embedding technique turns the narrative authority over to the physician, who thus becomes responsible for the transmission of the internal stories. Finally, by having embedded narratives that are not directly related to medical questions, the texts extend the power of the physician beyond the medical into the general. This can be seen in another story, *The Well of Life* ('Ayn al-Hayât), in which the physician narrator tells the story of a woman she had examined while practicing medicine in Jordan.[71]

In these four cases of embedded narratives, the stories, both internal and external, are about women. In all four cases, moreover, a physician narrator presents the saga of a woman who might not, because of her social situation, have the opportunity for literary self-expression. The physician, as a figure of social power, thus serves as a literary conduit that allows the other voices to speak out.

Here again, medicine as a vehicle of empowerment for individual women is set against the more general context of relative female powerlessness. But something far more subtle and more culturally encompassing is being intimated. As cultural critics beginning with Michel Foucault have shown repeatedly, medicine acts as a special discourse, itself a form of power.[72] Like the writer, the physician interprets a reality, codifies it, explains it, and then reports and transmits it to other physicians. In the Saadawian corpus, the social power of the physician merges with that of the writer.

In "Qissa min Hayât Tabîba" (A story from a woman doctor's life), a third-person narrator introduces the text: "Dr. S. wrote in her diary"[73] This statement is followed by the first-person narrative of Dr. S. and the permanent disappearance of the third-person narrator from the story. This is an odd coincidence, indeed, the initial S. standing, among other things, for El Saadawi. In any event, the story that Dr. S. proceeds to recount is as follows: A young girl is sitting in her clinic, flanked by a tall young man, her brother. The brother asks the physician to examine his sister, wishing to be reassured about her, "since we are marrying her to her cousin next week." The girl cuts her brother off, insisting that she does not love this man and does not wish to marry him. The brother, however, responds that she does not want to marry him for "another reason, Doctor . . . I think you understand"—a clear allusion to the possibility of her having already lost her virginity.

Observing the fright in the young girl's eyes, the physician asks the brother to leave the room so that she can perform the examination. Alone with the doctor, the girl refuses to be examined, but begs her to save her from this brother, who, she says, will surely kill her. The physician decides that she cannot proceed without the girl's permission and tells her that she will so inform the brother. The girl objects, insisting that he will simply take her to another doctor. She then asks the physician to claim that she examined her and found her "honorable." Her brother, she again says, will kill her otherwise. But she is in love with another man and will marry him in a month. She swears to the physician that nothing dishonorable has occurred between them. (Similarly, a young woman had visited the narrator of *Memoirs of a Woman Doctor* in search of protection from murderous male relatives.[74])

Examining her own conscience and the medical code of ethics, the physician in the story calls in the brother and declares to him that his sister is honorable. As she explains it later, she believes that the girl is honorable: "Medicine can only distinguish between disease and non-disease. It cannot distinguish between honor and dishonor." She makes the brother apologize to his sister for doubting her, and the two leave. The physician then writes her own oath: "I swear that my humanity and my conscience will be my rules in my work and my art," adding, "I put down my pen and felt an ease I had not felt for a long time."

The framing technique here is little more than a preface to the physician's written words; its absence would not alter the essential plot of the story. Hence, its presence is quite eloquent. This physician narrator needs a third-person narrator as an intermediary to introduce the writing process itself. The recording of the story in writing differs from the oral and epistolary framings analyzed, although like them it requires mediation. Like the other protagonists whose sagas need to be narrated by the physician, these two characters from the countryside would not have access to the written word. The female physician is once again the means by which silent voices can tell their stories.

But this particular framing highlights an important element that redefines the other enframed narratives. The opening phrase, "Dr. S. writes in her diary," is followed by the account of a clinic visit: the two characters enter, pose the problem, the physician makes her "diagnosis," the two leave, and the physician writes her notes. The story functions as a medical case history. When viewed in this light, the other physician-mediated narratives take on a different cast: they, too, become case histories of sorts.[75]

The rewriting of the oath is suggestive as well. Rather than adhering to traditional professional values, this physician redefines what medicine should be by setting down her own creed. This act is subversive, calling into question the authoritarian structure of professions like medicine, all of whose members are tied by this bond. Is this a feminist redefinition of medicine? It could very well be!

With the brother-sister pair, El Saadawi has put her medical finger on a deep societal problem. Brother-sister jealousy is pervasive in Arabo-Islamic culture. In fact, the noted Arab folklorist Hasan El-Shamy has boldly argued that brother-sister sexual attraction, with the attendant jealousy, is so powerful in Arab culture that it replaces in its psychological centrality the Oedipus conflict of Western society.[76] This conflict-laden brother-sister relationship appears in texts ranging from medieval to modern, literary to philosophical.[77]

The sister in this Saadawian short story is frightened by her brother. Twice she tells the physician that he will kill her—a not unrealistic expectation, as we will see again in the case of *The Circling Song* (Chapter 4). The motivating force behind the visit to the physician is the girl's honor. The female body must be certified as honorable before it can be handed over to the would-be husband. The brother is attempting to control woman's body, which becomes a pawn in intricate social gender games. But he knows little about women's solidarity. Thus the physician is able to defeat this man's desire and give the young woman back her body. Again medicine as social power for the female comes to the rescue.

In this short story, the brother's concern for his sister's virginity is preeminent. Her body is a commodity whose honor, if absent, will surely lead to her death. The Syrian male writer Zakariyyâ Tâmir, in his short story "al-'Urs al-Sharqî" (The eastern wedding), savagely attacks the marital customs that turn the female into a commodity. There, the price of a young girl is agreed upon, so much per kilo, and she is taken to the marketplace and weighed in.[78] Tâmir thus approaches El Saadawi, who in *Memoirs* likened the vocabulary used in the marriage ceremony to that used in the rental of an apartment, store, or other property.[79] The marriage-as-commerce metaphor is repeated when the narrator of *Memoirs* wonders if people expect her to sit and wait while some man decides to buy her as one buys a cow.[80] Woman's body is a commercial object, the value of which is linked to its "honor."

Dr. S.'s new oath, with which she closes her case history, calls for humanity and conscience not only in her work but in her art as well. Medicine and art are once again joined in an eloquent proclamation. Yet it is through medicine that she has saved the sister from the death threats of her brother. Social justice becomes fused with the physician's art, understood in the broadest sense.

The story of Dr. S., like *Memoirs of a Woman Doctor*, shows us the potential power of an upper-class woman in Egyptian society. She may be able to save herself. She may sometimes be able to save others. But what we glimpse already in these medical narratives is another female type: the lower-class woman who loses control over her body and who, if she attempts to regain it, will meet with physical destruction. These two types, and the intense emotional electricity that is created when they meet, receive their most powerful expression in the searing novel *Woman at Point Zero*.

CHAPTER THREE

# The Physician
# and the Prostitute

*Woman at Point Zero*: A prostitute convicted of murder
and awaiting execution speaks. Her name is Firdaws, Paradise, yet her
life seems the earthly antithesis of that other world.[1] Her story is spell-
binding. Just as riveting is the literary creative process that gives birth to
her discourse. An external physician narrator, a Shahrazâdian character
already familiar in El Saadawi's fiction—here, a psychiatrist—draws out
the story of the prostitute.[2] Prostitution, sexuality, religion, politics,
male-female roles, even a lesbian subtext: these are the ingredients that,
mixed together with a hauntingly repetitive style, create a world-class
narrative. *Woman at Point Zero* (Imra'a 'ind Nuqtat al-Sifr) is perhaps
the most dramatic and accessible novel penned by Nawal El Saadawi.
It is also the one that has generated the greatest interest among Western
critics working with the translated text.[3]

*Memoirs of a Woman Doctor* illustrated the literary ambiguities inher-
ent in a work entitled *Memoirs* in which the first-person narrator
remains unnamed and, like the work's author, is a female physician.
Despite these features, *Memoirs* is not an autobiography. An intrusive
first-person narrator also enframes the haunting *Circling Song* (see
Chapter 4).

Nowhere in the Saadawian fictional corpus, however, is the problem
of the biographical and the novelistic clearer than in *Woman at Point
Zero*. Indeed, critics have had too great a tendency to see this master-
piece in biographical and documentary terms. Firdaws's meeting with
the external narrator–psychiatrist thus becomes a meeting directly with
Nawal El Saadawi.[4] Firdaws "assures the author" of her acts.[5] Is El

44

Saadawi herself partly to blame here? In her introduction to the English translation of the book, she explains the circumstances that led to the writing of this work. There was indeed a prostitute in the Qanâtir prison, there was indeed a meeting between this prostitute and Nawal El Saadawi, and there was indeed a telling of her life by this prostitute. That prison is the one El Saadawi would herself enter as a prisoner in 1981.[6] The odds seem to be overwhelmingly in favor of the narrowly biographical.

Such a judgment, however, would reduce a superior work of art to a documentary, to occult its literary characteristics. In her author's preface, El Saadawi consistently refers to the work as a novel. El Saadawi could just as easily have penned a case study of Firdaws, as she does with other female cases in *Woman and Psychological Conflict*.[7] But no. For only in a novel, *Woman at Point Zero*, can the prostitute's narrative and her relationship with the psychiatrist-narrator come to full bloom. The novelistic form is no textual accident.

The external narrator begins by explaining her interest in the case of one of the prisoners, a prostitute. But the prisoner is elusive, refusing to see anyone, and even refusing to sign an appeal of her sentence. The prison doctor assures the psychiatrist that he himself does not believe Firdaws is a killer: "If you look in her face and eyes, you could not imagine that this gentle woman could kill."[8] Firdaws does eventually agree to speak to the psychiatrist; the bulk of the novel, then, consists of her telling of her life story.

Firdaws comes from a poor family. Clitoridectomy is performed on her young body. Her paternal uncle, a traditionally educated Azharite, molests her. He does look after her education, however, and takes her with him to Cairo after she is orphaned. When he marries his Azharite teacher's daughter, Firdaws is sent off to boarding school. There, she participates in a political demonstration, becomes infatuated with a female teacher, and graduates with superior grades. The problems arise when she is back in her uncle's house. Firdaws overhears a conversation between her uncle and his wife over her future: the university is not only too expensive, but it will also allow her to mix with young men. The solution? Marry Firdaws off to her step-aunt's maternal uncle, Shaykh Mahmûd. Yes, he is retired, but he is alone, and the step-aunt does not feel that he is too old for Firdaws. The young woman runs away. But at night she does not know what to do. Two eyes are watching her and she is frightened.

Before we know it, Firdaws is married to Shaykh Mahmûd. He is over sixty, she is not yet nineteen. The old man is not only physically repulsive, but he is an incredible miser as well. He watches his young wife incessantly to make sure she wastes nothing, even searching the garbage for anything thrown away. On one occasion, he finds a piece of food in the refuse and beats Firdaws in punishment.

Firdaws runs away again, this time to her uncle's house. There, she is told that men beat their wives, especially religious men. This brief interlude is followed by her return to Shaykh Mahmûd. More beatings and misery lead Firdaws to run away yet again.

She lands in a cafe, whose owner, Bayyûmî, takes her in, and she lives with him.[9] When she sees a group of schoolgirls and tells them that she has a secondary school degree, they take her for a madwoman. She confronts Bayyûmî with her desire to work, but he beats her and locks her up in the apartment. Then comes the use of Firdaws's body by Bayyûmî and his friends.

A female neighbor helps Firdaws escape, this time on the road to prostitution. She meets Sharîfa, a woman to whom she tells her story and who then takes her under her wing. Sharîfa, whose name means Honorable One (its implications, along with those of the name Firdaws, Paradise, will be analyzed below), is a madam who initiates Firdaws into the profession, at the same time providing her with luxurious physical surroundings. The experience is a rebirth for Firdaws. Sharîfa teaches the young woman the hard truth about men and life.

A prostitute's existence is no holiday, Firdaws and we learn. She never goes out of the house, day or night, but remains "crucified on the bed." One trick follows another—until Fawzî comes along. Firdaws overhears him speaking to Sharîfa about her. He wants to take her away, but Sharîfa will not allow it. Is he a pimp? We are not told, but we do know that he has already taken one of Sharîfa's other girls and that he partakes of the madam's body as well.

Firdaws does not wait but takes the occasion to run away. A policeman propositions her. She refuses, showing him her secondary school degree. He threatens to turn her in and, after exploiting her, does not even pay her for her services.

Once again on the street, in a downpour, Firdaws gets picked up by a rich man in a car, who, however, does pay her ten pounds for her favors. This is a turning point in her life. She realizes the worth of money, she is able to eat her fill, she is able to get a clean house with a library in which she places her framed degree. At age twenty-five, she becomes her own boss.

Things seem to be going well for Firdaws until Diyâ' comes along.

In bed, he wants to talk. She replies that he will have to pay like anyone else. He replies sarcastically: "As though I were in a physician's office! Why don't you hang a price list in the waiting room? And do you also have a quick examination?"[10] Firdaws asks if he is making fun of her profession or that of a doctor. Both, responds Diyâ'. Finally he declares that the major difference between the two occupations is that that of Firdaws is not respectable.

This assessment convinces the prostitute to reevaluate her life. She attempts to escape sexual slavery by working in an office as a secretary.[11] She falls in love, only to meet with disappointment when the man in question marries the boss's daughter. Firdaws returns to the streets, becoming a successful and sought-after object of men's desires. When a pimp attempts to run her life, however, she ends up killing him. She is taken to her execution at the end of the narrative. In the epilogue, the psychiatrist concludes that she herself is no better than the prostitute.

The physician narrator begins her literary frame with the assertion that "this woman is real, of flesh and blood."[12] This "real" woman, the voice that will enter the narrative and control her own saga, is defined first and foremost through her body. The physicality that the psychiatrist highlights in describing Firdaws will in the end sustain the narrative.

The reality of this prostitute murderer is, however, problematic: her narrative entrance and exit are couched in uncertainty. When the female jailer runs to the psychiatrist to announce the good news that Firdaws will talk to her, the physician likens the jailer's voice to the voices one hears in dreams,

> . . . and her mouth also became big, and her two large lips move in front of my eyes like two panels of a large door that is opening and closing, and then opening and closing.[13]

The lips/panels of the mouth/door, indicating a repeated opening and closing, are an eloquent metaphor for the oral process that will follow. The female jailer is but a herald for things to come. In fact, the psychiatrist will enter Firdaws's narrative through her mouth/door.

But the jailer's large lips and large mouth also stand for woman's vulva. Firdaws's narration is announced through woman's body, and it is through, and for, the body that she will articulate her own saga. The vaginal metaphor is extended as we discover that the narration takes place in a hermetically sealed cell, a womblike structure whose window and door are closed. The two women are the only things in it.

This vaginal space is also a space of water. The psychiatrist imagines that the coldness she feels from sitting on the bare floor is like that of the ocean she swims in as in a dream.[14] This dreamlike oceanic world in which the naked psychiatrist is swimming, though she does not know how to swim, is reminiscent of the "underwater world of the woman artist's imagination," heralding a "submarine lesbian utopia" that Jane Marcus discusses in her analysis of Virginia Woolf.[15] The dynamics of the Saadawian universe differ, but Firdaws is most certainly a siren luring the psychiatrist with her voice. It is her orders to the medical practitioner that transport the latter into that dream universe and into the potentially enclosed world of the homosexual couple.

The real fluidity of water also allows for another fluidity, in narrative roles. The psychiatrist is able to cede her place to the prostitute as she becomes the listener to the tale. But the physical space that is created for the two women and in which they will both share in Firdaws's saga is also a narrative space that will engender a potentially lesbian relationship.[16] The closeness, the privacy in the womblike atmosphere that is the hallmark of Firdaws's narration, is but an external sign of the intimate relationship established between prostitute and psychiatrist.

Firdaws's initial refusal to see the psychiatrist unleashes a host of emotions in the medical professional. Her sense of involvement is intense. Unable to move, she feels that the earth is on top of her and not she on top of it; the sky becomes like the earth and is also pressing on her:

> A feeling I did not experience in my life, but once, and several years back, when I loved a man who did not love me. His refusal of me became not the refusal of one human being in a big world full of millions of humans, but the refusal of me by the entire world, with all that is in it and all who are in it.[17]

When the female jailer announces Firdaws's willingness to see the psychiatrist, her feelings swing in the opposite direction. The physician is elated, the sky is blue, and she feels that the entire world is hers:

> A feeling I did not experience in my life, but once, several years back, when I was in love for the first time, and I went for the first appointment to meet my lover.[18]

She straightens her clothing before going in to meet Firdaws.

In her reaction to the prisoner's refusal and then willingness to see her, the psychiatrist has delineated an important bond between them: that of lovers. This is not a case of mere fascination on the doctor's part.

The entire episode has sexual overtones. The gender of the lover in her comparisons is clearly identified: it is male.

Redefining the prisoner-psychiatrist duo in terms of lover and beloved is pivotal in the narrative. It smacks, on a most superficial level, of a homosexual encounter between the two females. The attraction on the part of the psychiatrist is clear, the underlying sexual tensions are present. Whether Firdaws is party to this redefinition, however, remains a mystery.

An intricate game of sexual roles and reversals takes place in the prologue (and in the epilogue as well). The physician begins the narrative as the active member who initiates the discourse, who will give the prostitute a chance to tell her life. This superior position is not maintained for long, however. Firdaws becomes the lover, assuming the active role and converting the hitherto active psychiatrist into the passive beloved, initially scorned and then satisfied. The prostitute narrator becomes the active member of the duo.

This "male" Firdaws fits her role well. When the physician first faces her, she feels

> as if I had died in the first moment when my eyes met hers. Two killer eyes, like a knife, penetrating/piercing, deep, steady.[19]

This penetrating knife is certainly phallic; but it is also violent, echoing Firdaws's murder of a pimp, committed with a knife. The instrument, as we shall see below, will be made to pierce the male body over and over again, in a final triumphant show of reverse sexual penetration.

Concomitant with this role reversal between physician and prostitute is a parallel shift in the discourse. The psychiatrist, whose existence permits Firdaws to articulate her own narrative, becomes the passive listener to the prostitute's saga. Never does this medical practitioner interrupt the story to ask a question or to alter the flow of the discourse. Rather, the opposite takes place. Once the physician has entered that hermetically sealed space, she herself becomes the subject of Firdaws's orders: "Close the window"; "Sit on the ground"; "Let me speak and do not interrupt me."[20]

The relationship that unfolds between the two women, with its sexual subtext, does not come about easily or without resistance on the psychiatrist's part. She must constantly remind herself that she is "a scientific researcher."[21] But perhaps this is part of the function of the dreamlike state introduced with the jailer's voice ("like the voices I hear in dreams")[22] and maintained in the prologue and the epilogue. The psychiatrist sits on the ground of the jail cell. She is "as someone who moves while asleep." The ground under her is cold, but with a coldness that does not reach her body, "like the coldness of the ocean in a dream." Firdaws's voice is "like those voices which we hear in dreams," seeming to come from afar though they are near, or to come from close by though they are far away.[23] The uncertainty of their provenance (from up or down? from the left or the right? from the earth or the sky?) reinforces the dreamlike state. When Firdaws's narration comes to an end, her voice "stopped suddenly as voices in a dream stop." The psychiatrist moves her body "as someone who moves while asleep." Though Firdaws's voice disappears, its echo remains "like those voices which we hear in dreams." Once again, where these voices come from seems obscure. Firdaws's narration comes to a close with the identical phrases that opened it, all of which are imbued with the world of dreams.[24]

The narrative encounter between the psychiatrist and the prostitute may partake of the unreal, but Firdaws, inside her own story, is "real, of flesh and blood," as the external voice assures us in both the opening and the closing of the frame.[25] Indeed, the tension between dream and reality lies at the heart of the frame of *Woman at Point Zero*. Has the reader simply been witness to a dream? What is the relationship between dream and reality? Reality is associated with "the flesh and blood" of Firdaws, a corporality that defines her as a body. It is her voice that belongs to the ethereal and uncertain realm of dreams. Her body and her voice interact in a narrative game that overturns the reality of the body flanked as it is by the uncertainty of the voice; ultimately, that voice emanating from the world of dreams is responsible for the narrative. The narrative is what is "real" for the reader, and for the psychiatrist listener. The flesh and blood, the elements of Firdaws's corporality, will be destroyed when the death sentence is carried out. Her voice will be choked off by the hanging.

The dreamlike state may heighten sexual ambiguities, but it is the "real" Firdaws who aggravates them in her own story. In the boarding school, the young woman becomes infatuated with a female teacher, Iqbâl. A chance meeting, a furtive touching of hands, tears on both sides: this event marks Firdaws. One of her fellow students, Wafiyya, even asks her if she is in love with Iqbâl. When Firdaws answers in surprise, "Me?" Wafiyya responds, "Yes, you, and who else?" When Wafiyya points out that Firdaws speaks about Iqbâl every night, Firdaws answers, "Never, O Wafiyya." Yes, Firdaws agrees, Iqbâl is a wonderful teacher, "but she is a woman. Is it possible for me to love a woman?"[26] The rhetorical question answers itself.

Later in her career, when the young prostitute attempts to reform herself by working as a secretary in a company, a similar adventure befalls her, but this time with a man, Ibrâhîm. Here again we find the chance meeting, the furtive touching of hands, the tears on both sides. Asked by her friend Fathiyya if she is in love with Ibrâhîm, who is a dedicated revolutionary, Firdaws answers, "Yes. But I am a junior employee. Is it possible for Ibrâhîm to love a poor young woman like me?"[27]

The two episodes are more than just isolated narrative exposés of Firdaws's amorous adventures. A complicated literary process turns similarity into identity. The two adventures are similar in uncanny ways. In both, Firdaws is confronted with an emotional attachment, one that she quickly disavows. In both, moreover, this confrontation is the work of a female friend. Finally, the names of the two supposed beloveds begin with the same "I": Iqbâl, Ibrâhîm.

Yet there is an essential difference between the two relationships: one is a socially sanctioned potential heterosexual coupling, the other is a nonsanctioned, but equally potential, homosexual coupling. Firdaws's denial of the possible existence of the two relationships is revealing: the first, with Iqbâl, is rejected on grounds of gender; the second, with Ibrâhîm, on those of class. A woman's love of another woman is just as improbable as a high-level male employee's love of a lower-level female one.

The way Firdaws phrases the rejections is telling. In the case of Iqbâl, it is Firdaws who does the loving. In the case of Ibrâhîm, it is he who does the loving. In the male-female relationship, Firdaws is the passive party. In the female-female relationship, she is the active party—a position that should not surprise us, since it conforms to the role she has in the novel's prologue. But despite her protestations, the relationship with Ibrâhîm does develop further than the one with Iqbâl. Firdaws goes so far as to fall in love with him, and he, we assume initially, falls in love with her.

Lesbian attraction may be part of Firdaws's universe, but it is the heterosexual unit that receives the bulk of the narrator's attention. What a view of male-female relations, though! From the old Shaykh Mahmûd, through the sexually exploitative Bayyûmî, to the pimp, men are hardly positive figures in her story. Tempting as it might be to agree with Heong-Dug Park's assessment that all males in the novel are evil, that conclusion is unfortunately not true.[28] A slight glimmer of light exists with the male prison doctor in the prologue of the novel. He does not believe Firdaws is guilty. He even writes a petition to have her sentence commuted, which she refuses to sign. Nevertheless, even though this man is not a negative character, his power and authority are subverted by female power and female bonding. He is, in fact, proven wrong when Firdaws finally agrees to speak to the psychiatrist. And it is no literary accident that her willingness to do so is announced not by the male doctor but, as we have seen, by the female prison guard.

In a sense, Firdaws may be correct in refusing to sign the petition—a refusal that will lead to her physical destruction. Her previous experiments with potentially liberating situations were all unsuccessful. Was she not a great success in school, and to what end? The conversation she overhears between her uncle and his wife teaches her that her secondary school degree is useless. Bayyûmî knows about her degree, but that does not keep him from exploiting her body and turning it into an object of exploitation for all his friends.[29] When Firdaws insists to the schoolgirls in the street that she has a secondary school degree, they mock her.[30] For the policeman who takes her sexually, it is her role as a prostitute that defines her, not her education. (We will meet a similarly corrupt official in Chapter 4.)

Ironically, her status as a successful woman who sells her body is precisely what allows Firdaws to live in luxurious surroundings, in a house where her degree holds pride of place in its expensive frame.[31] And although this degree opens the door to that other bastion of respectability, the company in which she works as a secretary, that door, too, closes as Firdaws's love affair with Ibrâhîm comes to naught. The school and the company are merely mirages on Firdaws's road to destruction. It is here that the two relationships, with Iqbâl and with Ibrâhîm, turn out to be identical in their futility. Firdaws is doomed to endure a vicious circle of sexual slavery.

But what is sexual slavery if not the exploitation of woman's body? Indeed, one of the most important leitmotifs of *Woman at Point Zero* is woman's body. Who owns it? Who controls it? Does Firdaws have a right to it?

Even as simple a bodily function as eating becomes problematic. In Firdaws's literary universe, eating combines with gender in provocative ways (though as we will see in Chapter 4, food can also serve as an important class marker). For the prostitute hero, as for the narrator of *Memoirs of a Woman Doctor*, eating becomes associated with power and a male universe.[32] The young girl watches her father eat—but not before her mother has hidden the food from the children. Firdaws once stretches her hand to the dish, but her father hits it. She does not cry, because she is so hungry; instead, she watches him eat. "My eyes followed his hand from the moment it landed on the dish until it went up and entered his mouth. His mouth was big, like a camel's mouth." Then comes a graphic description of the father's jaws chewing the food and his tongue rotating in his mouth and stretching out to lick loose food from his lips and beard.[33]

The connection between food and the male is clear: the mother hides food from the children so that the father may consume it. The father's body parts pick up a life of their own. The young girl watches his hand as it moves up and down, seemingly of its own volition. The cavity that this hand enters, his mouth, is compared to the mouth of a camel, an unflattering image to say the least. Is it any surprise, given this link of food and male power, that Firdaws's husband, Shaykh Mahmûd, watches her eat?[34] Or that when she prepares food for Bayyûmî, she provides him with the choicest morsels, keeping for herself, in the case of fish, only the head and tail or, in the case of a rabbit, only the head?[35] As Carol J. Adams demonstrates in *The Sexual Politics of Meat*, such behavior is by no means unusual for women.[36]

Only when Firdaws earns her first ten pounds from a sexual encounter does she become free to eat with no one watching her. She orders a roasted chicken. As the waiter places the dish in front of her and his eyes move away from the food, she realizes that she is eating for the first time in her life from a dish into which no one is staring. Here, Firdaws is much like the first-person narrator of *Memoirs of a Woman Doctor*, for whom eating unhampered by society's constraints was also a significant act. Firdaws wonders if it is money that makes this possible. When she takes the cash from her purse to pay for her meal, the waiter's eyes play the same game as those of her husband, Shaykh Mahmûd, when, during his prayers, he would be praying and his eyes would wander to the table looking for her dish, or as her uncle's hand, which, while he was reading, would stretch from behind the book in search of her legs:

> The waiter was still standing, while the money was still in my hand, looking at its movement out of the corner of one eye, and with the other eye averting his gaze in shame as someone who averts the glance from a forbidden 'awra.[37]

With a single word—'awra—Firdaws redefines the game that men (and society) are playing. As we saw in Chapter 2 with *Memoirs of a Woman Doctor*, that highly loaded Arabic word 'awra can be extended beyond its meanings of the genitals or something shameful that must be covered to include the body as a whole. Firdaws now expands the discussion still further. In her universe, 'awra refers to money, which is made to possess the same shameful properties as a body part that must be covered. Thus, she realizes that she herself had looked away from money as though it were 'awra.[38]

"Averting the gaze" is part of the cultural baggage associated with the word 'awra. To avoid exposing oneself to the shame of an object defined as 'awra, one must avert one's gaze and not look at it. "Say to the believers that they cast down their eyes and guard their private parts" is the famous Qur'ânic injunction from the Sûrat al-Nûr, repeated in each grammatical gender to apply equally to men and to women. The literary and cultural echoes of this injunction have survived centuries, in sources ranging from the poetic to the religious.[39] The perceived power of the glance is of deep concern even today among the more religiously minded thinkers in the Middle East. It is no surprise that one finds the issue discussed in almost every contemporary work devoted to the proper dress and behavior of a Muslim woman.[40]

From the religious domain of the glance and the private parts to the economic domain of money—that is quite a semantic jump! Yet, by turning money into an object that is 'awra, Firdaws has effectively tied money to sex. This linkage is logical given the economic circumstances in the narrative. After all, did not Firdaws earn that money by selling her body? One bodily function, sex, thus permits the accomplishment of another, equally important bodily function: eating. This linkage is interesting. Selling one's body is not a socially sanctioned activity, though in principle eating is. In Firdaws's universe, however, eating freely was not permitted her; now it is only because she earns money from selling her body that she can purchase food and eat it unhampered by the male glance. It is no accident that the waiter's act was placed in the same universe as the acts of her uncle and her husband. The husband's scopic activity is linked to eating, the uncle's actions are those of male violation. Money liberates her from male oppression in both domains.

This bisociation (the bringing together of two elements not normally associated with each other) of eating and the sexual act is not alien to Firdaws, as we see in an earlier description of her husband's sexual advances:

At night, he would wrap his arms and legs around me. I would let his sweaty hand violate all of my body, not leaving anything. Like the hand of a hungry man who has not seen food for years, there he would be wiping the dish, licking it, and not leaving anything in it.[41]

This quasi-obsession with the oral activity of taking nourishment accords with the general orality of the narrative. In fact, the orality in Firdaws's saga is a double one: there is, on the one hand, the recounting of the story and, on the other, the activity of eating. And both are central. Only after the incident with the waiter does Firdaws, having realized the importance of money, begin on her independent path as a woman of the world. Now she can walk with her head high and look at money without shame.[42]

Firdaws's narrative is a verbal, oral attempt to reclaim her body. But society is more powerful, we learn. Ultimately, this female body will be annihilated. Were it not for the persistent psychiatrist, it would not be only the prostitute's physical body that would disappear, but her narrative as well. "Let me speak and do not interrupt me," orders the prisoner at the outset, "for I have no time to listen to you."[43] Firdaws takes control, and the physician becomes the passive recipient of the discourse.

Telling her story, we discover, is essential to Firdaws's existence, impermanent though it may be. But not telling the story to just anyone. Confiding in men leads nowhere. After all, did not the young woman reveal her previous life to Ibrâhîm? And that all-too-brief tryst only led Firdaws back to the streets. Female-to-female narration, however, is a different matter. It is salutary, when not positively life-giving.[44] Firdaws's escape from Bayyûmî and his circle of exploitative male friends would not have been possible without the help of the sympathetic female neighbor to whom she told her story.[45] When she meets the madam who will train her in the world's oldest profession, Firdaws learns that all men are identical, no matter what their name. She tells this newfound friend her story as well. The madam treats her to a bath, combs her hair, dresses her. Firdaws's body becomes "soft like the body of a child born an instant ago." When she opens her eyes and sees herself in the mirror, "I realized that I was born anew, with a soft clean body."[46] Just as recounting her tale to the madam permits her to shed the old Firdaws, telling her story to the psychiatrist will also bring about a rebirth of sorts, this time in the form of narrative.

Firdaws's road to sexual slavery begins in much the same way as that

of many of her colleagues worldwide. Bayyûmî's initially solicitous atti-
tude fits Kathleen Barry's discussion in *Female Sexual Slavery* of certain
means of procurement.[47] In some of its descriptions, Firdaws's account
of her life with the madam resembles other accounts of lives of prosti-
tution.[48] It is when she embarks fully in the profession that Firdaws's
path diverges. Her life of sexual slavery is a solitary—and lonely—one.
Save for the madam, other prostitutes are absent from the novel. Only
once, and casually at that, is another of the madam's girls mentioned.
Yes, there are pimps. Yes, a pimp has a physician friend who helps him
out when one of his "girls" gets pregnant. But the prostitutes remain
faceless. In this, Firdaws's story is quite different from other prostitution
accounts. In *La dérobade* by the French prostitute Jeanne Cordelier, to
take but one example, female solidarity dominates. This woman begins
her narrative journey in jail, surrounded by other prostitutes. All get
locked up together; they face the police system together. Affection for
one's coworkers is manifest.[49] This is in strong contrast to the atmo-
sphere of *Woman at Point Zero*.

Why this solitude? Why this lone voice? Because having other vic-
tims of sexual slavery would only confuse matters. Firdaws's narrative,
presented on its own, permits her plight to become more universal. She
is everywoman. When she first introduces herself to the physician, she
comes close to expressing this idea. After describing her expensive
makeup and visits to the hair salons, she adds:

> I did not belong to the upper class except by my makeup, my hair, and
> my expensive shoes. And I belong to the middle class by my secondary
> school degree and my suppressed desires. And I belong to the lower
> class by my being born to a poor, peasant father who did not read or
> write.[50]

The superficial aspects of the upper-class Firdaws underscore her inabil-
ity to escape her class of birth. The secondary school degree, that
worthless piece of paper that did not liberate her as she thought it
would, stands as a symbol of the middle class, likewise unattainable.
Only the profession of prostitute permits Firdaws to have access to the
makeup and hair salons that her lower-class origins otherwise denied
her.

Try as she might to escape, Firdaws is still fundamentally a member
of the lower class. As such, she is the social opposite of her co-hero, the
psychiatrist. These two—the middle- or upper-class woman and the
lower-class woman—are favored Saadawian heroes. The middle-class

character is able to fight her way to independence and have a career should she so choose, as the narrator in *Memoirs of a Woman Doctor* did. Firdaws, however, by her lower-class origins, resembles the female character in *The Death of the Only Man on Earth* (Mawt al-Rajul al-Wahîd 'alâ al-Ard), for whom "liberation" can be had only through murder and whose lot is destruction.[51]

It is not a literary accident, then, that Firdaws's awakening comes at the same time in her life that it did for the narrator of *Memoirs of a Woman Doctor*. At age twenty-five, after the episode with the waiter, Firdaws the prostitute realizes the value of money and begins to refuse customers at will. At age twenty-five, the female physician, with the help of the old peasant patient, realizes that she has spent her years unaware of her womanhood and begins her quest for love.[52] Both women have an intermediary in this awakening: the waiter for Firdaws, the patient for the physician. The disparity between the two paths—that of prostitution and that of a fulfilling medical career and romantic life—dramatically highlights the dilemmas of the Saadawian heroes.

Part of the literary tension and the success of *Woman at Point Zero* derives from the textual coexistence of these two types of heroes in a narrative relationship of enframing. This technique is not unusual in the Saadawian fictional corpus, as we saw in Chapter 2. The internal narrative in "The Man with Buttons," in fact, sheds some light on the prostitute Firdaws's tale. In that work, the physician narrator tells us that she published a story entitled "My Husband, I Do Not Love You,"[53] to which a reader replied by letter presenting her own story.[54]

The owner of this internal epistolary voice, like the internal narrator of *Woman at Point Zero*, is named Firdaws. The Firdaws of the short story is not a prostitute or a murderer, but she does have certain experiences in common with the Firdaws of the novel. For both women, the marital state provokes scorching criticism of male-female relations in general, and of man's body in particular. The husband of the epistolary Firdaws, like his counterpart in the novel, and out of the same miserly concern, watches his wife eat.[55] The short story narrator is obsessed with her husband's *zabîba* (lit. raisin), the prayer bump on a Muslim's forehead that results from the forehead repeatedly touching the ground during the five ritual daily prayers. This black *zabîba*, which is visible in the dark, constantly hits her own forehead whenever "that thing" occurs.[56]

This *zabîba* eloquently links the world of sex with that of religion. The sexual act that consists of the male penetration of the female is paralleled by the bump's hitting her forehead. Penetration becomes an act involving more than a man's sexual organ. Thus, rather than being a sign of piety (as it is normally assumed to be in Muslim society), the prayer bump becomes, for the female, a sign of unwanted male aggression.

The novelistic Firdaws, more violent than her literary namesake in the short story, also centers on a facial characteristic: a tumor on her husband's lower lip. The physical aspects of this tumor are graphically described, as only a physician's pen can do:

> under his lower lip was a big tumor with a hole in its middle that would dry on some days. On other days, like a rotten tap, red drops like blood or yellow or white drops like pus would fall from it.[57]

On dry days, Firdaws could feel the sore bumping against her during the sexual encounter, a contact that disgusts both her and the reader, as the old man, over sixty years of age, approaches his young wife, less than nineteen. When the sore was not dry, "a stink resembling the stink of a dead dog" would emanate from it and the young woman would move her lips and nose away.[58] Unlike its literary cousin, the *zabîba*, the sore is a protrusion from which liquid issues, bringing it closer to the male organ. Both Firdawses overtly connect the male physical oddity to the sexual act, as woman's body becomes but a tool at the hands of her husband. Both protrusions are felt physically as the male body approaches that of the female.

The husband's body in *Woman at Point Zero* is closer to that of an animal. The sore brings the human into the realm of the canine. More is at stake here, however. When Sharîfa, the madam, first encounters Firdaws, she asks, "What did the dog do to you?" The image of the male as dog might under other circumstances be considered as unremarkable as the English "son of a bitch." Sharîfa then extends the analogy by encompassing the entire male gender under it: "Which dog among them? They are all dogs under different names." When in her litany of names that of Bayyûmî surfaces, Firdaws cuts her off: "Bayyûmî!" Sharîfa laughs: "I know them all."[59] Like the rest of his gender, Shaykh Mahmûd had earlier been transformed into a "mad dog."[60]

The dripping sore that seems to define the Shaykh unites various corporal elements in Firdaws's marital universe. The Shaykh moves his hand over her body, an act we already saw linked to eating. And no sooner is the eating activity engaged than the sore reappears, hampering the movement of the old man's jaws.[61] Orality, we discover, does not belong to Firdaws alone; it is, rather, an essential part of her existence as a wife.

The Firdaws of the *zabíba* calls into question the "real" aspect of the nonfictional or documentary Firdaws in *Woman at Point Zero*. The juxtaposition of the two female characters reinforces the fictionality of both accounts. One Firdaws relates her saga in a jail cell, the other through a letter. Both women create private stories accessible initially only to the physician on the receiving end.

This onomastic identity may bring the two internal narrators close to each other, but it does not eliminate differences between the two external physician narrators. Yes, both induce other women to speak. But in *Woman at Point Zero*, the physician has a certain fragility that only accentuates Firdaws's power, allowing her to represent everywoman.

Yet this personal strength that is Firdaws's attribute when we first meet her had not always been part of her character. A striking aspect of Firdaws's personality for much of the narrative is precisely the opposite: her passivity. She is a reactive individual whose major actions are taken largely in response to those of other characters. Her dominant response in much of the early phase of her life is to run away. But even that has its limits. No sooner does she escape from the oppressive environment of her marriage to Shaykh Mahmûd than she returns to it. She expresses to Bayyûmî her desire to work only after she observes the young girls in the street. Her decision to seek a secretarial position in a company comes about only when Diyâ' tells her that she is not respectable.

Oddly enough, perhaps the only truly independent act Firdaws performs is the killing of the pimp, something she does when she perceives his fear. Her killing is a reversal of the male act of penetration. She grabs the knife from the pimp's hand and plunges it into his throat. Then she takes it out of his throat and plunges it into his chest. Then she takes it out of his chest and plunges it into his stomach, and into "all parts of his body."[62] This repeated act of penetration, graphically described with the pulling out and plunging in of the instrument, is nothing short of a reversal of the repeated male acts of aggression that for years metaphorically killed Firdaws. How interesting it then is to have her describe her own body as "dead" when she is the victim of Shaykh Mahmûd's and Bayyûmî's sexual advances![63] We now see the psychiatrist's reaction upon meeting Firdaws for the first time in a new light: "As if I had died in the first moment when my eyes met hers. Two killer eyes, like a knife, piercing, deep, steady."[64] The glance, penetration, death: all are brought together in that moment when the fragile physician meets the powerful prostitute.

How ironic that a prostitute should represent everywoman! But are we not repeatedly told by this committed narrator that all women are prostitutes?[65] Certainly, the woman-prostitute-victim nexus is a central motif in this text. A woman who earns her living by selling her body has simply chosen that path consciously.[66] Firdaws brings this point home persuasively. She describes her uncle and his wife having sex while she listens intently and participates vicariously. She describes in exactly the same terms and grammatical constructions the pimp having sex with the madam, again while she, Firdaws, listens. There is no difference in the two acts, we learn: sexual relations in a legal marriage are identical to those between a prostitute and her pimp. Even more important, a similar terminology emerges in Firdaws's descriptions of her sexual experiences with both Bayyûmî and Shaykh Mahmûd. From the specific, one moves to the general: it is no longer Bayyûmî or Shaykh Mahmûd or even the pimp who is in question, but the entire male gender's relationship with the female one. When Ibrâhîm comes to Firdaws many years after their breakup, she asks him to pay the normal rate, which he, with shaking hands, does. She realizes then that he had never really loved her but had only come to her every night because he did not have to pay.[67]

As a prostitute, Firdaws can hire servants, lawyers, doctors. A charitable donation even leads to her appearance in a newspaper. Honor and fame are not difficult to obtain: they simply demand money.[68] And it is this newfound status that permits Firdaws finally to play in the domain of real politics. Yes, as a student she had taken part in political demonstrations and screamed slogans calling for the downfall of the government.[69] Yes, she had even thought she might someday become a head of state.[70] Ultimately, however, it is the economic liberation resulting from the sale of her body that permits Firdaws to muse about nationalism and politics. When a certain ruler from an unnamed country desires her, she refuses. A policeman, sent daily to convince her to change her mind, argues that Firdaws's refusal will create bad relations between the two countries (as she cynically puts it, "nationalism required of me that I go to him"). Her response? "I told the policeman that I knew nothing about nationalism and that the nation had given me nothing but had taken everything from me, even my honor and my dignity." Indeed, Firdaws habitually declines to go to these rulers. "My body is my property. As for the fatherland, it is their property." On one occasion, her defiance even earns her a stint in jail.[71] This aside is a jab at the present situation in Arab capitals like Cairo, where it is well known among the local inhabitants that rich male Arabs from the Gulf often use their wealth to partake of young Egyptian women.

Firdaws argues her own position cogently. She may once have dreamt of being a player in politics, but now her body is the pawn in these games. Ironically, it is one of these "princes" or "rulers" who turns her in as a murderer. He tells her that he can afford her because he is "an Arab prince." She responds, "I am a princess also." Looking into his eyes, she sees from his fear that he is indeed a prince or a ruler. She therefore exacts an enormous sum of money from him, to which he agrees. To his repeated question "Do you feel pleasure?" she closes her eyes and answers, "Yes." Stupidly, he believes her. Eventually, though, she gets angry and answers, "No." She is still angry as she takes the money from him and proceeds to tear it into pieces. His response? "You are a princess, indeed! Why did I not believe you from the beginning?" In the ensuing discussion Firdaws tells this latest john that she has killed a man. He laughs, refusing to believe her. When she asks him why, he says, "Because you are gentle." She replies, "And who said that killing does not need gentleness?" To convince this disbelieving male that she can indeed kill, Firdaws slaps him. His cries bring the police, and Firdaws is arrested.[72] It is the political system that will eventually bring about Firdaws's demise.

Like the pimp, then, this client becomes the victim of Firdaws's violence. And just as the killing of the pimp had gender implications, so the hitting of the customer transforms gender roles. After the prostitute raises her hand and slaps him, she asks him if he now believes her capable of killing; and before she raises her hand to slap him a second time, he screams for help, "like women screaming for help."[73] From the male who violates the body of the female, repeatedly asking her if she receives pleasure from his violation, this prince has been reduced to the role of victim, to the role of a woman.

This incident involves more than just the prince, however. As Firdaws rips up the money this royal trick has paid her, it is

> as though I were tearing my uncle's piaster, and tearing my husband's piaster, and tearing my husband, and tearing my father, and tearing Marzûq, tearing Bayyûmî and Diyâ' and Ibrâhîm, and tearing all the men I have seen, and tearing the remains of the piaster of every man on my finger, and tearing my finger too.[74]

This tearing of all the men with whom Firdaws has come into contact, culminating in her finger, ties her and them indelibly to the sexual act. This narrating prostitute has already sensitized her listener (and the reader) to the fact that male fingers play a large part in her violation by the male gender, whether by Bayyûmî or by the policeman. Her own finger, which touched the money from the sexual act, must itself be ripped to permit Firdaws finally to liberate herself completely and utterly. It is thus no accident that the prince will be her last customer before she is arrested and condemned to death.

If fear in the eyes of the male is what permitted Firdaws to kill the pimp, it is fear of her that motivates the male police system to condemn her.

> They condemned me to death not because I killed . . . but they condemn me to death because they are afraid of my life, and they know that if I were to live that I would kill them. My life means their death and my death means their life.[75]

When her royal customer tells Firdaws that she is indeed a princess, she denies it:

> He said: "I thought you were a prostitute." I said: "I am not a prostitute. But my father, and my uncle, and my husband trained me from the beginning to be a prostitute."[76]

Patriarchy, represented by the abusive and exploitative figures of male authority, is blamed for Firdaws's selling of her body. This is hardly surprising. After all, she was subject to repeated abuse by all the males with whom she came in contact. She is only echoing Sharîfa's position that all men are dogs and answering once again the madam's question posed during their first encounter: "Who began: your father, your brother, your maternal uncle, your paternal uncle?" At that time, Firdaws had answered: "My paternal uncle."[77] Now, her answer is more categorical: the male figures are multiple.

If blame is to be distributed, however, society in its entirety is responsible for Firdaws's dilemma. Her mother participated in the performance of the clitoridectomy when she was a young girl.[78] This operation leads in the novel to a nostalgic sense of lost desire, to an absent sense of corporal pleasure.[79] Firdaws asks Sharîfa about feeling and pleasure. The madam replies with a set of rhetorical questions, all of which center on a single issue: Is not Firdaws feeling pleasure from all the material goods she enjoys? Interestingly enough, the first item Sharîfa isolates is food: "Do you not feel pleasure when you eat roast chicken stuffed with rice?"[80] Unbeknownst (or perhaps not so unbeknownst!) to Sharîfa, she has put her finger on one of Firdaws's central concerns as a woman: eating. By moving from the sexual domain of pleasure (the implied area of Firdaws's concern) to that of eating, Sharîfa reinforces the by-now familiar bisociation between eating and sex. We should not be surprised, then, that the restaurant food that played such an important role in Firdaws's economic and psychological liberation was roast chicken. American readers (and eaters) think of chicken as a less than prestigious meat. In Egypt, however, the opposite is true: chicken is the meat of choice for the well-to-do. Sharîfa and Firdaws here only echo their society's gastronomic values.

If female mutilation were not enough of a societal intrusion, the ideas on the impropriety of women mixing with men help keep Firdaws out of a university. Had she continued her education, her future might certainly have followed a different course. She might then have had the psychological luxury of worrying about her femininity, like her literary cousin, the narrator of *Memoirs of a Woman Doctor*. Instead she is married off to Shaykh Mahmûd in an abusive marital situation that, ultimately, leads to her downfall. It is after all her escape from this enforced and societally sanctioned male-female couple that leads her down the path of prostitution and to her doom.

Society, then, is responsible for making of Firdaws's life a hell, not the paradise that her name implies. Thus, we learn from names what we learned from the prayer bump, the *zabîba*: there is a difference between what society perceives and the reality of women's lives. Even the Arabic language becomes a pawn in this game of appearance and reality. Sharîfa, after stating that her sting is deadly, explains to Firdaws that life (*al-hayât*) and snakes (*al-hayya*) are one and the same. "If the snake [*al-hayya*] knows that you are not a snake like it, it stings you. And if life [*al-hayât*] knows that you do not sting, it stings you."[81] The two words come from the same Arabic root. The deadly snake is made to sit alongside life, the opposite of death.

On the surface, the madam's name, Sharîfa (Honorable One), like the name Firdaws (Paradise), is antiphrastic. Yet, in the context of the narrative and on a deeper level, the names are not so antiphrastic. Sharîfa indeed is a woman with honor: she listens to Firdaws and helps her escape some of the exploitative relationships she had endured. What would have happened to Firdaws had not Sharîfa appeared in her life? The same can be said for Firdaws. True, she is a prostitute; but she is unafraid of death and other negative forces of life. She is an inspiration, when not a life-giving force, for the physician. Ironically, the court, in releasing Firdaws from prison after she refuses to provide her services to a ruler, calls her an "honorable woman" (*sharîfa*).

Sharîfa and Firdaws are both true to their names. But herein lies the importance of the portrayal of the female characters in *Woman at Point Zero*. How tempting it would be to conclude in the universal virtue of the female gender and, conversely, the universal evil of the male gender. But just as the male characters are not categorically negative, so the females are not all positive. True, there is the female psychiatrist, there is the prison guard, there is the female neighbor who cries over Firdaws's fate and helps her to escape Bayyûmî's clutches: all these women are presented in a positive light. One negative female does stand out, however, and that is the step-aunt, who is instrumental in forcing Firdaws's marriage to the Shaykh.

What makes this woman different from the others? Is it that Firdaws does not form an intimate, narrating relationship with her? It is, after all, primarily storytelling that effects the female bonding so prevalent in the novel. Through her words, Firdaws forms relationships with women. The uncle's wife, however, is locked in a situation of sexual slavery, without being cognizant of it. Tellingly, she is the only female character in the novel whom the adult Firdaws encounters in a marital relationship.

This is not just any marital relationship, however. It is one in which the husband is a respected figure, educated in the Azhar, the internationally esteemed seat of Islamic learning. Yet this same uncle molested Firdaws as a young girl, a fact that gives her attack on the couple another dimension: it targets the convergence of marriage and religion.

After Firdaws, now married, is beaten by her older husband, she leaves him and returns to her uncle.

> But my uncle told me that all husbands beat their wives, and my uncle's wife told me that my uncle beat her. But I said to her that my uncle is a respected *shaykh* and a man who has a complete knowledge of religion, and it is not possible that he beat his wife. My uncle's wife said that the man who has a complete knowledge of religion is the man who beats his wife, because he knows that religion makes beating the wife permissible and that the pious wife should not complain about her husband. Her duty is complete obedience.[82]

The complete religious knowledge of the husband is matched by the complete obedience of the wife. But through her revelations, Firdaws has once again unwittingly (or wittingly?) entered into another contemporary religious debate: on the legality of beating one's wife. When the uncle's wife argues that men with a complete knowledge of religion are the wife beaters because religion sanctions their action, she is alluding to part of a Qur'ânic verse from Sûrat al-Nisâ': "And those [women] you fear may be rebellious / admonish; banish them to their couches, / and beat them."[83] Much ink has been spilled in Islamic debates over this question of wife beating; usually, it is argued that the beating should not be unduly violent and is better avoided.[84] Clearly, in both marriages, that of the uncle and his wife and that of Shaykh Mahmûd and Firdaws, wife beating was commonplace.

This abuse of women remains a sore point for the hero of *Woman at Point Zero*. When she becomes aware of her intense hatred of men, she realizes that the man she hates most is the one who envisions himself as a hero and tries to save her from her state as a fallen woman. She rejects this heroism, asking why no such man sought to save her when she was an abused wife.[85]

This is not to say that this work advocates the destruction of the male-female couple and the creation of a female-female one. Nor is it the first Arabic novel with a prostitute as a major character. To take but one example, Firdaws must vie with Hamîda, the young woman who turns to prostitution to satisfy her material desires in Najîb Mahfûz's *Midaq Alley* (Zuqâq al-Midaqq).[86] Nevertheless, differences exist between Firdaws's saga and the stories of her sister prostitutes in the Arabic and North African literary corpus. As Amy Katz Kaminsky argues in "Women Writing About Prostitutes," men and women writers differ markedly in their literary portrayals of prostitute subjects.[87] Firdaws had the good fortune to emerge from a feminist's pen, a fact that may account for the consistency and universality of the message in her saga.

The narrative style in which repetition dominates, in which events merge one with another, creates a sense of quasi-synchronicity. The identity in *Woman at Point Zero* between the beginning and the end, the prologue and the epilogue, closes the textual circle. But other circles close as well. When the police came to take Firdaws to her execution, "they surrounded her in the shape of a circle." This physical circle is symbolic of the circularity of the narrative. Firdaws leaves it as she entered it.

The literary linkage between the external and the internal narrator is the embodiment of their common female condition. Firdaws's impassioned first-person narrative is nowhere interrupted by the psychiatrist listener. Only once does a break in the narration occur, when Firdaws suddenly begins to address a second person, "you." Emile Benveniste, in his essay "La nature des pronoms," has already shown us that the two pronouns "I" and "you" are mutually determinative.[88] What is surprising here is the unexpected ungrammaticality (to use Riffaterre's term) in the text, the sudden shift with the conscious appearance of the "you" in Firdaws's narration.[89] Who is this "you"? Is it the reader? Or is it the psychiatrist listener? Let us ourselves listen to Firdaws:

> All women are deceived. Men oblige deceit upon you and then they punish you because you are deceived. Men oblige you to fall into ruin and then they punish you because you have fallen into ruin. Men impose marriage upon you and then they punish you with beating and abuse and continuous servitude. Except that the least deceived women are the prostitutes. And for the sake of marriage or love, woman receives a greater punishment.[90]

The individual addressed is clearly a woman. The male gender has been turned into a collective category whose punitive actions are imposed on the single female individual who is the "you" There is a haunting quality to Firdaws's language, in which the acts of men imposed on women and the resulting punishments are repeated. Does it matter who the woman is? Firdaws's point is clear: the lot of all women is essentially the same. The psychiatrist's silence is striking: she has been assimilated to the generalized group that is woman.

This common victimization unites womankind. We should not be surprised, then, to discover that the physician and the prostitute respond almost verbatim to the identical provocation. When the male physician tells the psychiatrist in the prologue that he does not feel that Firdaws is a murderer because "you cannot imagine that this gentle woman could kill," the psychiatrist responds: "And who said that the operation of killing does not need gentleness?" When Firdaws's royal trick finds it difficult to believe that she could kill because, as he tells her, "you are gentle," she retorts: "And who said that killing does not need gentleness?"[91]

The two women, though textually not yet acquainted with each other, reply in the same way to two male speakers. And this identical answer addresses the one aggressive act that the prostitute hero performs in the novel. This rejoinder unites them even before the narrative, with its homosexual subtext, is set in motion. When another of Firdaws's customers makes a comparison between prostitute and physician, he has hit pay dirt.[92] Physician and patient alike are caught in the coils of sexual politics.

The psychiatrist and the prostitute are a powerful couple, divided by class but united by gender. In *The Circling Song*, Nawal El Saadawi reverses the proposition. There, as we will see in the next chapter, the problematic pair of brother and sister is united by class but divided by gender.

# Boy-Girl, Brother-Sister

Firdaws's narrative, enframed by that of the psychiatrist in *Woman at Point Zero*, seemed to emanate from the world of dreams. Yet the story that Firdaws tells is not very dreamlike. Her saga, like that of her literary cousin in *Memoirs of a Woman Doctor*, has an inherent diachrony. We see her as a young woman soon to undergo excision. We follow her as she becomes first a student, then a wife, then a prostitute. We leave her as she is taken to her death by the police. At the same time, *Woman at Point Zero*, helped by the psychiatrist's prologue and epilogue, displays a circularity approaching that of another Saadawian novel, *The Circling Song* (Ughniyyat al-Atfâl al-Dâ'iriyya).[1]

*The Circling Song* is one of Dr. El Saadawi's more elusive novels. A work with a fragmented plot, *The Circling Song* boasts a first-person narrator who enframes a haunting narrative within a children's song. Life in *The Circling Song* merges with death, and past with present. Characters die but come alive again. Time is not stable. The closing of the narrative reflects its opening.

Even so, certain overarching categories govern the text, specifically, gender and the body. The literary universe of this Saadawian novel revolves around Hamîdû and Hamîda, a male-female pair that calls into question sexual boundaries. What is the male body? What is the female body? In the parallel trajectories of the sibling heroes, gender combines with class issues and social concerns to create an explosive literary mixture. Rather than stabilizing the differences between the two genders, *The Circling Song* actively subverts the gendering of the human body.

But as with so many of El Saadawi's texts, *The Circling Song* subverts not only cultural constructs but also the cultural artifacts that carry them. This powerful novel effectively rewrites and reinterprets one of the key gender-defining cultural "texts" of modern Egyptian society, the popular ballad of "Shafîqa wa-Mitwallî." In that narrative, a brother murders his sister after her sexual improprieties have dishonored the family and wins social approval for his act.

Unlike many other Saadawian first-person narrators who tell the stories of others, the first-person narrator in *The Circling Song* is not a physician, nor is the gender of this narrator divulged immediately. At the start of the novel, this narrator watches as a circle of children's bodies goes round and round, singing a refrain about Hamîda: Hamîda gave birth to a baby boy, whom she called 'Abd al-Samad. She left him on the side of the canal, and a kite snatched his head.

A child pulls away from this circle—a girl, we learn. The narrator asks her her name: it is Hamîda. Hamîda does not answer when the narrator asks, "Are they singing to you?" but instead disappears through a wooden door. The narrator follows her and describes a sleeping Hamîda. The girl is then raped. The mother, upon discovering her pregnancy, sends her from the village on a train. The father then dispatches Hamîdû, the girl's twin brother, to kill her and, hence, to wash out the shame. In the city (which we discover to be Cairo), the hungry Hamîda is raped by a policeman, who catches her trying to steal bread. Eventually she becomes a household servant and is raped again. Her brother, Hamîdû, arrives in the city and is taken into military service. Although he dies, as does Hamîda, both reappear in the novel. Hamîdû's path merges with hers when she finds herself in his arms. Hamîda becomes a woman of the night and Hamîdû kills his father. But then he awakens as from a dream and joins the other children in the circle, while they are singing the refrain about Hamîda and her baby, 'Abd al-Samad. The narrator is there as well, to watch a girl come out of the circle and to close the narrative.

Hamîda's song sets the entire story in motion. It heralds the narrator's entrance into, and exit from, the narrative. Indeed, Nawal El Saadawi, both as an adult and as a child, actually heard children singing this tune in her native village of Kafr Tahla in the Egyptian delta.[2] But the distance from this refrain to the powerful text of *The Circling Song* is more than mere intertextuality. The song the children sing in El Saadawi's novel is in Egyptian dialect, and thus is set off from the literary Arabic that dominates the bulk of the narrative. The dialect vouches for the popular, local Egyptian nature of the song. Yet on another level, it also speaks to the innocence of the children, for whom the language of the song is the language they speak. This use of dialect is not accidental. When Hamîda is about to get raped by the policeman in Cairo, she asks him who he is and begs him to let her go: all in dialect.[3] Her entreaties are, of course, to no avail: she becomes the innocent victim of the official.

The song does much more than permit a linguistic game. It is the action of Hamîda emerging from the singing circle that will identify the gender of the narrator and effect an identity between the narrator and the little girl. In looking at the face of this child who has broken away from her cohort, the narrator realizes that it is not a boy. Up until that point, the narrator had spoken of this individual using the grammatically male gender. But "it was a female. I did not know for certain that it was a female. For the faces of children are like the faces of old people: they have no gender."[4] (We shall return to this issue of gender.) This face is not strange to the narrator: the narrator recognizes her own face staring at her. Thus is the gender of the narrator established, along with her identity with the girl, Hamîda.

The song also foregrounds corporality in its opening line. Hamîda is introduced as someone who gives birth, and, in typically Middle Eastern fashion, the baby is a male. In fact, corporality is the first element that the reader encounters, with "a circle of small children's bodies" opening the novel.

Hamîda is, hence, doubly defined as being of the body. And it is her female body that will subject her to multiple rapes. The first physical violation, that of the sleeping child, is perhaps the most important. Its social and corporal impact resounds throughout the narrative. The narrator, who has followed Hamîda as she disappears behind the wooden door, describes her sleeping body: she is sucking on a sweet hidden under her tongue. She is still asleep as rough fingers lift up the galabiyya from her white thighs. Then the dream changes:

> The piece of sweets melted under her tongue. And the shopkeeper began to ask her for the piaster. She opened her hand but did not find the piaster. The boorish shopkeeper grabbed a stick and began to run after her.

The child runs away but suddenly feels, as one does in dreams, that her body has become heavy, as if it had turned to stone. The blows of the stick land between her open legs with a violence unknown to her. Hamîda screams, but no sound comes out of her mouth. A big broad hand blocks her mouth and nose, choking her. Now she becomes aware that she is not dreaming and that a large body smelling of tobacco is glued to hers.

> Her eyes were closed, but she was able to see the features of the face. She perceived that they resembled the features of her father, or her brother, or her paternal uncle, or her maternal uncle, or her maternal cousin, or any other man.

When Hamîda awoke the next morning, the dream was not forgotten like previous dreams. The fingers had left red and blue traces on her arms and legs. "The blows of the stick still caused her pain between her thighs, and the smell of tobacco still stuck to her skin."[5]

Hamîda's molestation is initially portrayed as a dream. The image of the candy melting in the young victim's mouth renders the act that much more odious—though we shall see below that the candy has yet another function. The act of penetration is described as blows of a stick on the child's thighs. Despite her closed eyes, Hamîda recognizes the perpetrator of the crime. The rapist, like his cousin in Firdaws's narrative, is a generic male whose specific identity is irrelevant: he could be any male. What determines his role as rapist is precisely his gender.

But like Firdaws's narrative, in which a dream state was concretized by a woman of flesh and blood, the dream for Hamîda turns out to be no dream. This fluidity between reality and unreality should not surprise us. After discovering the girl's name, the narrator jokingly asks her if the group is singing to her. By this simple question, the narrator has created a deliberate confusion between a character in a song and a character whom the narrator meets. It is no wonder, then, that the rape turns out to be real. Its effects are corporal; the male's aggression leaves physical traces. The tobacco functions in contrast to the piece of candy that Hamîda is enjoying, its smell representing man.

What about the first-person narrator? She enters the room directly after the young girl, completely familiar with the surroundings. She does not even knock first: "I did not touch the knocker, as is the custom of strangers when they knock on closed doors. I knew my way." In fact, she trips on the way in, as she has "every time."[6] The narrator is clearly no stranger to Hamîda's abode.

After entering, she declares: "I saw her asleep on the straw mat." What does the presence of the narrator at this crucial moment mean? She stands by in the darkness, like a voyeur, observing the rape. She does not stop it but seems content simply to relate it. Only after the rape and after Hamîda's mother has made the girl rest for a day, think-ing she might be ill, does the narrator reenter the narrative.

There is, of course, more to this narration, which at first glance seems routine and even-handed, than meets the eye. Hamîda, despite her closed eyes, is able to recognize the perpetrator of the molestation. It is Man (with a capital *M*). Hamîda, the victim, has a face resembling that of the narrator. Her identity is, therefore, not so singularized as it is generalized. Might she not represent every woman, as the rapist repre-sents every man? If so, then her physical violation would be the viola-tion of the generic category of woman. This congruence facilitates the presence of the female narrator during the rape, for on a certain level she, too, is a victim of the unwanted sexual act, along with Hamîda.

The assault leads to Hamîda's pregnancy, which inevitably is discov-ered. The progress of the young girl's physical changes is indicated by means of her outer clothing. Just as the narrator was present for the rape, so is she the first person to have an inkling about the changes in Hamîda's body. She can distinguish Hamîda from the other children by the blood spot on the back of her garment. Hamîda washes this gar-ment and, while it is drying, dons another galabiyya. This garment eventually becomes too tight; when Hamîda has trouble squeezing her stomach into it, her mother realizes what is going on. The clothing seems to define the young girl. Hence, also, when the mother sends Hamîda away on the train she gives her a black headcloth, a piece of clothing that becomes synonymous with the older woman.

For Hamîda, as it was for her literary cousin, Firdaws, this childhood violation is but the first in a set of male aggressions. And just as Firdaws was raped by a corrupt policeman, so is Hamîda. In Cairo, the hungry young girl grabs some bread and is about to eat it. But "a large hand with long fingers wrapped itself around her arm." The male figure of authority leads her away—to the police station, we are initially led to believe. As the pair enters a narrow street, however, the violation begins:

> The long fingers were still wrapped around her arm. But they were not five fingers as they had been. They became four fingers. As for the fifth finger, it had separated itself from the rest of the fingers and climbed all alone higher up, over the soft arm, cautiously, like a thief, then it buried its rough black tip under the soft, childlike armpit in which no hair had yet grown.

Hamîda tries to pull her arm away. But the finger is insistent, progress-ing from the armpit to her breast.[7]

This event is but a prelude to the rape that will follow. What a prelude, though! This corporal aggression parallels the male invasion of the female. The lone finger seems to have a life of its own as it proceeds to defile the young girl's body, in nothing short of an act of penetration. This finger with its rough tip is like the male organ, and the victim's soft and as yet hairless armpit, like a child's vagina—the absence of hair only making the act that much more odious. The finger as unwanted male sexual organ is not alien in El Saadawi's fiction; it was, as we have seen, a recurrent image in Firdaws's world.

Unlike the first rape, in which Hamîda was asleep, here she is quite awake. No dream ameliorates the harsh reality in this instance. The physical surroundings in which this second violation occurs are quite unsavory, and the man's clothing, like his independent finger, seems to come alive. Hamîda looks at the suit hanging on a nail in the room:

> [The] yellow brass buttons shone in the darkness like open eyes afflicted with a viral liver infection. On the ground the heavy boot settled with its long neck, like an animal without a head. Next to it was a white pair of pants whose back had yellowed and whose belly had blackened, and from them emanated a smell of old urine.[8]

The clothing is turned from inanimate object to live body. But this is not just any body: it is a body dissected by a physician's pen, creating at once revulsion and threat. The buttons that are like diseased eyes "afflicted with a viral liver infection" function because of the power of the medical image. The long boot is endowed with a neck. And the pants become synonymous with the bottom half of a male torso: they have a back and a belly, like the human body, and their odor is that of a bodily excretion.

The actual naked male body appears before Hamîda. This time she spots "the sharp hard instrument that had been hiding in his pocket."[9] No doubt lingers in Hamîda's mind now: "There was no shopkeeper beating with a stick." Instead, the stick has given way to the "instrument." The two violations are distinct; yet they are united by another common element: the second male body also reeks of tobacco.[10]

Yet, there are differences between the two rapes. In the first, the generic male aggressor had choked off Hamîda's scream with a big hand placed over her mouth and nose. In the second, the victim is not silent:

> She said in a weak cracked voice:
> —Who are you?
> He replied in a commanding harsh voice:
> —I am the government.[11]

The identity of the aggressor is extracted from him by his female prey. The contrast between her voice and his—weak and cracked versus commanding and harsh—is eloquent.[12]

As Susan Brownmiller demonstrates in *Against Our Will*, sexual violation of the female body by officers of the law is not unusual.[13] In identifying himself as "the government," however, this Saadawian male has expanded the boundaries of his transgression. From an act committed by a single individual, rape is turned into a global violation, one encompassing the entirety of the patriarchal political structure. When this "government" victimizes the child Hamîda because of her attempt to satisfy her physical hunger, that victimization takes on much larger proportions. To the gender dimension of rape are added class and political ones.

The class dimension of female corporal violation is amplified in the case of Hamîda's rape by her master. Someone seeing Hamîda walk with an uneven gait while carrying a heavy basket might think she was lame. But no, the narrator assures the reader; Hamîda was not lame, she was simply hungry. She stretched her hand into the basket and moved her fingers under the vegetables until she could feel the fresh meat. "She tore off a piece and shoved it between her teeth before anyone could see her." Her mistress, however, smelled the crushed meat. Hamîda denied what she had done, but a small piece of meat had lodged between her teeth, giving her mistress solid proof.

The task of beating the servant fell this time to the master. Hamîda sat in the kitchen awaiting her punishment. The master's fingers started by lifting her galabiyya above her waist. The young girl resisted, kicking with her feet. Her master grabbed a foot.

> He perceived for the first time the form of a woman's foot. For the foot had five toes, each one separated from the other. Her mistress's foot did not have toes, since her toes were stuck one to the other in a soft fleshy mass, like a camel's hoof.

The male also discovers that the young woman's muscles move, unlike those of her mistress, "in which his fingers sank without resistance, as they would sink into a bag of cotton." (The narrator is quick to add here that this was natural given the fact that the mistress had already died in the bedroom.) Hamîda's live flesh turns her master into "a pig who suddenly gets out of a ruined environment in which he has been living for years on cadavers and remnants of corpses." He then proceeds to rape her.[14]

The repeated experiences of molestation begin to echo one another. Once again, Hamîda's body is the target of an unscrupulous male. The master even resembles the previous violator. His eyes are initially described as yellow, shining with a brassy light—the mirror image of the policeman's brassy buttons that were like diseased eyes. During this rape, Hamîda recalls "a first beating." Her eyes fix on a stick, hiding under his clothing or behind his back. The stick, of course, echoes the initial molestation in the village, an event that changed Hamîda's life permanently.

Another element links the last two violations: death. After the government official has performed his vile act, there is "a moment of silence resembling death."[15] And death lurks in the background as the master defiles the young female servant, with the mistress's corpse lying close by. The nexus of death and sexuality is not foreign in modern Arabic literature. Yûsuf Idrîs, for example, exploited it in a short story, "The Greatest Operation" (al-'Amaliyya al-Kubrâ), where, although the sexual act is not a rape, copulation takes place in the presence of a dying patient.[16]

The male culprits in *The Circling Song* share something else besides: as the rapes proceed, they are relegated, by means of a powerful imagery that ever ascends in complexity, to the realm of animals. In the village, the rapist enters the room like a "panther."[17] After the sexual act, the "government" lapses into snoring, which, increasing in intensity, "becomes like the gurgling of an old waterwheel pulled by an exhausted sick bull."[18] We have already seen that the master is transformed, at the sight of Hamîda's flesh, into a pig who has only fed on dead bodies. Thus the animal imagery proceeds from panther to bull to pig. The panther is in itself not a negative image: quite the contrary, in fact. The image bespeaks courage in the male and can serve as an ideal to which young boys should aspire.[19] The bull might function similarly, though here the text subverts the image by calling the animal sick and exhausted. The pig is the most fascinating symbol of the three. In Muslim societies, the pig is a filthy animal that combines religious prohibition with popular disgust. To liken Hamîda's master to a pig is to relegate him to the lowest possible rank, even among animals.

The three rapes, despite their similarities, in fact represent different forms of violation. The first rape, with its generic male culprit, calls attention to the gendered nature of the act. The second rape, with the "government" as culprit, underscores the patriarchal and political nature of male aggression against the female. To the question of gender has

been added that of patriarchy and politics. With the third violation, per-
petrated by an upper-class "master" on a poor woman, the circle is
complete. Class is now attached to gender and politics to unite the
three dimensions of male violation of the female body.

Hamîda's body serves other, equally important functions, however.
In the last incident, her live (read: young) body is contrasted with that
of her dead mistress. But corporality does more than separate youth
from old age, life from death. As the master examines Hamîda's body
parts, he realizes that they are different in essence from those of his wife.
The mistress's foot, for instance, is one mass of flesh, closer to a camel's
hoof than to a human foot. Hamîda's foot, on the other hand, possesses
five toes that are distinct one from the other, as they should be.
Hamîda's body testifies to her humanity, whereas that of her mistress
testifies to the older woman's animality.

Hamîda's humanness is not what instigates the rapes, however.
Another form of corporality does that, another bodily function that is
intimately tied to the violation of the female: eating. In the first rape,
Hamîda, the innocent child, is sucking on a sweet, for which she has
not paid. In the second, Hamîda, the hungry girl in the alien city, is
about to bite into a piece of stolen bread. In the third, Hamîda, the
household servant, has chewed on a forbidden piece of meat. The oral
act of eating on the part of the female engenders sexual aggression on
the part of the male. It is as though woman is not meant to indulge in
the corporal activity of eating. In a sense, however, this is not just any
kind of food consumption. In all three cases, Hamîda acquired the food
by dishonest means.

Does that mean that a system of justice is at work here? And that
Hamîda could participate in the activity of eating were she to acquire
her food in an honest way? We have already seen the problematic of
eating and the female operating in *Memoirs of a Woman Doctor*, where
the narrator had to complete her medical studies and then escape to the
countryside before she could indulge freely in the activity of eating. The
situation was not dissimilar for Firdaws in *Woman at Point Zero*, for
whom financial liberation meant liberation in the area of eating as well.

For Hamîda, as for her literary cousins, eating is a forbidden domain.
Unlike the physician narrator and the prostitute hero, however,
Hamîda's orality defines her social class. She is not like the upper-class
woman doctor, who is able to consume food freely, nor has she
descended to the level of Firdaws the prostitute, who can eat freely if
she sells her body. Hamîda is locked into a class situation that does not

permit her the luxury of partaking of food without enduring a parallel physical molestation. She does not sell her body to acquire the privilege of eating. Although the relation of body orifice (mouth) to body orifice (vagina) is present as it was for Firdaws, the dynamics have changed.

Gender and class come together in Hamîda's trajectory of physical violation. But to accentuate this relationship, especially as it intersects with food, the Saadawian narrator in *The Circling Song* creates images and bisociations that place her saga within a larger Egyptian cultural domain.

As Hamîda chews on the stolen piece of meat, the narrator explains that her teeth are small and white, but sharp. Able to tear raw meat and grind bones, they are

> primitive teeth that sprouted on top of her jaws centuries ago, before forks, knives, and other modern implements had been invented (it is because of these implements that her master's teeth lost their strength and his gums were afflicted with pyorrhea).[20]

Thus Hamîda's manner of eating is contrasted with that of her master. The disease that afflicts his mouth is interpreted as the result of modern technological advances. (The narrator draws a similar analogy focused on hearing and its loss.)[21]

Hamîda's attempt to consume meat and her subsequent punishment for this act is symbolic of much more. Meat eating and overeating are not just gender-related; they are also class-related. The narrator, in speaking about garbage that is the property of "meat eaters," says that people's rubbish increases as their rank in society goes up. The more one orifice takes in, the more another orifice lets out. Hamîda's master, we learn, is endowed with a huge stomach, hence he creates a great quantity of refuse. This material, the narrator tells us, is carted and "gathered in the shape of a high pyramid in a distant place in the desert," to be admired by tourists.[22]

In one stroke, the narrator of *The Circling Song* has savagely linked the eating habits of the wealthy with Egyptian civilization, turning Egypt's greatest tourist attraction into a refuse heap created by the bodily excrement of the upper classes. The tourists are not let off the hook, either: rather than appreciating an internationally acclaimed artistic monument, they unknowingly admire a pile of trash. And another linkage—the social process of garbage creation is fused with the biological one of human waste production, truly a body social.

The implications of these attacks on dining customs are not lost on the socially conscious Arabic reader of *The Circling Song*. The connection between meat eating and the upper classes is a topos in contemporary Egyptian culture, both literary and popular. One has but to listen to the songs of the leftist singer al-Shaykh Imâm, many of whose ballads are written by the popular dialect poet, Ahmad Fu'âd Najm.[23] In "On the Subject of Beans and Meat" ('An Mawdû' al-Fûl wal-Lahma), for instance, al-Shaykh Imâm reminds poor Egyptians that "those who eat meat will surely go to hell"—an effort to keep them from coveting and consuming this expensive product. Then there are the comic-strip heroes, the tubby Tanâbila, created and drawn by the prize-winning Egyptian cartoonist Ahmad Hijâzî. The adventures of the Tanâbila, whose universe in fact revolves around eating, are a searing commentary on politics and society in the Middle East. At one point, they are tricked out of hiding by an ostentatious display of Middle Eastern delicacies, including fancy meat dishes, all carried by figures in tattered clothing.[24]

But Nawal El Saadawi's closest literary neighbor here is perhaps the fellow Egyptian novelist, essayist, and short story writer Yûsuf al-Qa'îd (b. 1944). Like El Saadawi, al-Qa'îd hails from a small village, this one in the coastal district of al-Buhayra. And like his comrades on the Egyptian left, al-Qa'îd, an avowed Marxist and Communist, does not shy away from issues of social injustice in his fiction. Interestingly, some of his most powerful imagery revolves around eating and meat. When the night watchman in *War in the Land of Egypt* (al-Harb fî Barr Misr) greets the *'umda* (village chief), he focuses on the village chief's hand.

> As for the *'umda*'s hand, it was heavy, fat, warm, and full of flesh. I came close to the back of his hand to kiss it. My lips sank into the folds of flesh. I remembered that I had not eaten meat since the last feast. I got lost while I was trying to count how many months had passed since the last feast. My tired brain could not do the complicated accounting of the days and months. The *'umda* left his hand so that I could kiss it. He imagines that that will make us happy, and for this reason he leaves it until we become satiated from the kissing.[25]

The night watchman makes all the necessary links between the village chief's fat, fleshy hand and the eating of meat. In fact, he moves directly from the hand to the meat, the act of kissing being the intermediary. Thus the mouth, used both for kissing and for eating, becomes the body part uniting the two worlds. Orality has once again surfaced, this time to focus attention on class injustice. The poor are to become sati-

ated from kissing the fleshy hand, an act that substitutes the orality of
the kiss for that of eating and the fleshiness of the 'umda's hand for that
of real meat.

Later, when the same watchman is served an elaborate feast by the
village chief, the poor man sees the various dishes that include meat and
realizes that he has not eaten "for thousands of years." He is awed by
the eating utensils and, for fear of misusing them, restricts himself to
foods that can be consumed with a spoon: soup, rice, vegetables, salad.
In an ironic twist, therefore, his fear leads him to the nonconsumption
of the very food item he so desires: meat. As for the 'umda, the watch-
man describes his relationship with these foods as an old one:

> A friendship thousands of years old. A relationship of love I had lost.
> He approached the food. His facial characteristics appeared at ease
> while he stuffed his mouth with pieces of meat.[26]

Al-Qa'îd's powerful class-centered food imagery in *War in the Land
of Egypt* highlights some of El Saadawi's gender-related food images in
*The Circling Song*. Both Egyptian authors exploit the eating utensils,
but they do so to different ends. The male writer centers on the dis-
comfort of the watchman, ill at ease before these implements, a dis-
comfort that subsequently prevents him from benefiting from the food
presented to him. Al-Qa'îd's literary exploitation reminds one of that
in Tâhâ Husayn's classic autobiography, *The Days* (al-Ayyâm). Here,
eating implements become, for the blind protagonist, a savage com-
mentary on the situation of the visually handicapped in both East and
West and their inability to partake of food in the same way that the
sighted do.[27] Civilizational issues merge with class ones because these
implements, developed in the West, are less commonly used as one
moves down the Egyptian social ladder.

The eating utensils function for al-Qa'îd's watchman as physical bar-
riers erected to maintain the separation of social classes. Indeed, they
symbolize the upper class. For Dr. El Saadawi, the situation is differ-
ent. In *The Circling Song*, eating utensils are not a sign of the superior-
ity of the wealthy over the poor; in fact, the opposite is true. The imple-
ments are responsible for the decay of the master's gums, leading to
pyorrhea. Hamîda's teeth, by contrast, are praised. They have no inter-
mediary between themselves and the food. After all, Hamîda rips up the
raw meat with her fingers and places it directly in her mouth. Rather
than signs of progress and of the success of the upper classes, the eating
utensils are symbols of their decadence, leading to their corporal decay.

In al-Qaʿīd's work one senses a nostalgia, a yearning on the part of the male-created lower-class watchman for the inherent supremacy of the upper-class ʿumda. The narrator of the feminist novel, however, has no such nostalgia. She subverts the positive valuations of the utensils by calling attention to their destructive nature.

El Saadawi's narrative also shares with that of al-Qaʿīd an awareness of the timeless nature of food-related activity. Again, however, the two writers' agendas differ. In the case of the male leftist, the thousands of years are attached to both the watchman and the village chief. The thousands of years of absence of food from the life of the former is paralleled by the thousands of years of friendship with the various foods in the life of the latter. There would seem to be no exit from this culinary class antagonism.

Despite superficial similarities in the situation linking El Saadawi's Hamīda and her master, this lower-class woman's plight is quite distinct from that of the Qaʿīdian watchman. In *The Circling Song*, the young female servant embodies a corporal strength that is centuries old, her sharp, primitive teeth having sprouted on her jaws that long ago. Her eternal qualities are positive. By contrast, the master's teeth have evolved, but for the worse. Thanks to technological advances, they have lost the sharpness that defines the female teeth and are accompanied by diseased gums. In the corporal class-based struggle, the female is superior. And, despite his avowed Marxism, al-Qaʿīd's system is static, while that of his feminist compatriot is dynamic.

The pairing of the male and the female in this food-related game in *The Circling Song* is not a literary accident. Male and female are what make this textual world go round. This is not to say that class issues are not important; they are simply superseded by gender-related ones. Here again, Yūsuf al-Qaʿīd makes a good foil. His *War in the Land of Egypt* revolves, like El Saadawi's *Circling Song*, around two characters. But whereas for the feminist, these two characters are male-female identical twins, for the male leftist, they are two males, who, though not quite identical twins, share enough characteristics to allow one to substitute for the other in the army. These young men are, respectively, the son of the powerful village chief and the son of the watchman—a juxtaposition between social classes that allows for a searing attack on the social and political system of Egypt.[28]

The preeminence of gender means that the most powerful pair in *The Circling Song* is the brother-sister couple of Hamīda and Hamīdū. As brother and sister, they are of the same class. Hamīda is raped and becomes pregnant. Her mother banishes her by sending her on the train that will carry her to the city and to more exploitation. When Hamîdû becomes aware of her absence, he realizes that

> he does not know how he will live without Hamîda. For she is not a normal sister, but his twin. And twins are of two types. A type that grows from two embryos living in one womb, and another that grows from a male and a female inside one embryo.
> Hamîdû and Hamîda were one embryo growing inside one womb. From the beginning, they had been one thing, or one cell. Then every-thing split into two. The features split into two, even the small muscle under each eye split into two. And it was no longer possible for anyone to know Hamîdû from Hamîda. Even their mother used to mix them up.[29]

Hamîdû is not given the opportunity to muse about this problem. He is sent after Hamîda, also on a train, but this time by the father. The paternal figure, giving Hamîdû something "long, hard, and sharp that shone in the darkness like a knife," admonishes him harshly: "Shame is only washed out by blood."[30] His orders are clear: Hamîdû is to avenge the dishonor that has befallen the family from Hamîda's act, and this through the shedding of her blood in murder.

This responsibility, falling as it does on the shoulders of the brother, makes of Hamîdû a normal phenomenon in the Arabo-Islamic cultural and literary sphere: a brother accountable for maintaining his sister's, and hence the family's, honor. But the plot of *The Circling Song* could not be more Egyptian. The story of the murderous brother is told in such popular ballads as "Shafîqa and Mitwallî" and its variant, "The Girgâwî Affair."[31] Indeed, the ballad of Shafîqa and Mitwallî has enjoyed such status as a model of appropriate behavior (on the part of the brother, that is) that another Egyptian feminist, Laylâ Abû Sayf, felt the need to compose an alternate ballad in which the brother does *not* kill his sister.[32] Nawal El Saadawi's own rewriting of this narrative is even more daring than that of her compatriot.

This narrative topos of sinful sister and avenging brother goes beyond the popular ballad, however, to more elite literary forms. It occurs, for example, in the famous novel *Bidâya wa-Nihâya* by the Egyptian Nobel Laureate Najîb Mahfûz. There, the brother drives his prostitute sister to suicide, then follows his own parallel suicide.[33] Mah-fûz's *Trilogy* exploits similar themes as well.[34] Hamîdû in *The Circling Song* is launched into the role that the brother took upon himself in El

Saadawi's "A Story from a Female Physician's Life," where, as we saw, the brother was apparently prepared to murder his sister if the doctor found that she had besmirched the family honor.

The forces pushing Hamîdû are really beyond him. When his father utters the phrase "Shame is only washed out by blood," he unwittingly fuses social and corporal concerns. The social notion of shame becomes tied to a bodily fluid like blood through sets of civilizational and cultural mental structures whose common denominator is woman's body. Hamîda's forcibly impregnated body becomes the locus of the family shame. The spilling of her blood will rectify this gap in the collective honor.

The command from father to son to wash away the shame is heard more than once in the novel. Its most eloquent manifestation, however, occurs when brother and sister are united in an incestuous embrace. Hamîda is lying in someone's arms. She asks him who he is, and he replies, "Hamîdû." Closing her eyes so that "he does not recognize them," she leaves his arms around her and his breath warming her. When he asks her who she is, she does not reply. Instead she makes believe that she is asleep and hides her head in his abundant chest hair. "And when she felt the big fingers lifting the dress from her, she held her breath. Her chest stopped rising and falling. She became dead." When the warm sun falls on her eyes in the morning, she sees the long body next to hers:

> His shoulders are uneven, resembling her shoulders. His fingers are swollen, ulcerated from the wash water like her fingers. His nails are black like her nails. She knew immediately that he/it was her body, so she hugged him with all her strength.

She then feels his leather wallet and discovers in it a picture of herself wearing the black headcloth and looking like her mother on her wedding night, as well as a command in her father's handwriting reminding Hamîdû of the "washing out of the shame."[35]

Brother and sister have enacted a scenario declared taboo by social and cultural norms: they are in each other's arms.[36] The fear associated with this act is an ironic commentary on the importance of the brother-sister bond in Arab culture.[37] But El Saadawi has effected a stunning reversal of this centuries-old cultural obsession. Hamîdû is as much a victim of the consequences of Hamîda's initial rape as is she. He is also a passive party to the brother-sister incest. After all, Hamîda is cognizant of his identity, but he is not of hers. She allows the situation to proceed. At the same time, however, as the male is uncovering her body, she dies, rendering her unconscious to whatever acts are to follow.

On awakening, she discovers Hamîdû's wallet, with its written order from the father to Hamîdû to wash out the shame. Hamîda does not flinch when she reads this order. She simply pilfers the money from Hamîdû's wallet in order to buy food and outfit herself with some fashionable clothing.

Nevertheless, this injunction, now in written form, turns the incestuous episode between brother and sister on its head. After all, Hamîdû is ordered to kill his sister, not seduce her. Is this so inexplicable, however? Does it not link male jealousy with male desire? The father hands the young boy the instrument with which he is to avenge the family honor. This instrument is described as "something long, hard, and sharp," which shines in the dark like a knife. Hamîdû places this instrument in his pocket, where it falls to the bottom and "hung alongside his thighs."[38]

The killing tool, handed down from father to son, is intriguing, indeed. It represents nothing less than the male sexual organ. But this identity becomes manifest only in the context of Hamîda's (and Hamîdû's) larger trajectory outside the village. When prior to her rape Hamîda lifts her eyes and sees the government official standing naked before her, "the sharp, hard instrument that was hiding in his pocket became apparent."[39] And, of course, this instrument is the male organ. Or, when Hamîdû recognizes that certain individuals are male, it is because he is tipped off by, among other things, "the hard killing instruments hanging alongside their thighs."[40]

This virtual identity between the instrument of murder and the corporal instrument of sexual exploitation then permits a further game of identity, this time between Hamîda's rape and her virtual killing. As the incestuous situation progresses, Hamîda "became dead." Hamîdû has, in a sense, fulfilled his father's order to murder his sister: he has killed her. But the killing tool is not what it was at first glance. The penis, it seems, is as deadly as the knife. This murderous act on the part of the brother with its death imagery ties this sexual encounter to the other physical violations of the female, in which death, as we have seen, played such an important role.

More than the subversion of the patriarch's order is at work here. The illicit brother-sister episode plays a part in the gender game of identity between Hamîda and Hamîdû, a game with which the narrator has been involved throughout the narrative. Hamîda recognizes the body lying next to hers as her own body: it has the same uneven shoulders, the same swollen and ulcerated fingers, and the same black fingernails. This should perhaps not come as too great a surprise. The narrator had already delineated the identical nature of the twins, one of each gender, emanating from the same embryo; their facial features were so alike that even their mother mixed them up.

The initial identity between Hamîdû and Hamîda leads to a parallel in some of the essential events in the narrative. The mother sends Hamîda out of the village; the father sends Hamîdû out of the village. The two exits stand side by side in the narrative as corresponding and repeated actions. Just as the mother places her hand on Hamîda's mouth, so the father places his on Hamîdû's mouth. The time of night is identical, as is the quiet of the village. The two naked, big feet of the parents move in the same way on the ground. A major difference surfaces when mother and father give each child, respectively, an object before sending them on their way. The mother hands Hamîda the black headcloth; the father hands Hamîdû the long, hard instrument. The incest scene highlights these objects and redefines them. When Hamîda discovers Hamîdû's wallet, she sees a picture of herself wearing the black headcloth and looking like her mother on her wedding night. The headcloth that turns Hamîda into the image of her own mother and the knife that functions as a male sexual organ are signs of adulthood handed down by each parent: by the mother to the young girl and by the father to the young boy. Seen this way, the incest scene represents the coming of age of the two protagonists.

But what a coming of age! Is the narrator advocating an incestuous relationship so that male hero and female hero, brother and sister, can fulfill their narrative roles? Quite the opposite. This adult Hamîda-Hamîdû encounter in fact calls into question the entire notion of gender. The essential corporal identity between male and female heroes is posited. Hamîda's discovery that Hamîdû's body is like hers, indeed *is* hers, is only the culmination of a long debate in the narrative of *The Circling Song* over what constitutes the male and what constitutes the female body.

Male and female are not such obvious and clearly delineated categories, we learn from the astute narrator of this complex text. The narrator argues for the importance of precision in addressing even the most basic linguistic gender issues. A writer must be careful and not ignore a single dot. This is especially true in Arabic, where "male becomes female because of a dot or a slash." Thus also does a husband (*ba'l*) become a

mule (*baghl*)—a move that echoes previous human-animal bisocia-
tions—or a promise a scoundrel, and so on.[41]

It is when this grammatically correct linguistic discussion moves into
other domains, like the corporal, social, and religious, that it becomes
culturally more provocative. Is Hamîdû, as a male, a distinct bodily
entity from Hamîda? What differentiates his male body from her female
one? The young boy knew he was different from Hamîda and that, from
birth, his body was separate from hers. But he would still become con-
fused

> and think he was Hamîda. So he would hide behind a wall and lift the
> galabiyya from his thighs and look behind them. And when his eyes fell
> on the thin, small slit, he would know he was Hamîda.[42]

More than once, Hamîdû checks for the male organ.[43] Hamîda indulges
in the same activity: "She lifted her galabiyya from her legs and looked.
The old familiar organ was not there. Rather, there was a small slit."[44]

Hamîdû is able to imitate Hamîda's voice so well that she believes it
to be her own voice.[45] Hamîda, however, can actually turn into
Hamîdû. When she went out to buy tobacco for any one of the men in
her family, she would bring the tobacco close to her nose, which would
make her cough. As she coughed, the corners of her mouth would swell
like those of her father. She would then imitate his harsh voice and
stand in the courtyard as he did. "Those who saw her at that moment
used to think that she was Hamîdû. She herself used to think she was
Hamîdû."[46] Hamîdû, likewise, loved to be a woman at times.[47]

The male sexual organ, seemingly gender flexible, was, Hamîdû's
mother told him, a divine punishment placed on Adam because he had
committed the greatest sin: "And all of a sudden there was an ugly
organ growing between his thighs."[48] The narrator's allusion to divine
punishment links gender to religion. Hamîdû, at this point a dead body,
has time to think about the logic of what his mother had instilled in
him, namely: "How did Adam commit the sin before this organ was
created for him?" This question is left unanswered. Once again, though,
the Arabic language has a role to play. The narrator notes that as a dead
Hamîdû looks between his thighs he does not spot the sexual organ,
but finds in its stead "a small slit that resembles the slit he used to see in
Hamîda's body." He thought there was some confusion and that in the
final sorting they had given him a woman's body. There are always mis-
takes in the final sorting, the narrator is quick to add, because the offi-
cial in charge has weak vision. His duty is to move the names from the

first sorting to the final one. Some names share letters, and female names often differ from male names by only one letter, the Arabic "tâ' marbûta." Thus it is that "Amîn becomes Amîna, and Zuhayr becomes Zuhayra, and Mufîd becomes Mufîda, and Hamîdû becomes Hamîda. In other words, it is only a stroke of a pen, and the man becomes a woman."[49]

Linguistic coupling of the male and female names is based on their virtual identity but for the feminine suffix. When the narrator places Hamîdû and Hamîda next to each other and alongside other male-female onomastically identical couples, she has inadvertently transformed them all into brother-sister couples. In fact, these onomastic couplings based on identical names for brothers and sisters involved in problematic relationships are part and parcel of Arab folklore.[50]

Gender malleability (or could we call it "gender trouble," to use Judith Butler's phrase?)[51] is central to *The Circling Song*. Whether one has a slit or a killing instrument determines a body's allegiance to one gender or another. A mere linguistic categorization determines a host of cultural issues. The play between male and female, the corporal uncertainty of who is Hamîdû and who is Hamîda, is provocative. It is not a case of either of them being a hermaphrodite, of having both male and female sexual organs—a status not alien to Arabo-Islamic culture, in which their legal status was vigorously debated,[52] and some historians even went so far as to record their births.[53] No, Hamîda and Hamîdû are twins, one supposedly of each gender. It is simply that in their case gender is unstable, creating an androgynous situation. Yet this is not an androgyny like that of Ursula K. Le Guin's futuristic world of Gethen, where no male-female distinction exists (to take a case in the Western cultural sphere),[54] or even like that of Tahar Ben Jelloun's fiction, where an infant of one gender is disguised as the other (to take a case from the North African cultural sphere).[55] Hamîdû and Hamîda are distinct entities. Clothing only adds to the complexity in El Saadawi's literary universe. In Egypt (and other parts of the Middle East), traditionally dressed males often wear a long, loose-flowing garment that reaches the ankles, called in Egypt a *galabiyya* (in Morocco, it is a *jellaba*). The same garment also serves as the clothing of the traditionally dressed female.

Sartorial similarity facilitates the narrator's task in *The Circling Song*. At least as far as Hamîdû and Hamîda are concerned, the identity in clothing does not suggest cross-dressing. But gender games are larger than the brother-sister couple in this novel. In her new role as an independent woman, Hamîda is picked up by her master and taken to his secondary residence. After he undresses, he places one leg on the bed and the other on the floor. Hamîda happens to glance at him at that moment, and what does she see? Not the killing instrument but the "old blocked-up wound," a familiar textual reference to the female genital area (and to clitoridectomy—but more on that in Chapter 7). Hamîda then turns her head to the wall, where she is met by the image of "her mistress in her military clothes inside a gold frame."[56] Gender roles are again reversed: the male has lost his sexual organ, and the female has gained the external accoutrements of the male—military garb.

These transformations are perhaps not overly unusual within the narrative context of the book. After all, we have already seen Hamîdû transformed into Hamîda, and the reverse. Why shouldn't the master lose his male organ and the mistress be outfitted in military gear? The latter case, being a possible allusion to cross-dressing, is especially suggestive. As we will see in our discussion of El Saadawi's travel memoirs (Chapter 9), cross-dressing is a provocative act in an Arabo-Islamic setting.[57] Generally in *The Circling Song*, however, it is not so much the way the body is covered but the essential body parts—that is, the sexual organs—that define one as male or female. The mistress in uniform calls attention to the social gendering of government functions.

Even these, El Saadawi's novel tells us, are not that easily delimited. When toward the end of the narrative Hamîdû buries his head in his mother's chest, it turns out not to be the mother at all, but rather the father, whose voice Hamîdû hears saying, "Shame is only washed out by blood." Hamîdû approaches his father; the father moves back, the light of the lamp revealing his face. The father blows out the lamp, and everything becomes dark. The father trips but regains his footing. Hamîdû screams as a child would, but "his body was not the body of a child." He pulls out the "metal hard instrument" from his pocket, takes a deep breath, closes his eyes, and shoots his father. When he opens his eyes, he sees the body lying in the sun. Finding a piaster in the corpse's hand, he takes the money and goes to the store to buy tobacco. He buys a sweet and places it in his mouth. He turns around to leave, but the seller asks him for the piaster. He opens his hand and finds nothing, at which point the seller picks up a stick and runs after him.[58]

The transformation of the mother into the father who gives the avenging order effects a merging of the adult genders. But it is Hamîdû's subsequent murder of the father that is most provocative.

The paternal body that trips is identical to the anonymous male body that trips as it prepares to violate the young Hamîda in the first rape scene. After the patricide, Hamîdû, taking the piaster from the corpse, intends to use it to buy tobacco (which, as the reader by now knows, is associated with the male), but instead he buys a sweet—which is textually linked to the young Hamîda and her first rape. The fact that Hamîdû is then chased by the seller is parallel to the merchant's chasing of Hamîda during her initial violation. Hamîdû's body is as if "nailed to the ground," as had been the case with his sister.

What does this parallel activity mean? Certainly, there is an identity between Hamîda and Hamîdû, with their roles merging. In one case, the core of the action is the rape of Hamîda; in the other, it is the killing of the father. Are we to understand that Hamîdû was about to be raped, just as his sister was? Possibly. Or do the repetition and parallelism redefine the earlier physical violation of Hamîda, such that the perpetrator of the first rape—the event that sets the entire narrative in motion—becomes the father? This is not an unusual construction in El Saadawi's literary universe, as we will see in Chapters 5 and 8.

The patriarch, prior to being shot by his son, utters once more the injunction "Shame is only washed out by blood." Only now does Hamîdû fulfill this order—by killing the father. It is the patricide that will, indeed, wash out the shame of the initial rape. This is not at all what was meant to happen. Hamîdû, by the rules of his society, should have murdered his sister. But as the narrator cleverly puts it, redefining the entire issue, the shame was not Hamîdû's. He only had to wash it. That is why he is transformed into a servant whose fingers are "ulcerated from the wash water."[59] El Saadawi's feminist narrative has recast the entire problematic: it is not the female victim who must pay with her blood, but the male patriarchal perpetrator of the violation. To put it in political terms, "shame" can be eliminated only by destroying the patriarchal order itself.

And yet, when Hamîdû opens his eyes after being beaten by the seller, "he ascertains that what he saw was nothing but a dream."[60] He jumps off the straw mat and runs into the street. There he finds his friends among the neighbor children, playing as usual. They are forming a circle and singing the familiar song about Hamîda and her baby.

The repeating song echoes the repeated paternal command. Both are intertextual intrusions from the popular cultural sphere, in one case a children's song and in the other a popular dictum.[61] But the two operate in a dialectical relationship one to the other. The injunction, uttered as it is by the patriarch, represents an older generation; the ditty, sung by the children, represents a newer one. *The Circling Song* is, on one level, about a coming of age, in which the son must kill the father. This elimination of the older generation, however, is a reality too difficult to digest. Is it a wonder that Hamîdû opens his eyes "and ascertains that what he saw was nothing but a dream." The Arabic word for Hamîdû's action, *ayqana*, contains a sense of certainty, of conviction. No doubt exists for the young man: he did not kill his father, the children are singing their familiar song, the little girl comes out of the circle, the narrator closes the narrative as she began it.

With this declaration of certainty, the narrator reanchors Hamîdû in the real world. This is a literary necessity, since part of his trajectory, like that of his twin sister Hamîda, was peppered with allusions to another world, a world that is not here and now, the world of "that time." When speaking of the policeman, for example, the narrator uses the word *shâwîsh*, noting that this was the common name for a police-man "at that time."[62] Or when Hamîda buys a "minidress," the narrator reveals in an aside that this was the dress "common at that time."[63] Many are the textual references to "that time."[64] An astute reader, espe-cially one familiar with contemporary Egyptian society, will not be fooled by these allusions. The society of *The Circling Song* is that of the modern-day Middle East. This play with time, however, permits the narrator to indulge in certain games. How could she otherwise speak of the deities whose feet have that "familiar smell" that emanates from unwashed feet?[65]

Smelly feet turn the deities into corporal entities, not too different from the humans who hold them in awe. At the same time, feet as a body part contribute to creating the genderless universe of *The Circling Song*. As the narrator puts it, "Feet in childhood are like faces. They have no gender, especially if they are naked feet. Shoes alone are what delimit gender."[66] And we already know from an earlier comment by this same narrator that "the faces of children are like the faces of the old: they have no gender."[67]

Ungendering the body means denuding it of its sexual allegiance. The narrator of *The Circling Song* is not unlike her literary cousin, the female physician narrator of *Memoirs of a Woman Doctor*, who discov-ered by dissecting the human body that "woman is like man": "woman has a heart, a brain, and nerves exactly like man."[68] Male and female share the same body.

Hamîda and Hamîdû's corporal saga transcends that of the female physician, however. The body in *The Circling Song* is not simply ungendered; like the corpses in *Memoirs*, it is dissected. Whereas the bodies the female physician encountered were those of dead individuals, the situation is not so clear-cut in *The Circling Song*. There are two types of life, we are told, one that is alive, and one that is dead. Dead life is one in which a human being walks around devoid of bodily fluids—perspiration, urine, and so forth. People who are alive cannot imprison their urine forever, otherwise they will die.[69] It should not be a surprise then, as we have seen, that dead bodies inhabit the same narrative spaces as live ones in this novel. These assertions open the narrative, as they close it, reaffirming the circularity of the entire process—beginning with the children's song about Hamîda.[70]

Hamîda is thus no longer just a child who emerges from a closed circle of her peers in the Egyptian countryside. Along with her twin, Hamîdû, she has transported the reader on a gender journey inspired by deep Arabo-Islamic cultural and mental structures, while at the same time redefining the centuries-old problematic brother-sister duo. Willy-nilly, she has been recast as a hero in another saga, one more dramatic than any mere retelling of the popular honor ballads in El Saadawi's native Egypt.

It would be easy (though simplistic) to see much of El Saadawi's fiction as an attack on the male gender. In fact, the parallel trajectories of Hamîdû and Hamîda, the lower-class male and the lower-class female, show how the rituals of blood and shame imprison men *and* women. Hamîda and Hamîdû, sister and brother, are caught in the same gender web. Their liberation will come about only through the destruction of the patriarch.

# CHAPTER FIVE

# Rewriting Patriarchy

A double killing. A rape. The world of *The Thousand and One Nights*. The world of test-tube men. No, this is not the latest episode in a television serial. It is the literary universe of El Saadawi's *The Fall of the Imam* (Suqût al-Imâm). The female hero of this novel, like other lower-class Saadawian rebels, is ultimately killed. But unlike Firdaws in *Woman at Point Zero*, she rises again to continue the struggle. For *The Fall of the Imam* is not a social novel in the realist tradition. It is a daring mythical creation, a recasting of the patriarchal system that pervades the Islamic and Judeo-Christian religious traditions, as it does the Middle East and the West.[1] Among the most important weapons of this devastating attack on the collusion of political and religious patriarchy is a series of textual games played with the literary texts and the holy words of these traditions themselves, from *The Thousand and One Nights* to the Qur'ân.

Summarizing a metafictional postmodern novel like *The Fall of the Imam* would mean weaving a plot where one does not exist. In this text, first- and third-person narrators coexist. A single chapter can have up to three different voices. Events repeat; the identity of characters is cast into doubt.

An ambitious work of fiction, *The Fall of the Imam* creates a mythical world inhabited by, among others, a male ruler, the Imam. Surrounded by a coterie of ministers and the standard paraphernalia of male political power, the Imam rules over a land described as "the other world." His wife is a woman of Christian origin who hails from lands "beyond the sea" and who has converted to Islam. During the annual Victory Holiday, the Imam is killed, and at the end of the novel he goes to a heaven seemingly controlled by Christians. Parallel to the Imam is Bint Allâh, the Daughter of God. A student in a nursing school, she lays her paternity at the Deity's door. She also is killed, but her demise comes about during a religious holiday. Neither character dies only once, however. Each death, that of the Imam and that of Bint Allâh, is repeated obsessively throughout the novel in a complex cyclical pattern. Indeed, the novel combines synchronic discussions and aspects of the Imam's world with an overlay (or is it under?) of this mythic, even ritual, cycle of murder. Although this imaginary earthly kingdom is no specified place, it has the uncanny familiarity of a Middle Eastern country. This "other world" is visited by the test-tube man, whose previous love is the Christian wife of the Imam. He becomes part of the Imam's entourage, eventually returning to his own land.

The Imam who stutters when delivering his speech; the Victory Holiday during which he is killed: these are but two elements that point to a possible identity between Nawal El Saadawi's fictional creation and the real Egyptian president Anwar Sadat, whose assassination was brought into the homes of television viewers the world around. The male critic Sabry Hafez, in a review of El Saadawi's work, uses this resemblance to belittle her literary achievement.[2]

The political similarity is largely superficial, though, for the Imam is more than Sadat. "Imam" as a title, of course, refers to the Imam Khomeiny as well, perhaps the most visible and most formidable Middle Eastern religious leader in this century. His role as the patriarch par excellence (with his long beard, his hand raised in a blessing) fits in well with the male-dominated system of this Saadawian novel. Sadat on the one hand, Khomeiny on the other. But one would need more hands to cover the political world of *The Fall of the Imam*. Bint Allâh's brother is named Fadl Allâh. Is it an accident that this is also the name of a prominent Lebanese Shî'î religio-political leader?[3] The Imam's Christian wife recalls Queen Nûr of Jordan. The Imam's world is no single, identifiable land. It is a generic Middle Eastern country. It is the system laid bare, what one has after all the superficial differences are removed.

It is the universality of the patriarchal system that dominates. The Great Writer (this is how he is referred to in the text) tells us that when he received this title, the Imam provided him with gifts: a new house, a new wife, and the best possible furniture.[4] Note the gender implications of this series: the new wife is sandwiched between the new house and the best furniture. Not only is she a mere object handed over from one male to another, but she is embedded within the confines of the physical world of house and furniture. Her domestic existence is foregrounded. And what about the prize the Great Writer is also awarded during the "Literature and Arts Celebration?"[5] How familiar this sounds to anyone who has attended conferences in the Middle East at which these prizes are awarded!

(A personal anecdote: I saw Nawal El Saadawi in Cairo in November 1989, just after she had returned from Libya. There, she had received a prize from the Libyan leader: a gold embossed plaque extolling her virtues and the work she had done for the liberation of Arab women. I must admit that, like El Saadawi, I found the entire project ironic. In a sense, she had been made—though for but one brief moment—to join the great patriarchal political establishment. Though she was clearly flattered by the gesture, I could not help but wonder if it reminded her of her own fictional creation. Egypt, Iran, Lebanon, Libya—the differences are only superficial.)

But it is not only political regimes that resemble one another, however. The males who surround the Imam are also quasi-identical. There is, for example, the Body Guard, whose job it is to stand in for the Imam and who wears a false elastic face that looks like that of the political leader. So effective is the substitution that the Body Guard with his false face is the one who falls when the Imam is killed. No matter: another male is quickly substituted for the Body Guard/Imam, and no one is the wiser.[6] Then there is the Great Writer and the Leader of the Legal Opposition Party. School buddies of the Imam, they are nameless but for their descriptive appellations, which define their official function in the Imam's political and social world. Their identities remain tied to that of the ultimate father figure, causing an ambiguity in their individuality that helps to make of them but one character.

Unified though the political vision may be, it is far from immune to El Saadawi's savage wit. The Imam in fact appointed the Legal Opposition Party, we learn. Its leader was given a monthly allowance, a daily newspaper, a seat in the Parliament, and a palace on Mîdân al-Hurriyya (Liberty Square).[7] In the imaginary (and fictional) universe of the Imam, this is a most appropriate name—not too different from the famous Mîdân al-Tahrîr (Liberation Square) in Cairo, but different enough that the two are not linked immediately. How nice a commentary it also makes on many a square in many a Third World country, where the words *liberty* and *freedom* too often get bandied about in quite a cavalier fashion.

Beware, however. This is not a novel that denigrates the Middle East in favor of some Western political construct. This is a novel that questions the larger cultural and civilizational constructs of both the East and the West, centering on an issue common to both: the plight of women.

And what better place to explore the intersection of gender and the religio-political arena than with the onomastic references in the text? Bint Allâh, the Daughter of God, is the central female in *The Fall of the Imam*. She is flanked in the novel by her brother, Fadl Allâh, and her sister, Ni‘mat Allâh. All three grew up in the orphanage known as Bayt al-Atfâl, the House of Children. The names of the three siblings are all constructed with the word Allâh, God. Fadl and Ni‘mat both inherently convey the same relationship to the Deity: that of kindness, favor, and blessing. Both, moreover, are real names in the complex Arabic onomastic system, in which names constructed with the word *Allâh* abound.[8] Bint Allâh is the odd name out; directly connected to God, it poses both an onomastic and a theological problem.

Onomastic first. To someone who does not think about what the words mean, the name Bint Allâh *sounds* right—and well it should. It combines in mellifluous Arabic two name elements, each of which seems to be in its appropriate location. The first element, Bint or "Daughter of," is found in such female names as Bint al-Shâti', while Allâh is familiar as the second part of the ubiquitous ‘Abd Allâh. By a subversive game of paradigmatic substitution, Nawal El Saadawi has created a shocking onomastic ungrammaticality.

A slightly less disruptive version of this game is played in the names of the two political parties. The Imam's party is Hizb Allâh (the Party of God) and that of the opposition, the Hizb al-Shaytân (the Party of Satan). The Hizb Allâh, an Islamic party that has played (and continues to play) such an important role in the Lebanese Civil War, is by now a household name in the United States, and its leader is commonly mentioned as being Shaykh Fadl Allâh.[9] And the Hizb al-Shaytân? What a radical notion! This is not the name of some satanic cult that has crept into the novel; it is the name of the opposition party in the Imam's political universe, whose head he himself appoints. The names Hizb Allâh and Hizb al-Shaytân deliberately violate the unspoken rules of Arabic political semiotics. The success of this onomastic game (as in the case of Bint Allâh) relies on its exploitation of the rules of both the Arabic language and the Arabo-Islamic onomastic system: the replacement

in the grammatical genitive construction (on the one hand, a noun pre-
ceding *Allâh* and, on the other, a noun following *hizb*) are semantically
appropriate. After all, if one can have Fadl Allâh, why can one not have
Bint Allâh; and if one can have Hizb Allâh, why can one not have Hizb
al-Shaytân?

The combinations (Bint Allâh and Hizb al-Shaytân) border on sacri-
lege precisely because they violate unspoken cultural rules and call atten-
tion to a central theological problem, that of God's unity and transcen-
dence. The two highly loaded words *Shaytân* and *Allâh* often function
paradigmatically, as in the oft-repeated phrase "A'ûdhu bil-Lâh min al-
Shaytân al-Rajîm" (I seek God's protection from Satan the Damned).[10]
The paradigmatic relationship between Hizb Allâh and Hizb al-Shaytân
already exists in the Qur'ân (Sûrat al-Mujâdala, verses 19–22). There,
however, the terms refer not to political parties, but to the saved and
the damned, respectively. It is clear why a political party would want to
identify itself with the saved. But a party of the damned? Hizb al-
Shaytân by its very existence calls into question the whole notion of
Hizb Allâh—that is, the setting up of a relationship between the Deity
and a political party. Reattaching the Qur'ânic Hizb al-Shaytân to the
modern political context of Hizb Allâh makes the association of God
and political party seem almost absurd. It ridicules the collusion of pol-
itics and religion in patriarchal power—one of the principal targets of
*The Fall of the Imam.*

The subversion implied by the name Bint Allâh goes beyond poli-
tics. Among other things, it deftly exposes the patriarchal assumptions
of Christianity. If a son of God, why not a daughter of God? For Islam,
the challenge is more forthright. Bint Allâh is a theological *bid'a* or
innovation (understood as a negative term). Her mere name violates
the unity and transcendence of the Deity, *tawhîd*. This is a central doc-
trine in Islam, of which the proclamation—the creed—is the first pillar
of Islam. As John L. Esposito puts it, this creed "affirms Islam's
absolute monotheism, an unshakable and uncompromising faith in the
oneness or unity (*tawhîd*) of God."[11] So heretical is the name Bint Allâh
that a believing Muslim called it blasphemy in my presence. If we
understand the nature of *bid'a* properly, that to be accused of it is
"equivalent to the charge of heresy in Christianity,"[12] the shock of the
name for a Muslim reader becomes clear.

While one might overlook the more excusable political connections
to the Deity in the name Hizb Allâh, it is much more difficult to do so

with Bint Allâh, since her relationship to the Deity is literally more inti-
mate. Bint Allâh in fact asserts many times in the novel that her father is
God. But how can this be? We, as readers, know that Bint Allâh is con-
scious of the physical dilemma involved in having the Deity as father.
She relates an exchange she has with her sister, Ni'mat Allâh, after hear-
ing part of the first three verses, so famous, from the Qur'ânic Sûrat al-
Ikhlâs: "Qul, huwa Allâhu ahad, lam yalid wa-lam yûlad" [Say, He is
God, One, who has not begotten, and has not been begotten].[13]
Ni'mat Allâh poses the problem when she then turns to Bint Allâh and
asks, "Did God not beget Jesus Christ?"[14] Is it any wonder that the
Chief of Security upon hearing Bint Allâh's name says, "Your name is in
itself a crime of unbelief?"[15]

If giving God children is a frontal assault on the most fundamental of
all Islamic theological notions, endowing him with a daughter is a far
more subtle jab. Verses from the Sûrat al-Nahl, generally understood
as condemning the Meccan cult of a number of goddesses worshipped
as daughters of Allâh, read: "And they assign to God daughters; glory
be to Him!—and they have their desire; and when any of them is given
the good tidings of a girl, his face is darkened."[16] Among the arguments
of these verses is the notion of the incongruity of people who them-
selves do not respect the female child attributing daughters to God.

Given that preference for male offspring is far from extinct in Arab
society today, the name of El Saadawi's female hero plays, in its own
way, and of course on a totally different register, with this incongruity.
(Interestingly, Nawal El Saadawi told me with great pride that when it
came time to publish *The Fall of the Imam* in Cairo, the publisher, the
well-known Nasserite and leftist Muhammad Fâ'iq, asked her to change
Bint Allâh's name to something else. She staunchly refused, arguing
that it would alter the entire thesis of the book.)[17]

Once the complexities of the Saadawian onomastic system are uncov-
ered, once we understand that more is at issue here than mere naming,
we have entered a different realm. *The Fall of the Imam* becomes then a
heavily coded novel, whose intertextual games are not improper twists
of "universally known" facts (as Sabry Hafez argues)[18] but a rewriting
and recasting of the enormous Arabic literary and religio-cultural textual
tradition, whose weight one feels El Saadawi carrying on her shoulders.

Nowhere is this more visible than in the literary and religious inter-
text of *The Fall*. Verses from the Qur'ân and stories from the *hadîth*,
those quasi-anecdotal collections of sayings and actions of the Prophet,

are richly interspersed in this highly complex novel. Most provocative in this intertext is its reflection of powerful cultural and civilizational forces. Let us take two examples.

The Christian wife of the Imam, beseeching the Deity to protect her husband from his former wife and her magical attempts to turn him into a monkey, says, "Protect him, O Lord, from the guile of women. Indeed, their guile is great [*inna kaydahunna 'azîm*]."[19] By uttering this phrase, with the word *kayd* (guile), the Christian wife has inserted herself into the centuries-old world of Arabo-Islamic mental structures regarding women.

The twelfth Qur'ânic *sûra*, the Sûrat Yûsuf, relates the "most beautiful of stories," that of Joseph and his various adventures, including his problematic relationship with the wife of the ancient Egyptian ruler.[20] The biblical Joseph is transformed in Islam into a paragon of beauty, and the attempted seduction of him by the ruler's wife, who is unnamed in the Qur'ân but later acquires the name of Zulaykhâ, has entered the Muslim literary and cultural imagination. The Egyptian ruler, upon ascertaining Joseph's innocence, declares: "Indeed, your guile is great."[21] "Your guile" here is in the feminine plural; in using it, therefore, the ruler addresses the entire female gender.

"Indeed, their guile is great" also refers to a plurality of women and has had an uncanny ability to reappear in the Arabo-Islamic textual corpus, in locations varying from the frame of *Thousand and One Nights* to contemporary short stories, including one by Najîb Mahfûz.[22]

That this phrase should then surface in a recent Egyptian novel is perhaps unremarkable. Once again, however, Nawal El Saadawi has redefined the debate. In its "original" Qur'ânic form, the phrase referring to the great guile of women is uttered by a male, hence delineating a male-female gender distinction. In the Saadawian vehicle, however, a woman joins the ranks of men to pass this judgment on her own kind. The Christian wife of the Imam is there to remind the reader of patriarchy's great attraction.

It is not just the Muslim holy book, however, that inspires the characters in *The Fall of the Imam* to recast the centuries-long Arabo-Islamic textual tradition. Material from the *hadîth* makes an appearance as well. Bint Allâh reveals to the Chief of Security that her brother, Fadl Allâh, sacrificed himself for his country: "I fought with him in a single trench and I saw him with my own eyes while he was fighting the enemy." The Chief of Security replies:

"What did you say? You were with him in a single trench?" She said:
"Yes." He said: "The two of you only?" She said: "Yes." He said:
"That is another crime. Man and woman cannot be together in unlaw-
ful seclusion, except that the Devil be their third."[23]

Thus, the Chief of Security has put his finger on a societal concern
related to mixed male-female company. This concern is articulated in
the oft-quoted *hadîth* that when a man and a woman are together, the
Devil is the third.[24] This means that a heterosexual situation in which
the two individuals are not linked by a licit bond such as marriage is
potentially explosive—and illicit.

Once again, the Saadawian text questions and redefines. Bint Allâh
was fighting in the trench with her brother. Brother and sister are alone.
Hamîda and Hamîdû of *The Circling Song* already demonstrated with
their incestuous interlude that the Chief of Security's concern may not
be so far-fetched. And sure enough, in a chapter entitled "Together in
the Trench" a third-person narrator describes this run-in between
brother and sister in the trench. They hug each other and become glued
together as though each wanted to lose him- or herself in the other.[25]
This relationship is clearly problematic. By uttering the *hadîth*, the
Chief of Security has inserted this brother-sister pair into a larger Arabo-
Islamic discourse on male-female relations.

Islamic religious materials are reformulated, as are Christian ones.
Both these monotheistic religions seem to figure large in the world of
the Imam. And to complicate things further, more specifically literary
texts from the rich medieval Arabic corpus play a pivotal role in this
novel. As the Imam arrives at the gates of Paradise, the angel Ridwân
asks him if he has a permit, to which the Imam answers in the negative.
He cannot enter Paradise without it, he is told. The Imam waits awhile
and then notices a willow tree by the gate. He asks for one of its leaves,
which he will then have turned into a permit. But Ridwân refuses, argu-
ing that no leaf can be taken out of Paradise except by permission of
His Majesty.[26]

Is this simply another humorous bisociation (examples of which
abound in *The Fall of the Imam*) between a religious universe and a less
religious one? No. In playing with the notion of a permit to enter Par-
adise, El Saadawi's narrator—in this case the Imam himself—has entered
yet another Arabo-Islamic cultural and textual domain. One of the most
famous medieval Arabic treatises is the *Epistle of Forgiveness* (Risâlat al-

Ghufrân) by the blind fifth/eleventh-century Syrian literary figure, Abû al-'Alâ' al-Ma'arrî.[27] As Suzanne Pinckney Stetkevych puts it:

> The first part of the *Epistle* consists of an ironic and satyrical journey to an Arabo-Islamic Parnassus. In it the author places his protagonist, his fellow littérateur, the Aleppan Ibn al-Qârih in the heavenly Garden to discourse and carouse with those of the Arab poets and assorted litterati that have been granted salvation.[28]

As Ibn al-Qârih approaches the gates of Paradise, Ridwân asks him the same question he asked the Imam in a novel nine centuries later: does he have a permit? The medieval littérateur's answer is the same as the twentieth-century ruler's: no. And Ridwân's response in both instances is likewise identical: there is no way to enter without this permit. Like the Imam, Ibn al-Qârih spots a willow tree and asks for a leaf—a request that meets the same fate as that of the Imam: it is refused.[29]

There is more than superficial similarity hiding behind these two incidents. The identity in narrative brings with it a similarity in language. The contemporary Saadawian novel and its medieval predecessor, al-Ma'arrî's epistle, exploit much the same vocabulary to express identical actions. This intricate feminist game of intertextuality redefines the Imam's journey as it recasts that of his medieval predecessor, Ibn al-Qârih. El Saadawi's version, however, takes on an interesting political twist as the Imam's discussion with Ridwân continues. The contemporary leader speaks of his own well-attended funeral:

> The scene was awesome. Did you not see the picture on the cover of *Newsweek*? Ridwân said: I had not heard of *Newsweek* until now. I said: If you do not know *Newsweek*, then you do not know the greats or the Great Powers.[30]

The difference in registers between the two speakers, the angel Ridwân and the image-conscious Imam, should not be a surprise. After all, the intersection of the religious and the political has been a given in the patriarchal world of Nawal El Saadawi's *Fall of the Imam*. But by exploiting the Ma'arrian literary construct of a journey to Paradise, El Saadawi has foregrounded the clash of the religious and the political, thus adding another dimension to this encounter. Ridwân is not concerned with the Western-generated image of the Middle Eastern political leader. Nor has he advanced much beyond his medieval namesake. As an embodiment of the religious face of patriarchy, he signals that this element has not changed—hence his identical responses to these two seekers of Paradise, medieval and modern.

But al-Ma'arrî's text and those of the Qur'ân and the *hadîth* notwithstanding, the most important intertext in *The Fall of the Imam* is created by *The Thousand and One Nights*. The *Nights* in the Egyptian feminist's text come predominantly through the royal male character, Shâhriyâr. He is such a powerful patriarchal figure that he can transcend his original locus in *The Thousand and One Nights* and serve to unify the Imam's mythical universe with its counterpart, the lands "beyond the sea."

The Imam's land, as we have seen, is a place without a name, an unspecified territory that could obviously stand for any or many a Middle Eastern country. One could comfortably place it in Egypt—there are, after all, references to water buffalo. But this would not be what the narrative intends. The text is uncomfortable identifying the "sea" either as the Mediterranean or as the Nile. "They said: the names here differ. Time differs. But the place is one. And the sun is one."[31] This society is complete: populated by men, women, and children.

The other geographical locus is also unspecified, but for being "beyond the sea." We can conclude that it is the West, the place where the Imam's foreign Christian wife learned political science. It is also the place that creates test-tube babies, and where women give birth to books. This West makes its appearance through the narration of the test-tube man, whose beloved ran off to "the other world," that of the Imam, and about which he has heard "fairy tales and the stories of *The Thousand and One Nights*." He himself is an office employee whose male boss makes sexual overtures to him. The woman he marries has "a warm intellect and a cold womb." He warms her in the winter, and she keeps him cool in the summer. He will, however, go to the land of the Imam, play the role of philosopher in the ruler's court, and leave with his beloved.[32]

When the test-tube man (later to become the Philosopher in the Imam's world) is filling out forms in the Eastern environment, he is asked his mother's name. He replies: "I do not know. I am one of the test-tube children." "And what are test tubes?" he is asked, to which he answers: "They are the new wombs. They produce children innocent of sin, without sex, marriage, or sexual intercourse. Nothing but artificial insemination." (The high-tech version of the Virgin Birth!)[33] The Eastern response is one of horror: to his questioners, this is forbidden sexuality that confuses paternity.[34]

Two distinct geographical loci. Two distinct societies. Each represents the other as a transoceanic land (*warâ' al-bahr, warâ' al-bihâr*).[35] One is clearly the East, and one, the West. But unlike in Kipling's verses, East does meet West in the Saadawian narrative, and on many levels. To begin with, there is physical contact between the two societies, not only in the Imam's relationship with his foreign wife but also through the visit of the test-tube man. Western male fantasies of female control do not differ from Eastern ones; both are channeled—as we shall see momentarily—through an identity with Shâhriyâr, the gynocidal ruler of *The Thousand and One Nights*. El Saadawi has been accused of praising the West and addressing her fiction to a Western audience.[36] Would that life were so simple. Unfortunately, in *The Fall of the Imam* there are no good guys and bad guys. There are only bad guys. The West receives the same harsh treatment as the East. Both loci are turned into dystopian territories, in a unified vision in which male patriarchy has the upper hand.

Certainly, feminist dystopias are not new in women's literature. But here again, El Saadawi's vision differs. Can the Imam's world be stood up next to, for example, the Hitlerian universe portrayed in Katharine Burdekin's *Swastika Night*?[37] A futuristic society based on the Hitlerian superman ideology gone mad, Burdekin's male society isolates women and relegates them to the role of breeding animals. The woman-as-animal theme is to be found in the Imam's world as well, where "the price of a female water buffalo in the market is higher than that of a woman. A man owns four women but has only one female water buffalo."[38] The words themselves are more eloquent than any commentary.

Nor is El Saadawi's fictional universe quite the same as that of Margaret Atwood's *The Handmaid's Tale*. Atwood's world of Gilead superficially resembles that of the Imam. Gilead, a religiously conservative (if not fundamentalist) society, is a male-oriented world in which women are pushed into the role of non-thinking servants. The handmaids function as breeding animals, their identity becoming tied to the male household of which they form a part.[39]

When one places *The Fall of the Imam* alongside *Swastika Night* and *The Handmaid's Tale*, however, essential differences arise. The Western works project certain trends into the future to create a dystopian vision of what could be. El Saadawi's work takes place in the present, though this is an atemporal present in which one year revolves into the next and in which holidays merge one with the other. *The Fall of the*

*Imam* does not speak, as *The Circling Song* did, of an amorphous time, "that time," which creates a possible alternate narrative reality. Bint Allâh's time is not the same as that of Hamîda and Hamîdû.

*The Fall of the Imam* magnifies traits existing in the present and lays bare the fundamental characteristics of society through its mythic discourse. The work displays a cyclical organization: Bint Allâh dies on the first page of the book, as she dies on the last. Herein lies the most important difference between El Saadawi's novel, on the one hand, and, on the other, Burdekin's and Atwood's dystopian works—or even such utopian visions as Burdekin's *The End of This Day's Business* or Katherine V. Forrest's *Daughters of a Coral Dawn*.[40] The linear, historical vision of the Western writers, be it utopian or dystopian, is rooted in the Judeo-Christian (or more properly Abrahamic, for that includes Islam) tradition. Present developments lead to different futures, whether darker antifeminist ones or rosier feminist ones. If Nawal El Saadawi's essentially pagan cyclical vision is pessimistic from one point of view—because the hero Bint Allâh is constantly being killed in a seemingly endless process—it is optimistic from another—because she is just as constantly rising up to struggle again.

Even the treatment of artificial insemination runs counter to contemporary feminist expectations. A world devoid of heterosexual intercourse, a world with some kind of artificial insemination might generally be assumed to signal a feminist utopia rather than a dystopia. After all, do not the women in Charlotte Perkins Gilman's *Herland* propagate themselves through parthenogenesis?[41] And is not fertilization in Joanna Russ's *The Female Man* accomplished by the merger of two ova?[42] At the hands of the Saadawian narrator, however, artificial insemination becomes a Western procedure discussed in an Eastern setting. It is not a sign of the superiority of the West. Rather, it is commented upon as an aberration, and this commentary transforms what might be a utopian element in the imaginary Western location into a dystopian one.

So, where does Shâhriyâr fit in? And what gives us the right to link East and West under his sign? Nawal El Saadawi could not have chosen her male prototype better. This Shâhriyâr can leap across the ocean, spanning geographical territories, moving from East to West. It is no accident that of all Arabic literature, *The Thousand and One Nights* is perhaps the one text that can justifiably be said to be as much a part of the Western literary tradition as of the Eastern one. Burton's translation, Galland's translation—these are only two of the texts that helped give the *Nights* a permanent position in world literature.[43] Hence the appropriateness of Shâhriyâr as a universal male figure.

In *The Fall of the Imam*, as in the works of many other modern authors, Eastern and Western, male and female, the medieval text appears primarily through its frame. John Barth, Tawfîq al-Hakîm, Ethel Johnston Phelps, and Edgar Allan Poe are but a few of the names that can be cited in this context.[44]

What do we mean, however, by the "frame" of *The Thousand and One Nights*? Shâhriyâr, a mythical ruler, longs to see his brother, Shâhzamân. The latter, about to set off to see Shâhriyâr, catches his wife frolicking with a loathsome cook. He kills both, then proceeds to visit his brother. There, he discovers that his brother's wife is also unfaithful, but her perfidy is with a black slave. He eventually reveals this to his older brother and the two set out on a spiritual journey, abandoning the world. On this voyage, they are lured into sexual intercourse by an *'ifrît*'s young woman who was locked up by this creature who kidnapped her on her wedding night. After this sexual interlude, Shâhriyâr returns to his kingdom, has his wife and her black lover disposed of, and begins his series of one-night stands with virgins, whom he kills after the evening's entertainment. Shahrazâd enters the scene at this point and, with her sister's help, recounts stories that conveniently stretch past the break of day, keeping the king in suspense and herself alive. At the end of the storytelling cycle, we learn that she has given birth to three sons. The monarch lets her live and has her stories engraved for posterity. Her sister weds Shâhzamân, and the four live happily ever after.[45]

The narrative concentration on Shâhriyâr in the contemporary Egyptian feminist's text is suggestive. What a grim view we get of the male hero as he is transformed into the royal serial murderer! The test-tube man confesses to having heard "the stories of *The Thousand and One Nights*."[46] When his psychiatrist recommends travel, the test-tube man tells his wife that he is going to "the other world." After leaving her, he looks in the mirror and sees himself as "King Shâhriyâr. I will rape a virgin every night, and before dawn I will kill her before she kills me."[47] This last phrase expresses it well: male aggression against the female is reinterpreted as self-protection. We have already redefined the emotion underlying Shâhriyâr's relationship to his ex-virginal victims: fear of the female.

The test-tube man's identification with Shâhriyâr remains fairly superficial, maintained in the realm of the imaginary. The identification between Shâhriyâr and the Imam is more direct, more violent. In his own first-person narration, the Imam reveals that when in bed he loved reading books from the *turâth* (the cultural and literary heritage of the Arabs), especially *The Thousand and One Nights*.[48] He would put on his reading glasses and take off the Imam's face. Looking in the mirror, he would watch as physical changes—white skin and white teeth—transformed him into Shâhriyâr. "My heart is white like his heart, loving black slave girls. And my soul is innocent like his, not knowing that a woman can love a man other than her husband."

The Imam's body shivers when he sees Shâhriyâr's wife in bed with the black slave, "and in my dreams I see my wife in bed with one of my black slaves." He opens his eyes and instead sees his wife in bed hugging a book. Reassured, he runs to his black slave girl, stopping on the way under a tree. He enjoys being without his guards, in complete anonymity. But what does he see? A giant whom he takes to be either a jinni or one of his enemies from the opposition political party. He quickly climbs the tree, as he did when he was a child, and hides in the branches. The giant sits under the tree, opening a box with multiple locks. Inside this box is another box, from which the giant takes out a woman of bewitching beauty; he lays his head on her lap and falls asleep. The young woman spots the man in the tree and calls out to him to descend; he does, and she proceeds to have sexual intercourse with him.

Then follows a *Thousand and One Nights*–like conversation about the men's rings this woman has collected from previous, similar sexual interludes, including the reference to adding the ring of this most recent male to the others. The Imam/Shâhriyâr runs back to the castle, only to find his wife in bed with her lover. He kills the two "just as Shâhriyâr had done" and adds to this singular gynocide that of his other wives.

Thereafter, every month at the new moon, he marries a virgin, deflowers her, and kills her the same night. This he does for twenty years, until the people object and the young women flee. So he requests from his Chief of Security a virgin, whose description he reads to the Chief of Security from the *turâth* books. The Chief of Security is flabbergasted and begins to believe in reincarnation, saying to himself: "This is King Shâhriyâr's soul inhabiting the body of the Imam, or it is the Imam's soul inhabiting King Shâhriyâr's body." After a protracted discussion with the Imam, during which the Great Writer is also called in to discuss love, the Chief of Security goes out to search for this young girl.[49]

The girl turns out to be Bint Allâh, and at this point in the narrative it is no longer Shâhriyâr whose saga is in question but the Imam's. The bloodthirsty medieval ruler disappears now that he has fulfilled his role. Nevertheless, the complex relationship that then develops between the Imam and Bint Allâh picks up elements of the fantastic that, as we shall see, bring it close in spirit to some of the stories in the *Nights*.

Shâhriyâr provides an effective and potent model for the Imam's gynocidal instincts. Unlike the test-tube man, who only imagined himself to be the medieval Islamic ruler, the Imam becomes that ruler. The book that he is reading is transposed into the reality that he then lives. The Saadawian narrative becomes like a camera lens moving constantly from the world of one ruler to that of the other. When the Imam spots the giant, whom we know to be a character from the frame of *The Thousand and One Nights*, he takes him to be either a jinni or one of his enemies from the opposition party. By this mere thought, he brings the two worlds together. When he kills his wife, he does it "as Shâhriyâr had done."[50]

The differences between the subsequent behavior of the two rulers are perhaps as telling as the similarities. The sexual interlude between the Imam and the giant's mate takes place at an altogether different point in the ruler's adventure than does that between Shâhriyâr and the *'ifrît*'s young woman. The Imam encounters this sexually aggressive woman as he himself is on his way to his black slave girl. When he checks on his wife, it is to discover that she is sleeping alone, hugging a book. Only after his own seduction does he discover his wife in bed with her lover. This reshuffling of events shifts attention to the ruler's sexual behavior. It is his setting out to see his black slave girl that unleashes the unfortunate events, and not his wife's illicit conduct, as in the original *Nights*. El Saadawi's text has deftly overturned the frame of *The Thousand and One Nights*, even going so far as to have the modern male ruler frolic with a black slave girl, when in the original it was the medieval rulers' wives who had strayed, one of them with a black male slave.[51]

When the Saadawian text alludes to the Imam's killing his earlier, older wives,[52] it makes an indirect commentary on the original Shâhriyâr's monogamy: the medieval narrator, after all, speaks of only one wife, the unnamed perfidious female. Does this monogamy make the wife's act that much more inexcusable? It might, since the reader could then assume that she did not share her husband's sexual favors with other wives.[53] Whereas Shâhriyâr performs his murderous exploits on a daily basis, his modern-day follower transposes the act into a monthly one, performed at the time of the new moon. The Muslim calendar is, of course, a lunar one; when the killing cycle becomes monthly, the deflowering and murder of the virgin by the Imam is turned into a quasi-sacrificial act, opposed to the daily avenging act of his medieval predecessor.

The Chief of Security may be correct in reincarnating King Shâhriyâr and playing musical bodies with the souls of the two governing murderers. But let us not underestimate the constant tension, created by El Saadawi's recasting of the frame, between the past that is Shâhriyâr and the present that is the Imam.

And what better place for this tension to be embodied than in the woman? Where has Shahrazâd gone in this modern narrative? *Cherchez la femme* becomes a dictum as important for us as it is for the Imam's Chief of Security. The Shahrazâd of *The Thousand and One Nights* is occulted. The name Shahrazâd does appear once in *The Fall of the Imam*. Bint Allâh, in a chapter she narrates, speaks of an old grandmother who would tell the children stories. Her stories merged one into another, her voice never stopping—"as though the cutting off of the story meant the cutting off of her life, like Shahrazâd." To the question "Who is Shahrazâd?" the old grandmother, rather than answering, would simply begin her narration anew.[54] This allusion to narration as a lifesaving device is familiar to readers of the *Nights*. In fact, it forms an essential part of a certain analytical approach to the text.[55]

From a major character, the medieval teller of stories is transformed into a mysterious, shadowy figure. Her fortuitous appearance in El Saadawi's text does serve a function, though. She is a literary herald of sorts who signals to us, the readers, that intricate intertextual games are about to unfold. Then she can comfortably disappear, leaving the frame to her male counterhero, the ruler.[56]

How can this Shahrazâd be so passive, so invisible, we might well ask, given that we are dealing with a feminist text? Simple. In the frame of the *Nights*, Shahrazâd enters the scene as a woman in control. She has read books, she has memorized poetry, she is knowledgeable, intelligent, wise, an *adîba* (a woman learned in the arts of literature and society).[57] She is also independent, defying her father's advice not to venture into the monarch's bed, and above all, she is crafty, saving herself and her female kind. Nawal El Saadawi's novelistic agenda is radically different. Here, man is in control. It is man's murderous acts that chase the women from the kingdom. It is man who orders that the virgin be searched out. It is man who determines the characteristics that she will have, guided by descriptions in his cultural and literary heritage.

More significantly, the Shahrazâd of *The Thousand and One Nights* performs a critical role in changing the dynamics of male-female sexual relations, in redefining sexual politics. When she consciously takes on her shoulders the burden of saving womankind from the royal serial murderer, she has accepted an arduous task: that of educating this ruler in the ways of a nonproblematic heterosexual relationship. The Shâhriyâr of the *Nights*, after all, has thus far come in contact only with perfidious females. Shahrazâd's self-instigated entry into the narrative changes all that.[58]

The Imam's path is different. When he orders his Chief of Security to look for a virgin, it is not to alter his behavior. No single woman will save him from the collective perfidy of the female gender. His Shahrazâd does not exist. In effect, she has been replaced by Bint Allâh, a very different figure indeed, and one who conforms more closely to the description Fatima Mernissi incorrectly ascribed to Shahrazâd: "an innocent young girl whom a fatal destiny has brought into Chahrayar's bed."[59] The substitution of Bint Allâh for Shahrazâd is appropriate to El Saadawi's cyclical vision. The original Shahrazâd worked in a linear frame and effected a solution, one that recuperated criticism and ultimately sanctioned the patriarchal order.[60] El Saadawi's universe shows no such resolution: the struggle between Bint Allâh and the Imam goes on.

What is true for the Imam is also the case for his geographical cousin, the test-tube man. The two males are united by a common merger of personality with Shâhriyâr. Both fuse identities with the medieval serial murderer by looking into a mirror: an instrument of reflection. Both will sacrifice virgins at the altar of their male fear, eloquently expressed by the Western protagonist. Both have also shared the same woman, who is the beloved of the test-tube man and the wife of the Imam. In a sense, these two males are like the two brothers from the medieval frame, who have also shared the same woman, the *'ifrît*'s mate. East and West have once again met, this time through male identity and sympathy with the murderous principle of gynocide. Shâhriyâr survives not only the test of time but also that of place. Politics may vary, places may vary, but sexual politics, we are told, do not.

Shâhriyâr may bring the two patriarchal systems of the East and the West together, but as a model he still remains more effective in the East, the world of the Imam. His roots are Arabo-Islamic and will remain so. His adventures are part and parcel of the Arabo-Islamic heritage, affec-

tionately and proudly called the *turâth*. The chapter in which the Imam
is metamorphosed into Shâhriyâr is appropriately titled "The Revivifi-
cation of the Heritage" (Ihyâ' al-Turâth). And when this very same
Imam talks about his bedtime reading, it is his passion for the *kutub al-
turâth* (the books of the *turâth*) that he singles out.[61]

The *turâth* is, of course, centuries old, a complex and enormous col-
lection of texts ranging from the literary through the historical to the
theological and philosophical. There is in the Saadawian fictional uni-
verse an intimate relationship between men and this rich textual tradi-
tion. They can exploit it, as the Imam does; they can cite it. They are
clearly at home with it. More important, they often use it in a delicate
gender game. The search for the virgin, the ideal woman described in
the *turâth*, is perhaps the least ambiguous example. She is described in
the *turâth*, but she herself is not familiar with it. When the Imam asks
Bint Allâh whether she has read the *turâth* books, she answers in the
negative. What about *The Thousand and One Nights*? The answer is the
same.[62]

Not surprisingly, the identical situation occurs with the Imam's
Christian wife. When he confesses to her that he fears coming back and
finding her in bed with the Body Guard, à la Shâhriyâr, she asks: "Who
is Shâhriyâr?" He responds: "Do you not know Shâhriyâr?" to which
she answers: "No." To the further question of whether she has read the
*turâth* books, she again responds in the negative. This is a shortcoming
in her breeding, she is told; she must read.[63] Lest we be tempted to
excuse this lack of knowledge by the fact that this woman is not of the
East, the test-tube man is there to argue the contrary. He, a male, is, as
we have seen, perfectly cognizant of Shâhriyâr, even going so far as to
identify with the murderous ruler.

In a sense, Bint Allâh is more fortunate than the Imam's wife, if only
because she is told who Shâhriyâr is: "King Shâhriyâr, whose wife, white
like honey, betrayed him with a black slave." This betrayal becomes an
obsession in the mind of the Imam/Shâhriyâr, and his own parallel
betrayal with the black slave girl seems almost irrelevant. This is what
the old grandmother meant when she called man's actions a "lawful
perfidy."[64] We have come full circle.

But what a far cry this modern Egyptian pseudo-Shahrazâd is from
her literary predecessor! The twentieth-century Arabic hero is a player in
a literary game in which she ignores the identity of the other players.
Unlike her ancestor, whose appearance in the text is triumphally her-
alded with her in-depth literary and historical knowledge, Bint Allâh is

particularly vulnerable. It is not her knowledge that is exposed, but her ignorance.

Bint Allâh will pay dearly for this ignorance. Her intimate encounter with the Imam demonstrates her distance from her medieval ancestor. As the contemporary Imam meets the equally contemporary Bint Allâh, his fate parts ways with that of the medieval Shâhriyâr. The Chief of Security looks through the keyhole and sees Bint Allâh spraying the Imam with water and ordering him to turn into a sheep. This he does, and spends the night bleating. Before sunrise, she reverses the operation and turns him back into the Imam. The security chief trembles as he watches this reversal, realizing that she is able to perform magic, "like the women in the *turâth* books."[65] The reader acquainted with *The Thousand and One Nights* realizes that the Chief of Security is, of course, right. Other women in that text preceded Bint Allâh in transforming humans into animals.[66]

But Bint Allâh is not just any woman. In this instance, she is paradigmatically playing the role of Shahrazâd. Instead of the narrative role of her predecessor, however, hers is imbued with magic as she transforms the male ruler into a docile animal. She makes her reasons clear before undertaking this act: either she will live or she will sacrifice herself to the daughters of the nation and liberate them from the male ruler. The option that Shahrazâd had does not seem to be available to this contemporary hero—an unremarkable fact, perhaps, given Shahrazâd's occultation from the feminist novel.

The powerful encounter between the Imam and Bint Allâh transforms both characters. The Imam, himself consumed by desire, in turn corporally consumes Bint Allâh. He sucks her bones as she hands them to him one by one. Despite his insatiability, his body inflates with what he eats and bursts. Bint Allâh, eyes wide with surprise, watches his face fall to the ground; she then takes off like a gazelle, her dog at her heels.[67]

This violent cannibalistic interlude is far from innocent.[68] As the Imam consumes Bint Allâh, he destroys himself. Seen another way, the patriarch attempts to annihilate the female by incorporating her within himself, but in the process he self-destructs. The third-person narrator of this episode could not have devised a better way to express the struggle between patriarchy and the female gender. The entire episode functions as a powerful *mise-en-abîme*.

As Bint Allâh sits with the Imam preceding this event, the narrator describes the ruler holding a glass of wine and sitting on a Persian carpet into which is woven a picture of the Ka'ba. His elbow is making a dent in the holy shrine, and, the glass of wine shaking in his hand, some of the wine lands in that dent. The narrator does not let the situation rest, however. As the conversation with Bint Allâh becomes more heated, the glass in the Imam's hand shakes even more, and its entire contents spill, "drowning the sacred enclosure, the Ka'ba, and the Prophet's tomb."[69]

The unidentified narrator is being highly provocative here. The Imam's drinking of the illicit liquid (alcohol is forbidden in Islam) calls attention to his superficial religiosity. But consuming this liquid on a rug displaying the Ka'ba is downright sacrilegious.[70]

Perhaps this narrator is, like the female hero being described, ignorant of the religious and literary tradition. Bint Allâh plays the role of kingpin in the Saadawian game of religious intertextuality and redefinition of the *turâth* despite her perceived ignorance of the male-defined *turâth*. She is the first speaker in *The Fall of the Imam*, the first voice the reader encounters:

> The Night of the Big Feast. After the long pursuit and before the rise of dawn, one of them hit me from behind. I was running in the dark looking for my mother, and I had no one with me but my dog.[71]

So far, so good: we have a chase, a victim and her dog, and a set of events that take place during a religious holiday. Soon enough, though, this chase and this victim with her ubiquitous dog are redefined. A third-person narrator tells us in the next chapter that the crime took place in the dark. The victim, it turns out, remained alive,

> in the form of a stone in the belly of the earth. Year after year. She remained living in the form of a stone, and beside her was her dog. The live body turned into stone. (This is a scientific fact. In history, the People of the Cave lived with their dog in the belly of the earth for three hundred years.)[72]

With one quick parenthetical remark, Bint Allâh and her canine companion have been transformed. From a modern-day victim pursued by the police system of an unjust ruler, the girl and her faithful dog are cast into the wider religious universe of the People of the Cave.

The People of the Cave (Ahl al-Kahf, known also as the Ashâb al-Kahf) are the legendary Seven Sleepers of Ephesus. They, along with their dog, attempted to escape the anti-Christian persecutions of the Emperor Decius by hiding in a cave where they slept for over three hundred years.[73] The tale is in the Qur'ân, in a *sûra* named, appropriately enough, Sûrat al-Kahf.[74]

Why the People of the Cave? François Jourdan, in a comparative study of the tale of the Seven Sleepers, explains that this legend—central to which is the notion of resurrection—is equally important for Christianity as for Islam.[75] In a version of the tale told by the medieval writer al-Tha'labî in his *Stories of the Prophets* (Qisas al-Anbiyâ'), the Prophet's son-in-law and cousin, 'Alî ibn Abî Tâlib, is the storyteller; he relates the adventures of the Sleepers in response to an inquiry by a Jew who says that he will convert to Islam if he finds the account true to that in his own tradition. When the Sleepers awake, they find themselves in a kingdom ruled by two kings, one a Muslim and one a Christian.[76]

In *The Fall of the Imam*, where both these monotheistic religions coexist and conversion plays a role, no better legend could be found to encapsulate the story. The Christian wife of the Imam wavers between Christianity and Islam. When praying for the safety of her Muslim husband, she first makes the sign of the cross and then recites: "The Father, the Son, and the Holy Ghost. Protect him from his enemies, O our Virgin Mother. I seek God's forgiveness. Protect him O God and O Prophet."[77] This Christian convert to Islam seems unable to keep her religions straight. The heaven to which the Imam goes is also inhabited by Christians.[78] What we do not see in *The Fall* is a battle between Christian and Muslim, like that which takes place between the two rulers in the medieval variant of the legend. There, the Christian ruler claims that the Sleepers died Christians, whereas the Muslim claims that they died Muslims. The question is, what is to be built at the door of the cave, a mosque or a church? The Muslim wins, and a mosque is built. El Saadawi's religious universe, however, is not so clear-cut.

In *The Fall*, it is the very same Christian wife who reverses the religious gender expectations in the text. No sooner does she invoke the Mother, the Daughter, and the Holy Ghost than she asks God's forgiveness and invokes the Father, the Son, and the Holy Ghost.[79] Is nothing sacred, the reader might well ask. The confrontation of these two trinities, one female and one male, has its uses, however. It facilitates the confrontation of Bint Allâh and the People of the Cave.

Gender differences aside, Bint Allâh is a lone figure. Her trajectory does not reflect the semicommunal solidarity of the People of the Cave. Nor are their fates the same: although both she and her male legendary predecessors are pursued by a tyrant during a holiday, the males escape, falling into a centuries-long slumber, whereas she is actually killed. The collective nature of her murder and its semiritualistic aspects bring her closer to the sort of figure René Girard calls "a scapegoat."[80] The mortal threat that propels the Sleepers' escape never materializes, as they safely find a refuge. Yet their sleep redefines Bint Allâh's death, which itself is but a temporary state in the narrative. Resurrection is always around the corner for her, as it is for the People of the Cave.

For both female and male victims, the resurrection is also a rebirth of sorts. The cave is but a metaphor for the womb, and Bint Allâh was transformed into stone in "the belly of the earth." The Saadawian narrator takes great care to conflate the two events by applying the same terminology to the People of the Cave.[81]

Yet despite resurrection and the invocation of the Christian and Muslim Abrahamic religious traditions, El Saadawi's vision is essentially cyclical and pagan. The saga of the Sleepers of Ephesus is reasonably straightforward: they escape, they sleep, and they are resurrected. Theirs is a linear trajectory. Bint Allâh's path breaks with theirs here. She does not escape, she is killed, and she is resurrected only to be caught again, to be killed again, and to be resurrected again—and on and on. And it is this cyclical aspect that also differentiates Bint Allâh's sacrifice from that of Abraham's son, Ismâ'îl, also mentioned in *The Fall of the Imam*.[82] Tempting though it might be to turn her into this dutiful son, she is actually closer to the sheep whose slaughter no one can or will stop.

In the same way that El Saadawi parted ways with the feminist dystopias and their linear historical visions, so does she diverge from the Abrahamic religions. Her narrators are not exclusively monotheistic in their exploitation of monotheistic religious elements. When, after one of her numerous killings, Bint Allâh is buried, her heart continues to beat for three days following her death. For seven days, her soul continues to hover over the grave.[83] The Christian element here is clear: the three days in the grave during which Bint Allâh's heart continues to beat parallel the three days Jesus is in the tomb prior to his resurrection. The soul's hovering, however, evokes a different tradition: the pre-Islamic notion that the souls of those whose blood has not been avenged would linger around their grave, turning into owls not to be silenced until vengeance was complete.[84]

Bint Allâh herself, like her soul, hovers between the various religious traditions. During a religious lesson in the Bayt al-Atfâl, she listens to the teacher reciting Qur'ânic verses from the Sûrat al-Falaq:

Say: "I take refuge with the Lord of the Daybreak
from the evil of what He has created,
from the evil of darkness when it gathers,
from the evil of the women who blow on knots."[85]

Bint Allâh closes her eyes and sleeps and sees the women who are blowing (al-naffâthât), looking like black eagles soaring in the air. She then awakes to the voice of the teacher, coming through like the roar of a jet plane (al-naffâtha).[86]

The naffâthât in the Qur'ânic text are female sorcerers who would spit on knots while uttering certain words.[87] From the most sacred of Muslim texts, Bint Allâh moves to eagles and thence to jet planes, creating a bisociation (more correctly a trisociation) that exploits the gap between traditional and modern. (A similar bisociation occurs in a discussion between the Great Writer and the Leader of the Opposition. After the Imam makes a query—namely, whether a link exists between Judgment Day and atomic radiation—the two vie with each other in debate, citing the Qur'ân.)[88] The reference to female sorcerers (witches, if one wishes) is hardly insignificant: they were, after all, religious competitors of the male Prophet. At the same time, this citation is one that more religiously oriented contemporary Arabic readers sometimes ask about. One of the most popular genres in Islamist discourse today is the legal injunction, the fatwâ. A sort of religious "Dear Abby" column, the fatwâ involves a question posed to a religious authority who then provides an answer based on Islamic law and theology. Thus it is that Mûsâ Sâlih Sharaf, in his collection of contemporary fatwâs on women, responds to a query from a Moroccan man about the meaning of the Qur'ânic quote "and from the evil of the women who blow on knots." This query provides the male religious authority with the opportunity not only to explain the full import of the verse, but also to educate his reader on the negative role of magic in Islam.[89]

But in the Saadawian young woman's religious lesson, however, the sûra remains incomplete. The last verse is missing. Only when the Christian wife of the Imam is praying for the safety of her powerful husband does the missing thematic element appear. She prays: "Protect him O Lord from his enemies. From the envious males [al-hâsidîn] and the envious females [al-hâsidât]. From the evil of the women who blow on knots."[90] Though not a Qur'ânic citation, the prayer of the Christian wife nevertheless plays an uncanny game with the sacred text, the reference to "the women who blow on knots" being its most obvious tie to the incomplete *sûra*. The missing last verse of the Sûrat al-Falaq reads: "from the evil of the envier [*hâsid*] when he envies."[91] Though the missing verse is not truly restored, its thematic core, "the evil of the envier," is effectively supplied by this Christian convert to Islam, whose garbled religiosity seems essential to the completion of the Qur'ânic text.

True, the wife of the Imam has used the occulted thematic element from the *sûra*, but she has reversed the order of the material. After all, in the Qur'ânic text, the female sorcerers preceded the envious. Is this simply an aberration, without significance? Or is it something more symptomatic of women's relationship to the religious textual tradition?

Bint Allâh fell asleep during the religious lesson. Is it any wonder, then, that she is in no position to defend herself when she confronts the Leader of the Official Opposition? In an interchange, she reveals to him that she is without mother or father. "No father?" he asks in confusion. She answers: "Yes." He says: "This is a calamity from God. We try you with evil and good for a testing," citing part of a verse from the Sûrat al-Anbiyâ'.[92] When he discovers that Bint Allâh does not know the verse, he enjoins her to memorize it. He then writes the verse on a piece of paper, in the process reversing the two words *evil* and *good*. She thus memorizes the wrong verse, and when she is heard reciting it, she is confronted with her misknowledge. She reveals the source of the mangling, but to no avail: the Leader of the Official Opposition denies having generated the incorrect verse. The punishment? Her tongue is to be cut out.[93] What a savage commentary on the official uses of religion! Good and evil are reversed. Normal assumptions are overturned, and once again it is those in control of discourse who define good and evil.

But perhaps redefining the parameters of the sacred is the domain of the male. As the Great Writer is chastising his mother for her inability to stand up to her unfaithful husband, he quotes the religion teacher who "would recite the words of God, saying: an eye for an eye, a tooth for a tooth, treachery for treachery, fidelity for fidelity."[94] The Sûrat al-Mâ'ida, which lays out these equivalencies, in fact has nothing on treachery or fidelity. Simply, the Saadawian male transmitters of the sacred traditions have no qualms expanding the semantic range of a given religious dictum, even going so far as to reverse it if necessary. In berating his mother, the Great Writer is not unlike the narrator of El Saadawi's short story "Death of an Ex-Minister" (Mawt Ma'âlî al-Wazîr Sâbiqan), who also feels that his mother should have had the courage to stand up to the father.[95] The presence of the political figure, the ex-minister, reminds the reader of El Saadawi's corpus that the structures of patriarchy transcend the individual and cover the political as well as the religious.

The intertextual use—and even misuse—of religious material is not an innovation of El Saadawi's. It formed part and parcel of medieval Arabic anecdotal texts. But in the medieval context, the individuals who indulged in this practice were generally quite learned in the tradition with which they played, and their exploitation of it was invariably ludic.

To take but one example: the religious traditionist and litterateur al-Khatîb al-Baghdâdî (d. 463/1071) tells us in his *Book of Misers* that a bedouin came to visit a man who had a platter of figs in front of him. Spotting the visitor, the man covered the platter with his garment. The bedouin noticed this but sat down nevertheless. Asked if he knew something from the Qur'ân, the bedouin recited: "By the olive and the Mount Sinai." The man asked where the fig was, to which the guest replied, "Under your garment."[96] What the bedouin has done here is eliminate part of the Qur'ânic text, which, recited properly, should be: "By the fig and the olive and the Mount Sinai."[97]

The ludic is alien to the world of Bint Allâh. She is outside the tradition, outside the mainstream of knowledge, which remains locked up in the patriarchal hands of the Imam and his coterie of male followers. This makes of Bint Allâh a modern hero. She also differs greatly from her female ancestors in the medieval Arabic narrative world, where women were at home with the religious textual tradition and could exploit and manipulate it at will.[98]

With these gender-oriented intertextual games in *The Fall of the Imam*, El Saadawi has expanded the literary horizons of the contemporary Arabic novel. For the last two decades or more, Arabic writers have been experimenting with extremely interesting and provocative metafictional forms. At issue is the definition of modern Arabic prose and its relationship to its textual ancestors. The name most clearly linked to this indigenous wave in the novel is that of the Egyptian Jamâl al-Ghîtânî, by now an internationally recognized author. His literary games involve overt exploitation of the classical textual tradition, ranging from the mystical through the biographical to the historical. Al-Ghîtânî's great innovation has been to associate with Mamlûk and other premodern settings the appropriate prose styles, language, and formal compositional features of the texts of the period in question, to tell essentially modern stories.[99] His compatriot Muhammad Mustajâb, on the other hand, winner of Egypt's State Prize in Literature, mocks the entire classical onomastic and lexicographical tradition when, in his novel *From the Secret History of Nu'mân 'Abd al-Hâfiz* (Min al-Ta'rîkh al-Sirrî li-Nu'mân 'Abd al-Hâfiz), he carefully indicates to the reader how the name of his character should be pronounced—but in dialect.[100]

Not restricted to Egypt, these intricate intertextual games have appeared in fiction ranging from one end of the Mediterranean to the other. The Palestinian Emile Habiby sets his novel *Ikhtayyi* in a completely different context by opening it with a text from the historical and literary compendium *The Prairies of Gold* (Murûj al-Dhahab), by the tenth-century polymath al-Mas'ûdî.[101] The Tunisian Mahmûd al-Mis'adî performs a literary tour de force in his novel *Abû Hurayra Related Saying* (Haddatha Abû Hurayra Qâl).[102] Abû Hurayra was one of the famous companions of the Prophet and a *hadîth* transmitter; and in this instance, the very title of the book exploits the narrative structure of the *hadîth*.

Names can be multiplied, examples from the literary heritage expanded. Najîb Mahfûz, for example, puts the medieval Arabic picaresque hero Abû al-Fath al-Iskandarî to highly original use in his story cycle "I Saw as the Dreamer Sees" (Ra'aytu fîmâ Yarâ al-Nâ'im). Abû al-Fath appears in the Mahfûzian oneiric universe alongside the wise fool Juhâ and the prophet al-Khidr.[103]

Multiply though we might and expand though we might, rare would be the Arabic woman writer who—like Nawal El Saadawi—dares to break rank with the other women writers and join the male line-up in playing intertextual games with the literary and religious heritage. The Algerian Francophone novelist and film director Assia Djebar, for instance, has composed a novel that exploits early Islamic accounts, but although her vision is contemporary, her project remains anchored in the historical universe of early Islam. In addition, the transposition into French sidesteps the linguistic violations of the original sources that El Saadawi effects so deftly.[104]

Nawal El Saadawi's *The Fall of the Imam* does not favor one monotheistic tradition over another. Instead, the tendency is toward amalgamation. In some of its Muslim versions, as we saw, the People of the Cave story evokes Judaism as well as Christianity. In El Saadawi's text, the old church where the Virgin Mary is sighted is close to the mosque.[105] And is it mere coincidence that Ephesus, the legendary city of our Sleepers, is one of the locations where pagan cults were replaced by Christian ones specifically related to the Virgin Mary?[106] The Sûrat al-

Falaq, al-Qurtubî (d. 671/1272) tells us, was one of three *sûra*s (one of the others being the Sûrat al-Ikhlâs) with which the Prophet asked God's protection from Jewish magic.[107] And the verses from the Sûrat al-Ikhlâs relating to God's begetting and being begotten have generally been considered a refutation of the Christian notion of the Incarnation.[108]

If Islam and Christianity take the foreground, Judaism is present by implication. Nawal El Saadawi challenges the patriarchal tradition common to all three Abrahamic religions, but is not afraid to exploit it. After all, were it not for Allâh, there would be no Bint Allâh.

# CHAPTER SIX

# Between Heaven and Hell

Bint Allâh, the female hero of *Suqût al-Imâm*, argued that patriarchy is universal and that monotheism is but one aspect of this pervasive system. Nawal El Saadawi's *Jannât wa-Iblîs* (English translation published under the title *The Innocence of the Devil*) is ideologically much more ambitious.[1] Here, too, patriarchy dominates, but this time the religious intertext is supreme, redefining the political and social structures with which it comes into contact. This dynamic differs from that in *The Fall of the Imam*, where the political took pride of place, redefining the social and the religious. Religion in *The Innocence of the Devil* governs the quasi-totality of the narrative, affecting discourses as diverse as the onomastic and the homosexual.[2]

*The Innocence of the Devil* might seem to represent quite a departure from other texts of Nawal El Saadawi. In her first mature work, *Memoirs of a Woman Doctor*, she had attempted to venture into the domain of religion but had had her hand slapped by the censors, who excised what they perceived to be the offensive sections of the novel.[3] Gradually, she began tackling this sensitive cultural area. It is as if she had been testing the waters before fully jumping in with *The Innocence of the Devil*. El Saadawi accomplished this final move with great skill. Her task has been facilitated by political and civilizational factors outside her control. The Islamist movement has planted itself firmly in the region, its roots going deeper than most Western critics perceive. Secularized writers and intellectuals like El Saadawi are aware of the cultural impact of this religious movement. El Saadawi is responding with her own feminist interpretation of the centuries-long Arabo-Islamic textual tradition. She did not go into the verbal battle unarmed. She read deeply and widely in the religious normative texts, like the Qur'ân and the *hadîth*, commentaries, lives of the Prophets, as well as in the less religiously oriented materials.[4] The result, *The Innocence of the Devil*, is Nawal El Saadawi's tour de force novelistic foray into theology.

Jannât is the female lead, whose name, the plural of *janna*, means Paradises. Iblîs is the name of the Devil or Satan in the Muslim tradition. A male and a female, they are opposed by more than gender differences. Whereas the Devil in *The Fall of the Imam* played a backstage role as the inspiration for the name of a political party, in *The Innocence of the Devil* he is a major character around whom other individuals revolve. The Deity is also present, as are the three monotheistic religions. And this is not to mention a multitude of other subjects dear to the Arab feminist's heart: issues of gender as they relate not only to theology but also to language, history, patrimony, etc. It might be tempting to see *The Innocence of the Devil* as a continuation of the project set forth in *The Fall*: the subversion and reformulation of patriarchy. Or one might see it as the final articulation of a lesbian relationship only hinted at in other works, such as *Woman at Point Zero*. Certainly, these similarities are there, but to delimit *The Innocence of the Devil* in any way would be to impoverish this highly significant novel.

Unlike *The Fall of the Imam*, where the narration shifts between first- and third-person narrators of both genders, *The Innocence of the Devil* has but one third-person narrator, who remains cautiously outside the story. This narration, however, is perhaps the least problematic of the text's literary properties. The events of the novel move in a dizzying fashion between past and present, fantasy and reality. Different levels of the language add to this ambiguity: the dialogue is sometimes in literary Arabic, sometimes in Egyptian dialect, and in several cases it involves both levels of the language at once.

*The Innocence of the Devil* is set in a mental hospital, the *sarây*. Jannât enters this enclosure on the first page of the text. Her entrance is dramatic, silencing even the birds. The reader traverses the portal with her and, in the process, meets the cast of characters. In addition to Iblîs, there is an older man whom people address as Mawlânâ, Our Lord; a female patient named Nafisa; and the individuals in charge of the institution, including the male director and the female chief medical officer, "al-Ra'îsa." The Director prescribes the treatment for the newcomer: a solitary room under observation and three "sessions" a week. These sessions, it turns out, are electroshock therapy.

For the reader, meeting the characters involves learning about their past lives: interaction with family, school teachers, the religio-political system, and so forth. The chapters center on different characters, and although there is a clear progression in the novel from beginning to end, it is not a linear progression.

Toward the end of the book, Jannât's treatment is declared success-ful, and her exit from the asylum is as dramatic as was her entrance into it: she is transported in a coffin. Her consciousness remains, however, as the narrator continues her saga. Iblîs also dies, attempting to jump over the wall of the facility. The Deity, seeing the demise of his "scapegoat," is discovered dead at the end of the novel.

For the majority of characters in *Innocence*, the *saráy* allows no for-ward or future vision. Rather, it is a place where the past takes center stage, governing and delimiting people's actions. Jannât thinks back to her grandfather, a Muslim, and her grandmother, a Christian who con-verted to Islam but retained her Christian beliefs. We hear about her school days and her informal education at home, where the grand-mother's popular religiosity and superstitions come to the surface.

When Jannât first sets eyes on al-Ra'îsa, she asks: "Nirjis?" No; al-Ra'îsa shakes her head. But Jannât's intuition that al-Ra'îsa is something other than who she pretends to be is correct. Her identity?: Nirjis, the daughter of a civil servant, the barber to the King. She has received the Medal of Nationalism and Honor, which she proudly wears, even in the asylum. On her wedding night, she sheds no blood. To erase this shame, her father commits suicide. The Director of the facility uses her body, and when she tells him that although she was a virgin she shed no blood, he reassures her that her hymen was elastic.

As the narrative progresses the reader learns that Jannât's recogni-tion of Nirjis was more than serendipity. The two had had a friendship that bordered on lesbianism. When their schoolteacher asked Nirjis whom she loved most in the world, she replied: "I love Jannât." Rumors began to fly about this sinful love caused by Iblîs. But just as this hidden past is coming alive again for Nirjis, Jannât forgets it. She is declared cured. Nirjis/al-Ra'îsa, however, declares to the Director that she no longer wishes to have anything to do with men. He confronts her with her lesbianism and curses her. She runs away, becoming trans-formed into a white butterfly. Another white butterfly joins her and the two are shot, their saga ending in drops of blood.

Nafîsa, the third woman whose past we see unfold before us in the asylum, is said to be Iblîs's sister. After all, had she not as a child heard the male teacher, Shaykh Mas'ûd, call her brother "Iblîs" in school? Nafîsa's past is intimately tied to her mother, whose son died in military service. He, along with other young men, was recruited to fight, only to die. The mother was told that her son was in Heaven with his Lord, in the Garden of Eden with prophets and martyrs. As Nafîsa thinks about the loss of her brother, and about her own journey to Cairo to look for him, she utters over and over the invocation "Yâ Rabb" (O Lord). She is looking out the window of the women's ward, and who—of course— should hear her but the "Deity" in the *sarây*, who commands her to come downstairs. This Deity questions her about her virtue and then asks her to declare herself his servant. This she does, provoking yet more questions about his being the only man in her life, without associate. Satisfied with her answers, he then rapes her. Her scream brings out the medical staff of the asylum, who escort the culprit to the "electricity room," one assumes for electroshock therapy.

This Deity does not have a relationship only with Nafîsa. He earlier demonstrated that he was inextricably tied to Iblîs as well. He wakes him in the middle of the night and urges him to go out and do his duty, whispering to people and tempting them. Iblîs, wishing to sleep, tries to dissuade the Deity, but without success. He finally decides to kiss the Deity's head out of respect. He jumps out of bed, knocking the turban from the master's head; what looks to the other inmates like a fistfight between Iblîs and the Lord ensues. An individual carrying a book under his arm appears, shouting: "A tribunal." He is a judge, whose activities come to an end only when the asylum siren sounds, summoning the asylum medical staff.

The intimate relationship between the Lord and his antithesis, Iblîs, reaches a climax at the end of the novel. Iblîs is now deceased, and the Deity's remorse is beyond compare—so much so that he himself is discovered dead on the last page of the text. Before his demise, however, he in vain declares Iblîs's innocence: "Forgive me, my son. You are innocent! . . . Innocent! Innocent!" These are the last words he utters.

Incarcerating literary characters is certainly not new for El Saadawi. Her other confinements take place, however, in prisons, perhaps a more appropriate locus for a politically conscious writer like our Egyptian feminist, a prisoner herself for some time under Sadat. After all, Firdaws (Paradise), the parallel namesake for Jannât (Paradises), dies as a prisoner, convicted of murder.

But why an insane asylum? This is a complicated question for which answers exist on many levels. Placing patients in such a locus and subjecting them to electroshock therapy is not unusual in fiction, especially by women writers.[5] Yet the *saráy* also permits the unfolding of complicated literary games, not the least important of which is the game of fantasy and reality. Once Jannât has crossed the portal of the *saráy*, the rules of the reality game change. The reader knows that characters who inhabit this peculiar world may not be subject to the same regulations and dynamics under which the world outside operates.

When the "Lord" is wandering in the street, he almost gets hit by a car. The driver stops the vehicle and screams out the window:

—Can't you see, you ass?
—Don't you know who I am, you ass?
—Who might you be? Our Lord?
—Yes, it's me. But without the official clothing.[6]

Thus the driver, responding to what he believes to be a provocative question, asks what he considers to be a ridiculous question. Little does he realize, however, that in the world of this text (the world in which the driver himself after all exists) this individual indeed has been functioning as the Deity.

The incarceration of this Deity and his cohorts in the asylum permits innovative transgressions and violations. Since the reader enters the enclosed literary space on the first page of the novel, all subsequent narrative acts, whether inside or outside the asylum, are colored by the incarceration.

Theology is by far the most consistent undercurrent in both the pre- and post-asylum life of the characters, providing the subtext for the whole of *The Innocence of the Devil*. It governs the names. It governs the relationships. It governs the gender dynamics. It governs the linguistic system. And by virtue of this enormous textual power, it also permits the creation of irony, bisociation, and so on.

When the newcomer to the *saráy* is first asked her name, she replies, "Jannât." She is fond of her name. "Jannât. The plural of *janna*. This is what her father used to say."[7] When she asked what *janna* meant, he would open the book and recite: "'The Garden of Eden has flowing in it rivers of honey and milk.' She did not like the taste of honey and milk. She preferred instead sharp cheese and pickles."[8] The dynamics have been presented. Jannât's name, her onomastic identity, has been defined intertextually in terms of the Muslim Holy Book.

Rivers of milk and honey is a reference to the pleasures awaiting the believer in the Garden of Eden. The Qur'ân speaks in many places of rivers flowing in Paradise.[9] To take but one example:

> This is the similitude of Paradise
> which the godfearing have been promised;
> therein are rivers of water unstaling,
> rivers of milk unchanging in flavour,
> and rivers of wine—a delight
>   to the drinkers,
> rivers, too, of honey purified.[10]

These liquids of Muslim Paradise are discussed in great detail by Qur'ânic commentators. They are different from the same-name products existing in this world whose nature changes. The paradisiacal liquids will have been created ex nihilo in the rivers. The milk, for example, does not come from animals, and the purified honey differs from the honey of this world, which is mixed with beeswax.[11] More interesting, the Holy Book in the context of rivers also speaks of *jannât*, Gardens/Paradises, identical to the Saadawian character's name.[12]

The book's narrator, however, denudes this religious intertext of all possible metaphorical connotations when the reader is told that the young woman did not like the taste of honey and milk. Opposed to these two sweet and significant fluids are solid foods, both of which are distinguished by the strength of their taste: sharp cheese and pickles.

The name Jannât recasts the entire concept of the Garden of Eden. The plurality of her name elicits reactions from other characters in the novel. When Iblîs in the asylum hears her identify herself, he looks at her with wide, fixed eyes: "Her name is Jannât? While he dreams of one single *janna*?"[13] At another point Nirjis's mother tries to comfort her by telling her that Nirjis is the name of a beautiful flower. The child, however, responds: "But the name Jannât, Mother, is more beautiful. It is the plural of *janna*, not one single *janna*. So how is it with one orphan flower like *nirjis*?"[14]

But it is not simply the idea of the Garden(s) of Eden inherent in Jannât's name that links her to the religious domain. Lying in the coffin, Jannât sees her official name: Jannât 'Abd Allâh 'Abd al-Lâh. She asks herself: Is 'Abd Allâh her father's name and 'Abd al-Lâh that of her grandfather? Her memory awakens gradually. She hears her grandmother calling out to her grandfather: "Yâ 'Abd al-Lât." He jumps up and corrects her: "'Abd al-Lâh. Not 'Abd al-Lât!" Her grandmother was consistently changing the *h* to a *t*, and her grandfather just as consistently tried to correct her. "Al-Lâh! Not al-Lât!" He grabbed his wife's hand and tried to make her write the two letters, the *h* and the *t*, which look identical but for the two dots over the *t*. "The feminine has two dots over it!" Jannât, while asleep, heard her grandmother repeating the mistake. Her grandfather's voice rang out in the night: "The two dots, you ass!" Her grandmother's response? "The whole business is two dots! You are overturning the world for two dots! May God take you from this world!"[15]

The two dots on which this discussion hinges are really not so ideologically innocuous. True, in the domain of Arabic grammar and lexicography alone, the two dots simply signal the feminine gender. The narrator of *The Circling Song*, after all, already sensitized the Saadawian reader to the question of linguistic gender and the definition of what is male and what is female based on these same two dots. Hence, when the grandfather declares that the "feminine has two dots over it," he is correct—but only on one level.

Lest the reader miss the other connotations of this discussion, the narrator continues. The ever-curious Jannât now asks her grandmother whether Allâh is different from al-Lâh. "I don't know," replies the old woman. "Ask your father and grandfather." Jannât does: "And is al-Lâh al-Lât?" Her grandfather is upset: "I seek God's protection from Satan the damned [*a'ûdhu bil-Lâh min al-shaytân al-rajîm*]." We next see Jannât being made to write three times the words *I seek God's protection*: "A'ûdhu bil-Lâh. A'ûdhu bil-Lâh. A'ûdhu bil . . . " When she gets to the third "Lâh," two ink drops fall on the page, turning the *h* into a *t*. It is again as if the world were overturned. The teacher, Shaykh Basyûnî, looks at her notebook and loses control: "A'ûdhu bil-Lâh! A'ûdhu bil-Lâh!" He raps her on the knuckles and erases the dots so hard that he rips the paper. When his eyes spotted the two dots, the narrator confides, it was as if he were seeing "Iblîs face to face, not a drop of ink." He then makes the girls recite after him a Qur'ânic verse: "Have you seen al-Lât and al-'Uzzâ, and Manât is the third other. You have the male and not the female. That is the division of. . . ." He stares at the girls and continues: "Verily, those who do not believe in the next world call angels in the feminine. . . ."[16]

Jannât has indeed opened up a can of worms. Her inquiries innocently begin in the domain of language but finish up in that of theology. The Arabic language itself has only facilitated her task. The word *Allâh*, as is well known, is composed of two elements: the definite article, *al* (the), and the word for "deity," *ilâh*, which are elided into al-Lâh or Allâh, the Deity par excellence. To complicate matters, the pronunciation of this word varies according to the vowel that precedes it. If it is preceded by an *i*, as in *a'ûdhu bil-Lâh*, the phrase we hear repeated over and over by the male characters in this segment of the text, then the pronunciation is with an open *a*, bringing it close to the al-Lâh that Jannât inquires about. From there, it is an easy jump to the feminine al-Lât, a word in which orthographically the *h* picks up those two infamous dots.

The by-now familiar Saadawian obsession with grammar has been redefined. In *The Circling Song*, the narrator's concern was social and corporal: the two dots that distinguish grammatical male from female are but a symbol of the sexual organs that differentiate the male and female bodies. In *Innocence*, grammar transports the reader into the domain of theology. The distinction between male and female deities becomes as arbitrary, in the Saussurian sense of the arbitrariness of the sign, as the presence or absence of dots on a consonant.[17]

So what have Jannât and her grandmother done? On a most rudimentary level, they transformed a grammatically male deity into a grammatically female one. (It should be remembered, of course, that although the word *Allâh* is grammatically masculine, Muslim theologians have always argued that human categories like gender do not apply to God.) And these are not just any two deities. The female, al-Lât, is one of the pre-Islamic goddesses, who, along with her female cohorts, surfaces in the Qur'ânic verse recited by Shaykh Basyûnî.[18] It was precisely the elimination of these pagan deities that the Prophet Muhammad set out to accomplish in the seventh century.[19] Islam is a monotheistic religion one of whose central precepts, as we have seen, is the notion of *tawhîd*, the unity and transcendence of Allâh. How sacrilegious it then becomes to have the women play these gender games with male and female deities! Not only is doubt cast on the nature of the Deity, but in the process a pre-Islamic goddess has been unwittingly revived.

Is it a wonder, then, that the two individuals who respond to this, the grandfather and the school teacher—both males—react in the same way: with frustration and impatience? And for both, the transposition of the two letters turns the world upside down.

As well it should, perhaps. The relationship between women and the Muslim religious tradition seems tenuous at best. The female characters in *The Innocence of the Devil* are not unlike their literary cousins in

*The Fall of the Imam,* for whom this tradition also seemed unfathomable. The narrator in *Innocence* earlier explained that Jannât's grandfather had taught the grandmother how to perform ablutions and recite the Qur'ân. The grandmother had, however, kept a Bible hidden under a pillow. After his death she no longer prayed with the Qur'ân but simply crossed herself and recited the Christian prayers.[20] Clearly, his attempt to educate her in Muslim ways did not pay off; the wife remained suspended between the two monotheistic religions just like the Christian wife of the Imam. Jannât herself tears a page from a book, out of which to make a paper airplane. The grandfather, upon discovering what she has done, is horrified: "This is God's Book, you ass!" Her physical mangling of the Qur'ân earns her a sound whipping.[21] Nirjis/al-Ra'îsa, playing with her father's copy of the Qur'ân, elicits the same response from him: she gets beaten on the hand and told not to play with "God's book, you ass."[22]

This verbal and physical abuse of the female is clearly linked to the religious domain. But it is the "Deity" in the asylum who performs the ultimate violation of the female: rape. When the Deity, answering Nafîsa's call, beckons her to come down, she does so. He takes her hand and leads her to a dark corner of the garden. She has kept her eyes closed, in keeping with Shaykh Mas'ûd's words that "he who opens his eyes will lose his sight from the strength of the light."[23] During the interrogation leading to the rape, the "Lord" asks her to kneel and say, "I am your servant." As she does so and takes his hand, the narrator notes that his hand is

> softer than the hand of the *'umda.* Clean, trimmed nails. But in his galabiyya is a smell of perspiration. She had a moment of doubt. Does the Lord perspire like a human? Then certainty returned to her.[24]

To Nafîsa, clearly, the man she is dealing with is the Deity. Each time she responds to his questions, she inserts the words "Yâ Rabb" (O Lord) into her answer. This is the formula that caused the Deity to call her down to him in the first place. But, more than that, she is ascertaining to herself and to the reader that she believes she is indeed involved with the Deity. After all, she heeds Shaykh Mas'ûd's words, based as they are on a real belief in the blinding power of the vision of God.

The perspiration, a sure sign of the corporality of the being in question, causes her to hesitate for only a moment. It should cause the reader to pause for a longer period. With this simple phrase the narrator has effectively called the reality of Nafîsa's world into question. What is the certainty that returns to her? For her, it is that this man really is the Deity. The reader should by now know better. The manipulation of the gullible female is real, as is her rape. Had she opened her eyes, had she herself doubted what Shaykh Mas'ûd told her about the blinding power of the light, she might have avoided being raped. In the gender dynamics of this Saadawian text, however, Nafîsa's response is par for the course.

This woman-victim is, along with the Deity, an inmate of the institution. His reality, it could be argued, is hers. But what should we make of the size of his hands and his perspiration? The narrator compares the hand of the "Lord" to that of the *'umda*, or village headman. These corporal comparisons are not innocent. We have already seen that the body and its attributes function as important social markers in El Saadawi's fiction. When Nafîsa asks herself whether the Lord perspires like humans, she has, without realizing it, tumbled onto a most important theological issue that has long plagued Muslim thinkers, revolving around the question of God's attributes. The anthropomorphism of the Deity was vigorously debated in the Middle Ages, and it was Ahmad ibn Hanbal, founder of the most conservative legal school in Islam, who declared that these corporal attributes were to be understood "bi-lâ kayf" (without how).[25]

Of course, when the question was debated by medieval Muslims, the physical attributes of the Deity were more noble ones than perspiration. And although this bodily function merely sparks a doubt in Nafîsa's mind, it does much more for the discerning reader: it ridicules the theological discussions over God's attributes, and reminds us that if the Deity did possess these attributes in the first place, he would be a corporeal being who not only would sit on a throne but undoubtedly would perspire as well. Nafîsa has gone beyond what her literary predecessor, Hamîdû, experienced in *The Circling Song*, where the deities hanging from the sky had smelly feet. Hamîdû's religious universe, with its multiplicity of gods, is at a safe distance from the monotheistic world of Nafîsa, who, through her questioning about the Lord's body odor, accidentally stumbles onto a very sensitive theological issue.

Is the narrator turning Nafîsa into an advocate of Islamic theology? No; the narrator is playing a much more delicate game. Woman and theology, we learn, are an explosive mixture. Let us look more closely at this woman-victim. Nafîsa in this interlude is a passive player, heeding the Shaykh's advice. She is doubly the victim of male authority figures:

the Shaykh on the one hand, the Deity on the other. She does not dis-
obey Shaykh Mas'ûd's words but, rather, keeps her eyes closed lest she
be blinded by the light emanating from the Deity. In this way she differs
drastically from another literary woman, a medieval hero whom a thief,
disguised as the Angel Gabriel, attempted to rob. Instead the woman
locked him up in a closet, and when he beseeched her to release him,
she replied that she was afraid of becoming blind should she behold his
powerful light.[26] This medieval anecdote highlights the nature of Nafîsa
as victim who falls prey to notions instilled in her by the traditional reli-
gious teacher. Once Nafîsa has blindly (if the word may be excused)
accepted the Shaykh's teachings, she becomes the casualty of another
male, this time the Deity, who proceeds to rape her.

This physical violation differs from those of Hamîda and even Fir-
daws, for in Nafîsa's case no link with other bodily functions, such as
eating, exists. But Nafîsa's molestation, like that of her Saadawian co-
heroes, is embedded in an additional referential universe, this time that
of theology. Before the actual physical assault, the incarcerated Deity
subjects the woman-victim to two interrogations, in each instance plac-
ing his finger on major cultural and civilizational forces.

The first interrogation involves Nafîsa's relationship with Iblîs. Is she
a pious woman? Has Iblîs whispered anything to her? Has he visited
her, or she him? Nafîsa passes this examination. The association of
woman with the Devil, Iblîs, is not innocent. In the Arabo-Islamic
imagination, woman and the Devil are a lively pair, at times becoming
synonymous one with the other. Numerous are the references to their
intimate association, in works ranging from religious normative mate-
rial, like the *hadîth*, to the more secular poetic and proverbial corpus.[27]
The medieval polymath Ibn al-Jawzî (d. 597/1200), dedicated one of
his works to Iblîs's activities. Appropriately titled *Iblîs's Deception* (Tal-
bîs Iblîs), the work devotes a section to the Devil's attempts to lead
women astray. In Ibn al-Jawzî's words, "as for his deceiving women, it
happens a great deal." The medieval author feels it is sufficient to refer
his reader to his specialized work on women.[28] This traditional but
enduring construct that associates woman with Iblîs and his kingdom of
hellfire helps the twentieth-century reader to better understand the con-
temporary dialogue into which *The Innocence of the Devil* has inserted
itself.[29]

Nafîsa's second interrogation involves the Deity more directly. Is she
going to be his obedient wife? Is he the first man in her life? Is he the
one without a partner (*sharîk*)? No human or *jinn*? "I have to see the

proof," he declares. At first glance, the Deity's inquiries seem to be directed at Nafîsa's relations with other males, "a partner" referring to Nafîsa's possible sexual exploits. In fact, though, this question leads the reader to more theologically complicated issues. As soon as the Deity utters the word *sharîk*, he himself enters the domain of theological debate in Islam over God's unity. To provide the Deity with a partner (*sharîk*) is to draw away from his unity, *tawhîd*, and lapse into idolatry (*shirk*).[30] Nafîsa is oblivious to these larger issues. She merely parrots the Deity's questions, but in an affirmative fashion.

Following this interrogation, the Deity proceeds to "see the proof." Nafîsa, with eyes closed, feels her galabiyya going up and his fingers crawling on her body.

> Her heartbeats stopped under her ribs. She recited under her breath the verse: "Say: 'He is God, One, God, the Everlasting Refuge.'" And suddenly she felt something stinging like fire.[31]

Nafîsa's recitation of the Qur'ânic verse confirms the theological nature of the second interrogation.[32] What she mutters under her breath are the first two verses of the Sûrat al-Ikhlâs, ascertaining the unity of the Deity and juxtaposing the all-important theological notion with corporal violence against women. This same *sûra* inspired the dialogue in *The Fall of the Imam* between Ni'mat Allâh and Bint Allâh about the paternity of the Deity ("who has not begotten, and has not been begotten"), just as it inspired a recitation by Jannât's Christian grandmother in the presence of her Muslim husband.[33] Be it in the political patriarchy of the Imam or in the equally patriarchal insane asylum, the relation of monotheism to women is central.

Like Firdaws in *Woman at Point Zero*, Nafîsa feels those male fingers assaulting her body. But unlike Hamîda's rapes in *The Circling Song*, which are often perceived in terms of a stick, Nafîsa's violation is (not surprisingly given the theologically drenched context) described in a more theologically pregnant register: "She felt something stinging like fire." Contextually, the word for fire, *al-nâr*, can be read as both fire and hellfire.

The two interrogations, the first centering on Iblîs and the second involving the Deity himself followed by the rape, function on two levels, one literal, and the other metaphorical. In the world of the insane asylum, where the women coexist alongside the Devil and the Deity, it might not seem out of line to question Nafîsa about her relations with different males. But the text of *Innocence* is speaking to two readers: on the one hand, the one who stays on the surface of the text and follows a woman's victimization; on the other hand, the one who is able to discern a much deeper feminist theological commentary.

The Deity's rape of Nafîsa links the theological and the sexual. Monotheism, the concern of the male patriarchal establishment, is transmuted into an obsession that expresses itself in terms of sexual jealousy. The female is but a pawn in this game, with her body having to bear the burden of proof.

The Muslim Deity is not the only inhabitant of the gendered religious universe of *The Innocence of the Devil*. Women as a collectivity raise the specter of that other Deity, the Yahweh of the Old Testament. When their sons are called up for military service, the women wail: "Yâ Hûuuuuuuh . . ."—"as though," the narrator adds, "they were calling out to a Deity whose name is Yâ Hûh."[34] The second time this call is made by a woman, the narrator elaborates further: "As though she were calling out to a Deity whose name is Yâ Hûh. The god of earthquakes and volcanoes."[35] On the third try, the narrator is more comfortable making a final link: "As though she were calling out to a Deity whose name is Yahwih. She read about him in the Bible. The god of earthquakes and volcanoes."[36]

All three Abrahamic religions coexist in *Innocence*, but they do so in a distinct hierarchy. Clearly, the preference is for Islam. Yet Islam seems to be the property at once of the male and of the patriarchal system. When Iblîs would awaken Nirjis and whisper to her at night, she would hide her head under the covers and recite the Ayat al-Kursî. She asked God to help her, "but God used to leave her alone to Iblîs . . . Nothing but sleep would save her from Iblîs."[37] The prayers of the female are useless. God does not respond to them. When Nafîsa calls out "Yâ Rabb," she is told that the Deity does not answer women: "Even the Deity became their possession"[38]—*their* here being in the masculine plural. It is only in the enclosed world of the asylum that the Deity answers Nafîsa's call, and then to rape her.

This rape by the Deity is symptomatic of an aspect of male-female relations that the narrator of *Innocence* presents but at the same time seems to wish to subvert: that is, the normal power relationship in which the male dominates the female. Jannât's grandmother is a case in point, for although the grandfather believes he has successfully converted her to his religion, the reader knows the depth of his illusion.

The case of al-Ra'îsa is extremely significant here. When we first meet her, she is under the control of the Director of the facility. His power over her is both sexual and professional. At the outset, therefore, she seems to meet all the criteria for the perfect sell-out: she works within the system; she permanently wears its medal on her person; she tries to emulate the smiles of male leaders;[39] she refuses to admit her identity to her childhood friend. Her official mask as al-Ra'îsa seems complete. Even her name implies an "official" function, the equivalent of a female boss.

Soon enough, though, cracks begin to appear in this mask. The medal al-Ra'îsa received is the Medal of Nationalism and Honor. Yet honor is precisely the element that brings tragedy to her life. On her wedding night, when the *dâya* (midwife) tried to extricate the blood from her broken hymen, none appeared. Honor, the narrator quickly interjects, is the honor of males, with females acting as its evidence or proof.[40] Hamîda would undoubtedly agree. Was not her twin brother sent after her by their father to avenge the honor of the family? In the case at hand, we see that progress—if that is what one wishes to call it— is being made: Nirjis/al-Ra'îsa's father killed himself over this shame. She lifts her eyes, filled with tears, to the sky. "Her father was better than Sayyidinâ Ibrâhîm (the Prophet Abraham). He slaughtered himself and did not slaughter his daughter."[41] This revelation is al-Ra'îsa's, not the narrator's. It comes to her as she calls up the image of Abraham about to slaughter his son before the appearance of the scapegoat.[42]

Nirjis/al-Ra'îsa should have been killed when her honor was cast into doubt, but she was not. One of her functions seems to lie precisely in the questioning and subverting of these traditional values. Her task may be facilitated by the fact that she, unlike her female colleagues in the text, is outwardly a functioning member of the male establishment. There is an intimate paradigmatic relationship between her absent corporal honor and the symbolic medal of honor she always wears.

The ultimate subversion by Nirjis/al-Ra'îsa involves her sexual preference. When Jannât's cure is declared successful, the Director fills out the official papers and hands the order to al-Ra'îsa. But she does not extend her hand to take the order. She has done this for thirty years: "Thirty years, standing in front of him, head bent, unable to lift her eyes to him."[43] But this time, she lifts her head and stares at the Director's eyes.

—What's with you, girl, standing like a statue?
—My name is Nirjis, not girl.
—Since when?
He lifted his hand and hit her with a stick over her breast.
—Since when, girl?
—Since today!

—Prepare the beer and the *mazza* [appetizers]. I am coming to you tonight.

—I am walking out and leaving you everything.

—Where will you go? Do you have another man?

—I hate you and I hate all men.

—So now you love women?

—Yes.

—You will go to Hell with the People of Lot.[44]

—No, Sir.

—Lesbianism is *harâm* [forbidden], O Mrs. al-Rayyisa!

—No, Sir! It is not mentioned in the Book of God.

—You Fallen Woman![45]

This confrontation between al-Ra'îsa/Nirjis and the male Director goes to the heart of the matter. Al-Ra'îsa's first step in asserting herself is to establish her identity: she is not "girl"; she now has a name, Nirjis. This rebellion earns her a physical beating from the Director. His attempt to reestablish their relationship in its previous dynamics of master and servant fails, however. Finally he inquires about other men, clearly unable to see a woman in other than purely heterosexual terms. Nirjis's reply takes him by surprise. Yes, she loves women. Naming, a process that provides an individual with identity and subsequently personhood, to cite Phyllis Trible's term,[46] does more than that here. It also permits Nirjis to declare openly her sexual preference, to come out of the closet, as it were.[47]

Once Nirjis's attraction to members of her own sex is declared, the dialogue shifts registers. Up to this point it was dominated by the discourse of social power and male-female interaction; now, however, it enters the religio-theological realm. The mention of Hell and the People of Lot is the signal. The phrase "the People of Lot," is a reference to male homosexuality and alludes to verses in the Qur'ân in which Lot's followers are linked to male homosexual desire.[48] The narrator of *Innocence* had already sensitized the reader to this issue when the boy Iblîs recited the Qur'ânic verse about Lot and his followers: "And Lot, when he said to his people . . . ' . . . you approach men lustfully instead of women; no, you are a people that do exceed.' "[49]

In Muslim tradition, male homosexuality certainly earned its practitioners a place in Hell[50] (though this does not mean it was completely occulted in the literary culture).[51] The Director assumes that the punishment is identical for lesbianism. Nirjis's vehement "No, Sir" is pithily eloquent. He is not deterred, however, for he then declares that les-

bianism is unlawful (*harâm*). Nirjis will not be fooled: "No, Sir! It is
not mentioned in the Book of God." Nirjis shows herself to be a worthy
opponent, indeed. She is quite aware that the Muslim Holy Book makes
no mention of female homosexuality.[52]

The term the Director uses for lesbianism, *sihâq*, comes from the
root *s-h-q*, from which the more common word for tribady/lesbianism,
*musâhaqa*, is derived. The terminology for female homosexuality is
quite ambiguous in the Arabic language, where the term *musâhaqa*
refers to rubbing and hence to female masturbation as well.[53] In any
event, female-female sex is, like male homosexuality, not unheard of in
the Arabic literary tradition. The medieval writer al-Râghib al-Isfahânî
(d. 502/1108), to take but one example, deals with the issue quite
openly in his anecdotal compendium, the *Muhâdarât al-Udabâ' wa-
Muhâwarât al-Shu'arâ' wal-Bulaghâ'*.[54]

Nor is El Saadawi the first twentieth-century writer in the Middle
East to broach the topic of lesbianism among Arab women. There is a
hint of it in the male writer Majîd Tûbiyâ's novel *Rîm Dyes Her Hair*
(*Rîm Tasbugh Sha'rahâ*), and the female novelist Hanân al-Shaykh
treats the subject quite openly in her novel *Women of Sand and Myrrh*
(*Misk al-Ghazâl*), as does Alîfa Rif'at in a short story. Even collections
of interviews with Arab women, like *Both Right and Left Handed* by
Bouthaina Shaaban, mention lesbianism.[55]

Here again, the Egyptian feminist distinguishes herself. Her textual
lesbianism is not simply a question of female-female physical relations:
rather, it is heavily tinged with theology. The verbal duel between man
and woman on female homosexuality transcends the corporal and
moves into the domain of religion, much as the physical violations do as
well.

The interchange between Nirjis and her male opponent permits her
to correct his misperception about female homosexuality. The power
game has shifted: Nirjis now has the theological upper hand. The proof?
When she declares that the topic of lesbianism is not in the Book of
God, she changes linguistic registers. Up to this point, her interchange
with the Director had been in the Egyptian dialect. She utters this last
sentence, however, in *fushâ*, literary Arabic—a shift that alerts the Direc-
tor (and, of course, the reader) to the importance of her statement. The
Director's response? "You Fallen Woman [*Yâ Sâqita*]!"

Is the Director cognizant of the full import of his closing comment,
which seems to escape his mouth almost of its own volition? He may
not be, but the reader most certainly is. When that very appellation was

applied to Jannât, the narrator offered a flashback of her childhood. She remembered Shaykh Basyûnî explaining that *saqata* (he fell) is the past tense, with *saqatat* (she fell) as the feminine. Jannât is a fallen woman (*sâqita*) like her mother Eve.[56] The word *sâqita*, a fallen woman, embraces a notion of falling that is gender specific, we learn. The feminine has a plural, *sâqitât*, but no masculine plural exists. "Adam was not a fallen man [*sâqit*]. Man does not fall except in elections, or a military battle, or in the school examination while still a student."[57] These ideas reappear throughout the narrative.[58] Not surprisingly, they also conform to the earlier *Fall of the Imam* (Suqût al-Imâm, from the same Arabic verbal root), in which the Imam fell—but not in terms of virtue. In a strictly grammatical sense, the information the narrator provides is at best misleading: a plural for the masculine of *sâqit* does in fact exist— *suqqât*. Culturally speaking, however, this obviously not impartial narrator has hit the target perfectly: the term *sâqita* carries a mountain of gender-specific cultural baggage.

Jannât as a fallen woman is linked to her mother, Eve. When the narrator makes it clear that man can fall only in elections, military battles, or school examinations, s/he has recourse to Adam. Adam and Eve— the male-female couple whose sojourn in the Garden of Eden and whose fall from grace are central to the mental structures of all three Abrahamic religions. True, Islam does not lay the blame for the fall squarely at Eve's door, Adam being responsible as well.[59] Nevertheless, in a certain misogynistic strand of the Islamic religio-cultural system, Eve is the chief culprit.[60]

Jannât's grandmother read to her the biblical story of Eve and the serpent.[61] This from the Christian perspective. On the Muslim side, Nirjis's father explained to her mother that the Lord forgave Adam only: "God received from Adam certain words, so He forgave him alone." This particular verse from the Qur'ân was revealed in the singular, not in the dual. In different verses, however, the Deity uses the dual. Here, the father recites from the Holy Book:

> And We said, "Adam, dwell thou, and thy wife, in the Garden . . . but draw not nigh this tree . . ."
>    Then Satan caused them to slip therefrom. . . .
>    And We said, "Get you all down, each of you an enemy of each."[62]

The Saadawian narrator has tripped on—or walked deliberately into—a vigorously debated issue in Arabo-Islamic texts. Did God, after the Fall, forgive Adam only, or did He forgive both Adam and Eve?

The Qur'ânic citation uttered by Nirjis's father is from the Sûrat al-Baqara (the *sûra* of the cow). The events in the Holy Book begin with God's enjoining Adam and Eve to live in the Garden but not to partake of the tree. Satan, however, leads the two astray, and the Deity casts them out. All these actions take place in the grammatical dual, referring to both Adam and Eve. So far so good. But the first part of verse 37 of Sûrat al-Baqara reads: "Thereafter Adam received certain words from his Lord, and He turned towards him"—meaning that the Deity forgave him.[63] There is no grammatical ambiguity here: the pronominal suffixes in the original Arabic are in the masculine singular.

When first posing the problem, the Saadawian text reverses the Qur'ânic passage from the Sûrat al-Baqara. We are told that "God received from Adam certain words, so He forgave him alone."[64] Male actors are reversed: in the original, Adam is the recipient of the words; in the contemporary feminist variant, the Deity takes that role. Is this a slip on the father's part? Possibly, but not necessarily. The reversal certainly renders the Arabic text easier to comprehend. Now the actor in both parts of the sentence is the Deity: He receives the words, and He forgives Adam. In the Qur'ânic original, Adam receives the words, and He—God—forgives him. The mother, we assume, will find the message clearer in the reformulation.

The father is instilling a message in the mother (and in the reader). The Arabic reader of El Saadawi's text need not be told that the Qur'ân is considered by believing Muslims to be the unmediated word of God, perfect in every respect, including language.[65] Hence, when the father declares, "And God is cognizant of the Arabic language and the rules of grammar. It is not possible for him to have used the singular or the dual where they did not belong,"[66] he is justifying the position that, on a most literal level, Eve was not forgiven. For this contemporary Arab textual male, the issue is, therefore, clear-cut: the female remains outside the purview of the divine action.

In this interpretation, Nirjis's father differs from many premodern commentators who discuss the verse. El Saadawi chuckled with glee as she told me of her discovery of this Qur'ânic passage and its singling out of the male for special treatment.[67] One of the commentators who stood out in her mind was al-Tabarî. And well he should have. Al-Tabarî (d. 310/923), author of one of the most popular Qur'ânic commentaries, the *Jâmi' al-Bayân fî Ta'wîl al-Qur'ân*, makes it clear that it is Adam who is forgiven. Lest his reader wonder if it is possible for the pronoun to refer to Eve as well, al-Tabarî eliminates that option: "And the *hâ'* [the pronominal suffix] which is in *'alayhi* goes back to Adam."[68] Other commentators felt that the verse needed some explaining and were not as comfortable as al-Tabarî in restricting the divine forgiveness to the male gender. The most common reason some of them adduce for the presence of the masculine singular is its encompassing nature. Eve is clearly covered in the action of forgiveness, they rush to explain. This is how al-Qurtubî (d. 671/1272) and al-Baydâwî (d. 692/1293 or 716/1316), for example, explain the problem in their famous commentaries.[69]

Al-Qurtubî also heads off the question of why the Qur'ânic text moves from the dual to the singular, positing a stylistic reason. After all, the Deity began the interchange in the masculine singular: "And We said, 'Adam, dwell thou, and thy wife, in the Garden.'" When He completes the story, therefore, He does so with the same masculine singular.[70]

Al-Qurtubî's creativity is to be commended. But al-Tabarî's argument seems more convincing. When the Deity addresses the command "dwell" (*uskun*) in the masculine singular, He quickly adds to it "and thy wife." Eve has thus been overtly included in the action. Yet when Adam "received certain words from his Lord" and is subsequently forgiven, Eve is not mentioned.

The debate over who is and who is not forgiven by the Deity in the Muslim Holy Book is not simply the domain of the premodern commentators. Indeed, by raising this question Nawal El Saadawi has inserted her novel into yet another contemporary debate. A questioner from Abu Dhabi asks a religious authority why he could not find in the Qur'ân a single verse indicating Eve's forgiveness, whereas Adam was forgiven by the Deity. The complex answer boils down to the fact that Eve was forgiven along with Adam, an answer that would hardly surprise some medieval commentators.[71]

The Saadawian discourse in *Innocence* is not so reassuring. Holy books are stacked against the female. Yet childhood brainwashing does not seem to have permanently affected either of the two female leads. They will both be destroyed, and together at that, but not before putting up a fight. Nirjis courageously confronts the Director, affirming her onomastic and sexual identity and walking away from the male political structure of which she had been a part for thirty years. The case of Jannât is more complicated. She was a rebel from the minute she was born. In fact, she emerged from her mother's belly with her eyes open, whereas all other children are born with their eyes closed. On witnessing this event, her grandmother spat on the ground and uttered the familiar "A'ûdhu bil-Lâh min al-Shaytân al-Rajîm" (I seek God's protection from Satan, the Damned), wondering whether the creature was human or *jinn*.[72]

Jannât embodies the eternal woman, doomed to destruction. The color of her eyes is yellow, like that of the serpent's eyes. Her nose is like that of the Sphinx. Her skin is black like the face of Iblîs.[73] Thus women and the Devil are brought together in a combination already familiar to the reader of El Saadawi's works. The narrator follows up this association with references to the Bible and the Qur'ân, including the all-inclusive quasi-proverbial phrase we saw in Chapter 5, "Kayduhunna 'Azîm" (Their guile is great).

Jannât's relationship to Iblîs, then, is more than mere placement in a book title. As children they loved each other, and she even wrote him a poem: "I love you / Because you are the only one among the servants / You refused to bow down and you said: No."[74] Jannât's admiration here evokes the Qur'ânic verses in which Iblîs, unlike all the angels, refuses God's order to bow down before Adam.[75] As Jannât and Iblîs are playing together, she whispers in his ear, "Iblîs?" He replies denying that he is Iblîs or Satan. Nor is he an angel. He is merely a human, "like you completely."[76] By negating his true nature, the Saadawian Iblîs has inserted himself in another Islamic debate on the nature of the Devil. Is he an angel? Is he a *jinn*? Opinions have varied.[77]

Nawal El Saadawi's radical feminist vision is not only imbued with mainstream Arabo-Islamic religio-legal texts; it also comes close to a view of Iblîs prevalent in Islamic mystical traditions. There he is excused, a misunderstood victim. His refusal to bow before Adam, though an act of disobedience, is redefined, becoming "an affirmation of uncompromising monotheism," and his resulting martyrdom is thus a necessary part of the divine plan.[78]

Jannât does not, however, have a monopoly on Iblîs in El Saadawi's novel. He interacts with the characters who populate the *sarây*. He is Nafisa's brother. He is blamed for the illicit relationship between Jannât and Nirjis.

But Iblîs's most important act is, of course, the one he performs with the "Deity." The two are already engaged in a perennial tug-of-war in the Arabo-Islamic unconscious through the popular phrase "A'ûdhu bil-Lâh min al-Shaytân al-Rajîm" (I seek God's protection from Satan, the Damned). *The Fall of the Imam*, after all, exploited this association with the names of the two political parties, the Hizb Allâh and the Hizb al-Shaytân. That they should then appear in an intimate and complex relationship in *The Innocence of the Devil* is hardly a surprise.

Iblîs is the scapegoat par excellence. In a sense, the Deity is the one urging him on to unsavory acts. When the Deity attempts to awaken Iblîs from his sleep to go out and tempt people, Iblîs replies:

> —And if I didn't whisper to people, what would happen? Let everyone go to Paradise [*al-janna*]!
> —And hellfire, for whom did I make it, you ass?
> —Grill some lamb on it, brother.[79]

The Deity, it appears, has more interest in seeing the Devil perform his tricks than does the Devil himself. The latter seems just as happy to send everyone to Heaven. Does he not, after all, blame the serpent for the whole problem: "If it weren't for the serpent . . . we would all be in Paradise?"[80]

This vision of Iblîs as an innocent victim of the patriarchal religious structure is not entirely new in contemporary Arabic belletristic texts. The twentieth-century male writer Tawfîq al-Hakîm posed the problem in a short story titled "The Martyr," which appeared in 1954 in a collection, *Show Me God* (Arinî al-Lâh). In that story (which may also owe some inspiration to the Sufi traditions mentioned above),[81] the Devil wishes to repent and change his ways. At Christmas, therefore, he descends on the Vatican and requests an audience with the Pope. He expresses his desire to enter the "haven of faith," to which the Pope reacts in confusion. But the Devil is not to be swayed. He repeats his request and pleads with the pontiff to save him. The Pope refuses, arguing that

> the fiend is the pivotal point in the Holy Bible, Old and New Testaments alike. How could he be eliminated without destroying all the symbolism and legend, even the teachings about good and evil that quicken the hearts of the faithful and stimulate their imagination? What significance would the Day of Judgment have if the spirit of Evil were wiped out of Man's world?[82]

The Devil is sent away, but with the advice that he try the other religions. This he does, going next to the Grand Rabbi. This religious authority, realizing that "Satan's finding of faith would make the structure of Jewish privilege collapse, and destroy the glory of the sons of Israel,"[83] comes to the same conclusion as his Christian counterpart, but with the stated reason that Judaism does not "conduct missionary work."[84]

Next the Devil approaches the Shaykh al-Azhar, head of the international Muslim citadel of traditional learning. Like his earlier colleagues, the Shaykh ponders the question.

> If Satan were to become a Moslem, then how would the Koran be recited? Would people be able any longer to recite: "I seek God's shelter from the cursed devil"? And if this verse should be abrogated then it would follow that the same would have to be done to most other verses of the Koran . . .[85]

Again Satan's request is firmly refused.

As a last recourse, the Devil goes to the gates of Paradise. Not surprisingly, he is turned away by Gabriel, as he was by the earthly religious authorities. As he returns to the earth,

> a stifled sigh burst out from him . . . ; instantly, it was re-echoed by every one of the stars as though all were joining with him to cry out in agony:
> "I am a martyr—I am a martyr."[86]

Tawfiq al-Hakîm's Satan is, like his Saadawian counterpart, embroiled with the three monotheistic religions. And like his literary cousin, he is a victim. But his victimization does not come about through a direct encounter with the Deity, as it does in *The Innocence of the Devil*. In "The Martyr," the Shaykh al-Azhar realizes the importance of the God/Satan relationship when he ponders the phrase "I seek God's protection from Satan, the damned" (a phrase already familiar to the Saadawian reader). In al-Hakîm's vision, the Devil is doomed to exist eternally in this relationship with the Deity. Not so in El Saadawi's narrative. Here, both the incarcerated Deity and the Devil are destroyed. No eternal life can be had for either of them. And their destruction means the destruction of the patriarchal system from which they emanate.

Nawal El Saadawi has gone beyond her male compatriot. She has redefined the monotheistic struggle between God and the Devil, adding a feminist twist to the encounter. Her narrative is complicated not only by the various characters but also by the serpent—who, it turns out, has been there all along. It is physically present in a crack in the wall of the *saráy*.[87] It is there in the imagery evoked in the text. For example, the warm thread of menstrual blood running down Nirjis's legs were she to stand is compared to the tail of the serpent.[88]

Adam and Eve; Iblîs and the Serpent; a novel whose Arabic title, *Jannât wa-Iblîs*, not only evokes all these elements but also functions as an intertextual clue: what we are dealing with, in short, is the Garden of Eden. Is this to say that the *saráy*, the insane asylum, is the Garden of Eden? On a certain level, yes. This is, after all, where the serpent raises its head. This is where we find Iblîs hiding near a tree. This is where the Deity walks around. The signals that the narrator sends us about the locus are rather subtle, though. When Nafîsa's brother dies, her mother is told that he is in "the Garden of Eden."[89] When Nafîsa goes looking for her brother in Cairo, a man on the street tells her to look for him either in prison or in the insane asylum.[90] Is this brother Iblîs? That is what we are led to believe. If so, then he is in the insane asylum. Or is it the Garden of Eden?

To say that the *saráy* functions on one level as a metaphorical universe that evokes the Garden of Eden is tantamount to saying that the Adam and Eve story functions as a subtext for *The Innocence of the Devil*. But unlike the Garden of Eden of religious lore, a place that conjures up a specific historical moment, El Saadawi's literary creation does the opposite. Its historical framework, that is, is precisely the opposite of a specific moment: it speaks rather to the universality and everlasting nature of the religious and cultural paradigms it seeks to uncover. Ancient Egyptian deities and cultural artifacts sit side by side with those of the three Abrahamic religions. Even the *saráy* itself reaches that far back: "an old palace from the time of the Pharaohs."[91]

It is perhaps this extension back in time, coupled with the subtext on the Garden of Eden, which creates that sense of the past, that feeling of the absence of a future permeating *The Innocence of the Devil*. The characters are doomed to destruction. The Garden of Eden is certainly not a paradise.

CHAPTER SEVEN

# Of Goddesses and Men

---

The world of *The Innocence of the Devil*, like that of *The Fall of the Imam*, was one of monotheism. A contested monotheism perhaps, but one that structured both the theological arguments and their gender implications. Nawal El Saadawi's dissections of patriarchy, however, extend from the body of monotheistic religion to that alternate spiritual corpus which can be called polytheism or paganism. Nothing un-Egyptian in this. Modern intellectuals of the Nile have long been aware that behind the dominant and still-living Islamic tradition lies another, that of Pharaonic Egypt. Egyptian artists and intellectuals have varied in their attraction to the Pharaonic past. For the cineaste Shâdî 'Abd al-Salâm, ancient Egypt was a cultural ideal and a privileged pole of national identity.[1] For modern Islamists, however, *Pharaoh* remains a code word for tyranny, defined essentially by his negative role in the Qur'ân. Thus, after Sadat's assassination, the leader of the action exclaimed: "I am Khalid Islambuli, I have killed Pharaoh and I do not fear death."[2] In certain periods of modern Egyptian history (as between the wars), a cultural and aesthetic Pharaonism has been especially prominent.[3] Nevertheless, for the overwhelming majority of educated Egyptians the Pharaonic past remains a permanent part of the cultural landscape, and for artists an always available bag of artifacts.[4]

Ancient Egyptian religion featured a rich pantheon, and, as in most polytheistic systems, the female was an integral part of the divine: goddesses meet both gods and men. Nawal El Saadawi, however, avoids the facile juxtaposition of an oppressive patriarchal monotheism with a liberating polytheism (as has been done by some contemporary Euro-

141

pean opponents of monotheism).[5] For the Egyptian feminist, the world of Pharaonic religion is one of struggle between patriarchal and liberating, antipatriarchal forces. Little wonder, then, that familiar concerns surface in this largely new environment, from the physical realities of rape and clitoridectomy to the long shadow of the frame of *The Thousand and One Nights*.

How fortunate for us that the Egyptian writer and intellectual Tawfîq al-Hakîm should decide to write a play, *Izîs*, based on the Isis legend.[6] Al-Hakîm, whom we saw as the author of the theological short story "The Martyr," is far more famous as a playwright. Indeed, he is probably still the best known dramatist in the Arabic tradition. And El Saadawi had already isolated him elsewhere for special treatment.[7]

Nawal El Saadawi responded to her compatriot's dramatic production by writing her own *Izîs*.[8] In an impassioned introduction to her play, El Saadawi takes Tawfîq al-Hakîm to task, at the same time defending her right to present her own interpretation of the ancient Egyptian goddess.[9] El Saadawi strongly objects to al-Hakîm's argument that Isis[10] is the model of the faithful wife, who learned all she knew from her husband. She is much more than this, argues the contemporary feminist, for whom al-Hakîm's patriarchal thinking blocks his abilities to see Isis as more than a shadow of her husband:

> The Isis of Tawfîq al-Hakîm is not the ancient Egyptian Isis. She is not the goddess Isis whose philosophy and worship spread in Egypt and crossed the seas and the continents, to the east and west, to the north and south.[11]

Nawal El Saadawi's *Izîs* was, then, written in response to another *Izîs*. Who is this other Isis, and how does she differ from the Saadawian one? Both plays are, of course, based on the same legend, a legend that, though complex, can be reduced to the following elements: The deities Isis and Osiris, brother and sister, are destined to wed each other. Their marriage has one offspring, Horus. Osiris is murdered by the pair's brother, Seth. His body is thrown into the Nile and drifts out to sea, where it is discovered by Isis. Seth, however, retrieves the body and dismembers it, disposing of its parts in the Egyptian countryside. Not to be outdone, Isis finds the body parts and buries them once again. Horus wishes to kill his uncle but is dissuaded from doing so by Isis.[12]

El Saadawi, in her introduction to her play, calls for a rewriting not only of Isis but also of other female figures, such as Eve and the Virgin Mary. Isis has always had great appeal for feminist thinkers, some of whom even link her to the Virgin Mary.[13] El Saadawi's title notwithstanding, her text does more than create a new Isis. Patriarchy, religion, sexuality, violence—these and other issues dear to Nawal El Saadawi invade the play and help to redefine this ancient Egyptian goddess.

Tawfîq al-Hakîm's drama unfolds on the banks of the Nile. A group of women bemoans the exploitative nature of the Village Headman (Shaykh al-Balad): he robs them. Helpless against him, they plan to go and complain to the scribe Thoth[14] in the hope of receiving magical amulets for protection. Isis, in disguise, informs Thoth that her husband, the ruler Osiris, is missing. He attended a dinner at the home of his brother, Tîfûn,[15] who, however, disclaims any knowledge of his disappearance. Thoth's hands are tied: he is merely a scribe and can do nothing but register matters. Isis will undertake the search for Osiris herself.

We next watch as Tîfûn and the Village Headman dispose of a trunk, carried by four men, in a place in the river from which the current will carry it. Though we are not told, we understand that the trunk holds Osiris. Two boys observe this event, and one tries to retrieve the trunk.

The Village Headman, who is clearly working with Tîfûn, announces to the villagers the ascendance of the new king. He also warns them that a crazy woman will come looking for her husband. True to his words, Isis appears, requesting the villagers' aid. In the process of helping her, one of the village women uncovers the disappearance and death of the young man who had gone after the trunk. Isis, blamed for this incident, is expelled. The young man who watched his friend disappear after the trunk, however, takes pity on her and tells her what he saw. Isis sits and moans on the shore. A sailor then appears and reveals that he heard other sailors, whose ship was heading north to Byblos, speak of the trunk. The first act of al-Hakîm's play ends on an optimistic note as Isis cries out: "Byblos . . . Osiris!"[16]

Isis is now in Byblos beseeching the king's guards to let her speak to him. No sooner, however, does she hear about a "man from the west"[17] who has appeared at the court than she decides she would rather see him. It is Osiris. A happy reunion follows. Osiris tells of his brother's vile act of attempted murder, and the couple decides to return to their homeland—not, however, before they reveal their identities to the king of Byblos.

Three years later, Isis and Osiris (now called the "Green Man") are living in an isolated house on the banks of the Nile. They have a child, Horus. Two old supporters, the scribes Thoth and Mistât, arrive and talk to Isis. They wish to have Osiris regain the throne. Isis, however, reveals that someone has apparently been watching Osiris, and she is concerned. Her worries are not unfounded, for just then a messenger arrives bearing the news of Osiris's death. His body has been dismembered and its parts put on a ship headed south.

As the third act opens, it is fifteen years later. The Village Headman has changed allegiances and is now working with Isis; Horus is in training to fight Tîfûn. Mistât and Thoth are surprised to see Isis working with the Village Headman, given his utter lack of principles. Isis, however, is concerned only about the safety of her son and his success. Mistât is unsatisfied; his loyalty to Osiris's ideals keeps him from joining her struggle.

A fight takes place between Horus and his uncle, who has discovered the young man's identity. But just as Tîfûn is about to plunge an arrow into his nephew, the Village Headman suggests that, instead, the young man should be taken prisoner and tried in front of the populace. A tribunal convenes. Horus is challenged to describe his father, which he cannot do. Accusations fly back and forth between Tîfûn and his brother's family. Fortunately, the king of Byblos arrives and vouches for the sincerity of Isis's accusations. What is more, he himself kept the trunk in which Osiris was placed. Horus is proclaimed king and wishes to kill Tîfûn, but Isis restrains him. She has the last words in the play: she hopes that her husband, Osiris, is pleased with what they have done.

The reader of Tawfîq al-Hakîm's text is further directed to a certain vision of Isis. The dramatic text is surrounded by extratextual material that at once redefines it and recasts it. On the one hand, a book cover advertises Isis's virtues, the first of which is said to be her fidelity to her husband.[18] On the other, closing arguments and questions seal the drama that has just unfolded. A comparison is made between Isis and Shahrazâd, each of whom performed an important action for her spouse; Penelope is also mentioned, though she was more passive than Isis, sitting patiently awaiting her husband Odysseus's return. Al-Hakîm also muses about the writer and his role: Should he be committed to the principle, as Mistât clearly was, or to the problem, as Thoth was?

The Saadawian *Izîs* is more complicated. The first act opens on the god Ra talking to Seth. Patriarchy is firmly entrenched, and no one questions it but Isis and Osiris. Ra promises Seth that he will inherit the throne of the earth from his father, Keb, and should any problems arise, Isis and Osiris will be handled appropriately. Seth, because of his love for Isis, asks the deity to spare her. Presently Keb, the earth ruler, dies.

But no sooner is Osiris declared to be his replacement than he is killed and Seth takes his place.

In the marketplace, soldiers spot a young girl wearing an image of Isis. They tear it from her and, despite the mother's pleadings, take the girl away, to have her raped by the Military Leader (Ra'īs al-Jaysh). The mother calls out to Isis for help. Isis, in mourning, is sitting with Maat, goddess of truth and justice. She hears a voice calling to her and thinks it is Osiris. She seems to be incapable of accepting his death. The woman who lost her daughter comes seeking their help. Maat promises an amulet, and Isis promises that she will deliver the young girl.

We now see Seth with the Military Leader discussing various matters, including Osiris and Isis. Seth's obsession with his sister, Isis, leads to a debate on male-female relations, in which the Military Leader reveals his aggressive attitudes. Seth should rape Isis, he advises the leader: "Women love rape." Seth is not convinced; this is man's fancy. He loves Isis precisely because she is stronger than he is.

The last scene of the first act brings together Isis and Maat on the shore of the Nile. They overhear a sailor singing the praises of the goddess Isis. The two women decide to warn him of the new situation in the country. Isis, however, does not want her identity revealed: "I do not want him to see me in this state. He undoubtedly has in his mind an image of the goddess Isis that is more beautiful than this image."[19] Maat is obliging. She informs the sailor, who she discovers is newly arrived from Syria, that Isis is a woman who has just lost her daughter in the market.

No sooner do the two leave Isis than Seth appears. As he approached, however, he overheard a male voice. He insists that he will discover who this individual is and will tear his body to pieces. His conversation with Isis leads to a discussion of male-female relations, during which Seth declares his love to Isis and his desire to marry her. But she loves another. Seth's eventual departure signals the return of Maat and the sailor. The sailor, having overheard Seth threaten Isis, vows to challenge him. "No," begs Isis; Seth will "kill you behind your back as he did with Osiris."[20] Maat suggests that the two hide from the ruler. The sailor suggests a small house he owns in a village far away.

The second act finds the group in their new environment. Isis and Osiris now have a child, Horus. The only fly in the ointment is an old priest who wishes to live on alms. Osiris enjoins him to work like everyone else. The old priest is not pleased and abandons the village.

Seth is summoned by Ra, who, however, does not appear. The High

Priest informs Seth that the deity had found his favorite woman in bed with a black slave. Although she insisted that nothing had transpired between them and that she is carrying Ra's baby in her belly, the High Priest is skeptical. The truth, he says, will be revealed when the child is born. Ra finally appears. He has ordered the slave killed. First, though, he would like to see him castrated. Seth obliges, carrying out this deed. An extended discussion ensues between Ra, Seth, and the High Priest about women, sexuality, and procreation. How is one to tell the good woman from the bad woman? Should they be dunked in water? Should they be outfitted with a chastity belt? Why not perform a parallel operation to that carried out on the slave, the High Priest suggests. As the power brokers are debating these questions, in comes the old priest from Isis and Osiris's hide-out. He gives Ra a report on their activities and reveals all he knows. The decision is made: castrating operations will be performed on both women and slaves.

Soldiers appear in Isis and Osiris's village, accompanied by Seth. Seth examines Isis's husband and declares that he is not Osiris. Nevertheless, the man is castrated, beheaded, and his body cut into pieces. Maat, Isis, and Horus discuss what to do. Horus wants to avenge his father. Isis, however, proposes a public tribunal. Conditions in the land are now such that castration and clitoridectomy are common procedures. The Military Leader offers his help to Maat, confessing that he has left Seth (probably because of that ruler's savagery). The state of the country has worsened: it faces economic ruin; Ra's holy book is being misused; he himself is aging; and his designated successor, his son, does not even look like him. A tribunal it will be. At Isis's instigation, the head of the tribunal is elected democratically by a show of hands. Seth kills the Military Leader, and Horus castrates Seth, wishing to kill him. He is stopped in his murderous act by Isis. Forgiveness is de rigueur for the more powerful. The populace is joyous, singing the praises of Isis and Horus.

Like Tawfîq al-Hakîm's drama, that of El Saadawi is prejudged for the reader by the author's lengthy introduction. The feminist writer explains that she wishes at once to distance herself from her predecessor and to rewrite what she perceives to be his misogynist interpretation of the ancient Egyptian goddess. This she has done, despite some superficial similarities in the story line between the two texts—without which, of course, this would not be a true recasting. Where al-Hakîm, for example, has two male characters discuss the dilemma of the writer, in the Saadawian retelling it is Isis and Maat who undertake this debate.[21]

The two represent two different sorts of women, as seen, for instance, in their response to the woman whose daughter has been stolen: Maat promises an amulet, while Isis promises the return of the girl.[22] Isis's response to the bereaved mother is highlighted by the fact that Maat is the goddess of justice and truth; it should be she who is concerned with the recovery of the lost child.

Perhaps the major characteristic of the Saadawian vision of Isis is its all-encompassing nature. The story is extended, the characters developed, new relationships formed—all in such a way as to broaden the scope of the play into a generalized attack on patriarchy and patriarchal religion. Violence becomes but a tool of the male universe that El Saadawi creates.

Let us begin with Isis and Osiris, the major figures in this drama. But to say "Isis and Osiris" is to enter into a complicated game of identity, one in which gender plays a crucial role. Both figures are present in both plays. But each, male and female, is treated by its gender-associated scriptor in such a way as to become the stronger and the more important character for the text in question: the male Osiris for Tawfîq al-Hakîm, and the female Isis for Nawal El Saadawi.

When Isis first surfaces in al-Hakîm's play, she is looking for her missing husband, the ruler Osiris. But she appears in disguise, hiding her face behind a black *niqâb* or veil. The scribe Thoth, in fact, belittles her by saying to his colleague Mistât that she is undoubtedly missing a duck or has had a goat stolen. When she, her identity still hidden, reveals to them that in fact her husband is missing, Thoth sarcastically comments that this certainly goes beyond "the domain of the duck or the goose or the goat!"[23] Isis eventually confesses her identity. The later scenario with the villagers is not dissimilar, for again Isis comes looking for her husband, "hiding her face with her black *niqâb*."[24] She likewise eventually reveals herself to the villagers, but not before they accuse her of being a crazy, inauspicious woman. In Byblos, too, Isis is unknown and her identity (like that of Osiris) is not exposed until later. And yet again, before Tîfûn's palace, Isis, standing with Thoth, wears a robe that hides her face.[25]

Why all these disguises? Security might play a role: perhaps Isis does not want to reveal who she is for fear of bodily harm. But in the end she does precisely the opposite, disclosing her identity to those from whom she previously concealed it. In most cases, moreover, her name is not divulged until a negative judgment has been made about her character. The disguise, in essence, helps to prejudge the case for the reader, for whom Isis becomes a tiresome figure. Before being recognized as the widowed wife, she is joined to the ranks of women who complain about their missing animals, or, even more telling, she is transformed into an insane person. When the young man disappears, Isis is accused of being a magician and blamed for this event. The women, as a group, scream for her expulsion.

Al-Hakîm's Osiris, on the other hand, is a positive presence from his first appearance as a missing ruler. No pretense or disguises are needed: he has simply disappeared. He is the wronged individual whose brother tries to murder him and eventually succeeds. He is the mentor figure who trains the inhabitants of Byblos in various skills. He may acquire a new name, the Green Man, but his identity is never in question.

With Nawal El Saadawi, however, quite the reverse is true. For the feminist, the character Isis has much more solidity than her husband. Her sense of self never wavers. Even Seth argues in favor of her intellect. She is strong. She is fair. She is wise.

Instead, Osiris is the one whose identity is called into question. The arrival of the sailor from Syria will be problematic not only for Isis, but for Osiris as well. Osiris, we know, is killed early in the text. Yet he is resurrected to be killed once again. Or is he really? This crisis of identity commences with the sailor's appearance on the scene. After Isis and her fellow goddess, Maat, overhear the sailor singing to the goddess Isis, Isis decides that she does not want him to see her in this state. "He undoubtedly has in his mind an image of the goddess Isis that is more beautiful than this image," she tells Maat.[26] The latter promises not to inform the individual. The sailor persists in saying that Isis's face is one he has seen before. When he asks why she is sad, however, Maat answers that she has lost her daughter in the market and is looking for her night and day.

Seth's questioning of Isis after the departure of the sailor and her companion, Maat, is significant. When he asks her if she is alone, she answers in the negative.

> —Who was with you?
> —Osiris . . . was with me . . .
> —There was a man with you a few moments ago . . . I heard his voice from afar . . . Who is he?
> —It is Osiris.
> —Who is it, Isis? Who is the man whom you are meeting in the darkness of night, far away from people's eyes?[27]

Seth's suspicions must remain just that. Isis insists that the man she was with is Osiris. In a later confrontation between the two men, Seth rejects the sailor's assumed identity as Osiris. This Saadawian game of identity with Osiris mirrors al-Hakîm's game of veils with Isis.

But why is Seth so concerned with the identity of Isis's male companion? After she repeatedly insists that the stranger is Osiris, Seth finally responds that he will rip his body to pieces. This is more than male jealousy. Isis is his sister, and the motif of his sexual attraction for her reappears throughout the play. In fact, the entire story operates (as does the Isis legend) around a brother-sister sexual nexus.[28] We are already familiar with the centrality of the brother-sister relationship in Arabo-Islamic culture, a concern strongly reflected in Nawal El Saadawi's literary corpus. The brother-sister couple in "A Story from a Woman Doctor's Life" (see Chapter 2) and the Hamîda-Hamîdû duo of *The Circling Song* are but two such literary manifestations. Even Bint Allâh, in *The Fall of the Imam*, was chastised for having fought in a trench with her brother, their seclusion there having been clearly linked to sexual transgression.

The dynamics of this brother-sister relationship are, indeed, powerful. But what El Saadawi has done is to reverse them. In the patriarchal world of her play, Isis stands out as a strong and powerful female figure. When Seth and the Military Leader discuss male-female relations, the latter tells his ruler that women love rape and that this is perhaps what Seth should have done with Isis. Seth confesses that he tried but that it was "she who took me."[29] Similarly, on more than one occasion he recognizes the superior power of Isis's intellect.[30]

It is precisely this strength of intellect that distinguishes the Saadawian Isis. When Tawfîq al-Hakîm was contextualizing his female hero, he placed her alongside Shahrazâd, the medieval narrator of tales who has transcended her modest beginnings in Arabo-Islamic culture to become a major player in world literature. For al-Hakîm, Shahrazâd resembles Isis because both did something honorable for the sake of their husbands.[31] And, the male playwright is consistent in the vision he presents of his hero. The last words in the play are Isis's as she declares her hope that her husband Osiris will be "pleased with what we did."[32] El Saadawi, in her introduction to her own play, correctly interprets al-Hakîm's "philosophy" as patriarchal.[33]

What does this patriarchy really mean? Gender-conscious criticism has made us aware that Shahrazâd herself, despite her narrative role, remains imprisoned in the patriarchal order that gave her literary birth.[34] Appropriately enough, this teller of tales makes no appearance in El Saadawi's play. Instead, as in *The Fall of the Imam*, the frame of the *The Thousand and One Nights* functions as a backdrop against which some of the most important events of the drama are played out.

El Saadawi's play opens on a universe in which the goddess Nut has been defeated and the god Ra is now master. The opening words of the drama are his, addressed to Seth: "It has been proven to me from this last battle that you are a courageous, strong horseman."[35] Is it accidental that these are the words by which the third-person narrator describes the male ruler, Shâhriyâr?[36] Seth also resembles the medieval ruler and his royal brother in another way. Like his predecessors, the contemporary Saadawian earth ruler has voyeuristic impulses.[37] Just as the two brothers watched the royal wives copulating with their black consorts, so Seth confesses to the Military Leader that he watched Isis and Osiris in bed. Unlike the sexually energetic lovers in the *Nights*, however, Osiris would simply lie in Isis's arms like a child with his mother and she would give him her breasts to suckle.[38]

Seth may be courageous and strong, but he is weak when it comes to raping Isis. Is Ra any better? Not much, really. He is a victim, we discover, of the same ailment that affected his literary predecessors, the two royal brothers in the frame of the *Nights*: jealousy. A member of Ra's harem was caught in bed with a black slave, and not just any woman, but his favorite, already chosen to be his wife and to give birth to his successor.[39] Ra, though, does not follow in the footsteps of the younger brother in the *Nights*, who resorts to instant gratification by murdering the two culprits. Indeed, Ra's revenge may be sweeter from a male perspective: he orders Seth to castrate the culprit, declaring, "I want to see him in front of me as a body without masculinity and without manliness, just like the body of woman."[40] Seth obliges, and the black slave's sexual organs are duly removed. Ra takes pleasure in this castration and laughs. He wonders out loud about "this strange mutilated creature . . . Is he a female? Is he a hermaphrodite?"[41]

The dialogue that ensues between Seth, the High Priest, and Ra is highly charged with sexual politics. The deity compares slaves to women, to which Seth responds that "woman is by her nature perfidious and it is not possible for her to be satisfied with one man, even if he is the great god Ra." Ra then bemoans the fact that sons are needed to inherit the throne, and sons cannot be had without women. "If man could become pregnant and give birth, we could do completely without women," he muses. The High Priest replies that Ra indeed can make man capable of pregnancy and childbirth. But Ra thinks that life without women would be boring, and, in any case, it is easier to rule over women and dominate them than it is to have men become pregnant and give birth.[42]

What an interesting exchange, transporting us as it does from the realm of the *Nights* into that of male procreation. This dialogue will undoubtedly remind those readers familiar with medieval Islamic philosophy of the story of the king who had such an aversion to women that his sage-physician devised a method by which a son could be begotten from the king's semen alone.[43] One wonders what the priest would have suggested had the deity pursued that line of argument. For an instant, one comes perilously close to an all-male society.

So the problem becomes, what, then, does one do with women? Various solutions are proposed. The priest suggests dunking them in the Nile: the one who floats and is carried upstream is innocent. This does not appeal to the deity; he fears that all women will drown. Seth has another idea: locking woman's body in an iron chest. It can be called a chastity belt. The deity does not like this suggestion either. What if a slave or a servant acquired the key? In the end, only one solution, originally proposed by the priest, is deemed adequate: clitoridectomy.

Once again, *The Thousand and One Nights* plays a role. Placing a woman in a box is reminiscent of what the *'ifrît* does in the frame of the *Nights*. There, the demon has kidnapped the woman on her wedding night, and we meet her at the same time the two royal brothers do. Although the kidnapper, having released her momentarily from her captivity, is asleep with his head on her lap, she manages to seduce the royal pair. Clearly, we are to understand from this incident that the perfidy of women is endless.[44] More to the point, the story from the *Nights* proves Ra right a posteriori: locking up women will not work.

In the feminist's text, however, the box is linked directly to the chastity belt. This device, along with the technique of dunking women, is associated with the West.[45] It is no coincidence, for example, that the brilliant Palestinian novelist and politician Emile Habiby evokes the Western chastity belt when defending Arab culture against the charge of oppression of women.[46] Thus, the Egyptian god's outright rejection of these remedies seems quite consistent.

The solution to the problem of women's sexuality? Clitoridectomy. How appropriate that this technique should be suggested by the priest, the highest representative of the religious establishment.[47] His argument is conclusive: woman's desire is greater than her intellect, and that desire must be controlled—by removing the organ of desire. When Ra asks, "Do you wish to castrate women as we castrated that slave?" the Priest's answer is categorical:

> Yes, O Great God. With the difference that the operation of castration in the slave will keep him from procreating, whereas the operation of clitoridectomy in woman will deprive her of desire only, and she will remain able to procreate.[48]

The deity is worried that the disappearance of desire in woman will lead to the same phenomenon in man. No, the High Priest reassures him: "Man's desire will remain as it is. It may even increase."[49]

The brutal cynicism of this dialogue is easy to decode: the patriarchal paradise is populated by desiring men and desireless women. Other points are more subtle. Western forms of control are confronted with non-Western ones, though the linking of the Eastern image of the box with the Western chastity belt argues for a fundamental similarity.

With one brief dialogue, El Saadawi's *Izîs* has again transported the reader into a new realm, this time into that of woman's sexual desire and her sanctioned corporal mutilation through excision.

Female excision is a subject close to the heart of El Saadawi, one she treats in her fictional as well as her programmatic work.[50] Of course, she is not the first Egyptian writer to deal with this culturally sensitive issue. The female writer, Alîfa Rifʿat, does as well.[51] The male writer Sulaymân Fayyâd also treats female excision in his powerful novel *Aswât* (Voices). There, it is a Western woman newly arrived in the village whose life is sacrificed to this form of mutilation.[52] El Saadawi's position on clitoridectomy is not far from that of other feminists, like Mary Daly, or even other women writers from the Middle East, like Evelyne Accad.[53] More recently, the African-American novelist Alice Walker popularized the plight of the genitally mutilated woman in her novel *Possessing the Secret of Joy*, which tells of an African woman who undergoes excision as a child. Two components of her book set Walker's narrative in context: the first is an annotated bibliography that includes some Middle Eastern material; the second, a set of thanks, in which Nawal El Saadawi's name appears.[54] The international feminist world concerned with the physical mutilation of women is a small one indeed.[55]

There is, however, one crucial difference between El Saadawi and Western, or even non-Western (like Accad), feminists who deal with clitoridectomy: El Saadawi underwent the operation herself as a child. Only much later, after she had met her third husband, Dr. Sherif Hetata, and with his encouragement, was El Saadawi able to articulate her feelings about this mutilation.[56] Her powerful account of the procedure has appeared not only in scholarly discussions of women in Islam, but also in popular magazines like the American *Ms.*[57]

That it should be the priest in *Izis* who recommends this radical operation is consistent with the Egyptian feminist's position on patriarchy and the religious order. That it is an ancient Egyptian who justifies the act is more suggestive. The Islamic tradition on clitoridectomy is a long one; *hadiths* (traditions of the Prophet) have been produced on the procedure, advising, for example, on precisely how much flesh should be excised. The general stance of Muslim jurisprudence has been to call the act permissible or recommended but not required.[58] Even today, discussions of clitoridectomy make their appearance in religio-legal materials.[59] As a social custom, clitoridectomy has been common in some Islamic societies and largely unknown in others. The procedure varies from limited circumcision to complete excision.[60] It has also (as Walker's novel attests) been practiced in non-Islamic African societies. Egypt, of course, is both African and Islamic. In this context, it is striking that in the enormous corpus of her imaginative literature, Dr. El Saadawi has reserved the male justification of clitoridectomy to an ancient Egyptian. She thus roots the practice firmly in her native Egypt, while sidestepping the question of its relation to Islam.[61]

Linking excision to castration redefines both as equivalent mutilations, while suggesting new implications, new politics of both gender and class. On the one hand, this linkage extends the negative (and presently unacceptable) image of male castration to female excision; on the other, it shows men violated along with women. The castration of slaves is a product of social hierarchy. Attaching that practice to excision relates oppressions of class (or caste) to those of gender. And what could be more universal than castration, which has a long history in both Western and Eastern cultures?

The proposed use of excision in *Izis* to cut off women's desire is, to be sure, a response to a specific female act. Like the royal wives in *The Thousand and One Nights*, Ra's consort has been caught in bed with a black slave.[62] But whereas their fate was death, hers is corporal mutilation. The similarity in the narrative situation of the two royal couples with that of the deity and his female favorite redefines the two punishments imposed on the female culprits. Juxtaposing the killing in the

*Nights* with the clitoridectomy in *Izîs* turns the latter act into a sort of death of the female.

As with the *Nights*, all these corporal games revolve around desire. In the medieval text, it was homosocial desire between two men that set the entire narrative in motion. And of course, woman's perfidious acts there were the result of her misplaced sexual urges.[63] In the twentieth-century drama, desire is exclusively heterosexual. On the one hand, there is the desire of the deity for his female favorite, a desire that comes upon him suddenly in the middle of the day as he is immersed in the affairs of the kingdom. On the other hand, there is woman's desire, once again illustrated by her perfidious act. The physical mutilation will be put into effect precisely to combat woman's heterosexual longing. After all, does the priest not argue that "desire in woman is greater than her intellect?"[64]

To say that the *Nights* operates as a subtext in *Izîs* is not to negate any differences between the two constructions of patriarchy, medieval and contemporary. The same situation, after all, obtained in *The Fall of the Imam*. In El Saadawi's drama, the slave is endowed with a voice, unlike his medieval counterpart. He proclaims his innocence, but to no avail.[65] Endowing this victim with a voice personalizes him, provides him with an identity. His entreaties also cast doubt on the whole question of his guilt. The act of castration becomes that much more heinous.

In the *Nights*, there is no discussion of any offspring from the ill-fated couple that was the ruler's wife and her black consort. Neither royal brother seems concerned about this progeny. In fact, only with Shahrazâd's entry into the narrative is the procreative process restored and the continuation of the line guaranteed.[66] This is not the case in Nawal El Saadawi's play. There, the female favorite is chosen by the deity to bear him an heir.[67] Later, in a discussion between the High Priest and Seth over the woman's alleged liaison, the priest notes that the truth will be manifest after the pregnant woman gives birth: the newborn will have either black skin or white skin.[68] As it turns out, the child's nose decides the matter: it is not like that of the deity but rather closer to those of slaves.[69] The use of the nose rather than the more obvious skin color of the infant casts doubt on the woman's guilt.

This concern for clearly identifying a child's paternity is patriarchal.[70] Since we know that patriarchy has just ousted matriarchy in *Izîs*, Ra's obsession is but a visible manifestation of this man-made system. Interestingly enough, it is the children who are most tragically caught in the web of matriarchy and patriarchy. The young girl who is taken from her mother and raped by the Military Leader meets her fate because she wears an image of Isis, a clear sign of defiance against the patriarchal order.

What kind of a patriarchy is this? It is at once social, political, and religious. In this it is not unlike the dominating patriarchy of the Imam's world or of the universe of Jannât and Iblîs. In *Izîs*, the religious aspect of patriarchy is most suggestive, the play being first and foremost a commentary on patriarchal religion. Ra is, after all, a deity. His advisors include a high priest. What, then, is the inspiration for the religious intertext? The compelling religious references are ones that allude directly to the monotheistic religions. In typical Saadawian fashion, the play, though it gives preference to Islam, is quite comfortable mixing religions. This tendency to attach patriarchy to religious systems in general, rather than to any particular creed, is a hallmark of El Saadawi's literary corpus.

*Izîs* is replete with monotheistic references—to the unity of the deity, to a Holy Book. In the first scene of the first act, allusions are made to the fact that Ra is the only deity, and Keb, the only earthly ruler.[71] Ra himself declares his unity: "Anâ . . . anâ . . . . al-Wahîd . . . al-Wahîd . . . " (I . . . I . . . . am the One . . . the One . . . ).[72] When Seth is later appointed earth ruler, much the same declarations are repeated.[73] These professions of the unity of the deity, using a word from the Arabic root *w-h-d*, automatically call up in the mind of the reader the Islamic concept of *tawhîd* (transcendence and unity of God), derived from the same root. And sure enough, the term *tawhîd* itself appears, with Seth arguing that Ra in fact ordered its implementation.[74] The reader should by now be aware of that notion's significance in the Egyptian feminist's writings: Bint Allâh, after all, defied the doctrine of *tawhîd* in her very name.

When Seth presents his argument, reinforcing it with the assertion that the deity eliminated all types of multiplicities, Maat responds: "Except the multiplicity of wives [*ta'addud al-zawjât*],"[75] a clear allusion to polygamy. In Islamic law, a Muslim man can have up to four wives.[76] Maat's quip connects to another discourse in the contemporary Islamic world: that on "multiplicity of wives." In the streets of the Arab world and North Africa today, religious pamphlets abound on this topic. Some of these works are even distributed for free in religious bookstores and at stands in cities from Cairo to Fez.[77] By raising this issue, El Saadawi has once again inserted herself into an important twentieth-century religious debate.

Ra speaks of his need for "the Holy Book" (al-Kitâb al-Muqaddas) and of the fact that he (Ra) may appear to Seth in the future to give him messages (*rasâ'il*) for the people.[78] "Al-Kitâb al-Muqaddas" is, of course, the Arabic name for the Bible, and the delivery of messages is an allusion to the Prophet Muhammad, the *Rasûl* or Messenger (a word derived from the same triliteral root), who receives his revelations from God through the Angel Gabriel.[79] More suggestive still are the formulas used when referring to Ra: *bi-Sm Allâh al-A'zam* (In the name of God the great) and *al-Hamdu lil-Lâh al-A'zam* (Praise be to God the great).[80] These formulas, while clearly modeled on those used daily in the Muslim world, are carefully made distinct from them.

But like the onomastic games played in *The Fall of the Imam* with the names of the two political parties (the Hizb Allâh, the Party of God, and the Hizb al-Shaytân, the Party of Satan), the recasting of these phrases calls attention to the meaning of the original formulation and forces the reader to question it. Here again, El Saadawi is not targeting any specific religious construction. Her vision is more global: ancient Egypt is but a means to speak about both ancient societies and contemporary ones.

The religious aspect of patriarchy becomes all the more powerful when it combines with the social and political dimensions. The religious may be the easiest to isolate, the social and the political being at times coterminous. The world in which the deity Ra operates is a political world, representing in microcosm the universe of a ruler, his court, and subject population. The social is closely tied to this universe, reflecting as it does the gender hierarchies operative in society at large.

Yet these gender hierarchies are complicated and are intimately tied to corporal questions—questions that in turn will redefine the gender boundaries themselves. Sexual violence and physical mutilation are the domain of the male; their victims are initially women and slaves. The Military Leader rapes the young woman sporting an image of Isis. Women and slaves are two categories that seem to have much in common, when they are not turned into identical beings. When Ra orders the slave's castration, he declares: "I want to see him in front of me as a body without masculinity and without manliness, just like the body of woman."[81] Elsewhere, the deity, in speaking about slaves, adds that they are like women.[82] Is it a surprise that both should have their genitalia mutilated? Man and woman become assimilated to each other, a construct reminiscent of *The Circling Song.*

The physical violence under patriarchy is not restricted to women and male slaves, however. Osiris, before being dismembered, is castrated, his sexual organs fed to the fish. Seth chops off the head of the Military Leader. Horus castrates Seth. The men become themselves victims of the patriarchal system they created.

It is Isis who stops the violence. After her son has castrated his uncle, he prepares to cut off his head. Isis tells him: "Enough O Horus . . . Enough . . . Do not kill him."[83] Isis's reaction is interesting. Throughout the play her primary attribute has been intellect. Seth himself opposes her mental strength to his own mental weakness. In his discussion with the Military Leader on women, he says that Isis is a woman whom no man can rape. The Military Leader replies, "Her muscles are so strong, my Lord?" Seth answers him sarcastically: "The problem is not muscles! How do I explain it to you? My muscles are stronger than her muscles, but she is stronger than I am. Do you understand this?" The Military Leader admits that he does not.[84]

Isis, however, clearly fathoms this difference. At one point, Seth tries to convince Isis that woman's place is in the home and that she was not created for the life of politics and rule. "Woman is delicate, weak of body," he says. "The bodies of men are stronger." Isis replies, "If the one who is stronger of body is the one who governs, then why do not mules govern us? There is no doubt that the mule is stronger of body than you, O Seth."[85] Corporal strength in men, corporal weakness in women—this is part and parcel of an Islamic religious debate that extends from the body into the realm of law.[86]

Elsewhere, we were already exposed to the idea that woman is not even human and that under Ra's rule she has nothing left to do but peel onions and give birth to children in the manner of rabbits and cats.[87] This is, of course, precisely the state to which women are reduced in dystopias like Burdekin's *Swastika Night* and Atwood's *The Handmaid's Tale.* Seth is more naive in his view of what an ideal wife should be—among other things, an affectionate mother and a meek wife who awaits her husband with a smile. Seth's "ideal wife" (he even calls her that), whose heart and mind are occupied only by her husband, functions (despite its near-universal applicability) as a perfect transposition of the views widely disseminated in popular Islamic literature throughout the region.[88]

Yet, how far Isis is from Seth's view of the "ideal wife"! She is the victorious one at the end. Is this because, as Seth puts it, she is not merely a woman or a female, "she is intellect"?[89] She even questions Ra's corporal logic, in an argument that applies as well to Islam (and Judaism): How, she asks, could he have created the body in the most perfect way and then order the removal of parts from this body under the name of castration or excision?[90]

But Isis does not reinstitute matriarchy. At the end of the play, the people dance and sing the praises of Horus: "Horus our beloved, Horus our king." Has the cycle of violent patriarchy come to an end? One wonders, since without Isis's intervention, her son would have certainly killed his uncle after having castrated him. For one brief literary moment, it seemed that matriarchy and the rule of the intellect might triumph. But the pull of patriarchy is stronger. The murder and mutilation, we know, will continue.

CHAPTER EIGHT

# Prison

---

A modern-day Shahrazâd, Nawal El Saadawi spins her
prison memoirs at night. During the day, we learn, the prisoners are
guarded too closely.[1] How odd that the incarceration saga of this con-
temporary feminist writer should have so much in common with the
literary adventures of her medieval predecessor. Both texts are instigated
by a violation. Both female heroes are at the mercy of a male ruler. Both
escape death at the end of the narrative. Both tell stories imbued with
politics, sexuality, and the body. Both texts are sealed in a family
reunion.[2] Yet the centuries separating Shahrazâd from Nawal El Saadawi
are significant. *Memoirs from the Women's Prison* (Mudhakkirâtî fî Sijn
al-Nisâ') emanates not from a gilded cage, like that in which Shahrazâd
told her stories, but from one of Sadat's prisons. And unlike Shahrazâd,
who willingly takes herself into the wolf's den, El Saadawi is taken
against her will into the cell that will constitute her world from Sep-
tember 6 to November 25, 1981.[3]

This enclosed world of the prison will help create for the narrator an
intimate universe in which women exist as a homosocial unit. In a
ground-breaking study, *Between Men: English Literature and Male
Homosocial Desire*, Eve Kosofsky Sedgwick has cogently argued for the
importance of homosociality among males.[4] Male homosocial desire is a
central component of Arabo-Islamic society, and its ubiquity is such
that it surfaces in texts of all kinds, ranging from the literary to the
philosophical and mystical.[5] Interestingly, the dominance of male
homosociality in Arabo-Islamic discourse is not unrelated to the domi-
nance of male scriptors in that tradition.[6] With her radical feminist

vision, Nawal El Saadawi has simply reversed societal and literary expectations. The prison setting provides a textual opportunity for the creation of a female homosocial environment. The female microcosm, whose inhabitants range from killers and prostitutes to political prisoners and religious conservatives, is pitted against the male patriarchal establishment. The two are, of course, linked: patriarchy creates the female homosocial world through a series of violations. The female hero strikes back from within this space through counterviolations.

While physically confining, the homosocial space of the prison is socially liberating. It permits the female hero-character, Nawal, to manipulate the ideological and social identities of Dr. El Saadawi, the author.[7] In *Woman at Point Zero*, the connection between the physician and the prostitute-murderer is blocked by the bars of the prison. Now that the physician is behind those same bars, that social gap can be breached. Again the two characteristic Saadawian female types make their appearance: the middle-class professional woman and her lower-class counterpart. Common imprisonment permits the romantic dissolution of class differences implicit in homosocial bonding.

Dr. Nawal El Saadawi was certainly not unique in being singled out for incarceration by the Egyptian president. While breathing its dying breaths, the Sadat regime imprisoned a great number of intellectuals and political and religious activists. Of course, these intellectuals were both male and female. The Egyptian feminist simply chose to center her text on her fellow women prisoners—who included such long-time acquaintances and friends as Sâfî Nâz Kâzim, Latîfa al-Zayyât, and Amîna Rashîd.[8]

Though already age fifty, El Saadawi experienced prison as an important rite of passage. Her husband, Dr. Sherif Hetata, had, after all, spent thirteen years of his life in jail for his political convictions. In conversations, too numerous to list, El Saadawi has confessed to me that the prison experience was a crucial part of her own life. It should then perhaps come as no surprise that, though chronologically rather short—only two and a half months—the physical incarceration generated quite a literary legacy. Not only did El Saadawi publish prison memoirs, but she also authored a play based on her carceral experience, *The Human Being* (al-Insân).[9] Also subsequent to this incarceration, El Saadawi penned *The Fall of the Imam*, so heavily inspired by the Sadat regime and its demise.

To be sure, El Saadawi is not the only Arab writer to turn her prison experience into words. The jails of Nasser and Sadat have provided literary fodder for men and women from all walks of political life. The Muslim Brotherhood activist Zaynab al-Ghazâlî, for example, described her prison ordeal under Nasser in the by-now classic bestseller *Days from My Life* (Ayyâm min Hayâtî). More recently, the well-known leftist Farîda al-Naqqâsh, in *Two Tears and a Rose* (Dam'atân wa-Warda), and the equally well-known Muslim revivalist Sâfî Nâz Kâzim, in *On Prison and Freedom* ('An al-Sijn wal-Hurriyya), have also written of their incarcerations.[10]

Distinctive in El Saadawi's narrative are a number of cross-generic allusions. It goes without saying, however, that such peeks across the border cannot be understood if one does not know the generic ground on which one is standing. Unfortunately, in Arabic literary studies, that is not always the case. In a recent article in a special issue of *Mundus Arabicus* on the Arabic novel since 1950, one of the better-known scholars and translators of modern Arabic literature writes the following:

> The first Arabic novel to be translated was the touching autobiographical depiction of the early village life of a poor, blind Egyptian boy; by the distinguished blind literary critic, scholar and author Taha Husayn, it appeared in English under the title of *An Egyptian Childhood.* . . . A second volume of Husayn's memoirs, telling of his days as a student at al-Azhar, published in Arabic in 1939 appeared in English in 1943 entitled *The Stream of Days.* . . . A third part, appearing in Arabic in 1967, that portrays his entry into the Egyptian university and his studies and romance in France, came out in English as *A Passage to France.*[11]

Of course, Tâhâ Husayn's three-volume work is not a novel but an autobiography par excellence. In fact, the concept and limits of autobiography have long posed problems for critics of Arabic literature.[12]

The same critic also brings us to Nawal El Saadawi, because in the same article he notes that she "has several works in English translation; some of these are extended in length and partly imaginative and are therefore considered to be novels."[13] What these quotations demonstrate (aside from the methodological naïveté of their author) is that the novel is considered to be a clearly superior artistic form to the autobiography. Thus a well-crafted autobiography is transformed into a "novel," while feminist works are labeled novels only grudgingly.

Linguists know that so-called mistakes in popular speech are really the sign of another set of linguistic paradigms seeking to burst through the shell of outmoded rules. Similarly, these generic "mistakes" represent unspoken but erroneous assumptions. The first is that the novel is an artistically superior form to the autobiography, or, to put it another way, that the more literary merit a work has, the more it is a novel. We need to banish the notion that, because autobiography and memoirs purport to talk about true events, literary artifice and literary merit are somehow foreign to them. Second is the misapprehension (also shared by other scholars) that first-person narration marks autobiography, while third-person narration marks the novel.

Admittedly, El Saadawi has not always made the matter easy. As we have seen, her first adult novel, *Memoirs of a Woman Doctor*, boasts an unnamed first-person narrator who happens to be a physician. It is, however, clearly a novel.[14] In the English translation of *Imra'a 'ind Nuqtat al-Sifr* (Woman at point zero), perhaps El Saadawi's most-read work, she includes a preface in which she describes her encounter with a female prison inmate, much like the plot of the novel itself.

*Memoirs from the Women's Prison*, however, is essentially what its title suggests. The text operates much under the same literary pact that Philippe Lejeune poses for autobiography: identity between author, narrator, and central character.[15] Yet the work does contain an element of fiction, in that some of the prison inmates are identified by pseudonyms. Their relation to the other historically identified individuals remains ambiguous. Barbara Harlow has called attention to this fictionality in her recent work, *Barred: Women, Writing, and Political Detention*.[16] Those who know something about the conditions of El Saadawi's imprisonment could make a good guess as to the identities of several of these people. I discussed the true identity of these individuals with Dr. El Saadawi, but she asked that this information remain confidential. I reminded her that the religious character in her prison text, who is depicted as wearing the *niqâb*, does not do so in real life. Dr. El Saadawi's reply? "It is all right. I have changed a lot of things in the text."[17]

Fictionality is not the only literary game that El Saadawi plays in her memoirs. "Because I was born in a strange time . . . it was not strange that I should enter prison." Thus, does the first-person narrator, Nawal, introduce her prison memoirs.[18] It is unfortunate that this introduction was omitted from the English translation of the book, for this birth signals an important literary event. Unfolding before our eyes is a complex and sophisticated narrative that partakes at once of the memoiristic and the autobiographical: memoiristic because the text is a memoir; autobiographical because the birth of the protagonist in this first line could herald an autobiography. In fact, on numerous occasions the text departs from its dominant memoiristic mode to include snatches that function almost as fragments of an unwritten autobiography. This *Memoirs from the Women's Prison* has something in common with other of El Saadawi's works in which, as we saw, suggestions of autobiography peek out from within works in other genres.[19]

*Memoirs from the Women's Prison* is a finely crafted text that goes beyond the prison experience. Although it seems to follow a diachronic mode, beginning with an arrest and ending with a liberation, into this surface diachrony are embedded multiple layers of events. The prison world of El Saadawi is an intricate weave. Descriptions of prison life sit side by side with childhood memories. Killers and prostitutes are made to travel in the same literary universe as political activists and veiled Muslim women. Religion and secular politics inhabit the same textual world. Add to this complexity an attention to the human body and questions of life and death, and one has a literary masterpiece, whose narrative techniques span the spectrum from bisociation to repetition.

One of the most important underlying acts in El Saadawi's *Memoirs from the Women's Prison* is violation. There is violation in the arrest. There is violation in the writing of the memoirs itself. There is even violation in the literary techniques.

It is three o'clock in the afternoon on Sunday, September 6, 1981. Nawal is at home, engrossed in the writing of a new novel. She ignores the repeated knocks on the door. When this is no longer possible, she asks who it is and discovers it is the police. They order her to open the door. She refuses. At last she goes into her room to don a white dress—her "going-out dress"—and begins to walk around the apartment, making an emotional and physical inspection of the locale. Then, she writes, "I heard the sound of the breaking door as though it were an explosion."[20]

This breaking of the door by the officials of the Sadat regime is, of course, initially a way for them to penetrate into her house to arrest her. But this act takes on almost mythic proportions as the account unfolds. Barbara Harlow notes that El Saadawi "repeatedly, obsessively, recalls throughout the narrative" the destruction of the door by "the arresting officers."[21] But the repetition is more than a mere obsession. It occurs at vital junctures in the text. In the vehicle transporting her to the prison, the officer declares to Nawal that she has exhausted the arresting officers. She thinks back to the intrusion and the breaking of the door.[22] Upon entering her cell, she declares to her old friend Amîna

Rashîd, already an inmate, that her door was broken down.[23] When Latîfa al-Zayyât takes her turn in the cell, she, too, is informed of this act.[24] During an official inspection of the prison, Nawal once again remembers the incident.[25] A letter from home opens with the discovery of the broken door.[26] When called before a government investigator, Nawal insists on registering the police intrusion and the smashing of the door.[27] Finally, the death of the Egyptian president, the narrator notes, occurs one month after he sent his police to break down her door and take her to prison.[28]

Clearly, the breaking of the apartment door is a topos that comes in a way to define the narrator. Yet why does this act of aggression assume such importance? Clearly, we are not dealing here with a simple breaking of a door, whose repetition is merely a literary device. The police penetration into the author's inner sanctum, her home, is perceived as a violation. It is a metaphorical rape of sorts, which must be exorcised as much as possible in new narrative situations. The fact that she was wearing a white dress accentuates the drama of this "rape" (as in the West, brides in the modern Arab world don a white gown). And the telling of the act becomes as important as the act itself, at once emphasizing it and exorcising it.

This perceived physical violation is compounded by the narrator when she links it to the act of writing. She is absorbed in her novel as the ominous knocks begin. Each successive knock leads to a set of reminiscences, some of which relate to the act of writing. The search of her apartment then reveals the novel. She cries out: "This is a novel . . . Leave it alone . . . Don't touch it."[29] The violation has been extended to encompass not just the hero's home, but her writing as well.

Is it a surprise then that writing should take on its own momentum in *Memoirs from the Women's Prison*? Indeed, the very act of writing becomes a violation: a violation of the prison system that would forbid it. The task itself is far from easy. Nawal pens her memoirs at night, on toilet paper and cigarette paper.[30] The pencil is too short to grasp efficiently. The paper is light and dry. If she presses on it, it rips. If she does not press on it, however, the letters do not appear.[31] Writing is a trial indeed, difficult because forbidden. The pen is a weapon (*silâh*).[32] When the prisoners express their desire to write home, the official reply is that paper and writing instruments are forbidden: "A pistol is safer than paper and a pen."[33] As the female prison guard puts it so eloquently to Nawal, the inmate: "A single word written in the political ward is more dangerous than a pistol. Writing is more dangerous than killing, O Doctor."[34]

Killing with the pistol, writing with the pen—the officials of the
Sadat regime understand their power. To these tools of destruction,
however, Nawal adds a third. For the women who inhabit El Saadawi's
prison universe, it is not the pistol that is the most potent instrument of
death, but the hoe.

The hoe, according to Harlow, functions "as an agricultural imple-
ment, symbolic of the peasant's vital attachment to the Egyptian
land."[35] This symbolism is certainly present. Yet the hoe does much
more than evoke agriculture. The *shâwîsha* (female prison guard) graph-
ically describes how Fathiyya the Murderer hit her husband on the head
with a hoe, dismembered him, wrapped his body parts in a kerchief, and
threw them into the water for the fish to eat.[36] To return once more to
the *turâth*: This procedure of killing, dismembering, and throwing the
body parts into the nearest body of water was quite common in
medieval texts, but predominantly with female victims.[37] The reversal
described by El Saadawi is thus all the more stunning. In the contem-
porary feminist's text, moreover, this violent act was instigated by
Fathiyya's discovery of her husband having sexual intercourse with her
daughter.[38]

As Nawal looks at Fathiyya, she corporally subsumes her identity,
beginning with resemblance and moving to virtual identity. Fathiyya's
brown, strong fingers resemble those of Nawal. The heartbeats of the
two women are generated by the "same power." Nawal's eyes shine
with the "same glitter." "And my hand, when it grabs the pen, resem-
bles her hand when it grabbed the hoe and struck." The pen so dear to
our prisoner is transposed into a hoe. But this is not enough. Fathiyya's
killing hoe permits Nawal to turn her pen into a killing instrument. She
continues by saying that it is as though she were hitting with this pen a
black, corrupt head that wanted to violate her freedom and her life, to
mutilate her true self, and to make her sell her intellect, to force her to
say yes when she wanted to say no. "If my fingers had not known the
pen, they might perhaps have known the hoe," she writes.[39]

This paradigmatic relationship between pen and hoe is crucial for set-
ting the two tools in opposition to the pistol, the killing instrument par
excellence for Sadat's prison officials. Women, whatever their social
class, we learn, do not need a pistol to kill.

How close Nawal the writer has come to being like Fathiyya the
Murderer! Is it an accident that Fathiyya acts as the mail courier
between Nawal and her family?[40] The two types of heroes so beloved
to this feminist writer are brought together once more, as they were in
*Woman at Point Zero*. In that novel as well, Firdaws, the prostitute

hero, kills the male authority figure in charge of her life, her pimp. And there, too, the upper-class physician comes to identify strongly with the lower-class woman.

In fact, this identity in *Memoirs from the Women's Prison* between political prisoner and killer is but one facet of a more complex and intimate relationship that exists between Nawal's colleagues in the prison setting and her family members outside it. Voices, facial features, general behavior—all come together to bridge the gap between the world inside the prison and that outside it. The features of the young prisoner I'tidâl, are compared to those of Nawal's daughter.[41] The Islamist Budûr, in many of her characteristics, is likened to Nawal's country grandmother.[42] This grandmother's singing is indirectly compared to the singing in jail.[43] The voice of Sabâh the Beggar when she sings reminds Nawal of her Aunt Zaynab's voice.[44] The laugh of the *shâwisha* is like that of Nawal's paternal grandmother, a peasant.[45] The accent of the prisoners from the countryside is like that of the women of "my village," Kafr Tahla.[46] Even the physical settings in which these characters interact become identical. The courtyard of the prison reminds the narrator of the courtyard in her grandmother's house.[47] As the hero is heading for the official investigation, a colleague hands her a sandwich and tells her she should not go with an empty stomach. "Her voice is like my mother's voice," when her mother would give her a sandwich and tell her not to take an examination on an empty stomach.[48]

Literary comparisons and juxtapositions are never innocent, of course. As prison and village come together, they redefine each other. Village life thus becomes a sort of prison, from which we already know Nawal El Saadawi has escaped.

It is not just the family and the village that provide material for these comparisons. Characters and situations from Nawal's childhood are resurrected and made to stand alongside characters and situations from her prison experience. Women's laughter and voices in jail recall those of students in the secondary school. The eyes of the jail inmates resemble those of the young girl's colleagues at the Hulwân Boarding School.[49] Officials in the two institutions, school and prison, also bear an uncanny resemblance to one another.[50] In calling up childhood memories, the narrator alludes to the schoolmistress's discovery of a "crime" when young girls were found sleeping together in the same bed. Given that we shortly hear of this same schoolmistress's obsession with sexual improprieties, are we to conclude that the female inmates had sexual relations with one another? The narrator plants the seed and abandons it. In this, she is different from the narrator of the later *The Innocence of the Devil*, who tackled the question of female homosexuality without hesitation.

The full analogy between the external world and that of the prison comes to fruition when Nawal, returning after her appearance before the government investigator, senses a "strange desire" to see her prison colleagues and feels she is returning to the intimacy of her family.[51]

Incarceration becomes an alternate family structure. Logically, these comparisons can be read in two ways: family is like a prison; prison is one big family. Neither proposition would be incompatible with Dr. El Saadawi's thought as it has been articulated in a lifetime of writing. In *Memoirs of a Woman Doctor*, images of confinement merge with family images. One of the most memorable of these bisociations is that involving the mother's "imprisonment" of the first-person narrator's hair in braids.

If we look closely at the comparisons used in the prison memoirs, however, we see that it is the acts of communication and caring—those of a family—that are stressed. In the extensive Saadawian corpus, families are not always presented as positive forces. Heroes like Firdaws in *Woman at Point Zero* and Hamîda in *The Circling Song* were abused by family members. The homosocial family unit, we discover, is different. There are no males to abuse the women. And it is this bond of homosociality that helps to diminish the social gulf between Nawal El Saadawi, the internationally famous physician and writer, and the rural lower-class women sharing her incarceration.

Prisoners are more than surrogate family members for Nawal. They interact with one another in complex ways within the prison ward. The prison ward becomes the locus for highlighting, within a clear homosocial environment, the distances and tensions present in contemporary Egyptian society. The most unlikely pair, whose existences the narrator intertwines in a set of savage bisociations, is that of the Islamist Budûr and the leftist Fawqiyya. This is not to say that either of these individuals does not function as a separate character. They do. But it is when Budûr and Fawqiyya are brought together, most often on opposite sides of a given argument, that their two systems of advocacy—religion and politics—are juxtaposed and redefined one in terms of the other.

Religion and politics are not, of course, isolated systems. We have already seen them in literary texts operating as integral parts of the dominant patriarchal structure. But in El Saadawi's prison memoirs, the advocates of the two systems are painted as intransigent in their positions, increasing the drama of their bisociation. When the prisoners awake in the morning, they exchange smiles and wish one another a good morning. All but Budûr and Fawqiyya. Scowls dominate their faces. While Budûr refuses to laugh, considering it illicit, Fawqiyya is unable to laugh, finding no benefit in it.[52] Though dissimilar, their convictions are deep-seated: for Budûr, God is the prime mover; for Fawqiyya, economics is the deity.[53] Their ideological differences do not, however, keep either of them from behaving as bad prison citizens: neither takes care of her bed, neither washes her laundry or her dish after eating, both refuse to bathe in cold water. Both, in short, behave like spoiled brats.[54]

This parallel behavior turns into a paradigmatic relationship. Nawal's preconceived notions of prison as solitude and silence are shattered. She cannot "enjoy" either but for a period between midnight and the dawn call to prayer. Anyone who has lived for an extended period in the Muslim world knows that the dawn call to prayer (the first of five daily calls to prayer) is designed to awaken the sleeper. That Nawal should have her sleep disrupted would be but part of the ritual of the dawn call. After all, the muezzin declares that "prayer is better than sleep."

In the world of the prison, Budûr and Fawqiyya are equally responsible for disturbing the narrator's peace. No sooner does Budûr stop arguing with her colleagues than she begins to recite the Qur'ân in a loud voice. And when she goes to sleep, Fawqiyya awakens and begins to argue and preach. And when Fawqiyya goes to sleep, then Budûr gets up for the call to prayer. It is as if the two noisemakers, on opposite sides of the politico-religious spectrum, function at times as opposite but related characters. An intimate relationship is created by this narrator between the two types of advocacy: the religious and the political. In her own account, the Islamist activist and writer Sâfî Nâz Kâzim, who was imprisoned with Nawal El Saadawi, notes that she was placed in solitary confinement because the light by which she read the Qur'ân disturbed the other prisoners.[55] In her Islamic account, religion is light. In Nawal's secular version, it is noise.

Setting off Budûr, the Islamic militant, against Fawqiyya, the materialist leftist, as equally dogmatic and obnoxious figures is an ideologically curious option. By her life and work, Nawal El Saadawi is far closer to the leftist militant than to the Islamic one; and the placement of her namesake narrator equidistant from and above these two would mislead a reader who did not know the author's political history. But the prison narrator is not obliged to adopt the public positions of the author.

Prison acts as an almost redemptive space, liberating fantasy identifica-
tions. Hence the narrator can identify herself with the peasant murderer
rather than with the leftist militant. The quasi-occultation in Nawal El
Saadawi's prison narrative of the other well-known political activists
(after an initial mention), together with the narrator's romantic cross-
class identification with poor women of the ward, facilitates this realign-
ment.

Through her secular politics, Fawqiyya acts as a foil to Budûr. But
politics is not the only domain used to highlight religion. The homoso-
cial environment permits the appearance of other topics dear to Nawal
El Saadawi, of which the most important is probably the corporal.

Let us take as an example an incident involving Budûr. Toilet facili-
ties in the ward are described in a graphic (and, needless to say, dis-
gusting) manner. The prisoner using the lavatory would find herself
with water dripping on her head from the shower above and with her
feet sinking into the sewage water below. A little color was added by
the flying cockroaches. On numerous occasions Budûr would enter the
lavatory and then immediately jump out again, without "completing
her task," screaming: "Cockroach!" The other inmates, hearing her cry,
would run to her, plastic sandals in hand "like the sword, prepared to
hit the cockroach." One day she let out a scream from the courtyard,
and, as usual, the rescuers took off their sandals, readying for the
impending battle. What they saw was not a cockroach, however, but a
man. It turned out that Budûr was not wearing her covering and was
terrified that a man might glimpse her hair. From this moment on,
whenever her voice would ring out in a scream, her fellow inmates
would ask before taking off their plastic sandals: "A cockroach or a
man?" Once, running in her haste to cover her hair, she fell and broke a
front tooth. On very hot days, Budûr sat with her co-religionists in the
courtyard, without their appropriate covering. Each kept one eye on
the Qur'ân in her lap and the other on the open area. No sooner would
they spot the shadow of a man than they would run inside to cover
themselves.

A similar confusion came about, but in an opposite way, in the pros-
titutes' ward. There the women would run out *un*covering their hair
and winking at the men. Thus any man, even a garbage collector, took
on great importance, causing an uproar among the *munaqqabât*, on the
one hand, and the prostitutes, on the other.[56] (A *munaqqaba* is a
woman who dons the *niqâb*, clothing designed to completely envelop
the human body, including the hands which are normally covered with

gloves. The only part of a *munaqqaba*'s body that faces the outside world are the eyes, and those through a slit in the facial covering.)

The lavatory incident embodies many of the elements that not only make El Saadawi's prison memoirs a good read but also are of concern to the Egyptian feminist. We get, among other things, a glimpse of the prison conditions and of the solidarity of the prisoners, no matter what their religious or political stripe. More than that, the narrator creates sets of connections and possibilities that move outward from the body through religion to male-female relations, the entirety couched in lively imagery. The detailed description of the privy, with the human body hanging, as it were, between two sorts of water—the dripping shower above and the sewage below—and surrounded by flying cockroaches effectively calls attention to the corporal vulnerability of the female prisoners.

Who should be made to enter this space of disgust but the person most concerned with keeping her body private, the *munaqqaba* Budûr? Obviously, Budûr's fear of cockroaches is what launches the incident and permits it to function on a literary plane. When the narrator adds as an aside that Budûr runs out without "completing her task," she calls even more attention to the body as corporality. The comparison of the plastic sandals to swords raises the specter of killing instruments. It is not men who are killed here, of course; it is cockroaches. Nevertheless, although he is not the victim of a killing act, by a process of literary comparison man does become indeed like a roach.

Yet man is more than a possible source of fear. The human male animal is cleverly used to tie the world of the pious Budûr and her religious cohorts to the world of the prostitutes. The human male creates confusion among both groups. True, in one case it is a matter of repulsion and in the other of attraction, but that is almost irrelevant. Both the pious females and the female prostitutes have been linked and redefined under the sign of the male and sexuality.

Why, we might ask, did the privy have to be exploited at all here? After all, the incident that spurs the juxtaposition of these two very different groups of women involved Budûr in the courtyard, not in the privy. Might this be simply a way for the narrator to increase the derision directed at the young Muslim woman? Nawal had already exposed Budûr's fear of stepping into the lavatory because of the roaches in an earlier episode. And were it not for her constipation, we are told, she might have stayed away forever.[57] More is at stake here. The bodily functions associated with toilets are, of course, the most private of all corporal activities, and the ones most identified with soiling and various taboos. By linking the *munaqqaba* to the lavatory, Nawal has taken the corporally very private Budûr and unveiled her in a dramatic way by calling attention to this most intimate aspect of her corporality.

Yet to restrict the significance of the lavatory to Budûr and her anxieties would be misleading and would underplay the larger role that the lavatory plays in El Saadawi's prison memoirs. The lavatory attaches itself in a fundamental way to the entire project of the memoirs, penetrating to its essence. The toilet (overflowing with sewage and cockroaches) is, on a basic level, the symbol of the unsavory prison conditions, which the prisoners themselves petition to have changed.[58] We also know that Nawal's project of writing was itself accomplished partly on toilet paper.[59]

The lavatory is also the private space for the prisoner. It is there that Nawal reads the letter from her family, and then burns it.[60] It is there that she listens, glued to the transistor radio, to the news of Sadat's shooting.[61] When, during her interrogation, she is offered something to drink "from the buffet," she thinks back to her time with the Ministry of Health and the close relationship between the drink preparation and the toilet, with flies buzzing back and forth between the commode and the tea cups.[62]

But it is the lavatory as great social and political equalizer that goes to the heart of the memoirs. Improving the condition of the toilet unites everyone in the prison ward, both veiled women and unveiled ones.

> Fortunately, man's [the word here is *al-insân*, man, which serves to express the category of human being] bowels do not distinguish between right or left, or one religion and another. No matter how one individual differs from another intellectually or politically, their need for the toilet is one.[63]

Just as the narrator denuded Budûr and reduced her to her most banal corporality, so it is with all humankind. Intellectual matters, politics, religious affiliation—all these are shunted aside in favor of the corporal. Humans are reduced to their lowest possible common denominator: their bowels. Or, as the narrator of Margaret Atwood's novel *The Handmaid's Tale* puts it so well: "There is something reassuring about the toilets. Bodily functions at least remain democratic. Everybody shits."[64]

We should not be overly surprised at this attention to corporal functions in Nawal El Saadawi's homosocial universe. She is, after all, a physician; and attention to the body, as we have already seen, has always been part and parcel of her textual creations. Whether in the scientific world of medicine or in the Hamîdû-Hamîda gender games or in the prostitution universe of Firdaws—or, in fact, in any of her narratives— the human body never ceases to be pivotal in Saadawian discourse.[65]

In prison, however, Dr. Nawal El Saadawi loses her identity as physician and as individual. She becomes a mere number and is not permitted to practice medicine.[66] That function is assigned to a male, Dr. Sâbir Barsûm. This is not mere literary serendipity. It reinforces the female homosocial aspect of *Memoirs from the Women's Prison*. Nawal must not break rank, lest in so doing she break the essential female bonding so central to the narrative.

Nawal, it turns out, recognizes the male physician from her student days at the medical school, and the coincidence of their meeting again is far from a happy one for him, literarily speaking. He, like other male prison officials, receives a nice verbal whipping, as he becomes yet another victim of the prison narrator's wit. She describes in detail his peculiarities as a student: how he looked, how he walked, how he reserved himself a seat in the front row of the lecture hall, how he looked like a drowning man seeking rescue when he missed a word of the lecture. The other students nicknamed him Sâbir In Shâ' Allâh because of his habit of beginning every phrase he uttered with the expression *in shâ' Allâh*, God willing.

Dr. Sâbir Barsûm does not cut a better figure in the prison. There, it is clear, he functions as an instrument of the patriarchal male government. He also misdiagnoses patients and is so easily bought off that he earns himself another nickname, Sâbir Barsûm Bi-Sijâra—Sâbir Barsûm by a Cigarette, meaning that it took only a cigarette to get him to write almost anything in his medical reports. On the inmates' urging he is eventually dismissed from their ward. After her release, Nawal spots him on the street and again recalls him as a student, closing this second round of remembrances with the scene of him looking for help like a drowning man.[67]

The male physician is pitted against the female physician in an environment that is really unkind to both. He is painted as incompetent, while she is not permitted to practice. She is part of the homosocial universe of women, separate from that of the men. The onomastic game is quite interesting. Nawal is careful to explain Barsûm's two nicknames in the two contexts in which she comes into contact with him. Both appellations are, of course, derisive, designed to take him down a notch or two from his function as all-knowing medical specialist. The name from his school days hints at more. The savvy reader acquainted with the Middle East, upon hearing the name Sâbir In Shâ' Allâh, will certainly think of that Islamic buffoon Juhâ, who has survived centuries in anecdotes that portray him as, at best, a wise fool.[68] In one of his more famous stories, Juhâ, setting out to sell a donkey, is asked about his errand. He explains it. His listener admonishes him to use the phrase *in shâ' Allâh*. On the way to the market, the donkey is stolen. The next time Juhâ sets out to sell a donkey and is asked about his errand, he inserts an *in shâ' Allâh* after every word.[69] Sâbir Barsûm is not far here from Juhâ himself.

Yet the fact that this physician picks up a nickname even in the jail is significant. On the one hand, that name serves constantly to remind one of his corrupt nature. On the other hand, we know that names in the prison environment are endowed with special meaning. The narrator had carefully explained on an earlier occasion that the crime for which one was incarcerated became attached to one's name in such a way that it turned into an essential part of one's identity. Thus there was Fathiyya the Murderer, Fathiyya the Thief, Fathiyya Politics, if the prisoner was accused of being a political, and so on.[70] With a simple onomastic flip of the pen, then, Sâbir Barsûm Bi-Sijâra—Sâbir Barsûm by a Cigarette—is turned into one of the prison crowd, a criminal not unlike those incarcerated.

This male physician's trajectory in El Saadawi's prison narrative is circular. His initial identity is linked to a drowning man, and the same image is repeated with his exit from the memoirs. The physician has been effectively deflated, his existence as a medical professional a mere intrusion in the life of Sâbir Barsûm the student. Despite his necessary presence in the women's world as healer, he is made to remain outside that world, united as it is by female bonding.

The prison space, though romantic in some respects, is not exempt from danger. In a lengthy introduction preceding the textual entrance of this corrupt physician, the narrator amply discusses the conditions of prison medicine.[71] Illness in prison, we learn, is "worse than death. It is a type of slow, long death . . . or death hundreds of times instead of once."[72]

In El Saadawi's memoirs, however, death is not something that merely follows from illness. It is a pervasive state that begins as soon as she enters the prison enclosure. Silence there is compared to the silence of graves.[73] Going through an opening in a small door becomes the entry into a grave. The white dress here plays its role, not as a symbol of purity, but as the funeral shroud—white being the color of the burial cloth in which a corpse is wrapped in the Muslim Middle East. The hands of the officer helping her are like the hands of an undertaker. The scene feels familiar to the narrator: only later do we learn that it is in fact identical to her mother's burial.[74] Death imagery is everpresent in these opening pages. A light voice, for example, seems to emanate from a dead body. When a man stops talking, it is as though he had suddenly died.[75]

Prison is death. Beyond that, it turns humans into animals, in what seems to be a process of reverse evolution. The prisoners are behind bars like animals.[76] But this is not simply a literary conceit. The narrator notes that her nails have grown long, like claws. She has not, after all, cut them since entering the jail. One day Nawal looks at her long fingernails in surprise: "Are they my nails or the claws of an animal?" she wonders. Even her hair is like that of a lion. So far so good. Lest the reader think that these animal comparisons are natural, given that neither nails nor hair would have been trimmed, the narrator adds that her nose is like an elephant's trunk. She has indeed become fully animal![77]

What, we might well ask, is next? Death and animality would seem to be the end of our hero, as for the other female inmates.[78] But salvation is at hand. Sadat's death in the prison memoirs is not merely the path to liberation for our narrator; it is a transformative act for the entire prison population.

The demise of the Egyptian ruler takes on mythic proportions. Prison, we discover, plays elaborate games with one's notion of time. Certainly, Nawal is not unique here: Elissa D. Gelfand has demonstrated eloquently that this is a phenomenon one encounters in French women's prison texts.[79] For our Egyptian prisoner, incarceration transfers time into non-time; hours stretch without end.[80] At a certain point, Nawal wonders if she is a child playing in the dirt or a woman locked in prison.[81] In prison, it is clear, one loses any sense of history and time.[82]

Sadat's death will overturn everything. But this political patriarch does not die immediately. His demise comes in stages. First, the inmates hear of the shooting (a radio had been smuggled into the cell). Then they hear that his wound is not mortal. But his shooting alone is enough to effect changes. Budûr, the Islamist, who until now had considered the radio to be an instrument of the devil, wishes to hear the news. The inmates will not be disappointed: the voice announcing Sadat's death finally penetrates the prison.

> All the bodies jumped in the air. The radio fell on the ground and no one paid any attention to it.
>
> A moment outside time, and outside existence, which cannot be felt. Perhaps we lost our five senses, for we could no longer see or hear anything. . . .
>
> Things around me are going round and round. I grabbed my head. Dream or knowledge? And what is that going round me? The earth? The ward? Or is it I who am going round?
>
> I awoke to a strange scene. Budûr going in circles around herself, without a *niqâb* and without an outer covering. She is going around and dancing. Surrounding her are the *munaqqabât* colleagues. Dancing, hair naked, without *niqâb* or *hijâb*. The bodies sway with vehemence, the hips bend, the bellies shake, the heads bend, and the hair flies.
>
> And another, stranger scene. Fawqiyya, who had not done a single prayer prostration . . . I saw her sitting on the ground, lifting her hands on high while she cried out: "I praise you, O lord..." And around her, the other colleagues sitting in prayer.
>
> Calling out in one breath: "We praise you, O Lord."[83]

This critical event that is the death of Sadat has transformed the world of the prison ward. When Nawal says that she "awakened" on the two strange scenes, it is as if the announcement of the death had rendered her unconscious or as if she had entered another existence. The other inmates are just as emotionally and physically affected by the demise of the ruler. Once again it is Budûr and Fawqiyya, that duo we have met before, who are the two critical poles for the reactions. There is Budûr, the *munaqqaba*, for whom control of the body is primary and who had argued that woman should not shake her body.[84] What has Sadat's death done to her? Her entire demeanor is the exact opposite of that she has been advocating all along: hair flowing, body shaking. Even more important, she has brought her other *munaqqabât* colleagues into the scene. As for Fawqiyya, for whom prayer was utterly alien, there we find her practicing that which she has never done before in her life. Her deity is no longer economics but Allâh, the God whom Budûr has worshipped all along. Fawqiyya likewise has gathered around her a group of women who join her in prayer.

These exchanges of behavior are the fulfillment of the romantic blur ring of identities in the homosocial pact. But to say fulfillment is to say completion, ending. Sadat's death closes a cycle. Nawal's entry into the prison was, after all, a death. The physical assassination of the male ruler becomes a redemptive act that will save her. It is an almost primitive system of justice: a death for a death. She is sentenced to a sort of death from which she can be resurrected only by her imprisoner's death. His death will allow her to live. The death of a male saves the female from perdition. This is not unlike the autobiography of the contemporary Palestinian poet Fadwâ Tûqân. In *Rihla Jabaliyya, Rihla Sa'ba* (translated as *A Mountainous Journey*), Fadwâ's birth, an event whose date her mother seems to have forgotten, is linked to the death of a male. She tells her mother: "I will extract my birth certificate [*shahâda*] from the tombstone [*shâhida*] of your cousin."[85]

The male death as liberation is certainly not alien to the Saadawian literary universe. Numerous are her novels in which the patriarch must be killed. In the prison memoirs, this patriarch is inextricably tied to his own political machine, the state, which itself then functions as a patriarchy. It is the demise of the all-powerful male figure that opens the prison and permits the ensuing liberation. In the process, female homosociality is dissolved in the space between the two violations. A disruption has thrust the protagonist from her ordinary world into the special one of the women's prison. Like the end of the frame of *The Thousand and One Nights*, Sadat's death closes this parenthesis, implicitly restoring the world of before.

The redemptive act of Sadat's death does more than liberate the hero. It permits the previous violations to be rectified. When Nawal's door was first penetrated, a violation that set in motion the entire prison experience, she was interrupted in the act of writing. Her novel was discovered by Sadat's officials. No matter. Nawal El Saadawi will pen her prison memoirs while incarcerated, an act that is a violation of all that the prison officials hold dear. The death for a death has also instigated a book for a book.

Unlike Shahrazâd, with whom she initially seems to have so much in common, El Saadawi sets down her own story. She does not need, as did her predecessor, a male ruler to ensure that her tale is transformed into something permanent, a text. The contemporary feminist generates her own text. This exercise in violation and homosociality has created an object that survives the incarceration—its own text.

CHAPTER NINE

# Dreams of Flying

---

"What was the dream of my life? I would see myself on a white horse, flying in the air, and in my hand a sword with which I would strike enemies and liberate the homeland."[1] Thus does Nawal El Saadawi link the world of travel to that of politics (and eventually gender) in the opening pages of *My Travels around the World* (Rihlâtî fî al-'Alam). Like other of her works, her travel memoirs are far from innocent documentaries. The boundaries El Saadawi crosses are not merely geographical, but literary, political, and sexual—making *My Travels around the World* a text of transgression.

Plenty of Arab women travel. Yet in the popular unconscious of the Arab world, a woman traveling, especially alone, is problematic. Films reinforce this: in the popular *Hikâyatî ma'a al-Zamân*, the singer Warda al-Jazâ'iriyya has to be smuggled from Cairo to Beirut in a string-bass case. She does not, we discover, have her husband's permission to leave the country.[2]

Nawal El Saadawi not only travels; she also writes about it. In the case of a woman, however, the telling of the act seems almost more illicit than the doing. Yet in textualizing her travel memoirs, the Egyptian physician is following a centuries-old tradition of male travel literature. The idea of travel, of the *rihla*, was central to medieval Islamic mentalities. Scholars and intellectuals roamed from the eastern to the western borders of that great geographical and cultural expanse that was the world of Islam. The *rihla fî talab al-'ilm*, the journey in search of knowledge, was a de rigueur activity and forms part of the biography of most, if not all, prominent medieval Muslim intellectual luminaries.[3]

177

Many were the male medieval authors who set down their travel memoirs, most often records of their pilgrimage to and from Mecca. The fourteenth-century Ibn Battûta, whose narrative extends from his home country of Morocco to the Indian subcontinent, is perhaps the most famous of these travelers.[4] Others, like the Andalusian Ibn Jubayr (d. 614/1217), with his pilgrimage account, and 'Abd al-Latîf al-Baghdâdî (d. 629/1231–1232), who visited Egypt during a great famine, have entered the annals of classical Arabic literature as well.[5]

Many modern male travelers have gone beyond the confines of the Arab world, and descriptions of their adventures abound. Whether as part of student delegations, diplomatic missions, or as independent travelers, male authors have not shied away from setting down their impressions of the sights and societies they have seen.[6] Here too, of course, the pilgrimage account still holds pride of place.[7]

In the contemporary period, the period after all in which El Saadawi flourishes, travel seems to have come within the purview of everyone. Male travel accounts are numerous, some of which are not devoid of a humor, like those of Anîs Mansûr.[8] At the same time, though the airplane has effectively decreased geographical distances, cultural and religious factors seem to have increased them. One can no longer speak of a purely Arabo-Muslim *rihla fî talab al-'ilm*. Travel now includes the Western world, a locus of perdition and danger for some religious Muslim thinkers. Anti-travel guides and memoirs exist, and words of caution against the lure of Western civilization pepper other accounts.[9]

To understand the power of El Saadawi's travel account one must, therefore, also understand the discourse on the other side of the cultural divide in the Middle East today. In his book of legal injunctions dealing with women, *Min al-Ahkâm al-Fiqhiyya fî al-Fatâwâ al-Nisâ'iyya*, the well-known Saudi religious authority Shaykh Muhammad ibn Sâlih al-'Uthaymîn responds to a concerned Muslim who wonders: Is it permissible for a woman to undertake the *'umra* (a pilgrimage to Mecca that can be performed at any time, unlike the *hajj*, which occurs during a prescribed month) without being accompanied by a legal guardian, and may a woman undertake the *'umra* in the company of other women, in lieu of a legal guardian? The Shaykh does not beat around the bush. He seizes the occasion to tackle not only the specific question but also the entire issue of woman's travel in general, adducing sayings of the Prophet and explaining them to his reader. So far so good.

But Shaykh Muhammad ibn Sâlih al-'Uthaymîn, like his questioner, lives in a day of planes and long-distance travel. So his answer must extend beyond the bounds of the Mecca pilgrimage per se. He dismisses those who would argue that it is permissible for a woman to travel on a plane without a legal guardian so long as that guardian accompanies her to the airport. The scenarios that can lead to woman's perdition, he comments, are multiple. For example, the legal guardian who is to take care of the woman on her arrival might be late. Or, on the plane itself, the female traveler might find herself sitting next to a dissolute male who will attempt to take advantage of her.[10]

Works like that of al-'Uthaymîn typically occupy the shelves of religiously minded readers. They are, nevertheless, part of the literary and cultural fabric of the contemporary Arab world and North Africa. Nawal El Saadawi's *My Travels around the World* functions as a counter-narrative to these admonitions, her travel scenario at times reading like the fulfillment of the Shaykh's more dire prophecies. Her story reveals different, and feminist, possibilities for the travel experience.

But to talk about travel is not necessarily to write a travel account. Many authors of both genders have talked about travel, of course. Travel narratives are often embedded within autobiography—as in the case of the famous twentieth-century blind male Egyptian modernizer Tâhâ Husayn—where they are subordinated to the autobiography and forced to adhere to its generic rules.[11] The female Palestinian poet Fadwâ Tûqân discusses her stay in England as part of the larger autobiographical project she undertakes in her *Rihla Jabaliyya, Rihla Sa'ba* (Mountainous journey, difficult journey).[12] The word *rihla* in this title should not mislead us, however; the journey described is not that of a travel text. In fact, modern Arabic usage now normally dictates that the plural form of the word, *rihlât*—as in El Saadawi's title—is a clearer indication of a book's membership in the travel genre. Even so, such contemporary works as *Rihlatî min al-Shakk ilâ al-Imân* (My journey from doubt to belief), by the born-again Muslim physician-writer Mustafâ Mahmûd, and *Rihlatî min al-Sufûr ilâ al-Hijâb* (My journey from unveiling to veiling), by the born-again Muslim female activist Karîmân Hamza, function more as spiritual journeys than physical ones.[13]

Within this context, El Saadawi's project becomes even more extraordinary. The very title of her work, *My Travels around the World*, sets it off from other, more modest enterprises, like Karîma Kamâl's *Bint Misriyya fî Amrîkâ* (An Egyptian girl in America).[14] Modesty is not the key to *My Travels*. El Saadawi hops from continent to continent, most often as a single woman—a provocation in and of itself. In Paris, she sits in a café and casually sips a beer.[15] This is at least as incorrect and potentially shocking as the same act would have been in polite Western society a hundred years ago. Even in the contemporary Arab world, woman's drinking of alcohol is considered risqué. This is, of course, not to speak of the religio-legal injunctions against alcohol, even for men, among religious Muslims generally. Indeed, this action on the part of the single woman traveler might have no real equivalent in the parallel Western discourse. The taboos she is breaking are not only societal, they are also literary.

In a way, El Saadawi has an unfair advantage. She is a physician. She is a writer. She is a feminist activist. Her husband, also a physician and a writer, is a prominent figure in his own right. She gets to conquer in these various guises. She is invited to medical conferences. She participates in literary conferences. And her husband's work in India permits her to sojourn in, and travel around, that subcontinent.

Nawal El Saadawi the traveler first departs from her homeland to attend a medical conference in Algeria. Then it is on to Europe and the United States. North America is followed by Jordan. A stop in Helsinki and a visit to the Soviet Union and Central Asia come next, and then Iran. A long visit to India and a shorter one to Africa seal the travel account. At times, our traveler plays the role of tourist, at others, that of engagé writer. History, geography, sociology—the curious reader can find ample information in each of these areas to satisfy his or her curiosity.

Yet the first-person narrator of this complex text does not merely jump from place to place, recounting her impressions and reactions. *My Travels around the World* functions almost as the travel equivalent of a *Bildungsroman* (a form certainly not alien to El Saadawi's prose).[16] When we first meet this intrepid narrator, she is anxious to tell us about her childhood. It is not individuals she meets outside the borders of her homeland with whom she interacts in the first few pages of her travelogue, but family members (including a grandmother whom we shall come to know more intimately below). As the text evolves, the narrator meets her third husband and gives birth to a second child. She exits the memoirs as a United Nations advisor having an interchange with a prominent male African writer.

A *Bildungsroman* is a novel of development. But as with El Saadawi's earlier *Memoirs of a Woman Doctor*,[17] the hero of the travel memoirs remains nameless, as do the intimate members of her family. The autobiographical pact implicit in a text like *My Travels* is all that permits the identification of the individual characters with certainty.[18] The reader familiar with Nawal El Saadawi's personal life can easily attach names and faces to the sometimes elusive incidents the narrator speaks of. For example: "In the spring of the year 1964, we met. He and I alone. I asked him where he came from. He said: 'From prison.' " This meeting leads to a wedding ceremony attended by the narrator's daughter.[19] This "he" is, of course, Dr. Sherif Hetata, who had his share of imprisonment under both King Farouq and Nasser and whose prison experience led to fictional work.[20] He is the husband whom Nawal will also visit in India.[21] The young daughter is Munâ Hilmî, now a writer and activist in her own right.[22]

This onomastic absence, this namelessness, is not insignificant. The normal expectation (though obviously exceptions do exist) in a text of this sort is for the identity of the central character to manifest itself somewhere along the line—as it does, for example, in El Saadawi's prison memoirs. But it is precisely "identity" that is problematic in *My Travels around the World*: gender identity, racial identity, national identity. As this quasi-*Bildungsroman* progresses, as the narrator moves around the world, her sense of identity becomes stronger. True, she never acquires a name, but at least the reader concludes the text with a sense of who she thinks she is.

The prelude to the actual travel text posits this problematic. When Nawal told her grandmother her dream of flying in the air on a white horse and liberating the homeland with a sword, the grandmother responded:

—These are not the dreams of girls.
—And what do girls dream of, Grandmother?
—They dream of a husband and a wedding dress.
—But I did not ever dream of a husband and a wedding dress.[23]

Nawal's grandmother had bought her a wedding dress "ten years before the coming of the groom." And on every holiday, her father would bring Nawal a new dress and her brother a gun and a small mechanical airplane. On one occasion, spotting the fancy silk dress in its gift box, she screamed in anger:

"I want an airplane and a gun like my brother."
    But my mother said: "You will be pretty in the new dress."
    I shouted: "I don't like dresses."
    My grandmother yelled out: "This girl should definitely have been a male."[24]

Nawal would look up at the sky with the eyes of a ten-year-old child. "Will a day come when I will ride an airplane?" she would muse. "Can I fly in the air like a bird, far from this prison into which I was born?" Our narrator continues:

> In the dream, I used to fly without a plane. My body would rise in the air, and I would fly over the roofs of houses, the top of trees, and the oceans. . . .
>
> My grandmother would say: "Flying in dreams means success and you will marry an emir or a prince."
>
> I would yell into her face: "I hate the king and I hate marriage."[25]

Her grandmother would then angrily declare that she was as crazy as her mother. But her mother, Nawal is quick to add, hated King Farouq, whereas her grandmother hated only the British and would sing with the radio: "King of the Land, O Beautiful One, O Farouq, O Light of the Eye!"[26]

These outbursts by the young Nawal are not simply temper tantrums. Their literary function is to set the stage for the account to come. The young girl is being brought up in a traditional manner. When she has dreams that girls "do not have," she is informed of this fact. Nawal and the grandmother are both undaunted. When the latter hears the second dream, she understands it as a supernatural sign: flying means success. The grandmother, with this interpretation, is inserting herself into an oneiric system that is centuries old. She interprets the dream as it is interpreted in dream books that use the classical oneiric tradition as a base.[27] But for the young Nawal, a dream is the exact opposite: rather than something unreal to be interpreted, a dream is something tangible to be fulfilled.[28]

The girl's desire for male-defined gifts finally leads her grandmother to exclaim that she should have been a male—not a boy (*walad*), but a male (*dhakar*). With this word choice she goes to the heart of an issue dear to Nawal El Saadawi and one we have seen her develop amply in other work. The problem in essence is the conflict between the young girl and her brother. In *Memoirs of a Woman Doctor*, for example, the hero finds herself, from the opening of the text, in rebellion against her femininity (*unûtha*). In that novel, it was a corporal prison that the Saadawian character was attempting to escape.

Here, when the narrator wonders, "Can I fly in the air like a bird, far from this prison into which I was born?" the prison is extended from the corporal to the social. Females simply do not do what she wants to do. Their dreams are not hers. Airplanes and guns are not supposed to be substituted for frilly dresses. Otherwise, one is not a girl but a male.

That Nawal refuses to be a victim of this sort of thinking becomes even more definite when, on her return from New York, she buys a gift for her daughter: a toy plane, blue with delicate white wings. At the Cairo airport, a clumsy Egyptian official shakes the gift so hard that it falls out of his hand. "The delicate wings scattered like a white butterfly on the asphalt."[29] Nawal's attempt to break with custom and give her female child the male gift of an airplane is met with failure at the hands of a male government official.

Breaking custom is not as easy as having a dream. But of course, we know that Nawal will fulfill the dream of flying. Even though the fulfillment does not come about until long after her fiery exchanges with the grandmother, nevertheless, the literary placement of the fulfillment is directly after them. From hearing her grandmother's singing along with the radio, Nawal goes on to hear the sound of her own new black shoes as she walks in the Cairo airport "as though it were yesterday."[30] Time has been encapsulated: from childhood we have jumped directly to the adult Nawal battling her way through the airport formalities. The reader now knows for certain that the grandmother was talking rubbish. Nawal's message is clear: forget the dreams that girls are "supposed" to have, forget the traditional interpretations—breaking through the societal gender roles would appear to be easy.

Or is it? At the airport, a police official confronts the traveling Nawal. She may well have the state's permission to leave the country, but where is the husband's? She remembers that she is not married and informs the officer of this fact. He demands proof. She pulls a long sheet of paper out of her purse, which he examines.

> "Why did you not say from the beginning that you were divorced [*mutallaqa*]?" (He pronounced it with the *a* after the *l*.)
>      I said angrily: "I am not *mutallaqa* (with an *a* after the *l*). "But I am *mutalliqa* (with an *i* after the *l*)!"[31]

By changing the internal vowel on the word *mutallaqa* (divorced), Nawal has transformed it from passive to active. The woman is no longer the one who is divorced; she is the divorcer. It was fortunate for the traveling Nawal that the government official, looking at her with eyes like those of "an imprisoned animal," simply stamped her passport in response to her philological correction, allowing her to actually fly. The airplane is now no longer the object of dreams but a reality that will transport the narrator and eventually help to create the travel memoirs.

Although the grandmother was wrong about flying and airplanes, she did make a gender-related statement that is significant. "This girl should have been a male," the old woman had declared. Of course, there is no question about the female identity of the narrator of *My Travels around the World*. She is a woman. Yet there are elements and episodes in the text that complicate gender issues. There is identity with males, and there is cross-dressing.

In the Cairo airport, Nawal stands in line. Behind her are a number of foreign men and women. Obviously wealthy, they are tall and stand with their heads upright and their back muscles taut. Nawal's response? She lifts her head and tightens her back muscles. She is tall, like the men; "Their women are shorter than I."[32] The descriptions the Western women receive are far from kind. The Egyptian traveler's instinctive response is to identify with the male of the species. It helps that she herself is tall, permitting her to distinguish herself from the foreign women.

Nawal El Saadawi is by no means advocating a universe in which women should become men. Far from it. Simply, she seeks to expose and subvert the gender boundaries that dominate the thinking of most societies. On her way to the Jordanian front during the 1967 war, she explains that she had learned to shoot arms in 1956, during the Port Said incidents. She was a physician in the countryside, in Tahla, and the medical facility was turned into a military camp training people to either fire arms or nurse the wounded. She decided that rather than dress bandages she would carry arms. She learned to fire and hit the target. The military instructor was so surprised that a woman could do this on a first try that he began to call her "Captain," in the masculine, as a way to express her superiority. But Nawal refused the title of a man and held on to her name. The instructor was surprised.

> "But this is an honor for you when we endow you with the name of a man." So I called him by the name of a woman, and he got angry. But I said in surprise: "But this is an honor for you when we endow you with the name of a woman."

He responded by lifting his gun and pointing it at her head. So she lifted her gun and pointed it at his head—whereupon he immediately backed off. The moral of the story for the female physician? Men understand only weapons, and weapons can be defeated only with weapons.[33]

The lesson here is clear. Nursing the wounded is woman's domain.

Yet it does not need to be so. Indeed, a woman may not only learn to shoot weapons, but she may be excellent at it, so much so in fact that the male of the species is willing to turn her into an honorary male. Performing a male activity, however, does not mean becoming a man. Simply, a woman should learn to operate in the domain of the opposite gender.

These incidents take gender barriers to task. When Nawal travels to Thailand, she actually crosses this most intractable of societal and physical boundaries. The trip to Thailand, subsumed under the larger section on India, is a trip Nawal takes with her husband. Outside their hotel, her husband is unable to get rid of a man offering him a beautiful woman for the night. She finally says to him: "And don't you have a beautiful man for me tonight?" The man is frightened and dashes off.[34] So far so good. Clearly, Thailand is certainly living up to its reputation as one of the world's sex capitals.[35]

But Nawal is (fortunately) incapable of leaving well enough alone. She is fascinated by the "massage houses," the euphemism for houses of prostitution. A specialist explains to her that the houses outnumber the tourists and that competition among them is severe. Each house therefore hires a number of "tourist guides," whose job it is to entrap the tourists and lure them to the massage parlors. She would see these men standing in front of the hotels and on the streets repeating their come-ons and peddling their wares.[36] "The desire to know or the desire to explore overcame me. I want to see one of these houses from the inside. But it is forbidden for a woman to enter," our narrator muses. The only exception is if she works as a masseuse. The woman's role is to present the service or the product; consuming is the right of man alone.

> So I put on men's clothing and entered. An insistence on knowing and ripping aside the curtain from the unknown.
> The backs bend in front of me with humility. The slit eyes examine me with utmost respect. For the first time, I realized the meaning of being a man. That any movement can be turned into great respect, even if it is the movement of the two legs on the way to the nest of prostitution.
> I lifted my head haughtily and imagined that I was a man.
> Then I found myself standing between rows of men with white faces imbued with red. Our wide shoulders sticking to one another. Our feet touching. Our eyes fixed forward.[37]

An intellectual curiosity drives the female narrator to transform herself externally into a male. How does she acquire men's clothing? We do not know. Nor does she tell us. Yet in that one sentence—"I put on men's clothing"—she has changed the gender dynamics of the travel narrative. She is now a man. The use of the first person allows this transformation to take place without undue grammatical difficulties. The social advantages of this transformation become quickly apparent: a man is treated with greater respect.

Nawal has no problem fitting into this male role. Identity in gender, especially of the male kind, obliterates all other differences. The male faces surrounding her are white; the reader knows from earlier references that her own complexion is dark.[38] But this color difference does not stand in the way of her physical integration into the male group: her skin color is not mentioned. Instead she becomes one with the surrounding males. Now she can speak as a member of the group, and the first-person plural pronoun dominates the narrative: "Our wide shoulders sticking to one another. Our feet touching." Her entire body, from top (the shoulders) to bottom (the feet), has merged with that of the others. Her corporal entity as a female has been dissolved into the male unity. It is no longer in question. We have passed beyond simple cross-dressing into the shady area of male identity. Our narrator no longer has to imagine that she is a man. For the purposes of the text, she has become one.

What better activity, then, for our transvestite narrator to indulge in than that of the male gaze? The eyes signal this scopic activity initially: "Our eyes fixed forward."[39]

> Rows of young girls sitting in front of us, behind a glass pane as though they are small animals imprisoned inside a glass cage, like the products displayed behind the windows of stores. We see them without their seeing us. The legs are naked, white. The bosoms are protruding, with a number fastened over them. Like the numbers of prisoners inside a cage. The eyes of the men widen in stares, settling on a bosom, or a leg, or a thigh.[40]

The collectivity of the "we" begins to examine the merchandise. The one-way mirror makes it clear that the male scopic activity can go on undisturbed by a female gaze that might answer it back. And what better way to express the notion of woman as object than to have the prostitutes displayed like merchandise with price tags on them? The locution "the legs . . . the bosoms" detaches these corporal parts from their bodies and persons. The female narrator practices the male gaze herself, by speaking in the "we" long enough to convince the reader that the gender boundary has been effectively crossed.

Nawal soon breaks rank with her male cohorts, however, eliminating the use of that enveloping first-person plural pronoun. This occurs at a critical moment in the narrative, when the generalized male gaze is transformed into a specific body part: the eyes of the men widening in stares.

But the breaking of rank does not mean the elimination of the scopic. In fact, the opposite occurs. Nawal is now engaged in the ultimate game with the gaze. Her activity becomes the truly voyeuristic one, as her own literary gaze moves back and forth between the male performing the scopic activity and the "caged" female who is its object. Nawal's game is complex. She is faced with several choices: she can describe the men directly, she can describe the women directly, or she can describe the women as seen by the men. For the reader, this procedure is not clear-cut. Initially, the eyes of the men run over the female bodies "like pieces of glass over the soft complexion, white like the color of chalk."[41] This is a violent image. Normally, pieces of glass being run over skin would cut it. And there is a cutting of sorts of the female bodies, as they are scopically dismembered by the male gaze that moves from body part to body part, isolating each in turn.

But then, from the male eyes the narrator moves to the faces of the females. Their chalklike complexion gives them "the faces of dolls made of white plaster."[42] From the inanimate faces, Nawal continues to their cheeks and to their eyes.

> The eyelid rises for a moment and the glance looks down furtively. A glance filled with emptiness resembling sadness. Or with sadness resembling emptiness. Then the glance disappears quickly.[43]

Although female eyes may be matched by male eyes, it is clear that the male gaze is still the stronger of the two.

This exchange of unequal parts is, of course, effected by the narrator, and is but a part of that intricate game with the gaze. The complexities are visible in an eloquent passage involving the three levels of description.

> Their [fem. plur.] bodies are thin, small like the bodies of children. The sizes of the men are big, bulky like rhinoceri or dinosaurs. Their [masc. plur.] eyes are open, gazing or staring. Full of alertness, attention, and precision. They examine the head, the nose, and the lips. Then they descend to the neck and the two breasts. Then the stomach and the two thighs. Then the two legs and the two feet.
> Their [fem. plur.] feet are small, minute like the feet of swallows.

Did they place the foot from childhood in iron shoes, like the Chinese?[44]

Initially, it is the narrator's seemingly objective evaluation that the reader encounters: the bodies of the females (compared to children) versus those of the males (compared to ungainly beasts). The male eyes, which are at first the object of the narrator's description (open, gazing or staring), quickly enough begin their own action and trajectory: the examination of the female bodies. The narrator then metaphorically travels along with them as they descend from the head to the feet. At this point, the female bodies become one, as the eyes of the male traverse their various body parts, expressed linguistically as one body: a head, a nose, lips, a neck, two breasts, a stomach, two thighs, two legs, two feet. The individual females have become more effectively objectified, losing their identity as the plurality of their bodies becomes expressed in the singular. The singular body that is described at this point is the object of a doubly scopic activity: that of the narrator mediated through the male customer.

That it is the male gaze that is transforming the multiple bodies into one is made clear when Nawal, shifting the scopic activity, moves from the two feet that are the property of one corporal entity to the plurality of feet that expresses a number of individuals. "Their feet are small, minute like the feet of swallows."

We are no longer dealing—if we ever had been—with the simple one-way mirror of the massage parlor. The narrative mirror is a two-way, even a three-way mirror. From a direct description of both males and females, Nawal has moved to a description of the females as seen through the male eye, and then back to direct description of the women.

This narrative hesitation, this ability to move the critical gaze between the gaze of the male and that of the female, is perhaps but an external sign of the hesitation in gender role of our cross-dressed narrator. Is she a man or is she a woman? When Nawal sees a tall man suddenly lift his hand and point to a number, she watches as the chosen girl moves along a corridor toward a closed door. She opens the door, and the man enters behind her. Then the door is closed.

I stood confused, hesitating. Do I lift my hand and point or do I not lift my hand? Perhaps my hand moved (by reason of hesitation) with a sign that attracted attention.[45]

One of the men bows to her with great respect and asks: "May I do something for you? Would you like something, Sir?" "No. Thank you," she replies. She has forgotten that her "voice was not the voice of a man." The man is utterly taken aback, loses his look of respect, and escorts her to the office of the director.

The term "Sir" reminds the reader that, despite the games she has been playing with the gaze, Nawal is still functioning socially as a man. Witness her own hesitation when she sees one of her male cohorts point to a young girl. This is the true unspoken question of the narrative: What might have taken place but did not?

Ultimately, however, it is Nawal's voice that brings about her demise as a man and that ends her unusual search for knowledge. "I had forgotten that my voice was not the voice of a man." The reader may well wonder also: Was the narrative voice we have been hearing here the voice of a man all along? Does this mean that the narrative we have been experiencing is that of a man? Clearly, the issue is complicated. For one brief moment, Nawal has envisaged herself a man and has attempted to transmit that sense of identity to her reader. Fundamentally, of course, she remains female. Perhaps, had she called for a prostitute, she might have extracted yet another story, one that might have led her to more fictional creations à la Firdaws.

It is not the absence of the prostitute that should, in fact, grab the reader's attention but that of the husband. Where is he during this escapade? And, what was he doing, after all, in Thailand in the first place, since he appears in the beginning only eventually to disappear from the narrative?

A travel account, like an autobiography, is a literary text, as constructed and as sophisticated as a fictional form. Elements and characters fulfill functions and have roles to play. Nawal's husband is no exception here. His presence in Bangkok facilitates the creation of the discourse on prostitution. After all, he is accosted a number of times in the street with offers of "a beautiful woman" for the night. Nawal attempts to reverse and subvert this dominant male-centered discourse by asking for "a beautiful man" for the night. Of course, she will not get one. Instead, her curiosity and desire for knowledge drive her, disguised as a man, to a house of prostitution. Her narrative in the massage parlor testifies that, in fact, the "beautiful woman" does not exist. Women in this society have been turned into caged animals, small birds, to be consumed by the giant rhinoceri and dinosaurs, men. Nawal's last words before she donned men's clothing were: "As for consumption, it is the right of man alone."[46]

Thailand is neither a Middle Eastern nor a Muslim country. The brothel scene reminds us—if we needed reminding—that in the Saadawian conception, women's oppression is a universal, not a local, phenomenon.

Nawal's intrusion into the massage parlor earns her the fury of its director. She has crossed a gender barrier, a shocking act even in a sex capital like Bangkok.[47] It is not the entry into the forbidden world of the brothel that is shocking in the context of modern Arabic letters. From the Nobel Laureate Najîb Mahfûz to his fellow Egyptian Yûsuf Idrîs, accounts of prostitution and even the accompanying erotic display of the female body are not uncommon.[48] What violates the expectations of the modern Arabic reader is the mode of entry and description. For in this incident in Thailand, Nawâl has done more than simply don men's clothing. She has altered her behavior, even if only partially, to conform to male behavior and, hence, partake of male scopic activity.

Of course, Nawal did not invent cross-dressing. A long tradition of transvestism exists in the West, as Marjorie Garber demonstrates in *Vested Interests*.[49] Seen in Middle Eastern terms, however, cross-dressing is all that much more radical. It is not that transvestism does not exist. It does, but predominantly from the medieval period. Ample examples of cross-dressing on the part of both genders can be found in the literature, including *The Thousand and One Nights*. In the contemporary Arab world and North Africa, Tahar Ben Jelloun's novels *L'enfant de sable* and *La nuit sacrée* stand as particularly expressive texts of cross-dressing and the power of gendered clothing.[50]

From a religious Muslim perspective, however, transvestism was clearly shunned, and the Prophet Muhammad admonished against it amply. And despite the passing of centuries, the issue remains the subject of frequent condemnation today among religious-minded individuals of both genders, surfacing not only in guidebooks addressed to women but also in those by-now familiar legal injunctions promulgated by male religious authorities. These voices warn not merely against women wearing men's clothing but against their behaving like men as well[51]—which is precisely what Nawal did in the brothel.

This trespass is perhaps the most daring of Nawal's acts of violation. It reinforces the sense that *My Travels around the World* is about breaking bounds. One must cross all sorts of barriers, the narrator seems to be telling us, to acquire that precious commodity called knowledge.

The Iranian odyssey represents for the narrator another opportunity to transgress—this time not without a price.

November 1968. Iran before the revolution. Nawal is on a scientific mission, attending a medical conference in Tehran. Once again it is "knowledge" that drives the narrator outside the official confines of her visit, in search of Iranian writers. Looking for a literary figure, however, is not the same as investigating the seamier aspects of prostitution.

Nawal's efforts begin at the university, where she is told that the best writer in Iran is the dean of the Faculty of Letters. She buys a notebook and goes to meet him in his plush office. She sits with him for half an hour without registering a single word on literature. This is obviously a false lead. A more fruitful one is with a group of young university students who direct her to the famous writer Jalâl Al-e Ahmad. She meets him and his wife, Sîmîn Dâneshvar, at the time a professor at the University of Tehran and a writer as well. Nawal is very comfortable with these two intellectuals; "I feel as though I were in my home in Egypt."[52] The conversation gravitates around politics and literature.

Two years later, in 1970, Nawal is once again in Iran for a medical conference. Penetrating the country this time is a challenge. The Iranian embassy in Cairo denies her a visa. Officially she is told that the refusal is the act of the Iranian government. Unofficially, a sympathetic young man working in the press section of the embassy reveals to her as she is leaving the grounds that the Shah's secret service wrote reports against the article she published two years earlier in the Egyptian weekly *al-Musawwar*. "What article?" she wonders. The young man informs her that it is the piece she wrote on Jalâl Al-e Ahmad, in such and such an issue of the journal, with such and such a date. She is surprised at his precision, since she herself has forgotten the article. But the young man smiles: he liked her article, he is a fan of Al-e Ahmad, who is his favorite writer, and he was very saddened by his death. Nawal jumps: " 'He died?' He said in a low voice: 'Yes. Under obscure circumstances.' "[53] Nawal later confides in a male medical colleague, whose response is to laugh "with the sarcasm of physicians" and say to her:

> "You are a physician. So why do you write and make problems for yourself? There it is, one article, that will prevent you from traveling to Tehran and attending this important world conference."[54]

Nawal decides to attend anyway, taking one of the conference's advisory statements to heart: those who cannot get a visa in time can get one at the airport in Tehran upon arrival. This decision is not an easy

one. Our hero worries that the embassy might notify the airport author-
ities in Tehran. What if she is permitted to enter and then arrested in
Tehran? "Why do I expose myself to danger without cause?" she won-
ders.[55] She nevertheless enunciates an answer to this rhetorical question:
she is attracted by danger.

The word *obscure* in the young man's characterization of Al-e
Ahmad's end has also excited her imagination. She needs to know. In
Tehran, the Egyptian traveler meets Sîmîn Dâneshvar once again and
hears the story of Jalâl Al-e Ahmad's death while on vacation on the
coast of the Caspian Sea. He had just finished exercising, and his wife
was reciting him some poetry. He then placed his head on a pillow "and
was silent forever."[56]

Nawal attends conference proceedings and spends a great deal of
time with a woman she encountered on the previous trip, Mânî. The
latter explains the dangers inherent in political activity under the Shah
and tells Nawal about torture in the prisons.

It is now June 1984. Nawal is in London meeting with some Iranian
youths who fled the Khomeini regime. She finds out that her friend
Mânî was a victim of Khomeini's prisons. At the end of her meeting in
London, she is convinced that "another revolution will take place in
Iran."

Compared to Thailand, the Iranian journey does not at first seem to
represent a radical crossing of boundaries. But in fact, the frontiers our
traveler traverses are more real and potentially more life-threatening
than in the Thai case. After all, she goes against Iranian government
regulations that forbid her entry into the country by arriving at the
Tehran airport without a visa. She is gambling with her life, and the
gamble pays off.

The Iranian case also reminds us that *My Travels around the World* is,
first and foremost, a composed narrative. The narrator chooses events
and arranges information in ways that serve the agenda of the text. The
denial of the visa by the Iranian embassy in Cairo is one such example.
At first, all we know is that the hero has been refused entry into Iran. Is
there some sinister reason behind this action on the part of the Shah's
regime? Only when the young man mentions this forgetful narrator's
article on Jalâl Al-e Ahmad do things become clear. Obviously, the
Iranian government did not like what Nawal El Saadawi had to say. Nor
does the narrator volunteer anything about what she might have dis-
cussed in this occulted article.

This is apparently a game of selective memory, in which the purpose is to conquer new frontiers. The first trip to Tehran involves some sleuthing on Nawal's part to find Iran's most famous writer. Her unsuccessful meeting with the dean of the Faculty of Letters is a savage commentary on official government culture. It is only in the popular student hangout that she gets the lead on Al-e Ahmad. And let us not forget that the formal purpose of her first visit to Tehran—as of the second—is medicine. The familiar conflict between medicine and literature is lurking, with medicine being upheld and literature derided by a male physician. Yet on both occasions, Nawal breaks away from the medical congress and explores on her own. Literature, too, demands that frontiers be crossed.

Literature and gender: two seemingly different areas that are conquered in different geographical settings, Iran and Thailand. Yet the two conquests are brought together by this astute narrator not under the sign of "knowledge" generally, but under knowledge of a specific sort. The word *obscure* in reference to Al-e Ahmad's death excites the narrator: "I must know. And desire for knowledge is like the sinful [or wicked; *áthima*] fruit that Eve ate and then had Adam eat from."[57] In Thailand, when Nawal is taken to see the director of the massage parlor, they engage in a battle of wits. When he tells her that he is a Jew and believes in the Old Testament, she replies that she thought that Buddhism and Hinduism were the only religions there. The man responds by saying that it is his right to call the police. "Naturally," she answers.

> "It is your right. For you have caught me in the act [*in flagrante delicto*] of sinful desire, 'desire for knowledge.' And God cursed Eve in the Old Testament because she ate from the tree of knowledge."[58]

Both sorts of knowledge have now been cast together as wicked and forbidden. It may be more familiar to see cross-dressing and the entire episode in the massage parlor in this light, less so the Iranian case, but that is not for us to judge. The fact is that by referencing Eve and the forbidden fruit in both episodes, Nawal automatically juxtaposes and reinterprets the two, one through the other. Both represent hidden knowledge, and both become illicit activities.

The chapter on Iran is entitled "Iran before the Revolution." Yet, the epilogue to the chapter encompasses the post-Khomeini revolutionary period and takes place in London. Hence, Nawal does not actually enter the Middle Eastern country for this section; then again, the title of the chapter does not specifically speak of travel, as it might have had it been, for example, "Journey to Iran before the Revolution." The entire notion of a journey delimited by a geographical locus disappears, leaving one with an emphasis on the state of the country rather than the physical trip there. There is, however, a thread unifying the two trips to Iran and the epilogue in London, a thread combining literature, political activism, and the power of the writer.

The Iran episodes make it clear that travel is a fairly fluid concept. In fact, *My Travels around the World* presents the reader with various possibilities. The notion of entry into a place shifts meaning throughout the book. Sometimes the narrator describes the journey itself, right down to the plane ride, airport formalities, and so forth, before entering a specific destination. This is the case with Thailand.[59] At other times, a political situation instigates the physical trip, which then becomes subordinated, if not occulted. This is the case with Nawal's visit to the Jordanian front following the June 1967 war.[60] At still other times, the narrator delves directly into the description of a country without any evocation of a journey, as is the case with Finland.[61]

Europe, Asia, America—all precede the continent of Africa in the chronological world view of the African narrator. Yet Africa holds pride of place for Nawal because her own identity is so intimately tied to that locus. Another part of her identity—this time as a mother—is linked to New York, the city in which she gives birth to her son.[62] And in Paris, a young girl tells the narrator that she is beautiful ("Vous êtes belle, Madame"), a phrase the Egyptian traveler repeats to herself as she contemplates her own physical appearance and skin color:

> On every trip outside the homeland I would be surprised. My face always appeared more beautiful in the plane mirrors than in the mirrors in my house or in other mirrors in the homeland.[63]

Egypt may be part of Africa, but that does not stop Nawal's family and school colleagues from making fun of her physical appearance. Her dark complexion is a particularly sensitive point. Her aunt even bought her white powder with which to hide her dark skin.[64]

The trip to the African continent will clarify all this as it will shed a new light on the sojourn in America. The narrator muses on her belated discovery of Africa, even though it is "our continent":

> But our eyes and faces were always facing the Mediterranean, Europe, and America, with our backs toward Africa, toward ourselves. When someone turns his back on himself, when one is ashamed of one's brown or black complexion and attempts to hide it with white powder, how does he know himself?[65]

This is clearly a very personal declaration for Nawal. Her sojourn in Africa lasts three months, "a short time to enter into the heart of the African human being [insân], but it was enough for me at least to enter into my heart, to get to know myself and my being African."[66]

This trip to the African continent is perhaps the most important of the voyages of discovery for the narrator.

> I still remember, despite the passing of years, that from the moment I was born I realized two truths in which there is no doubt. The first of them is that I am a girl and that I am not a boy like my brother. The second of them is that my skin is dark and not white like my mother's. And with these two truths I realized something else even more important: that these two characteristics by themselves and without any other defects would be enough to cause failure in my future.[67]

The journey to Africa thus facilitates an internal salvation of sorts for the hero as she begins to feel comfortable with herself and her own skin color. The sense of familiarity she experiences gives her a chance to think back to a trip she made to North Carolina in 1965 and to an incident she "does not forget": finding herself facing segregated restrooms, one for whites and another for blacks.[68] We had already heard about a similar event in her account of the trip to the United States. When telling of the incident in its American context, she notes,

> I stood in front of the mirror, looking intently at the color of my skin. I did not know which of them [the two doors] to enter. Then I entered through the door of "the coloreds" [al-mulawwanîn].[69]

In the context of the African experience, however, the event changes.

> That day, I stood in front of the mirror, confused. Which door do I enter? The color of my skin was not white or black, but a middle color between white and black. And I did not know to which world I belonged, to the world of the whites or the world of the blacks.[70]

Are these the same events or different ones? The narrator tells us that she will never forget the incident in question. The inconsistency, if such it is, rests in whether or not she actually entered the restroom. The specific facts of the matter may not be crucial. What is important is that in Nawal's discourse, American racism is set off against African identity. In the American version of the story, she enters by the door reserved for blacks. Any hesitation would have shed doubt on her African connection, which by the time she pens the account is a certainty in her mind. In a sense, she had to enter by the "colored" door, not to instill a message about her identity, but to strengthen the discourse on American racism. The hesitation in the African variant of the story serves a completely different purpose. In Africa, Nawal learns to accept her dark skin and her African identity. The hesitation, rather than eliminating that identity, is an important step on the way to finding it.

The repetition of this obviously important incident reinforces the political allegiance of Nawal El Saadawi's travel text. All her visits, in fact, have a political tinge, when they are not strictly defined by politics, as the visit to the Jordanian front clearly is. She visits Lenin's tomb, she meets with Indira Gandhi, she denounces imperialism.[71]

But it is perhaps the regime of her political *bête noire*, Anwar Sadat, that comes most under attack. Once again, it is the wealth of the African experience that allows Nawal to enrich her political discourse and attack the Egyptian political system. Chapter 9 of *My Travels around the World* is entitled "Haile Selassi and the Revolution." This chapter, however, opens with a denunciation of Sadat's rule and the internal situation in Egypt. Under him, she writes, "I feel I am in exile in my own country. . . . Things reversed themselves in our lives. Danger became security. And freedom, dictatorship."[72] It is, however, the effects of Sadat's famous economic open door policy (*infitâh*) that the narrator dwells on:

> And we began to see beer and Israeli eggs in the Egyptian stores. A flow of American advertisements poured out for Kent cigarettes and Seven-Up and Schweppes and artificial eyelashes.
> The national products disappeared from the market.[73]

This Egyptian introduction to Haile Selassi's country is more than a literary flourish. Nawal asks a friend to fill her in on Ethiopian history and the successful revolution against Selassi. "All I know," she adds, "is that he used to rule with the force of God, like Sadat in our country."[74] The comparison has been drawn. We should then not be surprised to learn that Sadat even borrowed the euphemism for prison, "the safe place," from the Ethiopians.[75] When Nawal, on hearing Haile Selassi's story, responds that it resembles the stories of *The Thousand and One Nights*, she brings more than just the two rulers together: Selassi now joins his Egyptian cohort as a possible mythical leader inhabiting the kingdom of Nawal El Saadawi's novel *The Fall of the Imam*. The deep corruption of Selassi's regime serves as a commentary on Egypt, as Egypt does on Ethiopia.

Africa brings us full circle. It redefines Nawal's homeland, just as it redefines her. Her last encounter in the book is with the Senegalese writer Sembene Othman, a critic of President Senghor's notion of "négritude." "There is not a culture that springs from black skin and another culture that springs from white skin," Othman says. "Culture springs from the brain, and there is no black brain and white brain." Nor is he in favor of Senghor's politics, which he compares to the politics of Sadat. As for Nasser, he is beloved of all Africans. Nawal replies: "That is true."

> He said: Are you a Nasserite?
> I said: No.
> He said: Are you a Marxist?
> I said: No.
> I said: I do not like to attribute myself to a person, whoever he may be. I am for justice, equality, and freedom for woman, man, and the nation. 'Abd al-Nâsir was great, but his mistakes were also great. Marx was a great thinker, but his ideas were also deficient, in particular concerning the position of women.[76]

These are Nawal's last words in the book. She has effectively declared her intellectual and political independence both from Middle Eastern political heroes and from Western ones. Her travels to the East and to the West have helped seal not only her cultural but also her political identity.

# CHAPTER TEN

# Toward an
# Arab Feminist Poetics

It is difficult to understand how the male critic Sabry Hafez, writing in 1989, could argue that from her first novel, *Memoirs of a Woman Doctor* to her then latest novel, *The Fall of the Imam*, Nawal El Saadawi's fiction had not undergone any "artistic and intellectual development."[1] In fact, from the nameless first-person narrator of *Memoirs* to the multivoiced narrative of *The Fall*, the Egyptian feminist effects quite a literary trajectory.[2] And this does not even include the other texts she has authored, including the play *Izîs*, the prison texts, her travel narrative, and her recent novels *The Innocence of the Devil* and *al-Hubb fî Zaman al-Naft* (Love in the time of oil). Readers willing to follow El Saadawi as she leads them on the intense literary journey that is her textual corpus will watch as the multiple faces of patriarchy are uncovered. The female physician writer creates and recreates a complex feminist discourse that seems to have the uncanny ability to articulate and redefine some of the most sensitive issues in Arab society today.

At the same time, Nawal El Saadawi's female heroes are memorable literary figures. The medical student in *Memoirs of a Woman Doctor* who becomes a successful physician is the first of her characters to posit the problematic relationship between science and art, a dilemma that continues to plague many a Saadawian figure. It is perhaps no accident that the female physician becomes, in El Saadawi's early fiction, a literary mediator, a narrator who empowers other characters to speak. Thus it is that a powerful female narrator, this time a psychiatrist, permits the prostitute Firdaws to tell her story in *Woman at Point Zero*. This Firdaws, abused by males, is not unlike another Firdaws, the teller of another tale, this one also enframed by a physician and also relating a negative male-female relationship.

The first Firdaws reveals her story to an enraptured psychiatrist in the closed environment of a jail cell. Incarceration becomes an important topos for Saadawian heroes. The Egyptian president Anwar Sadat facilitates this for the Egyptian feminist by imprisoning her, along with many other Egyptian intellectuals and activists, prior to his assassination in 1981. This real incarceration, rather than silencing El Saadawi, only adds to her vocal courage. Her post-prison narratives take the patriarchal bull by the horns and attempt textually to destroy him. She pens *Memoirs from the Women's Prison* and a play, *The Human Being*, both based on her jail experience. She pens *The Fall of the Imam*, heavily inspired by Sadat and his regime. But the faces of patriarchy in that novel are as multiple as the text's multiple narrators; the unnamed ruler is not merely Sadat, but a generic Middle Eastern ruler. *The Fall of the Imam*, with its heavily encoded cultural and religious subtext, leads easily to *The Innocence of the Devil*, another incarceration narrative, set this time in an insane asylum.

But Nawal El Saadawi does not need enclosed spaces to expose the many facets of patriarchy. Her patriarchal constructions, at once religious, social, and political, span centuries and continents. Set in ancient Egypt, *Izís* exposes a multifaceted patriarchy gone mad, mutilating women and slaves alike. Oddly, that same Isis travels to the contemporary world of twentieth-century Arabic literature to act as a textual foil to another Isis, constructed this time by the male Egyptian playwright Tawfîq al-Hakîm. The reader learns from the more contemporary setting of *The Fall of the Imam*, imbued as it is with such technological wonders as test-tube babies, that the same male phantasms of power exist simultaneously in the East and in the West.

Yet, despite these geographical and chronological distances, certain narrative threads hold the complex Saadawian discourse together. Unraveling these threads leads the critic on yet another journey, this one cultural and literary, in which we see how, from *Memoirs of a Woman Doctor* to *The Innocence of the Devil*, the Egyptian feminist has worked to recast and redefine centuries-old textual materials. One may well sense that in *Memoirs* she was merely dipping her toes in this intertextual water. No matter. She progressively placed the rest of her body into it, until, with *The Innocence of the Devil*, she was swimming in the *turâth*, that beloved Arabo-Islamic cultural tradition.

The power in El Saadawi's feminist poetics comes precisely from this game of redefinition. From concepts central to Arabo-Islamic gender expectations, through literary and religious texts, to popular folk materials, the Egyptian feminist leaves no area untouched. And she never forgets that if the formula is to be effective it cannot be restricted to gender alone. Thus it is that gender becomes intimately linked to class, and both in turn are inextricably tied to sexuality and the body.

As the female heroes follow one another into the Saadawian literary pantheon, each picks up something from her predecessors and carries it further. The textual fabric of Nawal El Saadawi's literary corpus is transformed into layers, parts of which overlap and parts of which do not. It is as if the reader were climbing the famous step pyramid of Sakkara in El Saadawi's home country, where each step is dependent on the ones below it and yet built away from them enough for the climber to finally reach the apex of that pyramid. At the same time, a complex dialogue is taking place between all of El Saadawi's texts, as concepts and mental structures appear and reappear in different and yet similar guises.

Perhaps the most compelling issues in El Saadawi's works relate to the corporal. Some of these are tied to age-old concepts in the Arabo-Islamic tradition, such as *'awra*, while others are part of the social condition of being a female.

The young first-person narrator of *Memoirs of a Woman Doctor* expands the word *'awra*, that which is shameful and must be covered, to her entire body. Firdaws in *Woman at Point Zero* carries the *'awra* further, this time into the economic domain. *'Awra* also appears and reappears in *The Fall of the Imam*, delimiting the world of the hero and setting her off against the male gender.

A similar game plays itself out with eating. In *Memoirs of a Woman Doctor*, for example, this bodily function serves as a gender and social divider, separating the female narrator from her brother. Only when she is finally an adult in the countryside can she perform this function audibly. For Firdaws in *Woman at Point Zero*, eating is the bodily function that defines her heterosexual relationship with her miserly husband. Only when she finally gains financial independence from selling her body can she perform this bodily function freely. For Hamîda in *The Circling Song*, the stakes with eating are even higher: her physical molestations are intimately tied to this life-sustaining activity.

How does a woman extricate herself from this vicious cycle of eating and male violence? In fact, it is only a homosexual woman, Nirjis in *The*

*Fall of the Iman*, who is finally able to break this disastrous relationship between women and food. As she asserts her onomastic identity with her given name and her sexual identity with her love for women, she is able to refuse the male's order to go and prepare his food. Her refusal is far more effective than the protestations of the unnamed hero in El Saadawi's first novel, whose childhood was imbued with ideas about woman's role in food preparation and for whom man and eating become virtually fused.

Consuming food is not a preoccupation of El Saadawi alone. It is a topic that goes to the heart of contemporary Egyptian letters. Only when the female physician writer is placed alongside her male compatriots, however, do significant differences arise. For the leftist writer Yûsuf al-Qa'îd, for example, the ability or inability to consume certain items, like meat, is part of the discourse of class, and this is manifest in his narrators' descriptions of human bodies in relation to the class status of individuals. For El Saadawi, gender cannot be isolated from class, and the two are played out in powerful imagery related to the everyday corporal function that is eating. Food in Egyptian letters, therefore, defines social classes, and its presence is part of the articulation of the class system. El Saadawi expands this class oppression by linking food to female oppression. Women, she makes abundantly clear, are oppressed just as are the members of the lower classes.

The issue of eating, thus, shows one of the ways in which Nawal El Saadawi fits into the world of modern Egyptian letters. Her earthy realism, like her politically uncompromising, frequently bleak visions of Egyptian society, show her to be the literary sister of such leftist-populist writers as Yusûf al-Qa'îd and Ahmad Fu'âd Najm, and even the cartoonist Ahmad Hijâzî. Indeed, in many ways she is closer to them than to most women writers in the region, who, even when they talk about women's problems, maintain a far more decorous tone. Dr. Nawal El Saadawi has taken the tough *engagé* style of the Egyptian left and added gender to its concern with social class. Her brew is rendered all the stronger, however, by her addition of secularism and philosophical questioning of religion—subjects handled in an infinitely more cautious way by a figure like Tawfîq al-Hakîm.

Eating, of course, cannot exist without the body, and bodies there are aplenty in the textual vision of the feminist physician. Male bodies, female bodies, young bodies, old bodies, diseased bodies, healthy bodies—all have a role to play in the Saadawian literary corpus. Narrators exploit body imagery. The body is the terrain on which games of power are played, whether of class, gender, medicine, or what have you. Nawal El Saadawi's training as a physician has a hand here: medical imagery reinforces the power of the corporal imagery in the feminist's literary corpus. Questions of femininity, masculinity, and the precise boundary of the body become part of the complex Saadawian world of gender. As Hamîda and Hamîdû, in *The Circling Song*, repeatedly lift their galabiyyas to verify the presence of their sexual organs, the reader is reminded of the fragility of gender boundaries.

Hamîdû and Hamîda are twins. Brother and sister, they are a problematic duo all too familiar from the Arabo-Islamic tradition, in which this male-female sibling relationship hides a dangerous incestuous possibility. Whether one wishes to go as far as Hasan El-Shamy and have the brother-sister relationship replace the Oedipal bond does not change the dynamics of this very Middle Eastern duo.

Other brother-sister duos keep Hamîda and Hamîdû company in the Saadawian universe. In the medical sphere, for instance, we find the concerned brother who wishes to verify the virginity of his sister. Brother and sister are part of the literary fabric of *Innocence* as well. In *Izîs*, El Saadawi turns the tables on the brother-sister duo: Isis is stronger than her brother Seth, and he is unable to rape her.

The pièce de résistance of brother-sister coupling comes in *The Fall of the Imam*. Bint Allâh mentions to the Chief of Security that she and her brother, Fadl Allâh, fought together in a single trench. The official, upon learning that the two were alone, tells the female hero that this constitutes a crime, and he cites the popular *hadîth* that when a man and a woman are together, the Devil is the third. If the reader had any previous doubts, this declaration dispels them: brother and sister are like any other male and female. If they are alone, they run the danger of an illicit union.

The use of this *hadîth* reminds us that the Saadawian literary universe is Middle Eastern and that the dominant referents for the Egyptian feminist are inspired by the Arabo-Islamic tradition. This is a literary fact of singular importance for Dr. Nawal El Saadawi, some of whose detractors dismiss her as a Western product. In fact, on the contemporary Arabic literary scene, it is difficult to think of a woman writer who has exploited the revered Arabo-Islamic textual tradition as thoroughly as she has.

From religious normative works to more literary texts, El Saadawi does not hesitate to tackle the predominantly male tradition of the Arabo-Islamic universe and intertextually turn it upside down. Verses from the Qur'ân, sayings from the *hadîth*, hidden references to such classics of medieval Arabic literature as the *Epistle of Forgiveness* of Abû al-'Alâ' al-Ma'arrî: these all enter the textual world of the Saadawian twentieth-century narrators. Thus it is that the Qur'ânic People of the Cave are transformed into a contemporary female hero in *The Fall of the Imam*, or that the popular ballad of "Shafîqa and Mitwallî" gets recast with the brother-sister twins Hamîdû and Hamîda.

But more than any other text, *The Thousand and One Nights* holds particular pride of place in Saadawian discourse. And it is especially the frame of the *Nights* that attracts the Egyptian feminist. Other writers, both Eastern and Western, have of course used this famous frame as well; but El Saadawi carves out her own unique turf in the special way she articulates that complicated intertext. In *The Fall of the Imam*, for instance, it is the king, Shâhriyâr, who takes center stage, rather than Shahrazâd. By foregrounding the male ruler instead of the female storyteller, El Saadawi locks on to patriarchy and defines it in universal terms. The medieval literary serial murderer is able, we discover, to transcend time and place as he becomes the locus of identity at once for the Eastern Imam and for the Western test-tube man. In *Izîs*, a royal wife's act of infidelity—cast as a parallel to that of her literary predecessor in the *Nights*—leads not to corporal death, but to corporal mutilation through clitoridectomy. Thus slaves and women alike are transformed into physically incomplete beings.

To the original focus in the frame of the *Nights*—sexuality and the body—El Saadawi has added another dimension: female excision. Nawal El Saadawi underwent this procedure as a young child, and she later wrote about it publicly at the urging of her husband, Dr. Sherif Hetata. But more than simply a biographical fact for the Egyptian feminist physician writer, this corporal mutilation is transmuted onto Saadawian literary heroines. For some of El Saadawi's female characters, excision is simply a fact of life, part of the reality of being female. For the prostitute Firdaws, for example, this mutilation is articulated as a nostalgia for pleasure no longer possible. For Hamîda, it is articulated corporally, as a wound that remains a physical symbol of the mutilation. Nowhere in Nawal El Saadawi's fictional corpus is the reader treated to a description of this act directed against the female body (as compared, for example, with the frequent explicit descriptions of rape). In this, El Saadawi differs from other contemporary female writers, such as Evelyne Accad in *L'Excisée*, where the operation is a graphic component of the narrative. The textual representation of female excision in the novels *Woman at Point Zero* and *The Circling Song*, moreover, differs from that in the play *Izîs*. Here, the excision is more visible, more englobing. Its intimate relationship to an overarching political and religious patriarchy makes of it an even more heinous crime.

Isis is, of course, a goddess. Her universe foregrounds religion. In this, the textual world of the ancient Egyptian deity is no different from that of almost all her co-heroines in the Saadawian literary system. From the jail cell in which Firdaws tells her story to the insane asylum in which the drama of the Devil and God unfolds, religion plays a central role in the narratives. In El Saadawi's writings, however, religion is a multifaceted and complex enterprise, much like patriarchy, of which it is a pivotal component. Islam, Christianity, Judaism—the three monotheistic religions sit alongside other religious constructs, like that of ancient Egypt or the multiple deities of Hamîdû's universe, to help mold an overarching religious patriarchy whose dynamics are universal.

Religion penetrates deeply, affecting everyday realities. It sanctions and perpetrates myriad injustices toward the female gender. Along with Firdaws, we learn (if we did not know it earlier) that wife beating is permissible in the religious and social system. No Qur'ânic citation is necessary (though one could easily have been adduced) to sanction this act of physical violence. Rather, its justification is done at the hands of women themselves. When Firdaws complains to her uncle's wife, the latter tells her that the act is legal. The validity of wife beating is thus transformed into a verbal enunciation handed down from woman to woman. The female gender, we discover, has incorporated religiously sanctioned violence against women into its own discourse of the female condition.

The religious intertext also becomes a pawn in the intricate Saadawian gender game. In *The Fall of the Imam*, for example, males seem to possess a more intimate knowledge of the scriptoral tradition (not insignificantly male in nature) and manipulate it as needed in the delicate game of controlling the female. The same situation initially obtains in *The Innocence of the Devil*, where the older males are involved in the consistent (yet hopeless) task of instilling in the females a proper appreciation for monotheism. One female is able to subvert this seemingly eternal alliance between males and the religious tradition: Nirjis. She accomplishes this stunning reversal in a dialogue with the male asylum administrator. Her own superior knowledge of the religious tradition is based on a fact related to her sexual orientation. The Muslim holy book, she informs her male interlocutor, does not discuss tribadism. The soundness of her argument hinges on this incontestable fact. Is it an accident that it is a woman who loves women who is able to overturn the cycle of male control of the religious tradition?

More than a mere game of religious intertextuality is at issue here. The physician feminist is in fact exploring some of the most important cultural debates in the contemporary Arabo-Islamic world. Can a woman travel alone, or must she be in the company of a legal guardian? While twentieth-century Islamist religio-legal experts discuss this question and issue legal injunctions about the social and moral dangers inherent in woman's travel, Nawal El Saadawi in her travel memoirs provides Middle Eastern women with an alternate model: that of a woman traveling alone and living to write about it. When a concerned Muslim wrote to a contemporary male religious authority asking him about the Qur'ânic omission of Eve's forgiveness, he was most likely unaware of El Saadawi's concern with this question in her novel *The Innocence of the Devil.*

The textual dialogue in which the Egyptian feminist imbricates herself not only relates to larger gender debates in the contemporary Arabo-Islamic sphere, but it also becomes a way for El Saadawi to question the precise modalities of male-female interaction. Here, the power of the scopic looms large. El Saadawi has a fascination with eyes that borders on obsession. Like the bodies of which they are a part, eyes are everywhere: male eyes, female eyes, diseased eyes, healthy eyes. Even one of her short stories is entitled "Eyes."[3]

In her fascination with the scopic, the Egyptian feminist is far from unique. Once again, however, it is the way she manipulates centuries-old cultural ideas that is significant. The male gaze is part and parcel of the complex Arabo-Islamic discourse on gender and sexuality. Legists, taking their cue from the Qur'ân, have tirelessly warned against the potentially socially destructive nature of this gaze.[4] Medieval opinions sit alongside contemporary ones warning against men looking at women.

This Arabo-Islamic cultural insistence on averting the gaze is part of a larger scopic regime.[5] As with many of her other violations, Nawal El Saadawi is engaged in the delicate game of subverting the scopic regime of the Arabo-Islamic universe. Like much that the Egyptian feminist deals with, the scopic is at once social and religious. It is social because it represents interaction between social groups, primary of which are the male and female. It is religious because the injunction to avert one's gaze is Qur'ânic. And of course, it is also about power.

The gaze becomes a tool in Saadawian male-female sexual politics.

The female hero of *Memoirs of a Woman Doctor* understands the social power of the scopic inherent in the position of the male physician. She latches on to that power by becoming a physician herself. For Firdaws in *Woman at Point Zero*, the scopic glance of the male invades her everyday activities, including eating. Her ability finally to perform this activity unhampered is linked to the absence of the male gaze. The hero of the short story "Death of an Ex-Minister" confesses to his mother that he was driven insane by a female employee's refusal to lower her eyes in his presence. As the male voices his concerns, he is in fact articulating his gender's response to the Saadawian reversal of the dominant cultural scopic regime: Saadawian female heroes have the uncanny ability of looking at men, thus disturbing, if not violating, the scopic space.

The female heroes may well violate scopic space, but it is their physical violation by males that is the moving force behind many of El Saadawi's texts. The violence in the violation varies. The nameless young girl in *Memoirs of a Woman Doctor* is molested. Hamîda in *The Circling Song* is raped. Nawal, the narrator of the prison memoirs, is metaphorically violated by Sadat's political police. And in the patriarchal universe of ancient Egypt, rape is the method of choice for the control of the female.

But physical violation, like other Saadawian literary elements, does not exist in isolation. The most incendiary combination is that of physical violation and religion. Woman's abuse becomes the physical manifestation of the religious patriarchal system that permits such abuse to exist. A narrator can reverse constructions long held dear, as when the prayer bump on a Muslim man's forehead, normally a sign of his extreme religiosity, comes to signify instead unwanted sexual penetration for the female. Examples of the nexus of violation and religion are many, but none is as effective as that ultimate violation in which the male Deity rapes the gullible female. This is, of course, what occurs in the closed world of the insane asylum in *The Innocence of the Devil*. True, that particular environment permits an ambiguity in identification to exist, leaving the reader to wonder if it is really the Deity or simply some old man who thinks he is the Deity. In a sense, that ambiguity is irrelevant, for once the physical violation occurs the seed has been planted in the reader's head: the monotheistic Deity is a rapist. Dr. El Saadawi made the point completely explicit in a taped interview.[6]

The nature of this monotheistic Deity in *The Innocence of the Devil* is intimately tied to the nature of the Arabic language. The grammatical gender categories that had fascinated the narrator of *The Circling Song* are here transmuted into the theological domain. The detailed gram-matical discussions remind us above all that Nawal El Saadawi is, first and foremost, an Arabic writer. Her literary vision and referential uni-verse are not those of Western authors. Rather, her textual feet are firmly planted in the centuries-old Arabo-Islamic scriptoral tradition. While many of the tensions that dominate her works may superficially resemble those addressed by other Arabic writers, her vision is distinct. The female hero of *Memoirs of a Woman Doctor* needed the country-side and nature to help her in her search for her own identity. Hence, for her, the urban-rural dichotomy was present. But the life of other Saadawian heroes is devoid of any nostalgia for the rural. Women are exploited, no matter what the environment. After all, the rape that drives Hamîda to the city and further exploitation occurred in the vil-lage. In this absence of nostalgia for the countryside, El Saadawi differs from some of her literary compatriots, for whom the countryside pro-vides an escape from the unsavory conditions in the city—as when, in a children's magazine, the Pharaonic hero Ramsîs flees to Upper Egypt to avoid the crowds and noise of Cairo.[7]

The distinct literary vision that is Nawal El Saadawi's extends into other domains. We saw, for example, that her dystopian project in *The Fall of the Imam* differed from that of Western feminist writers. If the urban versus rural dichotomy is not privileged in El Saadawi's literary universe, neither is the binary opposition of modernity versus tradition, so common among Middle Eastern and other third world writers. In fact, this division is so prevalent as to be almost a staple of contemporary Arabic letters.[8]

To say that these distinctions so dear to other writers are not crucial to the Egyptian feminist physician is to say that her literary agenda revolves around something that transcends such dichotomies. This "something" is patriarchy in all its ramifications. Religion, society, gen-der, class—all these are categories deeply influenced by patriarchy. The universality of patriarchy in the Saadawian system is such that many of the female heroes who pit themselves against it are destroyed. The upper-class heroes cannot break the power of patriarchy, though they can put a dent in it. If they are courageous, strong, and a little lucky, they can make a space for themselves. For lower-class women, even this is not possible.

One force can effectively battle this universality: the intensity of female-female relationships. This intensity can take the form of the pow-erful relationship between psychiatrist and prostitute in *Woman at Point*

*Zero*, a relationship that transcends class boundaries. Or it can manifest itself in the homosocial environment of the prison, as in *Memoirs from the Women's Prison*, this time transcending both class and politico-religious boundaries. Or it can articulate itself through the declared homosexual preference of the female hero of *The Innocence of the Devil*. But this female force, powerful though it may be, cannot destroy patriarchy. Woman in the Saadawian feminist literary construct is doomed to fight a battle she rarely wins.

# Notes

$EI^2$ refers to the *Encyclopaedia of Islam*, 2d ed. (Leiden: E. J. Brill, 1960–).

## INTRODUCTION

1. See Gilles Kepel, *Les banlieues de l'Islam: Naissance d'une religion en France* (Paris: Editions du Seuil, 1987), pp. 192–196.

2. On this ironic state of affairs, see Nawal El Saadawi, "Guarding My Tongue," *Guardian*, August 10, 1992, p. 21.

3. Georges Tarabishi, *Woman Against Her Sex: A Critique of Nawal el-Saadawi*, trans. Basil Hatim and Elisabeth Orsini (London: Saqi Books, 1988). El Saadawi had a chance to reply to Tarabishi in the same volume. For another critique of Tarabashi, see Sumayya Ramadân, "al-Radd 'alâ Kitâb *Unthâ Didd al-Unûtha*," in *al-Fikr al-'Arabî al-Mu'âsir wal-Mar'a* (Cairo: Dâr Tadâmun al-Mar'a al-'Arabiyya, 1988), pp. 125–131.

4. A great deal has been written on Yûsuf Idrîs. For book-length studies, see Sasson Somekh, ed., *Dunyâ Yûsuf Idrîs* (Jerusalem: Matba'at al-Sharq al-Ta'âwuniyya, 1976); P. M. Kurpershoek, *The Short Stories of Yûsuf Idrîs* (Leiden: E. J. Brill, 1981); Sasson Somekh, *Lughat al-Qissa fî Adab Yûsuf Idrîs* (Acre: Matba'at al-Sarûjî, 1984). The recent volume *Yûsuf Idrîs (1927–1991)*, ed. Samîr Sarhân and I'tidâl 'Uthmân (Cairo: al-Hay'a al-Misriyya al-'Amma lil-Kitâb, 1991), contains extensive bibliographical materials. See also Mona Mikhail, *Studies in the Short Fiction of Mahfouz and Idris* (New York: New York University Press, 1992).

5. See, for example, Michel Foucault, *Naissance de la clinique: Une archéologie du regard médical* (Paris: Presses Universitaires de France, 1963).

CHAPTER 1

1. For a slightly different discussion of some of the issues in this chapter, see Fedwa Malti-Douglas, "Writing Nawal El Saadawi," in *Feminism Beside Itself*, ed. Diane Elam and Robyn Wiegman (New York: Routledge, 1995), pp. 283–296.

2. Edward W. Said, "Embargoed Literature," *Nation*, September 17, 1990, p. 280.

3. See 'Abd al-Wadûd Shalabî, *Fî Mahkamat al-Ta'rîkh* (Cairo: Dâr al-Shurûq, 1986), pp. 31–45.

4. Hisham Sharabi, *Neopatriarchy: A Theory of Distorted Change in Arab Society* (New York: Oxford University Press, 1988), p. 33.

5. Our task here is not to make a catalogue of works that discuss Nawal El Saadawi. It is sufficient to glance at any study on women in the Middle East, both literary and nonliterary, in any language to find her included. See, for example, Nadje Sadig Al-Ali, *Gender Writing / Writing Gender: The Representation of Women in a Selection of Modern Egyptian Literature* (Cairo: American University in Cairo Press, 1993), and Issa J. Boullata, *Trends and Issues in Contemporary Arab Thought* (Albany: State University of New York Press, 1990), pp. 127–131.

6. See, for example, Heong-Dug Park, "Nawâl al-Saʿadâwî [sic] and Modern Egyptian Feminist Writings," Ph.D. diss., University of Michigan, 1988.

7. Jûrj Tarâbîshî, *Unthâ Didd al-Unûtha* (Beirut: Dâr al-Talîʿa, 1984). A recent Islamist polemic is Yâsir Farahât, *al-Muwâjaha: Dr. Nawâl al-Saʿdâwî...* (Cairo, al-Rawda, 1993).

8. See Miriam Cooke, "Arab Women Writers," in *The Cambridge History of Arabic Literature: Modern Arabic Literature*, ed. M. M. Badawi (Cambridge: Cambridge University Press, 1992), p. 453.

9. See Emmanuel Sivan, *Radical Islam: Medieval Theology and Modern Politics* (New Haven: Yale University Press, 1985), p. 182. The later expanded edition of this work (1990) solves the problem by eliminating reference to Nawal El Saadawi altogether.

10. See the short biography by Margot Badran and Miriam Cooke, "Nawal al-Saadawi," in *Opening the Gates: A Century of Arab Feminist Writing*, ed. Margot Badran and Miriam Cooke (London: Virago; Bloomington: Indiana University Press, 1990), p. 203.

11. Cooke, "Arab Women Writers," p. 454. The error here is understandable and is most likely due to a misreading of the Arabic original, since the Dâr al-Mustaqbal al-ʿArabî is on *Beirut* Street in Heliopolis (Misr al-Jadîda).

12. Hence, Lionnet's statement about El Saadawi—"These writers are all Western-trained feminist intellectuals or scientists (Koso-Thomas and Saadawi are physicians)"—is misleading, at best. The point is of larger cultural importance, however, since it shows the general inapplicability in the Arab world (but not only there) of Lionnet's assumption, developed in the same passage, that literacy dictates Westernization. See Françoise Lionnet, "Dissymmetry Embodied: Feminism, Universalism, and the Practice of Excision," in *Borderwork: Feminist Engagements with Comparative Literature*, ed. Margaret R. Higonnet (Ithaca: Cornell University Press, 1994), p. 23.

13. Nawal El Saadawi, "An Overview of My Life," trans. Antoinette Tuma, *Contemporary Authors Autobiography Series*, vol. 11 (Detroit, Mich.: Gale Research Co., 1990), p. 62.

14. Allen Douglas and Fedwa Malti-Douglas, "Reflections of a Feminist: Conversation with Nawal al-Saadawi," in Badran and Cooke, *Opening the Gates*, pp. 396–397.

15. El Saadawi, "Overview," p. 66.

16. Ibid., p. 70; Nawal El Saadawi, Personal communication, February 15, 1993. For the works on sexuality and gender, see Nawâl al-Sa'dâwî, *al-Mar'a wal-Jins*, 3d ed. (Cairo: Maktabat Madbûlî, 1974); idem, *al-Unthâ Hiya al-Asl* (Cairo: Maktabat Madbûlî, 1974); idem, *al-Rajul wal-Jins* (Beirut: al-Mu'assasa al-'Arabiyya lil-Dirâsât wal-Nashr, 1976); idem, *al-Mar'a wal-Sirâ' al-Nafsî* (Cairo: Maktabat Madbûlî, 1983).

17. Nawâl al-Sa'dâwî, *Suqût al-Imâm* (Cairo: Dâr al-Mustaqbal al-'Arabî, 1987); translated by Sherif Hetata as *The Fall of the Imam* (London: Methuen, 1988). See Chapter 5 below.

18. Nawal El Saadawi discusses this association in her introduction to *Women of the Arab World: The Coming Challenge*, ed. Nahid Toubia, trans. Nahed El Gamal (London: Zed Books, 1988), pp. 1–7. The volume constitutes papers presented at an AWSA conference in Cairo.

19. I am grateful to Nawal El Saadawi for many of these biographical details.

20. Nawâl al-Sa'dâwî, *Ma'raka Jadîda fî Qadiyyat al-Mar'a* (Cairo: Sînâ lil-Nashr, 1992).

21. Douglas and Malti-Douglas, "Reflections," p. 399.

22. Nawâl al-Sa'dâwî, *Mudhakkirât Tifla Ismuhâ Su'âd* (Cairo: Manshûrât Dâr Tadâmun al-Mar'a al-'Arabiyya, 1990).

23. Nawâl al-Sa'dâwî, *al-Hubb fî Zaman al-Naft* (Cairo: Maktabat Madbûlî, 1993).

24. El Saadawi, "Overview," p. 66.

25. For the complexity of these issues, see, for example, the essays in Chandra Talpade Mohanty, Ann Russo, and Lourdes Torres, eds., *Third World Women and the Politics of Feminism* (Bloomington: Indiana University Press, 1991). The linked issues of nationalism and feminism are also dealt with in Kumari Jayawardena, *Feminism and Nationalism in the Third World* (London: Zed Books, 1986). Deniz Kandiyoti's edited volume *Women, Islam, and the State* (Philadelphia: Temple University Press, 1991) contains much relevant information as well. See also, for example, Afaf Lutfi al-Sayyid Marsot, "The Revolutionary Gentlewomen in Egypt," in *Women in the Muslim World*, ed. Lois Beck and Nikki Keddie (Cambridge, Mass.: Harvard University Press, 1978), pp. 261–276; Thomas Philipp, "Feminism and Nationalist Politics in Egypt," in ibid., pp. 277–294; and Leila Ahmed, "Early Feminist Movements in Turkey and Egypt," in *Muslim Women*, ed. Freda Hussain (New York: St. Martin's Press, 1984), pp. 111–123.

26. See, for example, Fatima Mernissi, *Beyond the Veil: Male-Female Dynamics in a Modern Muslim Society* (Cambridge, Mass.: Schenkman, 1975), pp. 99–102. See also the pamphlet by Muhammad Fahmî 'Abd al-Wahhâb, *al-Harakât al-Nisâ'iyya fî al-Sharq wa-Silatuhâ bil-Isti'mâr wal-Sahyûniyya al-'Alamiyya* (Cairo: Dâr al-I'tisâm, 1979).

27. See, for example, Frantz Fanon, *A Dying Colonialism*, trans. Haakon Chevalier (New York: Grove Press, 1967), pp. 35–67, 99–120; and Kaci, *Bas les voiles* (Paris: Editions Rochevignes, 1984), inside cover. Of course, there is nothing sociologically unique or even particularly Islamic in this development. After World War II in the United States, for instance, women who had entered the work force in the national emergency were eased back into more domestic roles. For a discussion of this issue in other Middle Eastern materials, see Allen Douglas and Fedwa Malti-Douglas, *Arab Comic Strips: Politics of an Emerging Mass Culture* (Bloomington: Indiana University Press, 1994), pp. 143–149, 184–188. See also Bouthaina Shaaban, *Both Right and Left Handed: Arab Women Talk About Their Lives* (London: Women's Press, 1988), pp. 158–159 (quotation, p. 159); Val Moghadam, *Modernizing Women: Gender and Social Change in the Middle East* (Boulder, Colo.: L. Rienner, 1993); and Deniz Kandiyoti, "Identity and Its Discontents: Women and the Nation," in *Millennium: Journal of International Studies* 20, no. 3 (1991): 429–443.

28. Cf. Nawal El Saadawi, "Women's Resistance in the Arab World," in *Women in the Middle East: Perceptions, Realities and Struggles for Liberation*, ed. Haleh Afshar (London: Macmillan, 1993), pp. 139–145.

29. I have been present at lectures and participated on panels with Dr. El Saadawi on many occasions at which she has enunciated these positions.

30. Mary Daly, *Beyond God the Father: Toward a Philosophy of Women's Liberation* (Boston: Beacon Press, 1973), p. 5.

31. Joanna Russ, *How to Suppress Women's Writing* (Austin: University of Texas Press, 1983).

32. For a recent attempt to link Orientalism and feminist approaches to the study of Middle Eastern women, see Edward W. Said, *Culture and Imperialism* (New York: Alfred A. Knopf, 1993), pp. xxiv–xxv. See also Minh-ha T. Trinh, *Woman, Native, Other: Writing Postcoloniality and Feminism* (Bloomington: Indiana University Press, 1989); and Leila Ahmed, *Women and Gender in Islam: Historical Roots of a Modern Debate* (New Haven: Yale University Press, 1992), pp. 144–168. Many of the studies in Judith Tucker, ed., *Arab Women: Old Boundaries, New Frontiers* (Bloomington: Indiana University Press, 1993) deal, on one level or another, with some of these questions.

33. We shall have ample occasion to see this in many of the chapters below (e.g., Chapters 5, 6, and 7).

34. This objection has been made orally to me on many occasions by both Arabs and non-Arabs.

35. The negative image of Arabs in the West has been much studied. One of the most interesting works in this regard is that of Jack G. Shaheen, *The TV Arab* (Bowling Green, Ohio: Bowling Green State University Popular Press, 1984).

36. See, for example, Malika Mehdid, "A Western Invention of Arab Womanhood: The 'Oriental' Female," in Afshar, *Women in the Middle East*, p. 48.

37. Fedwa Malti-Douglas, "Dangerous Crossings: Gender and Criticism in Arabic Literary Studies," in *Borderwork: Feminist Engagements with Comparative Literature*, ed. Margaret Higonnet (Ithaca: Cornell University Press, 1994), pp. 224–229.

38. See, for example, 'Abd al-Wahhâb, *al-Harakât al-Nisâ'iyya*; Mustafâ Mahmûd, *al-Mârksiyya wal-Islâm*, 6th printing (Cairo: Dâr al-Ma'ârif, 1987); and idem, *Li-Mâdhâ Rafadt al-Mârksiyya?*, 3d printing (Cairo: Dâr al-Ma'ârif, 1989).

39. See Malti-Douglas, "Dangerous Crossings."

40. See Fedwa Malti-Douglas, *Woman's Body, Woman's Word: Gender and Discourse in Arabo-Islamic Writing* (Princeton: Princeton University Press, 1991).

41. University of Texas Press, "Readable Books: Prose and Poetry, Literary Criticism, Linguistics, and Language" (advertising flier), January 1991, p. 6.

42. For a discussion of this phenomenon in much of contemporary Arab culture, see Douglas and Malti-Douglas, *Arab Comic Strips*, pp. 217–227.

43. See, for example, the discussion in Roger Allen, *The Arabic Novel: An Historical and Critical Introduction* (Syracuse: Syracuse University Press, 1982), pp. 13–18.

44. It would be equally vain to speak of an authentic medieval Arabic culture, if by this one meant one untainted by influences from Greece to Persia. The historic greatness of Arabic culture, indeed, has been its capacity to act as the cosmopolitan vehicle for the integration of diverse civilizational strands.

45. Trevor Le Gassick, "The Arabic Novel in English Translation," *Mundus Arabicus* 5 (1992): 59 (special issue entitled "The Arabic Novel since 1950," ed. Issa Boullata); emphasis added.

46. Sabry Hafez, "Intentions and Realisation in the Narratives of Nawal El-Saadawi," *Third World Quarterly* 11, no. 3 (July 1989): 189. Perhaps because he is not a literary critic, Tarabishi is less concerned with formal generic issues. Instead he decides to treat El Saadawi's novels as autobiographical in order to make it easier for him to put the author and her characters on the couch together. El Saadawi has refuted this clearly in her response to the English translation of her book; see Nawal El Saadawi, "Reply," in Tarabishi, *Woman Against Her Sex*, pp. 189–191.

47. The most articulate statement on this topic is, again, that of Joanna Russ, *How to Suppress*.

CHAPTER 2

1. Nawâl al-Sa'dâwî, *Mudhakkirât Tabîba* (Beirut: Dâr al-Adâb, 1980), p. 5; ellipses in the original. The first chapter has been translated by Fedwa Malti-Douglas as "Growing Up Female in Egypt," in *Women and the Family in the Middle East: New Voices of Change*, ed. Elizabeth Warnock Fernea (Austin: University of Texas Press, 1985), pp. 111–120 (quotation, p. 111). The entire text has been translated as *Memoirs of a Woman Doctor*, trans. Catherine Cobham (San Francisco: City Lights Books, 1989).

2. Fuller discussion of some of the points in this chapter can be found in Malti-Douglas, *Woman's Body, Woman's Word*, pp. 111–143.

3. El Saadawi actually authored her first novel, *Mudhakkirât Tifla Ismuhâ Su'âd* (Memoirs of a girl named Su'âd), at the age of thirteen. This childhood novel, however, did not see the light of day until 1990.

4. Mahmûd and Hetata have yet to receive major critical attention. On Yûsuf Idrîs, see Kurpershoek, *Short Stories of Yûsuf Idrîs*; Somekh, *Lughat al-Qissa*; the introduction to Sasson Somekh, *Dunyâ Yûsuf Idrîs min Khilâl Aqâsisihi* (Tel Aviv: Dâr al-Nashr al-'Arabî, 1976); and Renate Wise, "The Concept of Sexuality in the Short Stories of Yusuf Idris," Ph.D. diss., University of Texas, Austin, 1992. On 'Abd al-Salâm al-'Ujaylî, see Fedwa Malti-Douglas, "al-'Anâsir al-Turâthiyya fî al-Adab al-'Arabî al-Mu'âsir: al-Ahlâm fî Thalâth Qisas," trans. 'I. al-Sharqâwî, *Fusûl* 2, no. 2 (1982): 21–29. Comparative references to other Arabic, or even European, texts are merely illustrative and not exhaustive. Nor are the discussions of aspects of El Saadawi's texts necessarily meant to imply the absence of similar elements in other modern Arabic texts.

5. For some of these relationships, see William Carlos Williams, *The Doctor Stories*, comp. Robert Coles (New York: New Directions Books, 1984); and Richard Selzer, *Rituals of Surgery* (New York: Harper's Magazine Press, 1974).

6. See, for example, Nawâl al-Sa'dâwî, "Lâ Shay' Yafnâ," in *Lahzat Sidq* (Beirut: Dâr al-Adâb, 1986), pp. 77–82; and idem, "Min Ajl Man," in *Hanân Qalîl* (Beirut: Dâr al-Adâb, 1986), pp. 123–127.

7. Tarâbîshî, in *Unthâ*, sees medicine chiefly as the line between life and death: "Was it [medicine] not chosen as a profession because it permits its practitioner to live with death on a daily basis and to stand night and day on the threshold separating it and life?" (p. 66). This point is an excellent example of the methodological weakness of Tarâbîshî's approach. One *could* choose medicine for this reason, but there is no real evidence in El Saadawi's corpus, nor does Tarâbîshî adduce any, for such an interpretation.

8. See Philippe Lejeune, *Le pacte autobiographique* (Paris: Editions du Seuil, 1975), esp. pp. 13–46.

9. For an analysis of this novel as a feminist recasting of Tâhâ Husayn's classic autobiography, *al-Ayyâm*, see Malti-Douglas, *Woman's Body, Woman's Word*, pp. 111–129. See also Tâhâ Husayn, *al-Ayyâm*, vol. 1 (Cairo: Dâr al-Ma'ârif, 1971); translated as *An Egyptian Childhood*, trans. E. H. Paxton (Washington, D.C.: Three Continents Press, 1981).

10. On the woman's *Bildungsroman*, see Annis Pratt, *Archetypal Patterns in Women's Fiction* (Bloomington: Indiana University Press, 1981), pp. 13–37 (chapter written with Barbara White).

11. On the general importance of nature for such resolutions, see ibid., pp. 16–24. This is paralleled in a short story "I Learned Love," where village life teaches the physician narrator that people are all alike and she subsequently learns to love; Nawâl al-Sa'dâwî, "Ta'allamt al-Hubb," in *Ta'allamt al-Hubb* (Cairo: Maktabat al-Nahda al-Misriyya, 1961), pp. 7–17.

12. For an important discussion of ellipses in women's writings, see, for example, Jane Marcus, "Afterword," in Helen Zenna Smith, *Not So Quiet . . .* (New York: Feminist Press, 1989), esp. pp. 272ff.

13. Al-Sa'dâwî, *Mudhakkirât Tabîba*, p. 10/"Growing Up," p. 114; ellipses in the original. In *al-Mar'a wal-Jins*, p. 50, El Saadawi cites an almost identical passage from "a diary of a ten-year-old girl." The provenance of material from various sources, including autobiographical, does not change the autonomy and integrity of the fictional text. It is, of course, not our task here to examine the compositional process of the author.

14. Al-Sa'dâwî, *Mudhakkirât Tabîba*, pp. 5–6/"Growing Up," pp. 111–112; ellipses in the original. Cf. Malek Chebel's description for the Maghreb: "Ainsi, comparativement à la liberté complète d'expression laissée au corps masculin, celui de la petite fille est très tôt soumis à un répertoire d'interdictions. . . . Le petit garçon peut se rouler dans tous les sens, lever ses jambes en l'air, procéder à la découverte complète de son corps et apprécier précocement ses possibilités et ses limites. La fille, par contre, ne peut ni se coucher comme elle aurait probablement tendance à le faire, copiant son petit frère, ou créant des positions originales, ni lever ses jambes en l'air, ni ouvrir ses cuisses, ni écarter les genoux quand elle est assise, ni sautiller si elle est plus grande"; Malek Chebel, *Le corps dans la tradition au Maghreb* (Paris: Presses Universitaires de France, 1984), p. 23.

15. Al-Sa'dâwî, *Mudhakkirât Tabîba*, p. 9/"Growing Up," pp. 113–114.

16. Ibid., p. 12/p. 115.

17. Ibid., pp. 17–19/pp. 118–119.

18. Ibid., p. 21/p. 119; ellipses in the original.

19. This negative attitude to the mother is not an aberration on the part of El Saadawi but can be seen in other Arabic texts written by women as well. See, for example, Fadwâ Tûqân, *Rihla Jabaliyya, Rihla Sa'ba* (Amman: Dâr al-Shurûq lil-Nashr wal-Tawzî', 1985); translated as *A Mountainous Journey: An Autobiography*, trans. Olive Kenny (London: Women's Press, 1990). For further discussion, see Malti-Douglas, *Woman's Body, Woman's Word*, pp. 164ff. In fact, the mother does not get much better representation even in such modern Arabic classics as Tâhâ Husayn's autobiography, *al-Ayyâm*, and Yahyâ Haqqî's novel *Qindîl Umm Hâshim* (Cairo: al-Hay'a al-Misriyya al-'Amma lil-Kitâb, 1975), to mention but two examples. How common this might be in other nondominant literatures remains to be investigated. Suffice it to say that the Anglophone Indian writer Ved Mehta follows the same procedure. See, for example, Husayn, *al-Ayyâm* 1:6, 120, 127–134; Haqqî, *Qindîl Umm Hâshim*, pp. 57–122; Ved Mehta, *Vedi* (Oxford: Oxford University Press, 1982), p. 125. For a discussion of this phenomenon, see Fedwa Malti-Douglas, *Blindness and Autobiography: "al-Ayyâm" of Tâhâ Husayn* (Princeton: Princeton University Press, 1988), pp. 76–77; idem, "al-'Amâ fî Mir'ât al-Tarjama al-Shakhsiyya: Tâhâ Husayn wa-Ved Mehta," *Fusûl* 3, no. 4 (1983): 72–75.

20. Al-Sa'dâwî, *Mudhakkirât Tabîba*, p. 22; ellipses in the original.

21. See Husayn, *al-Ayyâm* 1:6, 120, 127–134. For a discussion of this phenomenon, see Malti-Douglas, *Blindness and Autobiography*, pp. 76–77; Malti-Douglas, "al-'Amâ fî Mir'ât al-Tarjama al-Shakhsiyya," pp. 72–75.

22. The issue of the glance becomes tied to the entire question of woman's veiling and woman's role in the contemporary Islamic world. The number of pamphlets that deal with this issue is enormous and proliferating at an incredible rate. The spread of the Islamist movement has made this issue even more salient, not only in the Middle East but in Europe as well. See also Chapter 9 below.

23. See, for example, Ibn Qayyim al-Jawziyya, *Hukm al-Nazar lil-Nisâ'* (Cairo: Maktab al-Turâth al-Islâmî, 1982); also Malti-Douglas, *Woman's Body, Woman's Word*, pp. 43ff.

24. Mernissi, *Beyond the Veil*, p. 83.

25. Yûsuf Idrîs, " 'Alâ Waraq Silûfân," in *Bayt min Lahm* (Cairo: Dâr Misr

lil-Tibâ'a, 1982), pp. 31–51; translated by Roger Allen as "In Cellophane Wrapping," in *In the Eye of the Beholder: Tales of Egyptian Life from the Writings of Yusuf Idris*, ed. Roger Allen (Minneapolis and Chicago: Bibliotheca Islamica, 1978), pp. 169–189.

26. Nawâl al-Sa'dâwî, *al-Ghâ'ib* (Cairo: Maktabat Madbûlî, n.d.), p. 18; translated as *Searching*, trans. Shirley Eber (London: Zed Books, 1991).

27. Al-Sa'dâwî, *Mudhakkirât Tabîba*, p. 23; ellipses in the original.

28. Hans Wehr, *A Dictionary of Modern Written Arabic*, ed. J. Milton Cowan (Ithaca: Spoken Language Services, 1976), p. 656; Ibn Manzûr, *Lisân al-'Arab* (Cairo: al-Dâr al-Misriyya lil-Ta'lîf wal-Tarjama, n.d.), 6:290–299; al-Zabîdî, *Tâj al-'Arûs*, vol. 13, ed. Husayn Nassâr (Kuwait: Matba'at Hukûmat al-Kuwayt, 1974), pp. 154–170; Ibn Sîda, *al-Muhkam wal-Muhît al-A'zam fî al-Lugha*, vol. 2, ed. 'Abd al-Sattâr Ahmad Farrâj (Cairo: Matba'at Mustafâ al-Bâbî al-Halabî, 1958), pp. 245–249.

29. Al-Sa'dâwî, *Mudhakkirât Tabîba*, pp. 6–7/"Growing Up," p. 112.

30. See, for example, Abdelwahab Bouhdiba, *La sexualité en Islam* (Paris: Presses Universitaires de France, 1979), pp. 51, 53; Ibn Manzûr, *Lisân* 6:296; al-Zabîdî, *Tâj* 13:161; Ahmad ibn Hanbal, *Ahkâm al-Nisâ'*, ed. 'Abd al-Qâdir Ahmad 'Atâ (Beirut: Dâr al-Kutub al-'Ilmiyya, 1986), pp. 29ff. For a fuller discussion of this issue, see, also, Malti-Douglas, *Woman's Body, Woman's Word*. El Saadawi herself expands the boundaries of *'awra* when, in a short story entitled "And Love Died" ("Wa-Mâta al-Hubb," in *Hanân Qalîl*, p. 83), the narrator declares that "weakness is an *'awra*."

31. Once again, the literature here is extensive, ranging from guidance books for the proper behavior of women, in which invariably *'awra* is of central concern, to legal injunctions. See, for example, the debate between Karîmân Hamza and Yusriyya Muhammad Anwar: Karîmân Hamza, *Rifqan bil-Qawârîr* (Beirut: Dâr al-Fath lil-Tibâ'a wal-Nashr, 1985), pp. 53ff.; Yusriyya Muhammad Anwar, *Mahlan . . . Yâ Sâhibat al-Qawârîr: Radd 'alâ Kitâb "Rifqan bil-Qawârîr"* (Cairo: Dâr al-I'tisâm, 1403 A.H.), pp. 61ff. I am currently completing a study on this question in contemporary Islamist discourse.

32. Al-Sa'dâwî, *Mudhakkirât Tabîba*, pp. 42–47.

33. Ibid., p. 46.

34. Pratt, *Archetypal Patterns*, p. 21.

35. Al-Sa'dâwî, *Mudhakkirât Tabîba*, pp. 24–25.

36. Ibid., p. 25; ellipses in the original.

37. Ibid., p. 26; ellipses in the original.

38. Karîmân Hamza, *Rihlatî min al-Sufûr ilâ al-Hijâb*, 2d ed. (Beirut: Dâr al-Fath lil-Tibâ'a wal-Nashr, 1986), pp. 33, 82, for example, and for the quote, p. 189. See also Fedwa Malti-Douglas, "Gender and the Uses of the Ascetic in an Islamist Text," in *Asceticism*, ed. Vincent L. Wimbush and Richard Valantasis (New York: Oxford University Press, 1995), pp. 395–411. I am currently completing a book on Hamza's and other similar works.

39. Laylâ Ba'labakkî, *Anâ Ahyâ* (Beirut: al-Maktab al-Tijârî, 1965).

40. Nancy Huston, "The Matrix of War: Mothers and Heroes," in *The Female Body in Western Culture: Contemporary Perspectives*, ed. Susan Rubin Suleiman (Cambridge, Mass.: Harvard University Press, 1986), p. 120.

41. Al-Sa'dâwî, *Mudhakkirât Tabîba*, p. 27; ellipses in the original.

42. Ibid.

43. Ibid., p. 32; ellipses in the original.

44. Ibid., p. 35.

45. Ibid., pp. 37–39.

46. Ibid., pp. 47–51.

47. Ibid., p. 51.

48. Ibid., p. 52.

49. Ibid., p. 60; ellipses in the original.

50. Ibid., p. 64.

51. Ibid., pp. 76–85.

52. Ibid., p. 106; ellipses in the original.

53. Ibid., pp. 92–110.

54. Ibid., p. 105; ellipses in the original.

55. See C. P. Snow, *The Two Cultures and A Second Look* (Cambridge: Cambridge University Press, 1986).

56. Nawâl al-Sa'dâwî, "Shay' Akhar," in *Ta'allamt al-Hubb*, pp. 71–88.

57. Nawâl al-Sa'dâwî, "Hâdhihi al-Marra," in *Ta'allamt al-Hubb*, pp. 52–61.

58. Sharîf Hatâta, *al-'Ayn Dhât al-Jafn al-Ma'danî* (Cairo: Dâr al-Thaqâfa al-Jadîda, 1981); translated as *The Eye with the Iron Lid*, trans. Sherif Hetata (London: Zed Press, n.d.).

59. Nawâl al-Sa'dâwî, *Imra'atâni fî-Mra'a* (Cairo: Maktabat Madbûlî, 1983); translated as *Two Women in One*, trans. Osman Nusairi and Jana Gough (London: al-Saqi Books, 1985).

60. This dichotomy of art and science among physician writers is by no means peculiar to Nawal El Saadawi's fiction. See, for example, Theodora R. Graham, "The Courage of His Diversity: Medicine, Writing, and William Carlos Williams," *Literature and Medicine* 2 (1983): 15; and D. Heyward Brock, "An Interview with Dannie Abse," *Literature and Medicine* 3 (1984): esp. 18.

61. Nawâl al-Sa'dâwî, "Risâla Khâssa ilâ Sadîq Fannân," in *Mawt Ma'âlî al-Wazîr Sâbiqan* (Cairo: Maktabat Madbûlî, 1980), pp. 73–87; translated as "A Private Letter to an Artist Friend" in Nawal El Saadawi, *Death of an Ex-Minister*, trans. Shirley Eber (London: Methuen, 1987), pp. 97–111.

62. Nawâl al-Sa'dâwî, *al-Khayt*, in *al-Khayt wa-'Ayn al-Hayât* (Cairo: Maktabat Madbûlî, 1972), p. 41; translated as *The Thread* in Nawal El Saadawi, *The Well of Life and the Thread*, trans. Sherif Hetata (London: Lime Tree, 1993).

63. Nawâl al-Sa'dâwî, "Kullunâ Hayârâ," in *Ta'allamt al-Hubb*, pp. 144–148.

64. Nawâl al-Sa'dâwî, "Hînamâ Akûn Tâfiha," in *Hanân Qalîl*, p. 113.

65. Al-Sa'dâwî, *Imra'atâni*, p. 119; idem, *Mudhakkirât Tabîba*, p. 35.

66. *Kitâb Alf Layla wa-Layla*, ed. Muhsin Mahdi (Leiden: E. J. Brill, 1984); *Alf Layla wa-Layla*, 2 vols. (Cairo: Matba'at Bûlâq, 1252 A.H.); Richard F. Burton, *The Book of the Thousand Nights and a Night* ("Burton Club Edition"; n.p., n.d.). See also Malti-Douglas, *Woman's Body, Woman's Word*, pp. 11–28.

67. Nawâl al-Sa'dâwî, *Imra'a 'ind Nuqtat al-Sifr* (Beirut: Dâr al-Adâb, 1979); translated as *Woman at Point Zero*, trans. Sherif Hetata (London: Zed

Press, 1983). See also Evelyne Accad and Rose Ghurayyib, *Contemporary Arab Women Writers and Poets* (Beirut: Institute for Women's Studies in the Arab World, 1985), pp. 52–55.

68. Nawâl al-Sa'dâwî, "al-Rajul Dhû al-Azrâr," in *Kânat Hiya al-Ad'af* (Cairo: Maktabat Madbûlî, 1979), pp. 115–124; translated as "The Man with Buttons" in Nawal El Saadawi, *She Has No Place in Paradise*, trans. Shirley Eber (London: Minerva, 1989), pp. 103–111.

69. There is, in fact, a story by the same title in El Saadawi's collection *Ta'allamt al-Hubb*, pp. 135–143.

70. See Malti-Douglas, *Woman's Body, Woman's Word*, pp. 11–28.

71. Nawâl al-Sa'dâwî, *'Ayn al-Hayât*, in *al-Khayt*, pp. 59–112; translated as *The Well of Life* in Nawal El Saadawi, *The Well of Life and the Thread*.

72. See, for example, Michel Foucault, *Histoire de la folie à l'âge classique* (Paris: Editions Gallimard, 1972) and *Naissance de la clinique*.

73. Nawâl al-Sa'dâwî, "Qissa min Hayât Tabîba," in *Hanân Qalîl*, pp. 117–121.

74. In *Mudhakkirât Tabîba*, pp. 85–86.

75. For an interesting study of medical narratives and case histories, see Kathryn Montgomery Hunter, *Doctors' Stories: The Narrative Structure of Medical Knowledge* (Princeton: Princeton University Press, 1991).

76. See, for example, Hasan El-Shamy, *Brother and Sister Type 872*: A Cognitive Behavioristic Analysis of a Middle Eastern Oikotype*, Folklore Monographs Series, vol. 8 (Bloomington, Ind.: Folklore Publications Group, 1979), esp. p. 36; and idem, "The Brother-Sister Syndrome in Arab Family Life, Socio-Cultural Factors in Arab Psychiatry: A Critical Review," *International Journal of Sociology of the Family* 11 (1981): 313–323, esp. p. 320.

77. For a discussion of this phenomenon in differing literary contexts, see Malti-Douglas, *Woman's Body, Woman's Word*, chaps. 3 and 9.

78. Zakariyyâ Tâmir, "al-'Urs al-Sharqî," in *al-Ra'd* (Damascus: Manshûrât Maktabat al-Nûrî, 1978), pp. 71–79.

79. Al-Sa'dâwî, *Mudhakkirât Tabîba*, pp. 66, 71.

80. Ibid., p. 76.

CHAPTER 3

1. For an insightful perspective on this Paradise-Hell duo, see Assia Djebar, Preface to Naoual el Saadaoui, *Ferdaous, une voix en enfer*, trans. Assia Trabelsi and Assia Djebar (Paris: Des Femmes, 1981), pp. 7–24.

2. Al-Sa'dâwî, *Imra'a 'ind Nuqtat al-Sifr*. See also Accad and Ghurayyib, *Contemporary Arab Women Writers*, pp. 52–55.

3. See, for example, Peter Hitchcock, *Dialogics of the Oppressed* (Minneapolis: University of Minnesota Press, 1993), pp. 25–52; and Lionnet, "Dissymmetry Embodied." Although there are a few minor points of convergence between my own analysis and that of these critics (since the essential outline of the story we discuss is the same), the basic and major differences will be clear throughout this chapter. On the matter of literary analysis of a work in translation, see Chapter 1 above. Evelyne Accad discusses this novel briefly in "Rebel-

lion, Maturity, and the Social Context: Arab Women's Special Contribution to Literature," in *Arab Women: Old Boundaries, New Frontiers*, ed. Judith E. Tucker (Bloomington: Indiana University Press, 1993), pp. 234–238.

4. See, for example, Barbara Harlow, *Resistance Literature* (New York: Methuen, 1987), p. 138.

5. Park, "Nawâl al-Sa'adâwî," p. 221.

6. Nawal El-Saadawi, Author's Preface to *Woman at Point Zero*, pp. i–iv.

7. Al-Sa'dâwî, *al-Mar'a wal-Sirâ'*, pp. 85–159.

8. Al-Sa'dâwî, *Imra'a 'ind Nuqtat al-Sifr*, p. 6.

9. Hitchcock, *Dialogics*, p. 40, repeatedly refers to him as Baroumi.

10. Al-Sa'dâwî, *Imra'a 'ind Nuqtat al-Sifr*, p. 79.

11. I am borrowing the term "sexual slavery" from Kathleen Barry's excellent study *Female Sexual Slavery* (New York: New York University Press, 1979).

12. Al-Sa'dâwî, *Imra'a 'ind Nuqtat al-Sifr*, p. 5. An earlier version of some of this material appeared in Malti-Douglas, *Woman's Body, Woman's Word*, pp. 135–140.

13. Al-Sa'dâwî, *Imra'a 'ind Nuqtat al-Sifr*, p. 11.

14. Ibid., pp. 13, 114.

15. Jane Marcus, *Virginia Woolf and the Languages of Patriarchy* (Bloomington: Indiana University Press, 1987), p. 155. See also Trinh, *Woman, Native, Other*, p. 38.

16. I have found very useful here Marilyn R. Farwell's study "Heterosexual Plots and Lesbian Subtexts: Toward a Theory of Lesbian Narrative Space," in *Lesbian Texts and Contexts: Radical Revisions*, ed. Karla Jay and Joanne Glasgow (New York: New York University Press, 1990), pp. 91–103.

17. Al-Sa'dâwî, *Imra'a 'ind Nuqtat al-Sifr*, p. 10.

18. Ibid., p. 12.

19. Ibid., p. 13. The word *thâqib* (penetrating, piercing) can be constructed in an idiom, *thâqib al-nazar*, to mean perspicacious, sharp-eyed; see Wehr, *Arabic-English Dictionary*, p. 103. That is not the way it is used here, however, where, though eyes are present, *thâqib* refers to the knife.

20. Al-Sa'dâwî, *Imra'a 'ind Nuqtat al-Sifr*, pp. 13, 15.

21. See, for example, ibid., pp. 11, 12.

22. Ibid., p. 11.

23. Ibid., pp. 13–14.

24. Ibid., p. 114.

25. Ibid., pp. 14, 114.

26. Ibid., p. 36.

27. Ibid., p. 90.

28. See Park, "Nawâl al-Sa'adâwî," p. 220.

29. Al-Sa'dâwî, *Imra'a 'ind Nuqtat al-Sifr*, pp. 54–59.

30. Ibid., p. 56.

31. Ibid., p. 78.

32. For a fascinating study of the relationship of eating (especially meat) and male power, see Carol J. Adams, *The Sexual Politics of Meat: A Feminist-Vegetarian Critical Theory* (New York: Continuum, 1991), esp. pp. 25–61.

33. Al-Sa'dâwî, *Imra'a 'ind Nuqtat al-Sifr*, p. 23.

34. Ibid., p. 50.

35. Ibid., p. 56.

36. Adams, *Sexual Politics of Meat*, p. 26.

37. Al-Sa'dâwî, *Imra'a 'ind Nuqtat al-Sifr*, p. 76.

38. Ibid., p. 76.

39. *Al-Qur'ân* (Cairo: Mustafâ al-Bâbî al-Halabî, 1966), Sûrat al-Nûr, verse 30; A. J. Arberry, *The Koran Interpreted* (New York: Macmillan, 1974), 2:49. For discussion of some of the medieval materials on the subject, see Malti-Douglas, *Woman's Body, Woman's Word*, pp. 44, 60.

40. To list the texts that deal with this topic would be to make a catalogue of almost every pamphlet or work dealing with proper female behavior and resulting from the enormous literary production of the contemporary religious revival. See, for example, Hamza, *Rifqan bil-Qawârîr*, pp. 25ff.; and Anwar, *Mahlan . . .Yâ Sâhibat al-Qawârîr*, pp. 44ff. See also Muhammad Rashîd Ridâ, *Huqûq al-Nisâ' fî al-Islâm* (Beirut: al-Maktab al-Islâmî, 1981), pp. 178–180.

41. Al-Sa'dâwî, *Imra'a 'ind Nuqtat al-Sifr*, p. 50.

42. Ibid., pp. 76–77.

43. Ibid., p. 15.

44. Cf. Bonnie Zimmerman, " 'The Dark Eye Beaming': Female Friendship in George Eliot's Fictions," in Jay and Glasgow (eds.), *Lesbian Texts*, pp. 126–144.

45. Al-Sa'dâwî, *Imra'a 'ind Nuqtat al-Sifr*, p. 59.

46. Ibid., p. 61.

47. Barry, *Female Sexual Slavery*, pp. 4–5, 86–120.

48. See, for example, Paul Bailey, *An English Madam: The Life and Work of Cynthia Payne* (London: Jonathan Cape, 1982); and Sydney Biddle Barrows with William Novak, *Mayflower Madam: The Secret Life of Sydney Biddle Barrows* (New York: Arbor House, 1986).

49. See Jeanne Cordelier and Martine Laroche, *La dérobade* (Paris: Hachette, 1976), pp. 11ff.

50. Al-Sa'dâwî, *Imra'a 'ind Nuqtat al-Sifr*, p. 16.

51. Nawâl al-Sa'dâwî, *Mawt al-Rajul al-Wahîd 'alâ al-Ard* (Cairo: Maktabat Madbûlî, 1983); translated as *God Dies by the Nile*, trans. Sherif Hetata (London: Zed Books, 1985).

52. Al-Sa'dâwî, *Imra'a 'ind Nuqtat al-Sifr*, p. 77; al-Sa'dâwî, *Mudhakkirât Tabîba*, p. 50.

53. There is, in fact, a story by that title in El Saadawi's collection *Ta'allamt*, pp. 135–143.

54. Al-Sa'dâwî, "al-Rajul Dhû al-Azrâr," in *Kânat*, pp. 115–124.

55. Ibid., p. 122; al-Sa'dâwî, *Imra'a 'ind Nuqtat al-Sifr*, p. 50.

56. Al-Sa'dâwî, "al-Rajul," in *Kânat*, pp. 118, 120.

57. Al-Sa'dâwî, *Imra'a 'ind Nuqtat al-Sifr*, p. 50.

58. Ibid., pp. 50, 52.

59. Ibid., p. 60.

60. Ibid., p. 52.

61. Ibid., p. 50.

62. Ibid., p. 106.

63. Ibid., pp. 48, 58.

64. Ibid., p. 13.

65. Ibid., pp. 85, 101.

66. Ibid., p. 99.

67. Ibid., p. 98.

68. Ibid., p. 101.

69. Ibid., p. 30.

70. Ibid.

71. Ibid., pp. 99–100.

72. Ibid., pp. 107–110.

73. Ibid., p. 110.

74. Ibid., p. 109.

75. Ibid., p. 111.

76. Ibid., p. 107.

77. Ibid., p. 60.

78. For a fuller discussion of female mutilation, see Chapter 7 below.

79. See, for example, al-Sa'dâwî, *Imra'a 'ind Nuqtat al-Sifr*, pp. 17–18, 35, 38. See also Lionnet, "Dissymmetry Embodied."

80. Al-Sa'dâwî, *Imra'a 'ind Nuqtat al-Sifr*, p. 64.

81. Ibid., p. 62.

82. Ibid., p. 51.

83. *Al-Qur'ân*, Sûrat al-Nisâ', verse 34; Arberry, *Koran Interpreted* 1:105–106.

84. See, for example, Ridâ, *Huqúq al-Nisâ'*, pp. 52–54.

85. Al-Sa'dâwî, *Imra'a 'ind Nuqtat al-Sifr*, pp. 98–99.

86. Najîb Mahfûz, *Zuqâq al-Midaqq* (Beirut: Dâr al-Qalam, 1972); translated as *Midaq Alley*, trans. Trevor Le Gassick (London: Heinemann, 1966). See also Khalid Kishtainy, *The Prostitute in Progressive Literature* (London: Allison & Busby, 1982), pp. 63–73; Evelyne Accad, "The Prostitute in Arab and North African Fiction," in *The Image of the Prostitute in Modern Literature*, ed. Pierre L. Horn and Mary Beth Pringle (New York: Frederick Ungar, 1984), pp. 63–75; Miriam Cooke, "Men Constructed in the Mirror of Prostitution," in *Naguib Mahfouz: From Regional Fame to Global Recognition*, ed. Michael Beard and Adnan Haydar (Syracuse: Syracuse University Press, 1993), pp. 106–125.

87. Amy Katz Kaminsky, "Women Writing About Prostitutes: Amalia Jamilis and Luisa Valenzuela," in Horn and Pringle (eds.), *Image of the Prostitute*, pp. 119–131.

88. Emile Benveniste, "La nature des pronoms," in *Problèmes de linguistique générale*, vol. 1 (Paris: Gallimard, 1966), pp. 252–257.

89. See Michael Riffaterre, "Intertextual Scrambling," *Romanic Review* 68 (1977): 197–206.

90. Al-Sa'dâwî, *Imra'a 'ind Nuqtat al-Sifr*, p. 96.

91. Ibid., pp. 6, 109.

92. Ibid., p. 79.

CHAPTER 4

1. Nawâl al-Sa'dâwî, *Ughniyyat al-Atfâl al-Dâ'iriyya* (Cairo: Maktabat Mad-bûlî, 1978); translated as *The Circling Song* (London: Zed Books, 1989). The literal translation of the Arabic title is "The Children's Circular Song."

2. Nawal El Saadawi, Personal Communication, April 14, 1993. See also Nawal El Saadawi, Author's Introduction to *The Circling Song*, p. 2.

3. Al-Sa'dâwî, *Ughniyyat al-Atfâl*, p. 43.

4. Ibid., p. 11.

5. Ibid., pp. 15–19.

6. Ibid., p. 15.

7. Ibid., p. 41.

8. Ibid., p. 42.

9. Ibid., p. 43.

10. Ibid., pp. 18–19, 44.

11. Ibid., p. 43.

12. It is unfortunate that this parallel is missing in the English translation (*The Circling Song*, p. 32).

13. See Susan Brownmiller, *Against Our Will: Men, Women, and Rape* (New York: Bantam Books, 1986), esp. pp. 297–300.

14. Al-Sa'dâwî, *Ughniyyat al-Atfâl*, pp. 76–81.

15. Ibid., p. 44.

16. Yûsuf Idrîs, "al-'Amaliyya al-Kubrâ," in *al-Naddâha* (Cairo: Dâr Misr lil-Tibâ'a, 1982), pp. 113–137.

17. Al-Sa'dâwî, *Ughniyyat al-Atfâl*, p. 17.

18. Ibid., p. 44.

19. For an edifying children's story in which the male hero, known as al-Fahd (the Panther/Cheetah), is an extremely positive figure, see the Syrian children's magazine *Usâma*, 1982/334–1983/347–348. For a discussion of this story, see Douglas and Malti-Douglas, *Arab Comic Strips*, pp. 125–126.

20. Al-Sa'dâwî, *Ughniyyat al-Atfâl*, p. 77.

21. Ibid.

22. Ibid., p. 63.

23. On the poetry of Najm, see Kamal Abdel-Malek, *A Study of the Vernacular Poetry of Ahmad Fu'âd Nigm* (Leiden: E. J. Brill, 1990). Food imagery and its class connections are quite prevalent in Najm's corpus.

24. Food is an important element in much of Ahmad Hijâzî's comic-strip work; see, for example, *Tambûl al-Awwal* (Beirut: Dâr al-Fatâ al-'Arabî, 1981). For a discussion of food in Hijâzî's work, see Douglas and Malti-Douglas, *Arab Comic Strips*, pp. 61–82.

25. Yûsuf al-Qa'îd, *al-Harb fî Barr Misr* (Beirut: Dâr Ibn Rushd lil-Tibâ'a wal-Nashr, 1978), p. 62; translated as *War in the Land of Egypt*, trans. Olive Kenny, Lorne Kenny, and Christopher Tingley (London: al-Saqi Books, 1986). The Arabic has *yatrukunâ*, which is probably a typographical error for *yatrukuhâ*. See also idem, *Yahduth fî Misr al-An* (Cairo: Dâr Usâma lil-Tab' wal-Nashr, 1977); Fedwa Malti-Douglas, "Yûsuf al-Qa'îd wal-Riwâya al-

Jadîda," *Fusûl* 4, no. 3 (1984): 190–202; and idem, Afterword to *War in the Land of Egypt*, pp. 185–192.

26. Al-Qa'îd, *al-Harb fî Barr Misr*, pp. 72–73.

27. See Tâhâ Husayn, *al-Ayyâm*, vol. 3 (Cairo: Dâr al-Ma'ârif, 1973), pp. 68, 76–77; translated as *A Passage to France*, trans. Kenneth Cragg (Leiden: E. J. Brill, 1976). I have discussed incidents involving eating and their social importance elsewhere; see Malti-Douglas, *Blindness and Autobiography*, pp. 41ff.

28. See Malti-Douglas, Afterword to *War in the Land of Egypt*, pp. 185–192.

29. Al-Sa'dâwî, *Ughniyyat al-Atfâl*, pp. 30–31.

30. Ibid., pp. 20–35.

31. For these ballads, see Pierre Cachia, *Popular Narrative Ballads of Modern Egypt* (Oxford: Clarendon Press, 1989), pp. 269–322. According to my colleague and friend Hasan M. El-Shamy, the murderous brother is a common figure in Arab folklore generally.

32. Laylâ Abû Sayf, "New Ballads for Old," Public Lecture delivered at U.C.L.A. For a more traditional rewriting, see Shawqî 'Abd al-Hakîm, "Shafîqa wa-Mutawallî," in Shawqî 'Abd al-Hakîm, *Malik 'Ajûz* (Cairo: al-Dâr al-Qawmiyya lil-Tibâ'a wal-Nashr, n.d.), pp. 124–159.

33. Najîb Mahfûz, *Bidâya wa-Nihâya* (Beirut: Dâr al-Qalam, 1971).

34. See, for example, Hasan M. El-Shamy, "The Traditional Structure of Sentiments in Mahfouz's Trilogy: A Behavioristic Text Analysis," *al-'Arabiyya* 9 (1976): 53–74.

35. Al-Sa'dâwî, *Ughniyyat al-Atfâl*, pp. 105–106.

36. See, for example, Luciano P. R. Santiago, M.D., *The Children of Oedipus: Brother-Sister Incest in Psychiatry, Literature, History, and Mythology* (Roslyn Heights, N.Y.: Libra, 1973).

37. See, for example, El-Shamy, *Brother and Sister Type 872*, esp. p. 36, for the jealous brother; idem, "Brother-Sister Syndrome," pp. 313–323, esp. p. 320. For a discussion of this phenomenon in differing literary contexts, see Malti-Douglas, *Woman's Body, Woman's Word*, chaps. 3 and 9.

38. Al-Sa'dâwî, *Ughniyyat al-Atfâl*, pp. 34–35.

39. Ibid., p. 43.

40. Ibid., p. 54.

41. See, for example, ibid., p. 9.

42. Ibid., p. 31.

43. See, for example, ibid., pp. 57, 84.

44. Ibid., p. 66.

45. Ibid., p. 95.

46. Ibid., pp. 70–71.

47. Ibid., p. 57. For a discussion of cross-dressing, see Chapter 9 below.

48. Al-Sa'dâwî, *Ughniyyat al-Atfâl*, p. 56.

49. Ibid., pp. 56–57.

50. See El-Shamy, *Brother and Sister Type 872*.

51. Judith Butler, *Gender Trouble: Feminism and the Subversion of Identity* (New York: Routledge, 1990).

52. See, for example, Jean-Paul Charnay, "Communication et société: variations sur parole, amour et cuisine dans la culture arabe," in *L'ambivalence dans la culture arabe*, ed. Jacques Berque and Jean-Paul Charnay (Paris: Editions Anthropos, 1967), pp. 184–185; Paula Sanders, "Gendering the Ungendered Body: Hermaphrodites in Medieval Islamic Law," in *Women in Middle Eastern History: Shifting Boundaries in Sex and Gender*, ed. Nikki R. Keddie and Beth Baron (New Haven: Yale University Press, 1991), pp. 74–95.

53. See, for example, al-Sakhâwî, *al-Daw' al-Lâmi' li-Ahl al-Qarn al-Tâsi'* (Beirut: Manshûrât Dâr Maktabat al-Hayât, n.d.), 12:93–94.

54. See Ursula K. Le Guin, *The Left Hand of Darkness* (New York: Ace Books, 1969).

55. Tahar Ben Jelloun, *L'enfant de sable* (Paris: Editions du Seuil, 1985); idem, *La nuit sacrée* (Paris: Editions du Seuil, 1987).

56. Al-Sa'dâwî, *Ughniyyat al-Atfâl*, p. 115.

57. See Chapter 9 for a detailed discussion of cross-dressing and its heterodox nature in the Arabo-Islamic cultural sphere.

58. Ibid., pp. 118–120.

59. Ibid., pp. 74–75, 105.

60. Ibid., p. 121.

61. "Al-'âr mâ bi-yighsilush illâ al-dam" is the existing dialectical variant of the father's order in El Saadawi's text. I am grateful to Hasan M. El-Shamy for this information.

62. Al-Sa'dâwî, *Ughniyyat al-Atfâl*, p. 100.

63. Ibid., p. 106.

64. Ibid., pp. 57, 59, 82, to mention but three examples.

65. Ibid., p. 73.

66. Ibid., p. 28.

67. Ibid., p. 11.

68. Ibid., p. 32.

69. Ibid., pp. 9–10.

70. Ibid., pp. 9–10, 122–123.

CHAPTER 5

1. For an excellent analysis of patriarchy, see Gerda Lerner, *The Creation of Patriarchy* (New York: Oxford University Press, 1986).

2. Hafez, "Intentions and Realisation," pp. 192–196.

3. See, for example, Augustus Richard Norton, *Amal and the Shi'a: Struggle for the Soul of Lebanon* (Austin: University of Texas Press, 1987), pp. 102ff.

4. Al-Sa'dâwî, *Suqût*, p. 73.

5. Ibid., p. 73.

6. Ibid., p. 41.

7. Ibid., p. 35.

8. For an introduction to the complex Arabo-Islamic onomastic system, see, for example, Annemarie Schimmel, *Islamic Names* (Edinburgh: Edinburgh University Press, 1989). For the semiotic complexities of this system, see Fedwa Malti-Douglas, "Sign Conceptions in the Islamic World," in *Semiotics: A Hand-*

*book on the Sign-Theoretic Foundations of Nature and Culture*, ed. Roland Posner, Klaus Robering, and Thomas E. Sebeok (Berlin and New York: Walter de Gruyter, forthcoming). The name Ni'mat, short for Ni'mat Allâh, is very common in Egypt but less common in other Arab countries. I have known Egyptian women named Ni'mat, and El Saadawi's maternal aunt bore that name (El Saadawi, Personal Interview, Bloomington, April 15, 1993).

9. Norton, *Amal*, p. 103.

10. The old grandmother uses this phrase in *Suqût al-Imâm*, p. 54. Peter J. Awn, in his excellent work *Satan's Tragedy and Redemption: Iblis in Sufi Psychology* (Leiden: E. J. Brill, 1983), translates this phrase as "I seek refuge in God from Satan the Stoned" (p. 19).

11. John L. Esposito, *Islam: The Straight Path* (New York and Oxford: Oxford University Press, 1991), p. 89.

12. Ibid., pp. 84–85.

13. *Al-Qur'ân*, Sûrat al-Ikhlâs, verses 1–3; Arberry, *Koran Interpreted* 2:353. The Saadawian text is missing part of these verses, a literary accident not without significance, as we shall see.

14. Al-Sa'dâwî, *Suqût*, p. 26.

15. Ibid., p. 112.

16. *Al-Qur'ân*, Sûrat al-Nahl, verses 57–58; Arberry, *Koran Interpreted* 1:292. For commentaries on these verses, see, for example, al-Baydâwî, *Tafsîr al-Baydâwî/Anwâr al-Tanzîl wa-Asrâr al-Ta'wîl* (Beirut: Dâr al-Kutub al-'Ilmiyya, 1988), 1:547–548; al-Qurtubî, *al-Jâmi' li-Ahkâm al-Qur'ân* (Cairo: Dâr al-Kitâb al-'Arabî lil-Tibâ'a wal-Nashr, 1967), 10:116.

17. Nawal El Saadawi, Personal Communication, Cairo, January 11, 1988. See also El Saadawi's preface to *Fall of the Imam*.

18. Hafez, "Intentions and Realisation," p. 195.

19. Al-Sa'dâwî, *Suqût*, p. 34.

20. *Al-Qur'ân*, Sûrat Yûsuf.

21. For Joseph as the paragon of beauty, see, for example, al-Tha'âlibî, *Thimâr al-Qulûb fî al-Mudâf wal-Mansûb*, ed. Muhammad Abû al-Fadl Ibrâhîm (Cairo: Dâr al-Ma'ârif, 1985), p. 49.

22. *Kitâb Alf Layla wa-Layla*, ed. Mahdi, 1:64. See also, for example, Najîb Mahfûz, "Kayduhunna," in *Hams al-Junûn* (Beirut: Dâr al-Qalam, 1973), pp. 79–89; Na'îm 'Atiyya, "Kayduhunna 'Azîm," in *Nisâ' fî al-Mahâkim* (Cairo: Dâr al-Ma'ârif, 1980), pp. 82–88. Cf. the lines by Ghazi A. Algosaibi: "Here, life is a virgin still / who did not learn deceit / or woman's clever wiles" (*From the Orient and the Desert* [London: Oriel Press, 1977], p. 1). For an analysis, see Malti-Douglas, *Woman's Body, Woman's Word*, pp. 17–19, 22, 53–56.

23. Al-Sa'dâwî, *Suqût*, p. 112.

24. See, for example, al-Tirmidhî, *Sahîh al-Tirmidhî*, vol. 5 (Cairo: al-Matba'a al-Misriyya bil-Azhar, 1931), pp. 120–121; vol. 9 (Cairo: Matba'at al-Sâwî, 1934), pp. 8–10. For another modern example, see Idrîs, "al-'Amaliyya al-Kubrâ," p. 120. This *hadîth* also acts almost as a refrain in Karîmân Hamza's contemporary guide to the Muslim woman, *Rifqan bil-Qawârîr*, pp. 17–50.

25. Al-Sa'dâwî, *Suqût*, pp. 63–64.

26. Ibid., pp. 123–124.

27. Abû al-ʿAlâʾ al-Maʿarrî, *Risâlat al-Ghufrân*, ed. ʿAʾisha ʿAbd al-Rahmân (Cairo: Dâr al-Maʿârif, 1963).

28. Suzanne Pinckney Stetkevych, "Intoxication and Immortality: Wine and Associated Imagery in al-Maʿarrî's Garden," *Literature East and West* 25 (1989): 31 (special issue entitled "Critical Pilgrimages: Studies in the Arabic Literary Tradition," ed. Fedwa Malti-Douglas).

29. Al-Maʿarrî, *Risâlat al-Ghufrân*, pp. 261–262.

30. Al-Saʿdâwî, *Suqût*, p. 124.

31. Ibid., p. 14.

32. Ibid., pp. 83–88.

33. With regard to this highly ambivalent Saadawian narrative context in which artificial insemination surfaces alongside the Virgin Birth, cf. Mary Jacobus: "Ironically, the first artificial family was the Holy Family" ("In Parenthesis: Immaculate Conceptions and Feminine Desire," in *Body/Politics: Women and the Discourses of Science*, ed. Mary Jacobus, Evelyn Fox Keller, and Sally Shuttleworth [New York: Routledge, 1990], p. 21).

34. Al-Saʿdâwî, *Suqût*, p. 88.

35. See, for example, ibid., p. 85.

36. El Saadawi herself repeated these long-standing accusations to me in a telephone conversation on May 13, 1991. See also Chapter 1 above.

37. Katharine Burdekin, *Swastika Night* (New York: Feminist Press, 1985).

38. Al-Saʿdâwî, *Suqût*, p. 15.

39. Margaret Atwood, *The Handmaid's Tale* (New York: Ballantine Books, 1985).

40. Katharine Burdekin, *The End of This Day's Business* (New York: Feminist Press, 1989). Katherine V. Forrest, *Daughters of a Coral Dawn* (Tallahassee: Naiad Press, 1989). See also the special issue entitled "Feminism Faces the Fantastic," *Women's Studies* 14, no. 2 (1987); and Ruby Rohrlich and Elaine Hoffman Baruch, eds., *Women in Search of Utopia: Mavericks and Mythmakers* (New York: Schocken Books, 1984).

41. Charlotte Perkins Gilman, *Herland* (New York: Pantheon Books, 1979).

42. Joanna Russ, *The Female Man* (Boston: Beacon Press, 1975).

43. Burton, *Thousand Nights and a Night*; Georges May, *Les mille et une nuits d'Antoine Galland* (Paris: Presses Universitaires de France, 1986). On the questionable nature of May's entire enterprise, see Fedwa Malti-Douglas, Review of *Les mille et une nuits d'Antoine Galland*, by Georges May, *Journal of the American Oriental Society* 111, no. 1 (1991): 196.

44. John Barth, *Chimera* (New York: Fawcett Crest Books, 1972), pp. 9–64; Tawfîq al-Hakîm, *Shahrazâd* (Cairo: Maktabat al-Adâb, n.d.); Ethel Johnston Phelps, "Scheherazade Retold," in *The Maid of the North: Feminist Folk Tales from Around the World* (New York: Henry Holt, 1981), pp. 167–173; Edgar Allan Poe, "The Thousand-and-Second Tale of Scheherazade," in *Short Stories*, Greenwich Unabridged Library Classics (New York: Chatham River Press, 1981), pp. 491–502. See also Fedwa Malti-Douglas, "Shahrazâd Feminist," in *The Thousand and One Nights in Arabic Literature and Society*, ed. Fedwa Malti-Douglas and Georges Sabagh (Cambridge: Cambridge University Press, forthcoming). John Barth, of course, took on

another story cycle in *The Last Voyage of Somebody the Sailor* (Boston: Little, Brown, 1991).

45. *Kitâb Alf Layla wa-Layla*, ed. Mahdi, 1:56–72. Mahdi's edition does not contain the epilogue of the frame. See also *Alf Layla wa-Layla*, Bûlâq edition, 1:2–6, 2:619; and Burton, *Book of the Thousand Nights* 1:1–24, 10:54–62. For a gendered reading of the frame of the *Nights*, see Malti-Douglas, *Woman's Body, Woman's Word*, pp. 11–28.

46. Al-Sa'dâwî, *Suqût*, p. 83.

47. Ibid., p. 85.

48. One could argue about whether *The Thousand and One Nights*, which was not originally a high cultural product, should be included in the *turâth*. What matters here is that many today do include it, as does this narrator in *Suqût al-Imâm*.

49. Al-Sa'dâwî, *Suqût*, pp. 93–96.

50. Ibid., p. 94.

51. See Malti-Douglas, *Woman's Body, Woman's Word*, pp. 11–28. Cf. Bernard Lewis, *Race and Slavery in the Middle East: An Historical Enquiry* (New York: Oxford University Press, 1990), pp. 19–20.

52. Al-Sa'dâwî, *Suqût*, p. 94.

53. In certain medieval anecdotes, it is clear that physically sharing her husband with another wife was not something a woman relished. See, for example, al-Râghib al-Isfahânî, *Muhâdarât al-Udabâ' wa-Muhâwarât al-Shu'arâ' wal-Bulaghâ'* (Beirut: Dâr Maktabat al-Hayât, n.d.), 2:267; and for a discussion, Malti-Douglas, *Woman's Body, Woman's Word*, pp. 40–41.

54. Al-Sa'dâwî, *Suqût*, p. 53.

55. See Malti-Douglas, *Woman's Body, Woman's Word*, pp. 11–12.

56. For a comparative analysis of the Saadawian transformation of *The Thousand and One Nights* vis-à-vis that of Ethel Johnston Phelps, see Malti-Douglas, "Shahrazâd Feminist."

57. *Kitâb Alf Layla* 1:66.

58. Malti-Douglas, *Woman's Body, Woman's Word*, pp. 11–28.

59. Fatima Mernissi, *Chahrazad n'est pas marocaine* (Casablanca: Editions Le Fennec, 1988), p. 9.

60. Malti-Douglas, *Woman's Body, Woman's Word*, pp. 11–28.

61. Al-Sa'dâwî, *Suqût*, pp. 93–96.

62. Ibid., p. 99.

63. Ibid., p. 91.

64. Ibid., pp. 53–54.

65. Ibid., p. 97.

66. For a list of such transformations, see Nikita Elisséeff, *Thèmes et motifs des milles et une nuits: essai de classification* (Beirut: Institut Français de Damas, 1949), pp. 142–143.

67. Al-Sa'dâwî, *Suqût*, pp. 100–101.

68. For a fascinating study of the metaphors of incorporation, see Maggie Kilgour, *From Communion to Cannibalism: An Anatomy of Metaphors of Incorporation* (Princeton: Princeton University Press, 1990).

69. Al-Sa'dâwî, *Suqût*, p. 100.

70. The informed reader may also notice a potential incongruity, since the phrase in question appears to place together holy sites that are in two different cities. Combining them on a carpet would not, however, be unusual.

71. Al-Sa'dâwî, *Suqût*, p. 11.

72. Ibid., p. 14.

73. R. Paret, "Ashâb al-Kahf," *EI²*.

74. *Al-Qur'ân*, Sûrat al-Kahf, verses 9–26; Arberry, *Koran Interpreted* 1:316–319. For a commentary on these verses, see, for example, al-Baydâwî, *Tafsîr* 2:4–10; al-Qurtubî, *al-Jâmi'* 10:356–390. For an analysis of this *sûra*, see Mohammed Arkoun, "Lecture de la sourate 18," *Annales: Economies, sociétés, civilisations* 35, nos. 3–4 (1980): 418–435.

75. François Jourdan, *La tradition des Septs dormants: une rencontre entre Chrétiens et Musulmans* (Paris: Editions Maisonneuve & Larose, 1983).

76. The story of the Ahl al-Kahf recounted by 'Alî is but one of a series of answers he gives to queries addressed to him by three Jews, two of whom convert after their questions are answered. It is the third convert-to-be who demands the story of the Ashâb al-Kahf. See Al-Tha'labî, *Qisas al-Anbiyâ'/'Arâ'is al-Majâlis* (Beirut: Dâr al-Qalam, n.d.), pp. 413–416. The entire account is on pp. 411–428.

77. Al-Sa'dâwî, *Suqût*, p. 33.

78. Ibid., pp. 121–128.

79. Ibid., p. 34.

80. See, for example, René Girard, *Le bouc émissaire* (Paris: Editions Grasset & Fasquelle, 1982); idem, *La violence et le sacré* (Paris: Editions Bernard Grasset, 1972), esp. pp. 68, 125, 180.

81. Cf. Jourdan, *Tradition*, p. 113; al-Sa'dâwî, *Suqût*, p. 14.

82. Al-Sa'dâwî, *Suqût*, pp. 26–27.

83. Ibid., p. 69.

84. I am grateful to Jaroslav Stetkevych and Suzanne Pinckney Stetkevych for information on this question. See also T. Emil Homerin, "Echoes of a Thirsty Owl: Death and Afterlife in Pre-Islamic Arabic Poetry," *Journal of Near Eastern Studies* 44, no. 3 (1985): 165–184.

85. *Al-Qur'ân*, Sûrat al-Falaq, verses 1–4; Arberry, *Koran Interpreted* 2:354.

86. Al-Sa'dâwî, *Suqût*, p. 26.

87. Jalâl al-Dîn al-Mahallî and Jalâl al-Dîn al-Suyûtî, *Tafsîr al-Qur'ân* (Cairo: Mustafâ al-Bâbî al-Halabî, 1966), 2:381; al-Baydâwî, *Tafsîr* 2:632–633; al-Qurtubî, *al-Jâmi'* 20:257–259.

88. Al-Sa'dâwî, *Suqût*, pp. 55ff.

89. Mûsâ Sâlih Sharaf, *Fatâwâ al-Nisâ' al-'Asriyya* (Beirut: Dâr al-Jîl; Cairo: Maktabat al-Turâth al-Islâmî, 1988), pp. 176–177.

90. Al-Sa'dâwî, *Suqût*, p. 34.

91. *Al-Qur'ân*, Sûrat al-Falaq, verse 5; Arberry, *Koran Interpreted* 2:356.

92. *Al-Qur'ân*, Sûrat al-Anbiyâ', verse 35; Arberry, *Koran Interpreted* 2:19.

93. Al-Sa'dâwî, *Suqût*, pp. 119–120.

94. Ibid., p. 75.

95. Nawâl al-Sa'dâwî, "Mawt Ma'âlî al-Wazîr Sâbiqan," in *Mawt Ma'âlî al-Wazîr*, translated by Shirley Eber as "The Death of His Excellency the Ex-Minister," in *Death of an Ex-Minister*, pp. 17–18.

96. Al-Khatîb al-Baghdâdî, *al-Bukhalâ'*, ed. Ahmad Matlûb, Khadîja al-Hadîthî, and Ahmad Nâjî al-Qaysî (Baghdad: Matbaʿat al-ʿAnî, 1964), pp. 75–76.

97. *Al-Qur'ân*, Sûrat al-Tîn, verses 1–2; Arberry, *Koran Interpreted* 2:343.

98. See Malti-Douglas, *Woman's Body, Woman's Word*, chap. 2; idem, "Playing with the Sacred: Religious Intertext in *Adab* Discourse," in *Language and Cultural Context in the Near East*, ed. Asma Afsaruddin, Matt Zahniser, and Karl Stowasser (Winona Lake, Ind.: Eisenbrauns, forthcoming).

99. See, for example, Jamâl al-Ghîtânî, *al-Zaynî Barakât* (Cairo: Maktabat Madbûlî, 1975); idem, *Khitat al-Ghîtânî* (Cairo: Dâr al-Masîra, 1981).

100. Muhammad Mustajâb, *Min al-Ta'rîkh al-Sirrî li-Nuʿmân ʿAbd al-Hâfiz* (Cairo: Maktab al-Nîl lil-Tabʿ wal-Nashr, 1982), p. 4. See also Fedwa Malti-Douglas, "*Min al-Ta'rîkh al-Sirrî li-Nuʿmân ʿAbd al-Hâfiz* wa-Tadmîr Tuqûs al-Hayât wal-Lugha," *Ibdâ'* 1, nos. 6–7 (1983): 86–92.

101. Imîl Habîbî, *Ikhtayyi* (Cyprus: Kitâb al-Karmil, 1985), p. 9. See also Saʿîd ʿAllûsh, *'Unf al-Mutakhayyil fî Aʿmâl Imîl Habîbî* (Casablanca: al-Muʾassasa al-Hadîtha lil-Nashr wal-Tawzîʿ, 1986).

102. Mahmûd al-Misʿadî, *Haddatha Abû Hurayra Qâl* (Tunis: Dâr al-Janûb lil-Nashr, 1979). See also Mahmûd Tarshûna, *al-Adab al-Murîd fî Muʾallafât al-Misʿadî* (Tunis: La Maghrébine pour l'Impression, l'Edition et la Publicité, 1989).

103. Najîb Mahfûz, "Ra'aytu fîmâ Yarâ al-Nâ'im," in *Ra'aytu fîmâ Yarâ al-Nâ'im* (Beirut: Maktabat Misr, 1982), pp. 139–173. See also Fedwa Malti-Douglas, "Mahfouz's Dreams," in Beard and Haydar (eds.), *Naguib Mahfouz*, pp. 126–143.

104. Assia Djebar, *Loin de Médine* (Paris: Albin Michel, 1991). I discussed these and other questions relating to the rewriting of the *turâth* with Djebar as she was writing this novel (Assia Djebar, Personal Interview, Madison, Wisconsin, July 25, 1990). At the time, she had already published one chapter, which she was kind enough to share with me: "Celle qui dit non à Médine," *Algérie-Actualité*, no. 1273 (March 8–14, 1990).

105. Al-Saʿdâwî, *Suqût*, p. 86.

106. See, for example, Marina Warner, *Alone of All Her Sex: The Myth and the Cult of the Virgin Mary* (New York: Vintage Books, 1983), p. 208.

107. Al-Qurtubî, *al-Jâmi'* 20:251.

108. See, for example, ibid., p. 246. Cf. W. Montgomery Watt, *Companion to the Qur'ân* (London: George Allen & Unwin, 1967), p. 332; Watt writes that "*has not begotten*: presumably directed against the Arabian pagan belief in 'daughters of God.'"

CHAPTER 6

1. Nawâl al-Saʿdâwî, *Jannât wa-Iblîs* (Beirut: Dâr al-Adâb, 1992); translated as *The Innocence of the Devil*, trans. Sherif Hetata (London: Methuen; Berkeley and Los Angeles: University of California Press, 1994).

2. Some of these issues are discussed in Fedwa Malti-Douglas, "Introduction to *The Innocence of the Devil*: From Theology to Rape," in El Saadawi, *Innocence*, University of California Press ed., pp. vii–xlv.

3. I have discussed this issue with Nawal El Saadawi on many occasions.

4. Nawal El Saadawi, Personal Communication, April 14, 1993.

5. See the fascinating study by Elaine Showalter, *The Female Malady: Women, Madness, and English Culture, 1830–1980* (New York: Pantheon Books, 1985), esp. pp. 195–219. See also Hanân al-Shaykh, *Hikâyat Zahra* (Beirut:Dâr al-Adâb, 1989); translated as *The Story of Zahra* (New York: Anchor Books, 1994).

6. Al-Sa'dâwî, *Jannât wa-Iblîs*, p. 178.

7. Ibid., p. 11.

8. Ibid., p. 18.

9. See, for example, Muhammad Fu'âd 'Abd al-Bâqî, *al-Mu'jam al-Mufahras li-Alfâz al-Qur'ân al-Karîm* (Beirut: Mu'assasat Jamâl lil-Nashr, n.d.), pp. 180–182. For an analysis of how the medieval writer Abû al-'Alâ' al-Ma'arrî exploits some of these materials, see Stetkevych, "Intoxication and Immortality," pp. 29–48.

10. *Al-Qur'ân*, Sûrat Muhammad, verse 15; Arberry, *Koran Interpreted* 2:221.

11. See, for example, al-Mahallî and al-Suyûtî, *Tafsîr al-Qur'ân* 2:251–252; al-Tabarî, *Tafsîr al-Tabarî—Jâmi' al-Bayân fî Ta'wîl al-Qur'ân* (Beirut: Dâr al-Kutub al-'Ilmiyya, 1992), 11:313–314; al-Baydâwî, *Tafsîr* 2:402–403.

12. For a list of these verses, see 'Abd al-Bâqî, *al-Mu'jam al-Mufahras*, p. 182.

13. Al-Sa'dâwî, *Jannât wa-Iblîs*, p. 13.

14. Ibid., p. 98.

15. Ibid., pp. 156–157.

16. Ibid., pp. 158–160. The verses are from Sûrat al-Najm.

17. See, for example, F. de Saussure, *Cours de linguistique générale* (Paris: Payot, 1978), pp. 97–113.

18. *Al-Qur'ân*, Sûrat al-Najm, verses 19, 20, 27.

19. See T. Fahd, "al-Lât," *EI²*.

20. Al-Sa'dâwî, *Jannât wa-Iblîs*, pp. 22–23, 70–71.

21. Ibid., p. 20.

22. Ibid., p. 39.

23. Ibid., p. 65.

24. Ibid., p. 66.

25. See, for example, W. Montgomery Watt, *Islamic Philosophy and Theology* (Edinburgh: Edinburgh University Press, 1962), pp. 58–81; Cl. Huart and J. Sadan, "Kursî," *EI²*.

26. Ibn al-Jawzî, *Akhbâr al-Adhkiyâ'*, ed. Muhammad Mursî al-Khawlî (Cairo: Matâbi' al-Ahrâm al-Tijâriyya, 1970), pp. 208–209. For a discussion of this anecdote, see Fedwa Malti-Douglas, "Classical Arabic Crime Narratives: Thieves and Thievery in *Adab* Literature," *Journal of Arabic Literature* 19 (1988): 114–115.

27. See, for example, Ibn al-Jawzî, *Ahkâm al-Nisâ'* (Beirut: Dâr al-Kutub al-'Ilmiyya, 1985), pp. 33, 65–66. See also al-Tirmidhî, *al-Jâmi' al-Sahîh—Sunan al-Tirmidhî*, vol. 3, ed. Muhammad Fu'âd 'Abd al-Bâqî (Beirut: Dâr al-Kutub al-'Ilmiyya, 1987), p. 476; al-Maydânî, *Majma' al-Amthâl* (Beirut: Dâr

Maktabat al-Hayât, n.d.), 2:390; al-Tha'âlibî, *al-Tamthîl wal-Muhâdara*, ed. 'Abd al-Fattâh Muhammad al-Hulw (Cairo: 'Isâ al-Bâbî al-Halabî, 1961), p. 215. For a detailed discussion of these materials, see Malti-Douglas, *Woman's Body, Woman's Word*, pp. 48–49, 59.

28. Ibn al-Jawzî, *Talbîs Iblîs* (Cairo: Maktabat al-Mutanabbî, n.d.), pp. 402–404.

29. See, for example, Samîra 'Itânî, *Hal Sahîh anna Akthar Ahl al-Nâr Hum al-Nisâ'?* (Beirut: Dâr al-Fath lil-Tibâ'a wal-Nashr, 1979[?]); 'A'id ibn 'Abd Allâh al-Qarnî, *Makâ'id al-Shaytân* (Riyad: Dâr al-Diyâ' lil-Nashr wal-Tawzî', 1411 A.H.); and idem, *Bâqat Ward ilâ Fatât al-Islâm* (Riyad: Dâr al-Diyâ' lil-Nashr wal-Tawzî', 1411 A.H.), p. 29.

30. See, for example, Esposito, *Islam*, p. 14.

31. Al-Sa'dâwî, *Jannât wa-Iblîs*, pp. 66–67; and for the translation of the Qur'ânic verse, Arberry, *Koran Interpreted* 2:353.

32. The translation (El Saadawi, *Innocence*, p. 84) identifies this as the "first verse of the Koran," which is incorrect.

33. Al-Sa'dâwî, *Suqût al-Imâm*, p. 26; idem, *Jannât wa-Iblîs*, p. 73; Arberry, *Koran Interpreted* 2:353.

34. Al-Sa'dâwî, *Jannât wa-Iblîs*, p. 59.

35. Ibid., p. 78.

36. Ibid., p. 122.

37. Ibid., p. 90.

38. Ibid., p. 151.

39. Ibid., p. 35.

40. Ibid., pp. 36–37.

41. Ibid., p. 40.

42. For a brief overview of Abraham in the Muslim tradition, see R. Paret, "Ibrâhîm," *EI²*.

43. Al-Sa'dâwî, *Jannât wa-Iblîs*, p. 134.

44. The English translation (El Saadawi, *Innocence*, pp. 173) has "Lot's mother," which is incorrect.

45. Al-Sa'dâwî, *Jannât wa-Iblîs*, pp. 134–135.

46. For one reading on how naming can serve to create "personhood," see Phyllis Trible, *Texts of Terror: Literary-Feminist Readings of Biblical Narratives* (Philadelphia: Fortress Press, 1985), p. 15.

47. Eve Kosofsky Sedgwick, in *Epistemology of the Closet* (Berkeley and Los Angeles: University of California Press, 1990), has discussed many literary ramifications of the act of coming out of the closet.

48. See B. Heller and G. Vajda, "Lût," *EI²*.

49. *Al-Qur'ân*, Sûrat al-A'râf, verses 80–81; Arberry, *Koran Interpreted* 1:181.

50. See Charles Pellat, "Liwât," in *Sexuality and Eroticism Among Males in Moslem Societies*, ed. Arno Schmitt and Jehoeda Sofer (New York: Harrington Park Press, 1992), p. 152. This is an annotated version of the original *EI²* article, "Liwât," which was published anonymously.

51. See, for example, Everett K. Rowson, "The Categorization of Gender and Sexual Irregularity in Medieval Arabic Vice Lists," in *Body Guards: The Cul-*

*tural Politics of Gender Ambiguity*, ed. Julia Epstein and Kristina Straub (New York: Routledge, 1991), pp. 50–79; and idem, "The Effeminates of Early Medina," *Journal of the American Oriental Society* 111 (1992): 671–693. See also the various studies in Schmitt and Sofer (eds.), *Sexuality and Eroticism*.

52. See 'Abd al-Bâqî, *al-Mu'jam al-Mufahras*.

53. I am currently investigating the issue of female-female sex in the Arabo-Islamic tradition in a study in preparation.

54. Al-Râghib al-Isfahânî, *Muhâdarât al-Udabâ'* 3:273–274.

55. See, for example, Majîd Tûbiyâ, *Rîm Tasbugh Sha'rahâ* (Cairo: Maktabat Gharîb, 1983), p. 140; Hanân al-Shaykh, *Misk al-Ghazâl* (Beirut: Dâr al-Adâb, 1988); translated as *Women of Sand and Myrrh*, trans. Catherine Cobham (New York: Anchor Books, 1992); Shaaban, *Both Right and Left Handed*, p. 65, for example; and Alîfa Rif'at, "Sadîqatî," in Alîfa Rif'at, *Man Yakûn al-Rajul* (Cairo: Matâbi' al-Hay'a al-Misriyya al-'Amma lil-Kitâb, 1981), pp. 13–25.

56. Al-Sa'dâwî, *Jannât wa-Iblîs*, p. 28.

57. Ibid., p. 47.

58. Ibid., pp. 77, 130, 151.

59. For the Qur'ânic story, see *al-Qur'ân*, Sûrat al-Baqara, verses 35–38; Sûrat al-A'râf, verses 19–23; Sûrat Tâhâ, verses 120–121. For the Islamic Eve, see J. Eisenberg and G. Vajda, "Hawwâ'," *EI²*. Cf. John A. Phillips, *Eve: The History of an Idea* (San Francisco: Harper & Row, 1984), pp. 148–155. The book is, as a whole, quite interesting; the section on the Islamic Eve, however, is problematic. It is short and becomes enmeshed in the negative image of women in Muslim civilization, relying too heavily on Mernissi's *Beyond the Veil* and her sources in that study. See Malti-Douglas, *Woman's Body, Woman's Word*, pp. 45–46. For a recent discussion of the Muslim Eve, see Barbara Stowasser, *Women in the Qur'an, Traditions, and Interpretation* (New York: Oxford University Press, 1994), pp. 25–38.

60. See, for example, Ibn al-Batanûnî, "Kitâb al-'Unwân fî Makâyid al-Niswân," MS., Cairo, Adâb 3568. For a discussion of Ibn al-Batanûnî's misogynist vision, see Malti-Douglas, *Woman's Body, Woman's Word*, pp. 54–66.

61. Al-Sa'dâwî, *Jannât wa-Iblîs*, p. 73.

62. *Al-Qur'ân*, Sûrat al-Baqara, verses 35–36; Arberry, *Koran Interpreted* 1:33.

63. *Al-Qur'ân*, Sûrat al-Baqara, verse 37; Arberry, *Koran Interpreted* 1:34.

64. Al-Sa'dâwî, *Jannât wa-Iblîs*, p. 91.

65. Esposito, *Islam*, pp. 10–21.

66. Al-Sa'dâwî, *Jannât wa-Iblîs*, pp. 91–92.

67. Nawal El Saadawi, Personal Communication, April 14, 1993.

68. Al-Tabarî, *Tafsîr* 1:283.

69. Al-Qurtubî, *al-Jâmi'* 1:325; al-Baydâwî, *Tafsîr* 1:55.

70. Al-Qurtubî, *al-Jâmi'* 1:325.

71. Sharaf, *Fatâwâ al-Nisâ'*, p. 100.

72. Al-Sa'dâwî, *Jannât wa-Iblîs*, pp. 28–29.

73. Ibid., pp. 129–130.

74. Ibid., p. 170.

75. See 'Abd al-Bâqî, *al-Mu'jam al-Mufahras*, pp. 134, 344. See also A. J. Wensinck and L. Gardet, "Iblîs," *EI²*.

76. Al-Sa'dâwî, *Jannât wa-Iblîs*, pp. 171–172.

77. See, for example, al-Baydâwî, *Tafsîr* 1:53.

78. See Wensinck and Gardet, "Iblîs"; and Awn, *Satan's Tragedy*. Neil Forsyth's fascinating study *The Old Enemy: Satan and the Combat Myth* (Princeton: Princeton University Press, 1987) unfortunately omits the Islamic Satan as well as the Islamic Adam and Eve story.

79. Al-Sa'dâwî, *Jannât wa-Iblîs*, p. 52.

80. Ibid., p. 116.

81. Tawfîq al-Hakîm, "al-Shahîd," in *Arinî Allâh* (Cairo: al-Matba'a al-Namûdhajiyya, n.d.), pp. 13–29; translated by David Bishai and revised by Ronald Ewart as "The Martyr," in *Arabic Writing Today: The Short Story*, ed. Mahmoud Manzalaoui (Cairo: Dar al-Maaref, 1968), pp. 36–46. References below are to the English translation.

82. Al-Hakîm, "The Martyr," p. 39.

83. Ibid., p. 40.

84. Ibid., p. 41.

85. Ibid.

86. Ibid., p. 46.

87. See, for example, al-Sa'dâwî, *Jannât wa-Iblîs*, p. 17.

88. Ibid., p. 94.

89. Ibid., p. 60.

90. Ibid., p. 64.

91. Ibid., p. 6.

CHAPTER 7

1. The bulk of Shâdî 'Abd al-Salâm's cinematic corpus, including his documentaries, testifies to this. Shâdî 'Abd al-Salâm expressed to me on numerous occasions the appeal and importance of Pharaonic Egypt for his own work. See also Claude Michel Cluny, *Dictionnaire des nouveaux cinémas arabes* (Paris: Editions Sindbad, 1978), pp. 91–94.

2. See, for example, John L. Esposito, *The Islamic Threat: Myth or Reality?* (New York: Oxford University Press, 1992), p. 96; also Gilles Kepel, *Muslim Extremism in Egypt: The Prophet and Pharaoh* (Berkeley and Los Angeles: University of California Press, 1986).

3. Israel Gershoni and James P. Jankowski, *Egypt, Islam, and the Arabs: The Search for Egyptian Nationhood, 1900–1930* (New York: Oxford University Press, 1986), pp. 164–190.

4. See, for example, Douglas and Malti-Douglas, *Arab Comic Strips*, pp. 9–26, 154–155. Many modern Egyptian writers, from the Nobel Laureate Najîb Mahfûz to 'Alî Ahmad Bâkathîr, have exploited Pharaonic Egypt in their work.

5. See, for example, Allen Douglas, " 'La Nouvelle Droite': The Revival of Radical Rightist Thought in Contemporary France," *Tocqueville Review—La Revue Tocqueville* 4 (1984): 361–387.

6. Tawfîq al-Hakîm, *Izîs* (Cairo: Maktabat al-Adâb, 1985). The play was first published in 1955.

7. Nawâl al-Sa'dâwî, *'An al-Mar'a* (Cairo: Dâr al-Mustaqbal al-'Arabî, 1988), pp. 115–132.

8. Nawâl al-Sa'dâwî, *Izîs* (Cairo: Dâr al-Mustaqbal al-'Arabî, 1986).

9. Ibid., pp. 5–16.

10. When discussing these ancient Egyptian figures, I shall retain the most common Western spelling of their names.

11. Ibid., p. 15.

12. The legend is an important part of ancient Egyptian lore. See, for example, Grant Showerman, "Isis," *Encyclopaedia of Religion and Ethics*, ed. James Hastings et al., vol. 7 (New York: Charles Scribner's Sons, 1961), pp. 434–437. For slight variants, see Adolf Erman, *A Handbook of Egyptian Religion*, trans. A. S. Griffith (Boston: Longwood Press, 1977), pp. 25–36; and Roger Lancelyn Green, *Tales of Ancient Egypt* (New York: Henry Z. Walck, 1968), pp. 21–50.

13. See, for example, Jane Marcus's discussion in *Virginia Woolf and the Languages of Patriarchy*, p. 80; Evelyn Haller, "Isis Unveiled: Virginia Woolf's Use of Egyptian Myth," in *Virginia Woolf: A Feminist Slant*, ed. Jane Marcus (Lincoln: University of Nebraska Press, 1984), pp. 109–131; Lerner, *Creation of Patriarchy*, pp. 154, 159; Rosemary Radford Ruether, *Womanguides: Readings Toward a Feminist Theology* (Boston: Beacon Press, 1985), pp. 5–7, 13–18. See also Christine de Pizan, *The Book of the City of Ladies*, trans. Earl Jeffrey Richards (New York: Persea Books, 1982), pp. 76ff.

14. Tawfîq al-Hakîm has written "Tût," but the description fits the god Thoth, and we assume that is to whom he is referring.

15. This name is probably a rendition of Typhon, the Greek name for the god Seth. I am grateful to Dr. Jan Johnson for this information.

16. Al-Hakîm, *Izîs*, p. 58.

17. Ibid., p. 62.

18. On the importance of book covers, see Gérard Genette, *Seuils* (Paris: Editions du Seuil, 1987).

19. Al-Sa'dâwî, *Izîs*, p. 73.

20. Ibid., p. 87.

21. Al-Hakîm, *Izîs*, p. 142.

22. Al-Sa'dâwî, *Izîs*, pp. 50–51.

23. Al-Hakîm, *Izîs*, p. 21.

24. Ibid., p. 40.

25. Ibid., p. 112.

26. Al-Sa'dâwî, *Izîs*, p. 73.

27. Ibid., pp. 76–77; ellipses in the original.

28. Lerner (*Creation of Patriarchy*, p. 159) refers to Osiris as Isis's "brother-spouse."

29. Al-Sa'dâwî, *Izîs*, pp. 66–67.

30. See, for example, ibid., pp. 55, 64.

31. Al-Hakîm, "Bayân," in al-Hakîm, *Izîs*.

32. Al-Hakîm, *Izîs*, p. 137.

33. Al-Sa'dâwî, *Izîs*, p. 11.

34. See Malti-Douglas, *Woman's Body, Woman's Word*, chap. 1.

35. Al-Sa'dâwî, *Izîs*, p. 17.

36. *Alf Layla wa-Layla*, Bûlâq ed., 1:2; *Kitâb Alf Layla wa-Layla*, ed. Mahdi, 1:56.

37. On the voyeurism in the *Nights*, see Malti-Douglas, *Woman's Body, Woman's Word*, chap. 1.

38. Al-Sa'dâwî, *Izîs*, p. 65.

39. Ibid., pp. 96–97.

40. Ibid., p. 99.

41. Ibid., p. 101.

42. Ibid., pp. 101–102.

43. See Hunayn ibn Ishâq, "Qissat Salâmân and Absâl" (translated from the Greek), in Ibn Sînâ, *Tis' Rasâ'il* (Cairo: Maktabat Hindiyya, 1908), pp. 158–168. Henry Corbin summarizes the story in *Avicenne et le récit visionnaire* (Paris: Adrien-Maisonneuve, 1954). For a full discussion, see Malti-Douglas, *Woman's Body, Woman's Word*, pp. 97ff.

44. I am using Muhsin Mahdi's edition of the *Nights* here; see *Kitâb Alf Layla wa-Layla*, ed. Mahdi, 1:64. For a full discussion of this incident and the sexual politics of the frame, see Malti-Douglas, *Woman's Body, Woman's Word*, chap. 1.

45. On torture, see, for example, Edward Peters, *Torture* (Oxford: Basil Blackwell, 1985), esp. pp. 169–171 for a list of modern techniques; Elaine Scarry, *The Body in Pain: The Making and Unmaking of the World* (New York: Oxford University Press, 1985), esp. pp. 27–59. For a study that deals with various forms of torture in premodern Arabo-Islamic discourse, see Fedwa Malti-Douglas, "Literary Form and Ideological Content of 'Abbâsid Historiography: Al-Mu'tadid in Chronicle, Biography, and *Adab*," in *Early Islamic Historiography*, ed. Lawrence I. Conrad (Princeton: Darwin Press, forthcoming).

46. See Allen Douglas and Fedwa Malti-Douglas, "Literature and Politics: A Conversation with Emile Habiby," in *Mundus Arabicus* 5 (1992): 11–46 (special issue, "The Arabic Novel Since 1950").

47. Al-Sa'dâwî, *Izîs*, p. 103.

48. Ibid.

49. Ibid.

50. Nawal El Saadawi, Personal Communication, March 27, 1993. El Saadawi wrote of this experience in *al-Wajh al-'Arî lil-Mar'a al-'Arabiyya* (Beirut: al-Mu'assasa al-'Arabiyya lil-Dirâsât wal-Nashr, 1977), pp. 11–14. See also Nawal El Saadawi, *The Hidden Face of Eve: Women in the Arab World*, trans. Sherif Hetata (Boston: Beacon Press, 1982), pp. 7–11, 33–43. See also Chapter 3 above.

51. Alifa Rifaat, "Bahiyya's Eyes," in *Distant View of a Minaret and Other Stories*, trans. Denys Johnson-Davies (London: Quartet Books, 1983), p. 9; and Alîfa Rif'at, "Man Yakûn al-Rajul," in Alîfa Rif'at, *Man Yakûn al-Rajul*, pp. 97–104.

52. Sulaymân Fayyâd, *Aswât* (Cairo: Kutub 'Arabiyya, 1972).

53. See Mary Daly, *Gyn/Ecology: The Metaethics of Radical Feminism* (Boston: Beacon Press, 1978), pp. 153–177; Evelyne Accad, *L'excisée* (Paris: Editions l'Harmattan, 1982); translated as *L'excisée*, trans. David Bruner (Washington, D.C.: Three Continents Press, 1989).

54. Alice Walker, *Possessing the Secret of Joy* (London and San Diego: Harcourt Brace Jovanovich, 1992), p. 285.

55. For important works on female genital mutilation, see Asma El Dareer, *Woman, Why Do You Weep? Circumcision and Its Consequences* (London: Zed Press, 1983); Michel Erlich, *La femme blessée: essai sur les mutilations sexuelles féminines* (Paris: Editions l'Harmattan, 1986); Hanny Lightfoot-Klein, *Prisoners of Ritual: An Odyssey into Female Genital Circumcision in Africa* (New York: Haworth Press, 1989).

56. Nawal El Saadawi, Personal Communication, March 27, 1993.

57. See, for example, Juliette Minces, *La femme voilée: l'Islam au féminin* (Paris: Calmann-Lévy, 1990), pp. 97ff.; and Nawal El Saadawi, "The Question No One Would Answer," *Ms.*, March 1980, pp. 68–69.

58. "Khafd," *EI²*.

59. See, for example, Sharaf, *Fatâwâ al-Nisâ'*, pp. 43, 63.

60. For a typical Arabo-Islamic explication of this matter, see al-Tha'âlibî, *Thimâr al-Qulûb*, p. 303.

61. Such a position would be consistent with a tendency in the literature to distinguish between a more severe operation, often referred to as "Pharaonic," and a lesser one, whose proponents declare it to be in conformity with the *sunna* or Islamic legal tradition.

62. In Muhsin Mahdi's edition of the *Nights*, the first royal wife consorts with a cook; *Kitâb Alf Layla*, ed. Mahdi, 1:57.

63. See Malti-Douglas, *Woman's Body, Woman's Word*, chap. 1.

64. Al-Sa'dâwî, *Izîs*, p. 103.

65. Ibid., p. 100.

66. See Malti-Douglas, *Woman's Body, Woman's Word*, chap. 1.

67. Al-Sa'dâwî, *Izîs*, p. 97.

68. Ibid., p. 99.

69. Ibid., p. 121.

70. For an important in-depth analysis of these matters, see Lerner, *Creation of Patriarchy*.

71. See, for example, al-Sa'dâwî, *Izîs*, pp. 18, 23.

72. Ibid., p. 31; ellipses in the original.

73. Ibid., p. 54.

74. Ibid., p. 131.

75. Ibid., p. 131.

76. See, for example, Joseph Schacht, *An Introduction to Islamic Law* (Oxford: Oxford University Press, 1986), pp. 14, 162.

77. See, for example, Muhammad Mahmûd al-Sawwâf, *Zawjât al-Nabiyy al-Tâhirât wa-Hikmat Ta'addudihinna* (Cairo: Dâr al-I'tisâm, 1979). See also Hâshim ibn Hâmid al-Rifâ'î, "al-Kalimât fî Bayân Mahâsin Ta'addud al-Zawjât" ([Fez?], 1987). This is an offset publication I found in Fez in 1994 and which bears no publication data other than the date of publication.

78. See al-Sa'dâwî, *Izîs*, pp. 30, 31.

79. See Esposito, *Islam*, p. 22.

80. See al-Sa'dâwî, *Izîs*, pp. 34, 66. Although I have translated the descriptive *al-a'zam* as Great, it is grammatically an elative and should be rendered as "the Greatest."

81. Ibid., p. 99.

82. Ibid., p. 101.
83. Ibid., p. 134; ellipses in the original.
84. Ibid., p. 67.
85. Ibid., p. 84.
86. See, for example, Ridâ, *Huqûq al-Nisâ'*, pp. 45–48.
87. Al-Sa'dâwî, *Izîs*, p. 43.
88. See, for example, Ibrâhîm ibn Sâlih al-Mahmûd, *Kayf Taksibîna Zawjaki?!* (Fez: Maktabat wa-Tasjîlât al-Hidâya al-Qur'âniyya, 1991).
89. Al-Sa'dâwî, *Izîs*, p. 64.
90. Ibid., p. 132.

CHAPTER 8

1. Nawâl al-Sa'dâwî, *Mudhakkirâtî fî Sijn al-Nisâ'* (Cairo: Dâr al-Mustaqbal al-'Arabî, 1984); translated as *Memoirs from the Women's Prison*, trans. Marilyn Booth (London: Women's Press; Berkeley and Los Angeles: University of California Press, 1983), pp. 83, 113.
2. See Chapters 5 and 7; Malti-Douglas, *Woman's Body, Woman's Word*, chap. 1.
3. Al-Sa'dâwî, *Mudhakkirâtî fî Sijn al-Nisâ'*, pp. 15, 254.
4. Eve Kosofsky Sedgwick, *Between Men: English Literature and Male Homosocial Desire* (New York: Columbia University Press, 1985).
5. For a discussion of male homosocial desire as an essential component of Arabo-Islamic society, see Malti-Douglas, *Woman's Body, Woman's Word*, chaps. 1–5.
6. See Malti-Douglas, *Woman's Body, Woman's Word*, pp. 5–10.
7. As with critical discussions of autobiographical texts, I shall use the first name, Nawal, to refer to the character in the text and the full name, (Nawal) El Saadawi, to refer to the historical individual or the author.
8. Al-Sa'dâwî, *Mudhakkirâtî fî Sijn al-Nisâ'*, pp. 49–52.
9. Nawâl al-Sa'dâwî, *al-Insân: Ithnay* [sic] *'Ashar Imra'a fî Zinzâna Wâhida* (Cairo: Maktabat Madbûlî, 1982); translated into French as *Douze femmes dans Kanater*, trans. Magda Wassef (Paris: Des Femmes, 1984). In their brief (one-page) biography of El Saadawi introducing a translation of one of her short stories, Margot Badran and Miriam Cooke ("Nawal al-Saadawi," p. 203) mistakenly write that this French translation is of *Mudhakkirâtî fî Sijn al-Nisâ'*, the prison memoirs. At the same time, they note the existence of the Arabic original of the play, but without mentioning this translation.
10. For an interesting, though brief, comparative article, see Marilyn Booth, "Women's Prison Memoirs in Egypt and Elsewhere: Prison, Gender, Praxis," *Middle East Report*, no. 149 (November–December 1987): 35–41. See also Harlow, *Resistance Literature*, pp. 138–140, who briefly discusses El Saadawi's memoirs; Zaynab al-Ghazâlî, *Ayyâm min Hayâtî* (Cairo: Dâr al-Shurûq, 1987) (this is the ninth edition of this work); Farîda al-Naqqâsh, *al-Sijn: Dam'atân wa-Warda* (Cairo: Dâr al-Mustaqbal al-'Arabî, 1985); and Sâfî Nâz Kâzim, *'An al-Sijn wal-Hurriyya* (Cairo: al-Zahrâ' lil-I'lâm al-'Arabî, 1986).
11. Le Gassick, "The Arabic Novel," pp. 48–49.

12. See, for example, Sergei A. Shuiskii, "Some Observations on Modern Arabic Autobiography," *Journal of Arabic Literature* 13 (1982): 114; and Malti-Douglas, *Blindness and Autobiography*, p. 96.

13. Le Gassick, "The Arabic Novel," p. 59.

14. In this connection, see also the discussion of Tarabishi in Chapter 1 above.

15. See, for example, Lejeune, *Le pacte autobiographique*, pp. 13–46; and idem, "Le pacte autobiographique (bis)," *Poétique* 56 (1983): 416–434.

16. Barbara Harlow, *Barred: Women, Writing, and Political Detention* (Hanover, N.H.: Wesleyan University Press, 1992), p. 133.

17. Nawal El Saadawi, Personal Communication, April 14, 1993.

18. Al-Sa'dâwî, *Mudhakkirâtî fî Sijn al-Nisâ'*, p. 7.

19. For an excellent work on women's autobiography, see Domna Stanton, ed., *The Female Autograph: Theory and Practice of Autobiography from the Tenth to the Twentieth Century* (Chicago: University of Chicago Press, 1987). See also Malti-Douglas, *Woman's Body, Woman's Word*, pp. 144–178.

20. Al-Sa'dâwî, *Mudhakkirâtî fî Sijn al-Nisâ'*, p. 22.

21. Harlow, *Resistance Literature*, p. 139.

22. Al-Sa'dâwî, *Mudhakkirâtî fî Sijn al-Nisâ'*, p. 26.

23. Ibid., p. 51.

24. Ibid.

25. Ibid., p. 79.

26. Ibid., p. 186.

27. Ibid., p. 208.

28. Ibid., p. 235.

29. Ibid., p. 23; ellipses in the original.

30. Ibid., pp. 83, 113.

31. Ibid., p. 114.

32. Ibid., p. 8.

33. Ibid., p. 74.

34. Ibid., p. 103.

35. Harlow, *Resistance Literature*, p. 139.

36. Al-Sa'dâwî, *Mudhakkirâtî fî Sijn al-Nisâ'*, p. 96.

37. For a discussion of this phenomenon in the classical sources, see Fedwa Malti-Douglas, "The Classical Arabic Detective," *Arabica* 35 (1988): 59–91.

38. Al-Sa'dâwî, *Mudhakkirâtî fî Sijn al-Nisâ'*, p. 153.

39. Ibid., p. 156.

40. Ibid., p. 182.

41. Ibid., p. 167.

42. Ibid., p. 60.

43. Ibid., pp. 93–94.

44. Ibid., p. 92.

45. Ibid., p. 95.

46. Ibid., p. 92.

47. Ibid.

48. Ibid., p. 192.

49. Ibid., p. 129.

50. Ibid., pp. 130, 133.

51. Ibid., pp. 217–218.

52. Ibid., p. 168.

53. Ibid., p. 169.

54. Ibid., pp. 169–170.

55. Kâzim, 'An al-Sijn, p. 29.

56. Al-Sa'dâwî, Mudhakkirâtî fî Sijn al-Nisâ', pp. 121–122.

57. Ibid., p. 65.

58. Ibid., pp. 65, 66.

59. Ibid., pp. 113, 173. Cigarette paper is also mentioned on p. 113.

60. Ibid., pp. 185–186.

61. Ibid., pp. 228–229.

62. Ibid., p. 199.

63. Ibid., p. 65.

64. Atwood, The Handmaid's Tale, p. 327.

65. The body is such a constant for Nawal El Saadawi that it is almost redundant to cite the narratives in which it plays a major role.

66. Al-Sa'dâwî, Mudhakkirâtî fî Sijn al-Nisâ', pp. 43, 144, 146.

67. Al-Sa'dâwî, Sijn al-Nisâ', pp. 142–146. The repeated passage is missing from the English translation of the memoirs.

68. See, for example, 'Abbâs Mahmûd al-'Aqqâd, Juhâ al-Dâhik al-Mudhik (Cairo: Dâr al-Hilâl, n.d.).

69. This anecdote is extremely popular in the Arab world and is told orally by people all the way from Egypt to North Africa. It has even been recast in children's literature, with Juhâ and a neighbor of his as protagonists; see Ahmad Hânî Mahfûz, Mughâmarât Juhâ (Beirut: al-Maktab al-Islâmî, 1987), p. 38.

70. Al-Sa'dâwî, Sijn al-Nisâ', p. 95.

71. Ibid., pp. 139–141.

72. Ibid., p. 139.

73. Ibid., p. 41.

74. Ibid., pp. 41, 48.

75. Ibid., p. 34.

76. Ibid., p. 224.

77. Ibid., p. 179.

78. Ibid., p. 224.

79. Elissa D. Gelfand has demonstrated this phenomenon for French women's prisons texts; see Imagination in Confinement: Women's Writings from French Prisons (Ithaca: Cornell University Press, 1983), p. 123.

80. Al-Sa'dâwî, Mudhakkirâtî fî Sijn al-Nisâ', p. 135–136.

81. Ibid., p. 149.

82. Ibid., p. 181.

83. Ibid., p. 230

84. Ibid., p. 60.

85. Tûqân, Rihla Jabaliyya, pp. 14–15; Malti-Douglas, Woman's Body, Woman's Word, p. 166.

CHAPTER 9

1. Nawâl al-Sa'dâwî, *Rihlâtî fî al-'Alam* (Cairo: Dâr Nashr Tadâmun al-Mar'a al-'Arabiyya, 1987), p. 9; translated as *My Travels Around the World*, trans. Shirley Eber (London: Methuen, 1991).

2. The film, directed by Hasan al-Imâm, appeared in 1974. See 'Abd al-Mun'im Sa'd, *Mûjaz Ta'rîkh al-Sînamâ al-Misriyya* (Cairo: Matâbi' al-Ahrâm al-Tijâriyya, [1976?]), p. 55.

3. A glance at any medieval biographical compendium will show this to be the case.

4. Ibn Battûta, *Rihlat Ibn Battûta*, ed. Talâl Harb (Beirut: Dâr al-Kutub al-'Ilmiyya, 1987).

5. Ibn Jubayr, *Rihlat Ibn Jubayr* (Beirut: Dâr Sâdir, 1980); 'Abd al-Latîf al-Baghdâdî, *Kitâb al-Ifâda wal-I'tibâr* (Damascus: Dâr Qutayba, 1983).

6. See, for example, Albert Hourani, *Arabic Thought in the Liberal Age, 1798–1939* (London: Oxford University Press, 1970). The question of attitudes about Europe is central to Hourani's entire work. For an interesting analysis of pre-twentieth-century materials, see Bernard Lewis, *The Muslim Discovery of Europe* (New York: W. W. Norton, 1982).

7. See the fascinating studies in Dale F. Eickelman and James Piscatori, eds., *Muslim Travellers: Pilgrimage, Migration, and the Religious Imagination* (Berkeley and Los Angeles: University of California Press, 1990). See also the excellent collection *Adab al-Rihla wal-Tawâsul al-Hadârî* (Meknes: Publications of the Faculty of Letters and Human Sciences of the University Moulay Ismaïl, 1993).

8. Anîs Mansûr is considered the contemporary travel writer par excellence; Ahmad Yahyâ, back cover of Anîs Mansûr, *Anta fî al-Yâbân* (Cairo: al-Maktab al-Misrî al-Hadîth, 1984).

9. See, for example, Rabî' ibn Muhammad al-Sa'ûdî, *Zâd al-Musâfirîn ilâ Ghayr Bilâd al-Muslimîn* (Riyad: Dâr al-Fitya; Cairo: Dâr al-Sahwa lil-Nashr, 1988); 'Abd al-'Azîz ibn 'Abd Allâh ibn Bâz, *Fatâwâ lil-Muslim fî al-Mughtarab* (Washington, D.C.: Saudi Arabian Cultural Bureau, n.d.); Abû al-Hasan 'Alî al-Nadwî, *Ahâdîth Sarîha fî Amrîkâ* (Beirut: Mu'assasat al-Risâla, 1987); and Fedwa Malti-Douglas, "An Anti-Travel Guide: Iconography in a Muslim Revivalist Tract," *Edebiyât*, n.s., 4, no. 2 (1993): 205–213.

10. Shaykh Muhammad ibn Sâlih al-'Uthaymîn, *Min al-Ahkâm al-Fiqhiyya fî al-Fatâwâ al-Nisâ'iyya* (Fez: Maktabat wa-Tasjîlât al-Hidâya al-Qur'âniyya, 1991), pp. 22–25.

11. See Husayn, *al-Ayyâm* 3:79ff.; and Malti-Douglas, *Blindness and Autobiography*, esp. pp. 41–90.

12. Tûqân, *Rihla Jabaliyya*, pp. 169ff.; Malti-Douglas, *Woman's Body, Woman's Word*, chap. 9.

13. Mustafâ Mahmûd, *Rihlatî min al-Shakk ilâ al-Imân*, 9th ed. (Cairo: Dâr al-Ma'ârif, 1991); Hamza, *Rihlatî*. See also Malti-Douglas, "Gender and the Uses of the Ascetic." I am investigating these works in a book currently in preparation.

14. Karîma Kamâl, *Bint Misriyya fî Amrîkâ* (Cairo: Dâr Gharîb lil-Tibâ'a, 1988?).

15. Al-Sa'dâwî, *Rihlâtî*, pp. 45–46.

16. See Chapter 2 above.

17. For the idea of the female *Bildungsroman*, see Pratt, *Archetypal Patterns*, pp. 13–37 (chapter written with Barbara White).

18. We have already seen this pact in *Memoirs from the Women's Prison*; see Chapter 8, which also provides the necessary references.

19. Al-Sa'dâwî, *Rihlâtî*, p. 54.

20. See, for example, Hatâta, *al-'Ayn*; Hetata, *The Eye*.

21. As with the prison memoirs, I shall use the first name, Nawal, to refer to the character in the text and the full name, (Nawal) El Saadawi, to refer to the historical individual or the author. Regarding India, Hetata has himself authored a fascinating set of memoirs about his work and residence in the subcontinent, *Tarîq al-Milh wal-Hubb* (Cairo: Dâr al-Mustaqbal al-'Arabî, 1983).

22. See, for example, Munâ Hilmî, *Rajul Jadîd fî al-Ufq* (Cairo: Dâr Tadâmun al-Mar'a al-'Arabiyya, 1988).

23. Al-Sa'dâwî, *Rihlâtî*, pp. 9–10.

24. Ibid., p. 10.

25. Ibid.

26. Ibid.

27. See Al-Nâbulusî, *Ta'tîr al-Anâm fî Ta'bîr al-Manâm* (Cairo: 'Isâ al-Bâbî al-Halabî, n.d.), 2:62–63; and Ahmad al-Sabâhî 'Iwad Allâh, *Tafsîr al-Ahlâm* (Cairo: Maktabat Madbûlî, 1977), p. 186.

28. Al-Sa'dâwî, *Rihlâtî*, p. 9.

29. Ibid., p. 95.

30. Ibid., p. 11.

31. Ibid., pp. 12–13.

32. Ibid., p. 11.

33. Ibid., p. 100.

34. Ibid., p. 296.

35. See, for example, Gail Pheterson, ed., *A Vindication of the Rights of Whores* (Seattle: Seal Press, 1989), pp. 64–67.

36. Al-Sa'dâwî, *Rihlâtî*, p. 298.

37. Ibid., p. 299.

38. See, for example, ibid., pp. 11, 62. Later in the narrative the racial differences will loom larger; see below.

39. We have already seen the importance of the scopic in Nawal El Saadawi's fiction, as, for example, in Chapter 2 above.

40. Al-Sa'dâwî, *Rihlâtî*, p. 299.

41. Ibid.

42. Ibid.

43. Ibid.

44. Ibid., p. 300.

45. Ibid.

46. Ibid., p. 299.

47. A much more conformist description of Thailand and its sex industry is available to Arabic readers in Mansûr, *Anta fî al-Yâbân.*

48. See, for example, Yûsuf Idrîs, *Niyû Yûrk 80* (Cairo: Dâr Misr lil-Tibâ'a, 1980), pp. 5–74; and Mahfûz, *Zuqâq al-Midaqq*, p. 183.

49. Marjorie Garber, *Vested Interests: Cross-Dressing and Cultural Anxiety* (New York: HarperCollins, 1992).

50. Ben Jelloun, *L'enfant de sable* and *La nuit sacrée.*

51. See, for example, Anwar, *Mahlan . . . Yâ Sâhibat al-Qawârîr*, pp. 78–79; Muhammad al-Ghazâlî, *Qadâyâ al-Mar'a bayn al-Taqâlîd al-Râkida wal-Wâfida*, 3d ed. (Cairo: Dâr al-Shurûq, 1991), pp. 194–195; Sharaf, *Fatâwâ al-Nisâ'*, p. 11; and al-'Uthaymîn, *al-Fatâwâ al-Nisâ'iyya*, pp. 79–80.

52. Al-Sa'dâwî, *Rihlâtî*, p. 150.

53. Ibid., p. 155.

54. Ibid.

55. Ibid., p. 156.

56. Ibid., p. 160.

57. Ibid., p. 156.

58. Ibid., p. 301.

59. Ibid., p. 294.

60. Ibid., pp. 98ff.

61. Ibid., p. 110.

62. Ibid., pp. 83–86.

63. Ibid., pp. 48–50.

64. Ibid., p. 49.

65. Ibid., p. 308.

66. Ibid.

67. Ibid., pp. 308–309.

68. Ibid., p. 310.

69. Ibid., p. 62.

70. Ibid., p. 310.

71. Ibid., pp. 141–143, 277–282, 22, 308, 316, 356.

72. Ibid., p. 332.

73. Ibid., p. 333.

74. Ibid., p. 337.

75. Ibid., p. 343.

76. Ibid., p. 375.

CHAPTER 10

1. Hafez, "Intentions and Realisation," p. 189.

2. References to the various texts and concepts discussed in this chapter will be found in the above notes; they will not be repeated here. Only materials not previously cited will be referenced here.

3. Nawal al-Saadawi, "Eyes," trans. Ali Badran and Margot Badran, in Badran and Cooke (eds.), *Opening the Gates*, pp. 205–212.

4. See Malti-Douglas, *Woman's Body, Woman's Word.*

5. I am borrowing the concept of "scopic regime" from Martin Jay ("Scopic

Regimes of Modernity," in *Vision and Visuality*, ed. Hal Foster [Seattle: Bay Press, 1988], p. 3), who, in turn, takes it from Christian Metz.

6. Nawal El Saadawi, Personal Interview, August 15, 1986. When the interview was published (Douglas and Malti-Douglas, "Reflections"), the editors chose to omit this part of the discussion.

7. See Douglas and Malti-Douglas, *Arab Comic Strips*, pp. 15–26.

8. A classic narrative on the traditional-modern pattern is Haqqî, *Qindîl Umm Hâshim*. For some other discussions of this theme, see Malti-Douglas, "Al-'Anâsir al-Turâthiyya," pp. 21–29; and Malti-Douglas, *Blindness and Autobiography*, pp. 75–90.

# Works Cited

'Abd al-Bâqî, Muhammad Fu'âd. *Al-Mu'jam al-Mufahras li-Alfâz al-Qur'ân al-Karîm*. Beirut: Mu'assasat Jamâl lil-Nashr, n.d.

'Abd al-Hakîm, Shawqî. "Shafîqa wa-Mutawallî" In *Malik 'Ajûz*, pp. 124–159. Cairo: al-Dâr al-Qawmiyya lil-Tibâ'a wal-Nashr, n.d.

'Abd al-Salâm, Shâdî. Entire cinematic corpus.

'Abd al-Wahhâb, Muhammad Fahmî. *Al-Harakât al-Nisâ'iyya fî al-Sharq wa-Silatuhâ bil-Isti'mâr wal-Sahyûniyya al-'Alamiyya*. Cairo: Dâr al-I'tisâm, 1979.

Abdel-Malek, Kamal. *A Study of the Vernacular Poetry of Ahmad Fu'âd Nigm*. Leiden: E. J. Brill, 1990.

Abû Sayf, Laylâ. "New Ballads for Old." Public Lecture delivered at U.C.L.A.

Accad, Evelyne. *L'excisée*. Paris: Editions l'Harmattan, 1982.

———. *L'excisée*. Translated by David Bruner. Washington, D.C.: Three Continents Press, 1989.

———. "The Prostitute in Arab and North African Fiction." In *The Image of the Prostitute in Modern Literature*, edited by Pierre L. Horn and Mary Beth Pringle, pp. 63–75. New York: Frederick Ungar, 1984.

———. "Rebellion, Maturity, and the Social Context: Arab Women's Special Contribution to Literature." In *Arab Women: Old Boundaries, New Frontiers*, edited by Judith E. Tucker, pp. 224–253. Bloomington: Indiana University Press, 1993.

Accad, Evelyne, and Rose Ghurayyib. *Contemporary Arab Women Writers and Poets*. Beirut: Institute for Women's Studies in the Arab World, 1985.

*Adab al-Rihla wal-Tawâsul al-Hadârî*. Meknes: Publications of the Faculty of Letters and Human Sciences of the University Moulay Ismaïl, 1993.

Adams, Carol J. *The Sexual Politics of Meat: A Feminist-Vegetarian Critical Theory*. New York: Continuum, 1991

Ahmed, Leila. "Early Feminist Movements in Turkey and Egypt." In *Muslim Women*, edited by Freda Hussain, pp. 111–123. New York: St. Martin's Press, 1984.

————. *Women and Gender in Islam: Historical Roots of a Modern Debate.* New Haven: Yale University Press, 1992.

*Alf Layla wa-Layla.* 2 vols. Cairo: Matba'at Bûlâq, 1252 A.H.

Algosaibi, Ghazi A. *From the Orient and the Desert.* London: Oriel Press, 1977.

Al-Ali, Nadje Sadig. *Gender Writing/Writing Gender: The Representation of Women in a Selection of Modern Egyptian Literature.* Cairo: American University in Cairo Press, 1993.

Allen, Roger. *The Arabic Novel: An Historical and Critical Introduction.* Syracuse: Syracuse University Press, 1982.

'Allûsh, Sa'îd. *'Unf al-Mutakhayyil fî A'mâl Imîl Habîbî.* Casablanca: al-Mu'assasa al-Hadîtha lil-Nashr wal-Tawzî', 1986.

Anwar, Yusriyya Muhammad. *Mahlan . . . Yâ Sâhibat al-Qawârîr: Radd 'alâ Kitâb "Rifqan bil-Qawârîr."* Cairo: Dâr al-I'tisâm, 1403 A.H.

al-'Aqqâd, 'Abbâs Mahmûd. *Juhâ al-Dâhik al-Mudhik.* Cairo: Dâr al-Hilâl, n.d.

Arberry, A. J. *The Koran Interpreted.* 2 vols. in 1. New York: Macmillan, 1974.

Arkoun, Mohammed. "Lecture de la sourate 18." *Annales: Economies, sociétés, civilisations* 35, nos. 3–4 (1980): 418–435.

'Atiyya, Na'îm. "Kayduhunna 'Azîm." In *Nisâ' fî al-Mahâkim,* pp. 82–88. Cairo: Dâr al-Ma'ârif, 1980.

Atwood, Margaret. *The Handmaid's Tale.* New York: Ballantine Books, 1985.

Awn, Peter J. *Satan's Tragedy and Redemption: Iblîs in Sufi Psychology.* Leiden: E. J. Brill, 1983.

Ba'labakkî, Laylâ. *Anâ Ahyâ.* Beirut: al-Maktab al-Tijârî, 1965.

Badran, Margot, and Miriam Cooke. "Nawal al-Saadawi." In *Opening the Gates: A Century of Arab Feminist Writing,* edited by Margot Badran and Miriam Cooke, pp. 203–204. London: Virago; Bloomington: Indiana University Press, 1990.

al-Baghdâdî, 'Abd al-Latîf. *Kitâb al-Ifâda wal-I'tibâr.* Damascus: Dâr Qutayba, 1983.

Bailey, Paul. *An English Madam: The Life and Work of Cynthia Payne.* London: Jonathan Cape, 1982.

Barrows, Sydney Biddle, with William Novak. *Mayflower Madam: The Secret Life of Sydney Biddle Barrows.* New York: Arbor House, 1986.

Barry, Kathleen. *Female Sexual Slavery.* New York: New York University Press, 1979.

Barth, John. *Chimera.* New York: Fawcett Crest Books, 1972.

————. *The Last Voyage of Somebody the Sailor.* Boston: Little, Brown, 1991.

al-Baydâwî. *Tafsîr al-Baydâwî/Anwâr al-Tanzîl wa-Asrâr al-Ta'wîl.* 2 vols. Beirut: Dâr al-Kutub al-'Ilmiyya, 1988.

Ben Jelloun, Tahar. *L'enfant de sable.* Paris: Editions du Seuil, 1985.

————. *La nuit sacrée.* Paris: Editions du Seuil, 1985.

Benveniste, Emile. *Problèmes de linguistique générale.* Vol. 1. Paris: Gallimard, 1966.

Booth, Marilyn. "Women's Prison Memoirs in Egypt and Elsewhere: Prison,

Gender, Praxis." *Middle East Report*, no. 149 (November–December 1987): 35–41.

Bouhdiba, Abdelwahab. *La sexualité en Islam.* Paris: Presses Universitaires de France, 1979.

Boullata, Issa J. *Trends and Issues in Contemporary Arab Thought.* Albany: State University of New York Press, 1990.

Brock, D. Heyward. "An Interview with Dannie Abse." *Literature and Medicine* 3 (1984): 5–18.

Brownmiller, Susan. *Against Our Will: Men, Women, and Rape.* New York: Bantam Books, 1986.

Burdekin, Katharine. *The End of This Day's Business.* New York: Feminist Press, 1989.

———. *Swastika Night.* New York: Feminist Press, 1985.

Burton, Richard F. *The Book of the Thousand Nights and a Night.* 10 vols. "Burton Club Edition"; n.p., n.d.

Butler, Judith. *Gender Trouble: Feminism and the Subversion of Identity.* New York: Routledge, 1990.

Cachia, Pierre. *Popular Narrative Ballads of Modern Egypt.* Oxford: Clarendon Press, 1989.

Charnay, Jean-Paul. "Communication et société: variations sur parole, amour et cuisine dans la culture arabe." In *L'ambivalence dans la culture arabe*, edited by Jacques Berque and Jean-Paul Charnay, pp. 172–190. Paris: Editions Anthropos, 1967.

Chebel, Malek. *Le corps dans la tradition au Maghreb.* Paris: Presses Universitaires de France, 1984.

Cluny, Claude Michel. *Dictionnaire des nouveaux cinémas arabes.* Paris: Editions Sindbad, 1978.

Cooke, Miriam. "Arab Women Writers." In *The Cambridge History of Arabic Literature: Modern Arabic Literature*, edited by M. M. Badawi, pp. 443–462. Cambridge: Cambridge University Press, 1992.

———. "Men Constructed in the Mirror of Prostitution." In *Naguib Mahfouz: From Regional Fame to Global Recognition*, edited by Michael Beard and Adnan Haydar, pp. 106–125. Syracuse: Syracuse University Press, 1993.

Corbin, Henry. *Avicenne et le récit visionnaire.* Paris: Adrien-Maisonneuve, 1954.

Cordelier, Jeanne, and Martine Laroche. *La dérobade.* Paris: Hachette, 1976.

Daly, Mary. *Beyond God the Father: Toward a Philosophy of Women's Liberation.* Boston: Beacon Press, 1973.

———. *Gyn/Ecology: The Metaethics of Radical Feminism.* Boston: Beacon Press, 1978.

Djebar, Assia. "Celle qui dit non à Médine." *Algérie-Actualité*, no. 1273 (March 8–14, 1990).

———. *Loin de Médine.* Paris: Albin Michel, 1991.

———. "Préface." In Naoual el Saadaoui, *Ferdaous, une voix en enfer*, pp. 7–25. Translated by Assia Trabelsi and Assia Djebar. Paris: Des Femmes, 1981.

Douglas, Allen. " 'La Nouvelle Droite': The Revival of Radical Rightist Thought in Contemporary France." *The Tocqueville Review—La Revue Tocqueville* 4 (1984): 361–387.

Douglas, Allen, and Fedwa Malti-Douglas. *Arab Comic Strips: Politics of an Emerging Mass Culture.* Bloomington: Indiana University Press, 1994.

———. "Literature and Politics: A Conversation with Emile Habiby." *Mundus Arabicus* 5 (1992): 11–46 (special issue entitled "The Arabic Novel Since 1950," edited by Issa Boullata).

———. "Reflections of a Feminist: Conversation with Nawal al-Saadawi." In *Opening the Gates: A Century of Arab Feminist Writing*, edited by Margot Badran and Miriam Cooke, pp. 394–404. London: Virago; Bloomington: Indiana University Press, 1990.

Eickelman, Dale F., and James Piscatori, eds. *Muslim Travellers: Pilgrimage, Migration, and the Religious Imagination.* Berkeley and Los Angeles: University of California Press, 1990.

El Dareer, Asma. *Woman, Why Do You Weep? Circumcision and Its Consequences.* London: Zed Press, 1983.

El Saadaoui, Naoual. *See* El Saadawi, Nawal.

El Saadawi, Nawal [al-Sa'dâwi, Nawâl]. *'An al-Mar'a.* Cairo: Dâr al-Mustaqbal al-'Arabî, 1988.

———. *The Circling Song.* London: Zed Books, 1989.

———. *Death of an Ex-Minister.* Translated by Shirley Eber. London: Methuen, 1987.

——— [El Saadaoui, Naoual]. *Douze femmes dans Kanater.* Translated by Magda Wassef. Paris: Des Femmes, 1984.

——— [al-Saadawi, Nawal]. "Eyes." Translated by Ali Badran and Margot Badran. In *Opening the Gates: A Century of Arab Feminist Writing*, edited by Margot Badran and Miriam Cooke, pp. 205–212. London: Virago; Bloomington: Indiana University Press, 1990.

———. *The Fall of the Imam.* Translated by Sherif Hetata. London: Methuen, 1988.

——— [al-Sa'dâwi, Nawâl]. *Al-Ghâ'ib.* Cairo: Maktabat Madbûlî, n.d.

———. "Guarding My Tongue." *The Guardian*, August 10, 1992.

———. *God Dies by the Nile.* Translated by Sherif Hetata. London: Zed Books, 1985.

———. "Growing Up Female in Egypt." Translated by Fedwa Malti-Douglas. In *Women and the Family in the Middle East: New Voices of Change*, edited by Elizabeth Warnock Fernea, pp. 111–120. Austin: University of Texas Press, 1985.

——— [al-Sa'dâwi, Nawâl]. *Hanân Qalîl.* Beirut: Dâr al-Adâb, 1986.

———. *The Hidden Face of Eve: Women in the Arab World.* Translated by Sherif Hetata. Boston: Beacon Press, 1982.

——— [al-Sa'dâwi, Nawâl]. *Al-Hubb fî Zaman al-Naft.* Cairo: Maktabat Madbûlî, 1993.

——— [al-Sa'dâwi, Nawâl]. *Imra'a 'ind Nuqtat al-Sifr.* Beirut: Dâr al-Adâb, 1979.

——— [al-Sa'dâwi, Nawâl]. *Imra'atâni fî-Mra'a.* Cairo: Maktabat Madbûlî, 1983.

———. *The Innocence of the Devil*. Translated by Sherif Hetata. Berkeley and Los Angeles: University of California Press, 1994.

——— [al-Sa'dâwi, Nawâl]. *Al-Insân: Ithnay* [sic] *'Ashar Imra'a fî Zinzâna Wâhida*. Cairo: Maktabat Madbûlî, 1982.

———. "Introduction." In *Women of the Arab World: The Coming Challenge*, edited by Nahid Toubia, translated by Nahed El Gamal, pp. 1–7. London: Zed Books, 1988.

——— [al-Sa'dâwi, Nawâl]. *Izîs*. Cairo: Dâr al-Mustaqbal al-'Arabî, 1986.

——— [al-Sa'dâwi, Nawâl]. *Jannât wa-Iblîs*. Beirut: Dâr al-Adâb, 1992.

——— [al-Sa'dâwi, Nawâl]. *Kânat Hiya al-Ad'af*. Cairo: Maktabat Madbûlî, 1979.

——— [al-Sa'dâwi, Nawâl]. *Al-Khayt wa-'Ayn al-Hayât*. Cairo: Maktabat Madbûlî, 1972.

——— [al-Sa'dâwi, Nawâl]. *Lahzat Sidq*. Beirut: Dâr al-Adâb, 1986.

——— [al-Sa'dâwi, Nawâl]. *Al-Mar'a wal-Sirâ' al-Nafsî*. Cairo: Maktabat Madbûlî, 1983.

——— [al-Sa'dâwi, Nawâl]. *Al-Mar'a wal-Jins*. Third edition. Cairo: Maktabat Madbûlî, 1974.

——— [al-Sa'dâwi, Nawâl]. *Ma'raka Jadîda fî Qadiyyat al-Mar'a*. Cairo: Sînâ lil-Nashr, 1992.

——— [al-Sa'dâwi, Nawâl]. *Mawt Ma'âlî al-Wazîr Sâbiqan*. Cairo: Maktabat Madbûlî, 1980.

——— [al-Sa'dâwi, Nawâl]. *Mawt al-Rajul al-Wahîd 'alâ al-Ard*. Cairo: Maktabat Madbûlî, 1983.

———. *Memoirs of a Woman Doctor*. Translated by Catherine Cobham. San Francisco: City Lights Books, 1989.

——— [el-Sa'adawi, Nawal]. *Memoirs from the Women's Prison*. Translated by Marilyn Booth. London: Women's Press, 1986; Berkeley and Los Angeles: University of California Press, 1994.

——— [al-Sa'dâwi, Nawâl]. *Mudhakkirât Tabîba*. Beirut: Dâr al-Adâb, 1980.

——— [al-Sa'dâwi, Nawâl]. *Mudhakkirât Tifla Ismuhâ Su'âd*. Cairo: Manshûrât Dâr Tadâmun al-Mar'a al-'Arabiyya, 1990.

——— [al-Sa'dâwi, Nawâl]. *Mudhakkirâtî fî Sijn al-Nisâ'*. Cairo: Dâr al-Mustaqbal al-'Arabî, 1984.

———. *My Travels Around the World*. Translated by Shirley Eber. London: Methuen, 1991.

———. "An Overview of My Life." Translated by Antoinette Tuma. In *Contemporary Authors Autobiography Series* 11:61–72. Detroit, Mich.: Gale Research Co., 1990.

———. "The Question No One Would Answer." *Ms.*, March 1980, pp. 68–69.

———. *Al-Rajul wal-Jins*. Beirut: al-Mu'assasa al-'Arabiyya lil-Dirâsât wal-Nashr, 1976.

———. "Reply." In Georges Tarabishi, *Woman Against Her Sex: A Critique of Nawal el-Saadawi*, translated by Basil Hatim and Elisabeth Orsini, pp. 189–211. London: Saqi Books, 1988.

——— [al-Sa'dâwi, Nawâl]. *Rihlâtî fî al-'Alam*. Cairo: Dâr Nashr Tadâmun al-Mar'a al-'Arabiyya, 1987.

————. *Searching.* Translated by Shirley Eber. London: Zed Books, 1991.

————. *She Has No Place in Paradise.* Translated by Shirley Eber. London: Minerva, 1989.

———— [al-Sa'dâwi, Nawâl]. *Suqût al-Imâm.* Cairo: Dâr al-Mustaqbal al-'Arabî, 1987.

———— [al-Sa'dâwi, Nawâl]. *Ta'allamt al-Hubb.* Cairo: Maktabat al-Nahda al-Misriyya, 1961.

————. *Two Women in One.* Translated by Osman Nusairi and Jana Gough. London: al-Saqi Books, 1985.

———— [al-Sa'dâwi, Nawâl]. *Ughniyyat al-Atfâl al-Dâ'iriyya.* Cairo: Maktabat Madbûlî, 1978.

———— [al-Sa'dâwi, Nawâl]. *Al-Unthâ Hiya al-Asl.* Cairo: Maktabat Madbûlî, 1974.

———— [al-Sa'dâwi, Nawâl]. *Al-Wajh al-'Arî lil-Mar'a al-'Arabiyya.* Beirut: al-Mu'assasa al-'Arabiyya lil-Dirâsât wal-Nashr, 1977.

————. *The Well of Life and the Thread.* Translated by Sherif Hetata. London: Lime Tree, 1993.

————. *Woman at Point Zero.* Translated by Sherif Hetata. London: Zed Press, 1983.

————. "Women's Resistance in the Arab World." In *Women in the Middle East: Perceptions, Realities, and Struggles for Liberation,* edited by Haleh Afshar, pp. 139–145. London: Macmillan, 1993.

El-Shamy, Hasan. "The Brother-Sister Syndrome in Arab Family Life, Socio-Cultural Factors in Arab Psychiatry: A Critical Review." *International Journal of Sociology of the Family* 11 (1981): 313–323.

————. *Brother and Sister Type 872*: A Cognitive Behavioristic Analysis of a Middle Eastern Oikotype.* Folklore Monographs Series, vol. 8. Bloomington, Ind.: Folklore Publications Group, 1979.

El-Shamy, Hasan M. "The Traditional Structure of Sentiments in Mahfouz's Trilogy: A Behavioristic Text Analysis." *Al-'Arabiyya* 9 (1976): 53–74.

Elisséeff, Nikita. *Thèmes et motifs des milles et une nuits: essai de classification.* Beirut: Institut Français de Damas, 1949.

*The Encyclopaedia of Islam.* 2d ed. Edited by H.A.R. Gibb et al. Leiden: E. J. Brill, 1960–.

Erlich, Michel. *La femme blessée: essai sur les mutilations sexuelles féminines.* Paris: Editions l'Harmattan, 1986.

Erman, Adolf. *A Handbook of Egyptian Religion.* Translated by A. S. Griffith. Boston: Longwood Press, 1977.

Esposito, John L. *Islam: The Straight Path.* New York: Oxford University Press, 1991.

————. *The Islamic Threat: Myth or Reality?* New York: Oxford University Press, 1992.

Fanon, Frantz. *A Dying Colonialism.* Translated by Haakon Chevalier. New York: Grove Press, 1967.

Farahât, Yâsir. *Al-Muwâjaha: Dr. Nawâl al-Sa'dâwî.* Cairo: al-Rawda, 1993.

Farwell, Marilyn R. "Heterosexual Plots and Lesbian Subtexts: Toward a Theory of Lesbian Narrative Space." In *Lesbian Texts and Contexts: Radical Revisions*, edited by Karla Jay and Joanne Glasgow, pp. 91–103. New York: New York University Press, 1990.

Fayyâd, Sulaymân. *Aswât*. Cairo: Kutub 'Arabiyya, 1972.

Forrest, Katherine V. *Daughters of a Coral Dawn*. Tallahassee: Naiad Press, 1989.

Forsyth, Neil. *The Old Enemy: Satan and the Combat Myth*. Princeton: Princeton University Press, 1987.

Foucault, Michel. *Histoire de la folie à l'âge classique*. Paris: Editions Gallimard, 1972.

———. *Naissance de la clinique: une archéologie du regard médical*. Paris: Presses Universitaires de France, 1963.

Garber, Marjorie. *Vested Interests: Cross-Dressing and Cultural Anxiety*. New York: HarperCollins, 1992.

Gelfand, Elissa D. *Imagination in Confinement: Women's Writings from French Prisons*. Ithaca: Cornell University Press, 1983.

Genette, Gérard. *Seuils*. Paris: Editions du Seuil, 1987.

Gershoni, Israel, and James P. Jankowski. *Egypt, Islam, and the Arabs: The Search for Egyptian Nationhood, 1900–1930*. New York: Oxford University Press, 1986.

al-Ghazâlî, Muhammad. *Qadâyâ al-Mar'a bayn al-Taqâlîd al-Râkida wal-Wâfida*. 3d ed. Cairo: Dâr al-Shurûq, 1991.

al-Ghazâlî, Zaynab. *Ayyâm min Hayâtî*. Cairo: Dâr al-Shurûq, 1987.

al-Ghîtânî, Jamâl. *Khitat al-Ghîtânî*. Cairo: Dâr al-Masîra, 1981.

———. *Al-Zaynî Barakât*. Cairo: Maktabat Madbûlî, 1975.

Gilman, Charlotte Perkins. *Herland*. New York: Pantheon Books, 1979.

Girard, René. *Le bouc émissaire*. Paris: Editions Grasset & Fasquelle, 1982.

———. *La violence et le sacré*. Paris: Editions Bernard Grasset, 1972.

Graham, Theodora R. "The Courage of His Diversity: Medicine, Writing, and William Carlos Williams." *Literature and Medicine* 2 (1983): 9–20.

Green, Roger Lancelyn. *Tales of Ancient Egypt*. New York: Henry Z. Walck, 1968.

Habîbî, Imîl. *Ikhtayyi*. Cyprus: Kitâb al-Karmil, 1985.

Hafez, Sabry. "Intentions and Realisation in the Narratives of Nawal El-Saadawi." *Third World Quarterly* 11, no. 3 (July 1989): 188–198.

al-Hakîm, Tawfîq. *Izîs*. Cairo: Maktabat al-Adâb, 1985.

———. "The Martyr." Translated by David Bishai, revised by Ronald Ewart. In *Arabic Writing Today: The Short Story*, edited by Mahmoud Manzalaoui, pp. 36–46. Cairo: Dar al-Maaref, 1968.

———. "Al-Shahîd." In *Arinî Allâh*, pp. 13–29. Cairo: al-Matba'a al-Namûdhajiyya, n.d.

———. *Shahrazâd*. Cairo: Maktabat al-Adâb, n.d.

Haller, Evelyn. "Isis Unveiled: Virginia Woolf's Use of Egyptian Myth." In *Virginia Woolf: A Feminist Slant*, edited by Jane Marcus, pp. 109–131. Lincoln: University of Nebraska Press, 1984.

Hamza, Karîmân. *Rifqan bil-Qawârîr*. Beirut: Dâr al-Fath lil-Tibâ'a wal-Nashr, 1985.

————. *Rihlatî min al-Sufûr ilâ al-Hijâb.* 2d ed. Beirut: Dâr al-Fath lil-Tibâ'a wal-Nashr, 1986.

Haqqî, Yahyâ. *Qindîl Umm Hâshim.* Cairo: al-Hay'a al-Misriyya al-'Amma lil-Kitâb, 1975.

Harlow, Barbara. *Barred: Women, Writing, and Political Detention.* Hanover, N.H.: Wesleyan University Press, 1992.

————. *Resistance Literature.* New York: Methuen, 1987.

Hatâta, Sharîf. *See* Hetata, Sherif.

Hetata, Sherif [Hatâta, Sharîf]. *Al-'Ayn Dhât al-Jafn al-Ma'danî.* Cairo: Dâr al-Thaqâfa al-Jadîda, 1981.

————. *The Eye with the Iron Lid.* Translated by Sherif Hetata. London: Zed Press, n.d.

———— [Hatâta, Sharîf]. *Tarîq al-Milh wal-Hubb.* Cairo: Dâr al-Mustaqbal al-'Arabî, 1983.

Hijâzî, Ahmad. *Tambûl al-Awwal.* Beirut: Dâr al-Fatâ al-'Arabî, 1981.

Hilmî, Munâ. *Rajul Jadîd fî al-Ufq.* Cairo: Dâr Tadâmun al-Mar'a al-'Arabiyya, 1988.

Hitchcock, Peter. *Dialogics of the Oppressed.* Minneapolis: University of Minnesota Press, 1993.

Homerin, T. Emil. "Echoes of a Thirsty Owl: Death and Afterlife in Pre-Islamic Arabic Poetry." *Journal of Near Eastern Studies* 44, no. 3 (1985): 165–184.

Hourani, Albert. *Arabic Thought in the Liberal Age, 1798–1939.* London: Oxford University Press, 1970.

Hunayn ibn Ishâq. "Qissat Salâmân and Absâl" (translated from the Greek). In Ibn Sînâ, *Tis' Rasâ'il,* pp. 158–168. Cairo: Maktabat Hindiyya, 1908.

Hunter, Kathryn Montgomery. *Doctors' Stories: The Narrative Structure of Medical Knowledge.* Princeton: Princeton University Press, 1991.

Husayn, Tâhâ. *See* Hussein, Taha.

Hussein, Taha [Husayn, Tâhâ]. *al-Ayyâm.* Vols. 1 and 3. Cairo: Dâr al-Ma'ârif, 1971, 1973.

————. *An Egyptian Childhood.* Translated by E. H. Paxton. Washington, D.C.: Three Continents Press, 1981.

———— [Husayn, Tâhâ]. *A Passage to France.* Translated by Kenneth Cragg. Leiden: E. J. Brill, 1976.

Huston, Nancy. "The Matrix of War: Mothers and Heroes." In *The Female Body in Western Culture: Contemporary Perspectives,* edited by Susan Rubin Suleiman, pp. 119–136. Cambridge, Mass.: Harvard University Press, 1986.

Ibn al-Batanûnî. "Kitâb al-'Unwân fî Makâyid al-Niswân." MS. Cairo, Adâb 3568.

Ibn al-Jawzî. *Ahkâm al-Nisâ'.* Beirut: Dâr al-Kutub al-'Ilmiyya, 1985.

————. *Akhbâr al-Adhkiyâ'.* Edited by Muhammad Mursî al-Khawlî. Cairo: Matâbi' al-Ahrâm al-Tijâriyya, 1970.

————. *Talbîs Iblîs.* Cairo: Maktabat al-Mutanabbî, n.d.

Ibn Battûta. *Rihlat Ibn Battûta.* Edited by Talâl Harb. Beirut: Dâr al-Kutub al-'Ilmiyya, 1987.

Ibn Bâz, 'Abd al-'Azîz ibn 'Abd Allâh. *Fatâwá lil-Muslim fî al-Mughtarab*. Washington, D.C.: Saudi Arabian Cultural Bureau, n.d.

Ibn Hanbal, Ahmad. *Ahkâm al-Nisâ'*. Edited by 'Abd al-Qâdir Ahmad 'Atâ. Beirut: Dâr al-Kutub al-'Ilmiyya, 1986.

Ibn Jubayr. *Rihlat Ibn Jubayr*. Beirut: Dâr Sâdir, 1980.

Ibn Manzûr. *Lisân al-'Arab*. 20 vols. in 10. Cairo: al-Dâr al-Misriyya lil-Ta'lîf wal-Tarjama, n.d.

Ibn Qayyim al-Jawziyya. *Hukm al-Nazar lil-Nisâ'*. Cairo: Maktab al-Turâth al-Islâmî, 1982.

Ibn Sîda. *Al-Muhkam wal-Muhît al-A'zam fî al-Lugha*. Edited by 'Abd al-Sattâr Ahmad Farrâj, Husayn Nassâr, et al. 7 vols. to date. Cairo: Matba'at Mustafâ al-Bâbî al-Halabî, 1958–.

Idrîs, Yûsuf. "'Alâ Waraq Sîlûfân." In *Bayt min Lahm*, pp. 31–51. Cairo: Dâr Misr lil-Tibâ'a, 1982.

———. "Al-'Amaliyya al-Kubrâ." In *al-Naddâha*, pp. 113–137. Cairo: Dâr Misr lil-Tibâ'a, 1982.

———. "In Cellophane Wrapping." Translated by Roger Allen. In *In the Eye of the Beholder: Tales of Egyptian Life from the Writings of Yusuf Idris*, edited by Roger Allen, pp. 169–189. Minneapolis and Chicago: Bibliotheca Islamica, 1978.

———. *Niyû Yûrk 80*. Cairo: Dâr Misr lil-Tibâ'a, 1980.

al-Imâm, Hasan. *Hikâyatî ma'a al-Zamân*. 1974.

'Itânî, Samîra. *Hal Sahîh anna Akthar Ahl al-Nâr Hum al-Nisâ'?* Beirut: Dâr al-Fath lil-Tibâ'a wal-Nashr, 1979[?].

'Iwad Allâh, Ahmad al-Sabâhî. *Tafsîr al-Ahlâm*. Cairo: Maktabat Madbûlî, 1977.

Jacobus, Mary. "In Parenthesis: Immaculate Conceptions and Feminine Desire." In *Body/Politics: Women and the Discourses of Science*, edited by Mary Jacobus, Evelyn Fox Keller, and Sally Shuttleworth, pp. 11–28. New York: Routledge, 1990.

Jay, Martin. "Scopic Regimes of Modernity." In *Vision and Visuality*, edited by Hal Foster, pp. 3–23. Seattle: Bay Press, 1988.

Jayawardena, Kumari. *Feminism and Nationalism in the Third World*. London: Zed Books, 1986.

Jourdan, François. *La tradition des Septs dormants: une rencontre entre Chrétiens et Musulmans*. Paris: Editions Maisonneuve & Larose, 1983.

Kaci. *Bas les voiles*. Paris: Editions Rochevignes, 1984.

Kamâl, Karîma. *Bint Misriyya fî Amrîkâ*. Cairo: Dâr Gharîb lil-Tibâ'a, 1988[?].

Kaminsky, Amy Katz. "Women Writing About Prostitutes: Amalia Jamilis and Luisa Valenzuela." In *The Image of the Prostitute in Modern Literature*, edited by Pierre L. Horn and Mary Beth Pringle, pp. 119–131. New York: Frederick Ungar, 1984.

Kandiyoti, Deniz. "Identity and Its Discontents: Women and the Nation." *Millennium: Journal of International Studies* 20, no. 3 (1991): 429–443.

———, ed. *Women, Islam, and the State*. Philadelphia: Temple University Press, 1991.

Kâzim, Sâfî Nâz. *'An al-Sijn wal-Hurriyya*. Cairo: al-Zahrâ' lil-I'lâm al-'Arabî, 1986.

Kepel, Gilles. *Les banlieues de l'Islam: naissance d'une religion en France*. Paris: Editions du Seuil, 1987.

———. *Muslim Extremism in Egypt: The Prophet and Pharaoh*. Berkeley and Los Angeles: University of California Press, 1986.

al-Khatîb-al-Baghdâdî. *Al-Bukhalâ'*. Edited by Ahmad Matlûb, Khadîja al-Hadîthî, and Ahmad Nâjî al-Qaysî. Baghdad: Matba'at al-'Anî, 1964.

Kilgour, Maggie. *From Communion to Cannibalism: An Anatomy of Metaphors of Incorporation*. Princeton: Princeton University Press, 1990.

Kishtainy, Khalid. *The Prostitute in Progressive Literature*. London: Allison & Busby, 1982.

*Kitâb Alf Layla wa-Layla*. Edited by Muhsin Mahdi. Leiden: E. J. Brill, 1984.

Kurpershoek, P. M. *The Short Stories of Yûsuf Idrîs*. Leiden: E. J. Brill, 1981.

Le Guin, Ursula K. *The Left Hand of Darkness*. New York: Ace Books, 1969.

Le Gassick, Trevor. "The Arabic Novel in English Translation." *Mundus Arabicus* 5 (1992): 47–60 (special issue entitled "The Arabic Novel Since 1950," edited by Issa Boullata).

Lejeune, Philippe. *Le pacte autobiographique*. Paris: Editions du Seuil, 1975.

———. "Le pacte autobiographique (bis)" *Poétique* 56 (1983): 416–434.

Lerner, Gerda. *The Creation of Patriarchy*. New York: Oxford University Press, 1986.

Lewis, Bernard. *The Muslim Discovery of Europe*. New York: W. W. Norton, 1982.

———. *Race and Slavery in the Middle East: An Historical Enquiry*. New York: Oxford University Press, 1990.

Lightfoot-Klein, Hanny. *Prisoners of Ritual: An Odyssey into Female Genital Circumcision in Africa*. New York: Haworth Press, 1989.

Lionnet, Françoise. "Dissymetry Embodied: Feminism, Universalism, and the Practice of Excision." In *Borderwork: Feminist Engagements with Comparative Literature*. Edited by Margaret R. Higonnet, pp. 19–46. Ithaca: Cornell University Press, 1994.

al-Ma'arrî, Abû al-'Alâ'. *Risâlat al-Ghufrân*. Edited by 'A'isha 'Abd al-Rahmân. Cairo: Dâr al-Ma'ârif, 1963.

al-Mahallî, Jalâl al-Dîn, and Jalâl al-Dîn al-Suyûtî. *Tafsîr al-Qur'ân*. 2 vols. in 1. Cairo: Mustafâ al-Bâbî al-Halabî, 1966.

Mahfouz, Naguib [Mahfûz, Najîb]. *Bidâya wa-Nihâya*. Beirut: Dâr al-Qalam, 1971.

——— [Mahfûz, Najîb]. "Kayduhunna." In *Hams al-Junûn*, pp. 79–89. Beirut: Dâr al-Qalam, 1973.

———. *Midaq Alley*. Translated by Trevor Le Gassick. London: Heinemann, 1966.

——— [Mahfûz, Najîb]. "Ra'aytu fîmâ Yarâ al-Nâ'im." In *Ra'aytu fîmâ Yarâ al-Nâ'im*, pp. 139–173. Beirut: Maktabat Misr, 1982.

——— [Mahfûz, Najîb]. *Zuqâq al-Midaqq*. Beirut: Dâr al-Qalam, 1972.

Mahfûz, Ahmad Hânî. *Mughâmarât Juhâ*. Beirut: al-Maktab al-Islâmî, 1987.

Mahfûz, Najîb. *See* Mahfouz, Naguib.

al-Mahmûd, Ibrâhîm ibn Sâlih. *Kayf Taksibîna Zawjaki?!* Fez: Maktabat wa-Tasjîlât al-Hidâya al-Qur'âniyya, 1991.

Mahmûd, Mustafâ. *Li-Mâdhâ Rafadt al-Mârksiyya?* 3d printing. Cairo: Dâr al-Ma'ârif, 1989.

——. *Al-Mârksiyya wal-Islâm.* 6th printing. Cairo: Dâr al-Ma'ârif, 1987.

——. *Rihlatî min al-Shakk ilâ al-Imân.* 9th ed. Cairo: Dâr al-Ma'ârif, 1991.

Malti-Douglas, Fedwa. "Afterword." In Yusuf al-Qa'id, *War in the Land of Egypt*, translated by Olive Kenny, Lorne Kenny, and Christopher Tingley, pp. 185–192. London: al-Saqi Books, 1986.

——. "Al-'Amâ fî Mir'ât al-Tarjama al-Shakhsiyya: Tâhâ Husayn wa-Ved Mehta." *Fusûl* 3, no. 4 (1983): 72–75.

——. "Al-'Anâsir al-Turâthiyya fî al-Adab al-'Arabî al-Mu'âsir: al-Ahlâm fî Thalâth Qisas," translated by 'I. al-Sharqâwî. *Fusûl* 2, no. 2 (1982): 21–29.

——. "An Anti-Travel Guide: Iconography in a Muslim Revivalist Tract." *Edebiyât*, n.s., 4, no. 2 (1993): 205–213.

——. *Blindness and Autobiography: "al-Ayyâm" of Tâhâ Husayn.* Princeton: Princeton University Press, 1988.

——. "Classical Arabic Crime Narratives: Thieves and Thievery in *Adab* Literature." *Journal of Arabic Literature* 19 (1988): 108–127.

——. "The Classical Arabic Detective." *Arabica* 35 (1988): 59–91.

——. "Dangerous Crossings: Gender and Criticism in Arabic Literary Studies." In *Borderwork: Feminist Engagements with Comparative Literature.* Edited by Margaret Higonnet, pp. 224–229. Ithaca: Cornell University Press, 1994.

——. "Gender and the Uses of the Ascetic in an Islamist Text." In *Asceticism.* Edited by Vincent L. Wimbush and Richard Valantasis, pp. 395–411. New York: Oxford University Press, 1995.

——. "Introduction to *The Innocence of the Devil*: From Theology to Rape." In Nawal El Saadawi, *The Innocence of the Devil*, translated by Sherif Hetata. Berkeley and Los Angeles: University of California Press, 1994.

——. "Literary Form and Ideological Content of 'Abbâsid Historiography: Al-Mu'tadid in Chronicle, Biography, and *Adab*." In *Early Islamic Historiography.* Edited by Lawrence I. Conrad. Princeton: Darwin Press, forthcoming.

——. "Mahfouz's Dreams." In *Naguib Mahfouz: From Regional Fame to Global Recognition*, edited by Michael Beard and Adnan Haydar, pp. 126–143. Syracuse: Syracuse University Press, 1993.

——. "*Min al-Ta'rîkh al-Sirrî li-Nu'mân 'Abd al-Hâfiz* wa-Tadmîr Tuqûs al-Hayât wal-Lugha." *Ibdâ'* 1, nos. 6–7 (1983): 86–92.

——. "Playing with the Sacred: Religious Intertext in *Adab* Discourse." In *Language and Cultural Context in the Near East*, edited by Asma Afsaruddin, Matt Zahniser, and Karl Stowasser. Winona Lake, Ind.: Eisenbrauns, forthcoming.

——. Review of *Les mille et une nuits d'Antoine Galland*, by Georges May. *Journal of the American Oriental Society* 111, no. 1 (1991): 196.

———. "Shahrazâd Feminist." In *The Thousand and One Nights in Arabic Literature and Society*, edited by Fedwa Malti-Douglas and Georges Sabagh. Cambridge: Cambridge University Press, forthcoming.

———. "Sign Conceptions in the Islamic World." In *Semiotics: A Handbook on the Sign-Theoretic Foundations of Nature and Culture*, edited by Roland Posner, Klaus Robering, and Thomas E. Sebeok. Berlin and New York: Walter de Gruyter, forthcoming.

———. *Woman's Body, Woman's Word: Gender and Discourse in Arabo-Islamic Writing*. Princeton: Princeton University Press, 1991.

———. "Writing Nawal El Saadawi." In *Feminism Beside Itself*, edited by Diane Elam and Robyn Wiegman, pp. 283–296. New York: Routledge, 1995.

———. "Yûsuf al-Qa'îd wal-Riwâya al-Jadîda." *Fusúl* 4, no. 3 (1984): pp. 190–202.

Mansûr, Anîs. *Anta fî al-Yâbân*. Cairo: al-Maktab al-Misrî al-Hadîth, 1984.

Marcus, Jane. "Afterword." In Helen Zenna Smith, *Not So Quiet. . . .* New York: Feminist Press, 1989.

———. *Virginia Woolf and the Languages of Patriarchy*. Bloomington: Indiana University Press, 1987.

Marsot, Afaf Lutfi al-Sayyid. "The Revolutionary Gentlewomen in Egypt." In *Women in the Muslim World*, edited by Lois Beck and Nikki Keddie, pp. 261–276. Cambridge, Mass.: Harvard University Press, 1978.

May, Georges. *Les mille et une nuits d'Antoine Galland*. Paris: Presses Universitaires de France, 1986.

al-Maydânî. *Majma' al-Amthâl*. 2 vols. Beirut: Dâr Maktabat al-Hayât, n.d.

Mehdid, Malika. "A Western Invention of Arab Womanhood: The 'Oriental' Female." In *Women in the Middle East: Perceptions, Realities, and Struggles for Liberation*, edited by Haleh Afshar, pp. 18–58. London: Macmillan, 1993.

Mehta, Ved. *Vedi*. Oxford: Oxford University Press, 1982.

Mernissi, Fatima. *Beyond the Veil: Male-Female Dynamics in a Modern Muslim Society*. Cambridge, Mass.: Schenkman, 1975.

———. *Chahrazad n'est pas marocaine*. Casablanca: Editions Le Fennec, 1988.

Mikhail, Mona. *Studies in the Short Fiction of Mahfouz and Idris*. New York: New York University Press, 1992.

Minces, Juliette. *La femme voilée: l'Islam au féminin*. Paris: Calmann-Lévy, 1990.

al-Mis'adî, Mahmûd. *Haddatha Abû Hurayra Qâl*. Tunis: Dâr al-Janûb lil-Nashr, 1979.

Moghadam, Val. *Modernizing Women: Gender and Social Change in the Middle East*. Boulder, Colo.: L. Rienner, 1993.

Mohanty, Chandra Talpade, Ann Russo, and Lourdes Torres, eds. *Third World Women and the Politics of Feminism*. Bloomington: Indiana University Press, 1991.

Mustajâb, Muhammad. *Min al-Ta'rîkh al-Sirrî li-Nu'mân 'Abd al-Hâfiz*. Cairo: Maktab al-Nîl lil-Tab' wal-Nashr, 1982.

al-Nâbulusî. *Ta'tîr al-Anâm fî Ta'bîr al-Manâm.* 2 vols. in 1. Cairo: 'Isâ al-Bâbî al-Halabî, n.d.

al-Nadwî, Abû al-Hasan 'Alî. *Ahâdîth Sarîha fî Amrîkâ.* Beirut: Mu'assasat al-Risâla, 1987.

al-Naqqâsh, Farîda. *Al-Sijn: Dam'atân wa-Warda.* Cairo: Dâr al-Mustaqbal al-'Arabî, 1985.

Norton, Augustus Richard. *Amal and the Shi'a: Struggle for the Soul of Lebanon.* Austin: University of Texas Press, 1987.

Park, Heong-Dug. "Nawâl al-Sa'adâwî [*sic*] and Modern Egyptian Feminist Writings." Ph.D. diss., University of Michigan, 1988.

Pellat, Charles. "Liwât." In *Sexuality and Eroticism Among Males in Moslem Societies,* edited by Arno Schmitt and Jehoeda Sofer, pp. 151–167. New York: Harrington Park Press, 1992.

Peters, Edward. *Torture.* Oxford: Basil Blackwell, 1985.

Phelps, Ethel Johnston. "Scheherazade Retold." In *The Maid of the North: Feminist Folk Tales from Around the World,* pp. 167–173. New York: Henry Holt, 1981.

Pheterson, Gail, ed. *A Vindication of the Rights of Whores.* Seattle: Seal Press, 1989.

Philipp, Thomas. "Feminism and Nationalist Politics in Egypt." In *Women in the Muslim World,* edited by Lois Beck and Nikki Keddie, pp. 277–294. Cambridge, Mass.: Harvard University Press, 1978.

Phillips, John A. *Eve: The History of an Idea.* San Francisco: Harper & Row, 1984.

Pizan, Christine de. *The Book of the City of Ladies.* Translated by Earl Jeffrey Richards. New York: Persea Books, 1982.

Poe, Edgar Allan. "The Thousand-and-Second Tale of Scheherazade." In *Short Stories,* Greenwich Unabridged Library Classics, pp. 491–502. New York: Chatham River Press, 1981.

Pratt, Annis. *Archetypal Patterns in Women's Fiction.* Bloomington: Indiana University Press, 1981.

al-Qa'îd, Yusuf. *Al-Harb fî Barr Misr.* Beirut: Dâr Ibn Rushd lil-Tibâ'a wal-Nashr, 1978.

———. *War in the Land of Egypt.* Translated by Olive Kenny, Lorne Kenny, and Christopher Tingley. London: al-Saqi Books, 1986.

———. *Yahduth fî Misr al-An.* Cairo: Dâr Usâma lil-Tab' wal-Nashr, 1977.

al-Qarnî, 'A'id ibn 'Abd Allâh. *Bâqat Ward ilâ Fatât al-Islâm.* Riyad: Dâr al-Diyâ' lil-Nashr wal-Tawzî', 1411 A.H.

———. *Makâ'id al-Shaytân.* Riyad: Dâr al-Diyâ' lil-Nashr wal-Tawzî', 1411 A.H.

*Al-Qur'ân.* Cairo: Mustafâ al-Bâbî al-Halabî, 1966.

al-Qurtubî. *Al-Jâmi' li-Ahkâm al-Qur'ân.* 20 vols. in 10. Cairo: Dâr al-Kitâb al-'Arabî lil-Tibâ'a wal-Nashr, 1967.

al-Râghib al-Isfahânî. *Muhâdarât al-Udabâ' wa-Muhâwarât al-Shu'arâ' wal-Bulaghâ'.* 4 vols. in 2. Beirut: Dâr Maktabat al-Hayât, n.d.

Ramadân, Sumayya. "al-Radd 'alâ Kitâb *Unthâ Didd al-Unûtha,*" in *al-Fikr* al-'Arabî al-Mu'âsir wal-Mar'a, pp. 125–131. Cairo: Dâr Tadâmun al-Mar'a al-'Arabiyya, 1988.

Ridâ, Muhammad Rashîd. *Huqûq al-Nisâ' fî al-Islâm*. Beirut: al-Maktab al-Islâmî, 1981.

Rifaat, Alifa. "Bahiyya's Eyes." Translated by Denys Johnson-Davies. In *Distant View of a Minaret and Other Stories*, pp. 5–11. London: Quartet Books, 1983.

———[Rif'at, Alîfa]. *Man Yakûn al-Rajul*. Cairo: Matâbi' al-Hay'a al-Misriyya al-'Amma lil-Kitâb, 1981.

Rif'at, Alîfa. See Rifaat, Alifa.

al-Rifâ'î, Hâshim ibn Hâmid. "Al-Kalimât fî Bayân Mahâsin Ta'addud al-Zawjât." Offset publication. [Fez?], 1987.

Riffaterre, Michael. "Intertextual Scrambling." *Romanic Review* 68 (1977): 197–206.

Rohrlich, Ruby, and Elaine Hoffman Baruch, eds. *Women in Search of Utopia: Mavericks and Mythmakers*. New York: Schocken Books, 1984.

Rowson, Everett K. "The Categorization of Gender and Sexual Irregularity in Medieval Arabic Vice Lists." In *Body Guards: The Cultural Politics of Gender Ambiguity*, edited by Julia Epstein and Kristina Straub, pp. 50–79. New York: Routledge, 1991.

———. "The Effeminates of Early Medina." *Journal of the American Oriental Society* 111 (1992): 671–693.

Ruether, Rosemary Radford. *Womanguides: Readings Toward a Feminist Theology*. Boston: Beacon Press, 1985.

Russ, Joanna. *The Female Man*. Boston: Beacon Press, 1975.

———. *How to Suppress Women's Writing*. Austin: University of Texas Press, 1983.

al-Saadawi, Nawal; el-Sa'adawi, Nawal. *See* El Saadawi, Nawal.

Sa'd, 'Abd al-Mun'im. *Mûjaz Ta'rîkh al-Sînamâ al-Misriyya*. Cairo: Matâbi' al-Ahrâm al-Tijâriyya, 1976?

al-Sa'dâwî, Nawâl. *See* El Saadawi, Nawal.

al-Sa'ûdî, Rabî' ibn Muhammad. *Zâd al-Musâfirîn ilâ Ghayr Bilâd al-Muslimîn*. Riyad: Dâr al-Fitya; Cairo: Dâr al-Sahwa lil-Nashr, 1988.

Said, Edward W. *Culture and Imperialism*. New York: Alfred A. Knopf, 1993.

———. "Embargoed Literature." *Nation*, September 17, 1990.

al-Sakhâwî. *Al-Daw' al-Lâmi' li-Ahl al-Qarn al-Tâsi'*. 12 vols. Beirut: Manshûrât Dâr Maktabat al-Hayât, n.d.

Sanders, Paula. "Gendering the Ungendered Body: Hermaphrodites in Medieval Islamic Law." In *Women in Middle Eastern History: Shifting Boundaries in Sex and Gender*, edited by Nikki R. Keddie and Beth Baron, pp. 74–95. New Haven: Yale University Press, 1991.

Santiago, Luciano P. R., M.D. *The Children of Oedipus: Brother-Sister Incest in Psychiatry, Literature, History, and Mythology*. Roslyn Heights, N.Y.: Libra, 1973.

Sarhân, Samîr, and I'tidâl 'Uthmân, eds. *Yûsuf Idrîs (1927–1991)*. Cairo: al-Hay'a al-Misriyya al-'Amma lil-Kitâb, 1991.

Saussure, F. de. *Cours de linguistique générale*. Paris: Payot, 1978.

al-Sawwâf, Muhammad Mahmûd. *Zawjât al-Nabiyy al-Tâhirât wa-Hikmat Ta'addudihinna.* Cairo: Dâr al-I'tisâm, 1979.

Scarry, Elaine. *The Body in Pain: The Making and Unmaking of the World.* New York: Oxford University Press, 1985.

Schacht, Joseph. *An Introduction to Islamic Law.* Oxford: Oxford University Press, 1986.

Schimmel, Annemarie. *Islamic Names.* Edinburgh: Edinburgh University Press, 1989.

Schmitt, Arno, and Jehoeda Sofer, eds. *Sexuality and Eroticism Among Males in Moslem Societies.* New York: Harrington Park Press, 1992.

Sedgwick, Eve Kosofsky. *Between Men: English Literature and Male Homosocial Desire.* New York: Columbia University Press, 1985.

———. *Epistemology of the Closet.* Berkeley and Los Angeles: University of California Press, 1990.

Selzer, Richard. *Rituals of Surgery.* New York: Harper's Magazine Press, 1974.

Shaaban, Bouthaina. *Both Right and Left Handed: Arab Women Talk About Their Lives.* London: Women's Press, 1988.

Shaheen, Jack G. *The TV Arab.* Bowling Green, Ohio: Bowling Green State University Popular Press, 1984.

Shalabî, 'Abd al-Wadûd. *Fî Mahkamat al-Ta'rîkh.* Cairo: Dâr al-Shurûq, 1986.

Sharabi, Hisham. *Neopatriarchy: A Theory of Distorted Change in Arab Society.* New York: Oxford University Press, 1988.

Sharaf, Mûsâ Sâlih. *Fatâwâ al-Nisâ' al-'Asriyya.* Beirut: Dâr al-Jîl; Cairo: Maktabat al-Turâth al-Islâmî, 1988.

al-Shaykh, Hanân. *Hikâyat Zahra.* Beirut: Dâr al-Adâb, 1989.

———. *Misk al-Ghazâl.* Beirut: Dâr al-Adâb, 1988.

———. *The Story of Zahra.* Translated by Peter Ford. New York: Anchor Books, 1994.

———. *Women of Sand and Myrrh.* Translated by Catherine Cobham. New York: Anchor Books, 1992.

Showalter, Elaine. *The Female Malady: Women, Madness, and English Culture, 1830–1980.* New York: Pantheon Books, 1985.

Showerman, Grant. "Isis." In *Encyclopedia of Religion and Ethics,* edited by James Hastings et al., 7:434–437. New York: Charles Scribner's Sons, 1961.

Shuiskii, Sergei A. "Some Observations on Modern Arabic Autobiography." *Journal of Arabic Literature* 13 (1982): 111–123.

Sivan, Emmanuel. *Radical Islam: Medieval Theology and Modern Politics.* New Haven: Yale University Press, 1985; enlarged ed., 1990.

Snow, C. P. *The Two Cultures and A Second Look.* Cambridge: Cambridge University Press, 1986.

Somekh, Sasson. *Dunyâ Yûsuf Idrîs min Khilâl Aqâsisihi.* Tel Aviv: Dâr al-Nashr al-'Arabî, 1976.

———. *Lughat al-Qissa fî Adab Yûsuf Idrîs.* Acre: Matba'at al-Sarûjî, 1984.

———, ed. *Dunyâ Yûsuf Idrîs.* Jerusalem: Matba'at al-Sharq al-Ta'âwuniyya, 1976.

Stanton, Domna, ed. *The Female Autograph: Theory and Practice of Autobiography from the Tenth to the Twentieth Century.* Chicago: University of Chicago Press, 1987.

Stetkevych, Suzanne Pinckney. "Intoxication and Immortality: Wine and Associated Imagery in al-Ma'arrî's Garden." *Literature East and West* 25 (1989): 29–48 (special issue entitled "Critical Pilgrimages: Studies in the Arabic Literary Tradition," edited by Fedwa Malti-Douglas).

Stowasser, Barbara. *Women in the Qur'an, Traditions, and Interpretation.* New York: Oxford University Press, 1994.

al-Tabarî. *Tafsîr al-Tabarî—Jâmi' al-Bayân fî Ta'wîl al-Qur'ân.* 30 vols. in 12. Beirut: Dâr al-Kutub al-'Ilmiyya, 1992.

Tâmir, Zakariyyâ. "Al-'Urs al-Sharqî." In *al-Ra'd*, pp. 71–79. Damascus: Manshûrât Maktabat al-Nûrî, 1978.

Tarabishi, Georges [Tarâbîshî, Jûrj]. *Unthâ Didd al-Unûtha.* Beirut: Dâr al-Talî'a, 1984.

———. *Woman Against Her Sex: A Critique of Nawal el-Saadawi.* Translated by Basil Hatim and Elisabeth Orsini. London: Saqi Books, 1988.

Tarâbîshî, Jûrj. *See* Tarabishi, Georges.

Tarshûna, Mahmûd. *Al-Adab al-Murîd fî Mu'allafât al-Mis'adî.* Tunis: La Maghrébine pour l'Impression, l'Edition et la Publicité, 1989.

al-Tha'âlibî. *Al-Tamthîl wal-Muhâdara.* Edited by 'Abd al-Fattâh Muhammad al-Hulw. Cairo: 'Isâ al-Bâbî al-Halabî, 1961.

———. *Thimâr al-Qulûb fî al-Mudâf wal-Mansûb.* Edited by Muhammad Abû al-Fadl Ibrâhîm. Cairo: Dâr al-Ma'ârif, 1985.

al-Tha'labî. *Qisas al-Anbiyâ'/'Arâ'is al-Majâlis.* Beirut: Dâr al-Qalam, n.d.

al-Tirmidhî. *Al-Jâmi' al-Sahîh—Sunan al-Tirmidhî.* Edited by Muhammad Fu'âd 'Abd al-Bâqî. Beirut: Dâr al-Kutub al-'Ilmiyya, 1987.

———. *Sahîh al-Tirmidhî.* Cairo: al-Matba'a al-Misriyya bil-Azhar, 1931; Matba'at al-Sâwî, 1934.

Trible, Phyllis. *Texts of Terror: Literary-Feminist Readings of Biblical Narratives.* Philadelphia: Fortress Press, 1985.

Trinh, Min-ha T. *Woman, Native, Other: Writing Postcoloniality and Feminism.* Bloomington: Indiana University Press, 1989.

Tûbiyâ, Majîd. *Rîm Tasbugh Sha'rahâ.* Cairo: Maktabat Gharîb, 1983.

Tucker, Judith, ed. *Arab Women: Old Boundaries, New Frontiers.* Bloomington: Indiana University Press, 1993.

Tuqan, Fadwa. *A Mountainous Journey: An Autobiography.* Translated by Olive Kenny. London: The Women's Press, 1990.

——— [Tûqân, Fadwâ]. *Rihla Jabaliyya, Rihla Sa'ba.* Amman: Dâr al-Shurûq lil-Nashr wal-Tawzî', 1985.

Tûqân, Fadwâ. *See* Tuqan, Fadwa.

The University of Texas Press, Readable Books: Prose and Poetry, Literary Criticism, Linguistics, and Language, January 1991.

*Usâma.* Damascus: Ministry of Culture, 1969-present.

al-'Uthaymîn, Shaykh Muhammad ibn Sâlih. *Min al-Ahkâm al-Fiqhiyya fî al-Fatâwâ al-Nisâ'iyya.* Fez: Maktabat wa-Tasjîlât al-Hidâya al-Qur'âniyya, 1991.

Walker, Alice. *Possessing the Secret of Joy.* London and San Diego: Harcourt Brace Jovanovich Publishers, 1992.

Warner, Marina. *Alone of All Her Sex: The Myth and the Cult of the Virgin Mary.* New York: Vintage Books, 1983.

Watt, W. Montgomery. *Companion to the Qur'ân.* London: George Allen and Unwin Ltd., 1967.

Watt, W. Montgomery. *Islamic Philosophy and Theology.* Edinburgh: Edinburgh University Press, 1962.

Wehr, Hans. *A Dictionary of Modern Written Arabic.* Edited by J. Milton Cowan. Ithaca: Spoken Language Services, 1976.

Williams, William Carlos. *The Doctor Stories.* Compiled by Robert Coles. New York: New Directions Books, 1984.

Wise, Renate. "The Concept of Sexuality in the Short Stories of Yusuf Idris." Unpublished Ph.D. thesis, University of Texas, Austin, 1992.

*Women's Studies.* Special issue on "Feminism Faces the Fantastic," 14, no. 2 (1987).

Zabîdî (al). *Tâj al-'Arûs.* Edited by 'Abd al-Sattâr Ahmad Farrâj, Husayn Nassâr, et al. 22 vols. to date. Kuwait: Matba'at Hukûmat al-Kuwayt, 1965–present.

Zimmerman, Bonnie. "'The Dark Eye Beaming': Female Friendship in George Eliot's Fictions." In *Lesbian Texts and Contexts: Radical Revisions,* edited by Karla Jay and Joanne Glasgow, pp. 126–144. New York: New York University Press, 1990.

# Index

glance, 32; metaphorical, 5; of Nafîsa, 129; paradigms of, 1–7; physical, 4, 24, 70, 72, 77, 83, 88, 128, 133, 164, 206; sexual, 74

violence, 61, 70, 143, 147, 156–57, 206; corporal, 129; male, 200; physical, 204; religiously sanctioned, 204

virginity, 41–42, 103–4, 106–8, 120, 202

Virgin Mary, 116, 142–43

voice, 47, 73, 85, 91, 154, 166, 176, 189–90; of Budûr, 168–69; of dead body, 174; external, 50; of Firdaws, 48, 50; internal epistolary, 40, 57; of jailer, 47, 49; of mother, 166

vulva, 47

Wafiyya, 50

Walker, Alice, 152–53

*War in the Land of Egypt* (al-Harb fî Barr Misr) (al-Qa'îd), 78–80

weapons, 164, 184–85

*The Well of Life* ('Ayn al-Hayât) (El Saadawi), 40

West, the, 14, 22, 101, 107, 199

"When I am Worthless" (El Saadawi), 38

White, Barbara, 29

Williams, William Carlos, 21

*Woman and Psychological Conflict* (El Saadawi), 45

*Woman and Sex* (El Saadawi), 11

*Woman at Point Zero* (Imra'a 'ind Nuqtat al-Sifr) (El Saadawi), 3, 18, 39–40, 43–68, 76, 91, 119, 129, 160, 162, 165, 167, 198–200, 204, 206–8

women: Arab, 18; Egyptian, 61; eternal, 137; homosexual, 200; lower-class, 43, 166; middle-class, 160; Middle Eastern, 17; modesty of, 28; Muslim, 54, 163; as physical object, 35; travel of, 205; upper-class, 20, 43; as victims, 127–28

*Women of Sand and Myrrh* (Misk al-Ghazâl) (al-Shaykh), 133

"Women Writing About Prostitutes" (Kaminsky), 65

Woolf, Virginia, 48

writer: *engagé*, 19; leftist, 15

*zabîba*, 57–59, 63, 206

al-Zayyât, Latîfa, 160, 164

Zulaykhâ, 97

| | |
|---:|:---|
| Compositor: | ComCom |
| Text: | 10/13 Galliard |
| Display: | Galliard |
| Printer: | Haddon Craftsmen, Inc. |
| Binder: | Haddon Craftsmen, Inc. |